China Perspectives

The *China Perspectives* series focuses on translating and publishing works by leading Chinese scholars, writing about both global topics and China-related themes. It covers Humanities & Social Sciences, Education, Media and Psychology, as well as many interdisciplinary themes.

This is the first time any of these books have been published in English for international readers. The series aims to put forward a Chinese perspective, give insights into cutting-edge academic thinking in China, and inspire researchers globally.

To submit proposals, please contact the Taylor & Francis Publisher for China Publishing Programme, Lian Sun (Lian.Sun@informa.com)

Titles in sociology currently include:

Family Burden Coefficient in China
Exploratory Research and Application
Tian Feng

The Relationship Between Trust and Social Capital of China's Urban Residents
Zou Yuchun

Constructing Space
A Longitudinal Study of Immigrants from Wenzhou in Paris
Wang Chunguang

Structural Change and Evolution of China's Internet Society
Liu Shaojie

Two-Dimensional People
Lives, Desires, and Social Attitudes in a Changing Chinese Village
Tan Tongxue

For more information, please visit https://www.routledge.com/China-Perspectives/book-series/CPH

Two-Dimensional People

Lives, Desires, and Social Attitudes in a Changing Chinese Village

Tan Tongxue

LONDON AND NEW YORK

First published 2023
by Routledge
4 Park Square, Milton Park, Abingdon, Oxon OX14 4RN

and by Routledge
605 Third Avenue, New York, NY 10158

Routledge is an imprint of the Taylor & Francis Group, an informa business

© 2023 Tan Tongxue

The right of Tan Tongxue to be identified as author of this work has been asserted in accordance with sections 77 and 78 of the Copyright, Designs and Patents Act 1988.

Translated by Matthew A. Hale

All rights reserved. No part of this book may be reprinted or reproduced or utilised in any form or by any electronic, mechanical, or other means, now known or hereafter invented, including photocopying and recording, or in any information storage or retrieval system, without permission in writing from the publishers.

Trademark notice: Product or corporate names may be trademarks or registered trademarks, and are used only for identification and explanation without intent to infringe.

English version by permission of Social Sciences Academic Press (China)

British Library Cataloguing-in-Publication Data
A catalogue record for this book is available from the British Library

ISBN: 978-1-032-40354-0 (hbk)
ISBN: 978-1-032-40438-7 (pbk)
ISBN: 978-1-003-35307-2 (ebk)

DOI: 10.4324/9781003353072

Typeset in Times New Roman
by Newgen Publishing UK

Contents

Map of Cheng Village — vi
Kinship Charts — vii
Preface — xi
Acknowledgments — xiii

PART I
Text — 1

1 An Ancient Confucian Village — 3
2 A Centralist Cadre — 41
3 A Peasant Boss — 70
4 Two Intellectuals — 99
5 An Authoritarian Official — 132
6 An Ordinary Peasant — 163
7 The Younger Generation — 191

PART II
Reflections — 223

8 The Paradox of Transition — 225
9 From the Past to the Present — 254

References — 288
Index — 297

Map of Cheng Village

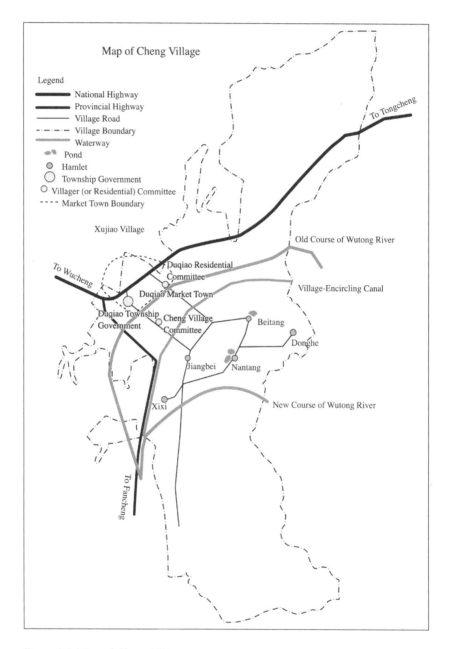

Figure 0.1 Map of Cheng Village

Kinship Charts

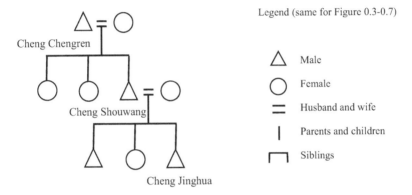

Figure 0.2 Cheng Chengren's Family (mainly discussed in Capters 2 and 7)

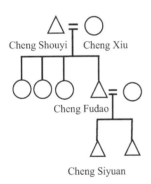

Figure 0.3 Cheng Shouyi's Family (mainly discussed in Chapters 3 and 7)

viii *Kinship Charts*

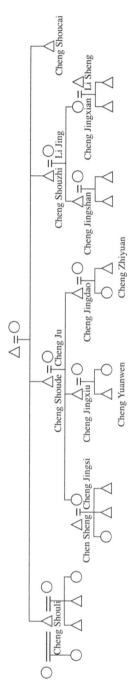

Figure 0.4 Cheng Shoude's Family (mainly discussed in Chapters 4 and 7)

Kinship Charts ix

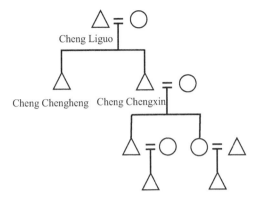

Figure 0.5 Cheng Chengxin's Family (mainly discussed in Chapters 2 and 5)

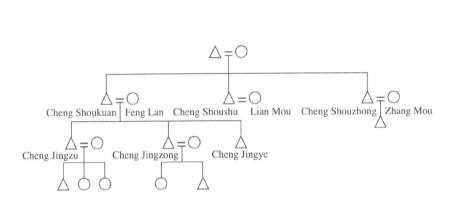

Figure 0.6 Cheng Shoukuan's Family (mainly discussed in Chapters 6 and 7)

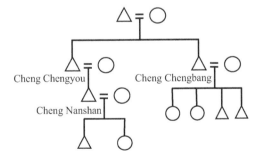

Figure 0.7 Cheng Nanshan's Family (mainly discussed in Chapters 2 and 6)

Preface

The main content of this book is divided into two parts composed of nine chapters. The first part, "Text," consists of seven chapters presenting the spatiotemporal layout of the village that I researched and the life histories of six categories of people. The second part, "Reflections," includes two chapters presenting a structural analysis of this empirical material from the perspectives of economy, politics, society, and beliefs, along with some reflections on "cultural awakening." The reasoning for this arrangement is as follows.

Empirical material is the primary basis for empirical scholarship. The interspersion of narrative and commentary would help to connect the expression of views more closely with the empirical material, but an overly rigid analytical framework might fragment material that would otherwise fit together holistically. This book therefore aims to emphasize the overall experience. More importantly, however, I hope to maintain the openness of empirical scholarship. For myself as researcher, the empirical is like a social book without words, that is why the first part is called "Text." The analysis in the second part consists merely of what I have learned through "reading" that text. My deeper cultural "reflections" on what I learned through reading are also a sort of self-questioning. From the same text, different readers may come up with completely different modes of analysis and of posing questions. Presenting the text first may therefore give readers more space for their own readings and reflections.

After sketching the spatiotemporal layout of Cheng Village, the following chapters draw inspiration from the *Records of the Grand Historian* in presenting the biographies, or life histories, of six categories of people.[1] Sima Qian's biographies combined the fates of individuals and philosophies of life with deeper structures, and with the spirit of the Spring and Autumn Era. In contemporary approaches to social research, there have been complex debates over the relationship between structure and agency, but history shows that biographies trace a path of interaction between these two. People are constrained by structures, but at the same time they change those structures to some extent, while also creating new ones. No doubt, there are mature models that may be consulted for the use of contemporary social science's structuralistic analytical frameworks to tame empirical material, and in fact this is already the norm for young scholars such as myself. It should be a worthwhile exploration, however, to present empirical details through biographical narratives before adding structural interpretation and teasing out their cultural significance. On this point, like many of my colleagues in the social sciences, I am deeply embedded within the frameworks of modern culture and academia, daring not to make empty statements about continuing some tradition, but I do believe that certain special words and modes of expression can better move and resonate with readers interested in Chinese culture.

Another reason for this type of presentation is the hope that this book may be accessible to a broader readership. (This is also why I have strived for a straightforward style of writing.) I hope that anyone with a basic high school education can understand the analysis, or can at least read the "Text" portion of the book. My intention is not to reject sophisticated scholarship altogether, and I do not believe that all such work may be presented in a popularized manner, but I am firmly convinced that a great deal of scholarship should be capable of presenting specialized ideas in a manner that ordinary people can understand. Especially when it comes to social and cultural scholarship about people (anthropology), if it has only one cold, standardized face, and if the pages are covered in jargon or nonsense that even the author does not understand, it will remain cut off from the people with whom it is concerned. How could such work be truly "professional" or "standardized"? In this sense, maybe we still need to move toward an anthropology for ordinary people. Of course, I cannot determine whether this book has achieved any success in this regard (that can only be determined by the readers), but I just hope that this attempt can give readers a few truly meaningful insights.

Note

1 *Translator's note:* The *Records of the Grand Historian* (*shiji* 史记) is a major set of records compiled by Han dynasty historian Sima Qian in the first century BCE dealing with 2,500 years of history and legend up to that time. Much of its content consists of biographies of specific historical personages.

Acknowledgments

When I began the research for this book in November 2007, I had just started my postdoctoral program in the Anthropology Department at Sun Yat-sen University under Ma Guoqing (whose doctoral dissertation advisor had been Fei Xiaotong). After I received a teaching position there in March 2010, I had the opportunity to work with Professor Ma for many years. In research and in life, he provided me with all kinds of support. I would also like to thank Zhang Yingqiang, Liu Zhiyang, Liu Zhaorui, Wang Jianxin, Zhang Zhenjiang, Zhu Aidong, and Tan Chee-Beng from the Anthropology Department for providing an excellent environment for my research. The South China Rural Research Center of Sun Yat-sen University was another place where I conducted research and found emotional sustenance. I would like to thank my colleagues there Liang Qingyin, Wu Chongqing, Zhang Huipeng, and Han Qi for all the help they provided. And if it were not for the support and encouragement of my close friends Xiao Lou, Ding Wei, Hu Yi and others from the "Three People Walking" reading group, I might have completely lost the confidence and endurance necessary to gradually grind away at this project long before its completion. Similar spiritual motivation and direct help often came from other friends such as Gao Peng, Huang Zhihui, and Zhang Liang.

By the time the Chinese edition of this book was published in late 2016, nine years had been devoted to this project. Throughout those years, far too many people provided support in various forms for a complete list to be enumerated here, but I must mention Dong Leiming, Huang Hai, Feng Gang, Liu Zhiwei, Gan Yang, Wang Mingming, Wu Fei, Liu Xin, He Ming, Zhang Peiguo, Zhu Xiaoyang, Chen Shaoming, He Yanling, Yu Guanghong, Sun Zhaoxia, Mao Gangqiang, Zeng Yun, Li Zhuofeng, Zhang Shaochun, Chen Daina, Lai Lili, Zhang Hui, Zhang Ningxi, Wang Dan, Hans Steinmüller, and Judith Farquhar, who each provided academic suggestions, reference materials, or helped with fieldwork.

The Chinese Scholarship Council provided funding for me to work at the London School of Economics Anthropology Department as a visiting scholar in 2014–2015. While there, I received academic and practical assistance from Hans Steinmüller, Charles Stafford, Stephan Feuchtwang, Wu Di, Lin Chun,

Xiang Biao, and Adam Yuet Chau. This book's manuscript was composed in the department's Seminar Room (Seligman Library) during that time.

Fieldwork for this book was conducted with support from many cadres and villagers in Duqiao Township and Cheng Village. It is a pity that the need to protect their confidentiality precludes me from listing their names here. I hope that their lives will get better and better!

Finally, I would like to thank Yang Zhenlin, Cao Yiheng, and Lü Xiayun for all their help on the Chinese edition of this book, and Lü Qiusha, Matthew A. Hale, and Hans Steinmüller for their help on the English edition.

Tan Tongxue
August 30, 2020
Golden Bamboo Library, Kunming

Part I
Text

1 An Ancient Confucian Village

The Old Village

In November 2007, due to a fortuitous opportunity, several friends and I visited Duqiao Township in Wu County, western Guangdong.[1] The township cadre responsible for receiving us, Wen Zhibin, mentioned that near the local market town was an "ancient village" called Cheng that had been preserved "extremely well." "What has been preserved there?" I asked. "Ancestral buildings," Wen replied, "mainly ancestral buildings." Wen turned out to be the township "*baocun* cadre" assigned to Cheng Village,[2] so he contacted the village committee director Cheng Qianjin, and the two of them took us down to check it out.

We soon arrived at the Great Cheng Clan Temple in a hamlet (*zirancun*) of Cheng Village called Beitang. A couplet on the doorway read, "The spring wind blows with dignity, the sound of a home of the School of Principle" (*chunfeng daomao, lixue jia sheng*).[3] Cheng Qianjin explained:

> This is our clan's ancestral temple. Everyone in our village is surnamed Cheng.[4] Look at this couplet: it means that we're descended from Cheng Hao.[5] It's said that he was famous and well-read.

Seeing that Cheng Qianjin had nothing else to say, Wen Zhibin stepped in and continued the story systematically.

From Wen's account we learned that, according to the *Cheng Clan Genealogy*, the village was established in the second year of the Ming dynasty's Yongle reign (1404 CE). Currently 45,000 square meters are occupied by "ancient buildings," mainly built in the Ming and Qing, along with a few structures built during the Republican era, known by the villagers as "ancestral buildings." These buildings were mainly constructed of blue brick, with red clay shingles in the outside and wooden beams and columns on the inside. All the buildings in this ancient village were arranged in a crisscross pattern with main roads 3 meters wide, and 1.5 meters between each house. The roofs were separated from each other by pot-shaped gables. The roads in and around the village had originally been paved with blue flagstones about

DOI: 10.4324/9781003353072-2

forty centimeters wide, but now many of the stones are gone, leaving only earthen paths. Less than a hundred meters of the road encircling the village remains, disconnected into patches. The irrigation ditches had originally been paved with flagstones or blue bricks, in picturesque disorder, forming a lattice-work connected to the outside world, but now much of it is buried or clogged up. The village had once been encircled by interlinked ponds, with four of them, each having a surface area over ten *mu* (0.6 hectare), at the entrances of three ancestral temples facing west, and one facing east. At the entrance to the Great Cheng Clan Temple facing west, there is still a sluice gate connecting the pond to the Wutong River (a branch of the Xi River, as this upstream portion of the Pearl River is called). Now, however, the pond has been filled in and used for construction. (After the Wutong diversion project was completed in 1978, the river was reduced to a depression with only a little water in the rainy season.) Most of the other ponds have also been filled and used for construction, growing vegetables, planting trees, or building roads, leaving only two ponds to the left and right of the westward-facing ancestral temple in Nantang Hamlet (three and one *mu* in area, respectively), and one 0.3 *mu* pond to the left of the eastward-facing temple in Beitang.[6]

Aside from differences in size, several of the temples and ordinary houses display basically the same architectural style. (The larger temples are one-story buildings seven meters high, while the houses are two-story buildings about six meters high.) Taking the Great Cheng Clan Temple for example, its outer walls are dense and heavy structures of blue brick, and its roof is covered in red clay shingles, with two higher fire-prevention walls on either side curving upwards in the shape of a crescent moon, and ceramic figures of various auspicious animals decorating the roof beam. The temple consists of a double-entrance structure (with two entrance halls separated by an atrium). Behind the entrance is a front hall and an upright folding screen that can be opened as a door. It is said that in "the old society" (before the 1950s), the screen could be opened only when an exalted person who had achieved the status of an imperial official entered the temple. Behind the screen is an atrium, after that a horizontal central hall, behind that a second atrium, and finally the inner hall (the main hall) and the ancestral shrine. On the shrine lies the memorial tablets of the Cheng clan ancestors, set with devotional candles and an incense burner. Corridors run along both sides of those rooms, its columns made of a composite of stone and wood. The eaves of all these rooms are decorated with sculptures and engravings of stone, wood, brick and stucco depicting various mythological beasts, folklore, and vegetation. On some of the walls under the eaves one can still see frescos of flowers and folktales, along with a few slogans and posters from the collective era (late 1950s to early 1980s) with now barely discernible words. Most of the remaining interior walls now reveal only a dull gray color, and the blue brick on the exterior has been severely eroded.

The village is equipped with wells to the north, south, east, and west. The largest, deepest well (about ten meters deep) is in the south. It is the earliest one to have been dug, its walls constructed of blue brick. Nowadays most

Figure 1.1 Aerial view of old houses in Beitang and Nantang, with new houses in the background.

villagers have dug their own artesian wells or use pipes to get spring water from the surrounding hills, so these older wells are now used mainly by a portion of the villagers to get water for washing clothes and bathing. Standing next to the wells are incense burners—traces of where villagers used to make offerings to the Water Deity.

Upon entering the ancient village, on the few houses that are still inhabited, one can see images of guardian deities affixed to the doorways, alongside the more common couplets. Couplets adorning the doorways of "public buildings" (smaller halls used for clan branch ceremonies) include the aforementioned "Spring wind blows with dignity, the sound of a home of the School of Principle," as well as:

> From the clan's source at the Luo River, its branches flourish like the parasol forest[7] (*yuanyuan zong Luoshui, zhiye fa Wulin*).
>
> The writings of the School of Principle endure eternally; peace and prosperity greet the millennium (*Lixue wenzhang liu wangu, guangfeng jiyue zhu qianqiu*).
>
> The School of Principle is worthy of Mount Ni,[8] both find their source in the Luo River (*Lixue pei Nishan, yuanyuan tong Luoshui*).

The couplets are written on bright red paper that has been affixed to the doorways only recently, judging by appearances. (During subsequent visits

6 *An Ancient Confucian Village*

Figure 1.2 View of old hamlet from Nantang's grain-drying ground and longan trees; pond to the left.

over the following years, I noticed that the couplets were changed periodically, but other than for special occasions such as weddings and funerals, the words were always the same.) Aside from a portion of the main road, most of the other roads and paths are surrounded by weeds as high as a person's waist, and the outer wall bases of the houses are covered in moss emitting a strong moldy smell. The public buildings are regularly cleaned by the village committee, but most of the houses are locked up, and through the windows you can see rooms overrun with tall stands of wild taro and sweet flag, fed by rainwater leaking in. In many places the houses are already in ruins. Cheng Qianjin pointed to a collapsed house and said, "This village of ours has always valued academic work. This is the old school where all the Cheng boys used to study." Wen Zhibin added, "Upholding the family through farming and scholarship is a traditional culture emphasized by the School of Principle Confucians. This village has produced great men of both the pen and the sword."

On the periphery of the old village, some of the houses are newly built on the sites of old houses that have been demolished. Especially beyond the Great Cheng Clan Temple and the eastward-facing temple in Beitang, many of the new houses are built on old sites, standing in stark contrast with the dilapidated old homes surrounding them. To the front of the Great Temple in Beitang and to the south of the old houses in Nantang, there are two grain-sunning grounds. The former was paved with concrete in 2002 (so it now doubles as a basketball court), while the latter still maintains its lime-covered surface from the 1960s. Next to the southern grain-sunning ground there are two large banyan trees, originally right next to the pond but now forty meters away (because part of the pond has been filled in). It is said that in between those trees and the grain-sunning field there used to be a large longan tree, but it was cut down in the late 1990s.

Later I obtained some materials produced by Duqiao Township for the promotion of tourism and took them, along with my own photographs, to consult with a few experts on Guangdong history and architecture. From their analysis, I learned some new information.

The overall construction of the old village was obviously planned with a great deal of precision. Although such a large village could not have been built at one time, it was all centered around the oldest public buildings, with all the houses on the west side facing west, and all the houses on the east side facing east. The spacing between buildings was uniform, and those houses that had obviously been built later conformed to the standard of the earlier ones. The temples, public buildings, and houses varied in their dimensions, but all shared the same basic style. Even the irrigation ditches had been designed with consideration for the village as a whole: high in the middle, low on the sides, and laid out in a harmonious pattern.

The houses' pot-shaped gables are reminiscent of Hui-style architecture, combining aesthetics with protection against fire. The brick carvings, porcelain, and stucco on the roof beams, the paintings on many of the walls, and the blue and white porcelain windows all show that the original owners must have been relatively wealthy and discerning in artistic taste, although this artwork is mainly intended to ward off evil spirits and attract good fortune. The temples are even more carefully designed. The folding screens, for example, have the geomantic (*fengshui*) function of redirecting the flow of energy, on the one hand blocking the entry of negative energy (*shaqi*) from the outside, while on the other hand preventing the family's energy from the leaving the house—in addition to adding a layer of privacy.

The old village's layout in relation to the surrounding landscape was clearly influenced by geomantic knowledge. It was built at a bend in the Wutong River, in the plain that stretches from the southeastern hills to the river. The Wutong flowed from the south through Jiangbei Hamlet before meandering to the west, then north along the western edges of Nantang and Beitang before moving on toward the east. In addition, the old village was surrounded by fishponds, so it resembled an island in the water, approaching the geomantic concept of "lotus land," symbolizing prosperity and fortune. The large-scale fishpond at the entrance to the temple also functioned geomantically to block negative energy and dispel evil spirits. At the same time, the fishponds linked to the Wutong River served the practical functions of drainage, transportation, prevention of fires, and protection against bandits.

8 *An Ancient Confucian Village*

Figure 1.3 Great Cheng Clan Temple, with new houses on each side and fishpond in foreground, originally linked to Wutong River.

Figure 1.4 Screen inside entrance to Jiangbei Cheng Clan Temple; women preparing dinner as offering to ancestors.

However, it is hard to say whether there is any direct evidence of a relationship between this old village and the Neo-Confucian School of Principle. Buildings such as the temples and public buildings embody the ideas about clans promoted by Confucianism in the Ming and Qing dynasties, undoubtedly. Moreover, later buildings had to adhere to the style and layout of the earlier ones so that the village layout as a whole could be administered effectively. Overall, this could demonstrate that a powerful clan organization was maintaining these architectural rules. On the other hand, the village layout and buildings themselves reflect a stronger influence of ideas from the *Book of Changes*. Furthermore, it is hard to find complete evidence of a lineage tracing back to Cheng Hao from the genealogical tablets alone. In this region of Southern China (Lingnan), it is extremely common for villages surnamed Li or Zhu to claim descendance from Li Shimin or Zhu Xi on the basis of their genealogical tablets, but rarely can this be verified. (A physical anthropologist told me that judging by their physical features, the Cheng villagers may be products of intermarriage between indigenous southerners and northern migrants, but that their southern features were more pronounced.) In any case, Cheng is smaller than many of the other villages claiming descent from Cheng Hao or Zhu Xi.

As for the preservation of this older section of Cheng Village, it has been far from perfect. One expert joked that, "If it weren't for the fact that a few old people still live there, the area could be described as 'ruins'." Indeed, I later learned that Wu Chongqing (2011), who has been studying rural South China for many years, had conducted systematic research on such old villages within a day's travel of Guangzhou. He discovered dozens of old villages much larger than Cheng, not even including those that had been renovated and promoted as tourist attractions. I also discovered that even in the vicinity of Cheng there were many old villages with similar-scale buildings in similar conditions of preservation, but they were further away from market towns and harder to access. For example, in a neighboring township there is one village on the banks of the Xi River where most of the families are surnamed Dou, with an ancestor who served as provincial governor (*xunfu*) in the Ming dynasty. As river transportation declined, the village fell into poverty, since it was remote from the new land transportation system, but its traditional buildings are larger than those in Cheng, and they are still better preserved. (Since its economic conditions are worse than those of Cheng, many of its villagers still live in the old section, which comprises over half of the buildings in the village.)

New Houses

As mentioned above, there are already a few new buildings both within and surrounding the old section of Cheng Village. In the words of cadres from Duqiao Township and Cheng Village, these newer structures have already "caused some destruction" to the old section's architectural style and layout.

The real problem, however, seems to be that the old village and all the roads leading to it are already surrounded by new buildings.

Regarding the spatial layout, these newer structures lack any sense of constituting a "village," instead standing scattered along several meandering roads and in open spaces among the fields. Since they were built according to the twists and turns of the roads, the houses are facing all different directions. Moreover, they were built on ancestral plots or sometimes even on farm plots, so the distance between houses varies considerably, from as much as several hundred meters down to only five centimeters (with two walls right next to each other rather than sharing one wall). The height of the houses varies from six stories reaching eighteen meters down to two-story houses only six meters high. For example, one of the first new houses was built by Cheng Shouyi, and it is five stories. Since the place where it was built was already at a high elevation, if you stand on the rooftop, you can survey most of the village. From a distance, it looks like a "chimney" (as Cheng Qianjin put it) perched atop the northeast corner of the village's older section. If you look from the edges of the old village or an even greater distance, however, several other new houses look like chimneys. Just across from the Great Cheng Clan Temple, opposite the basketball court, stand two new houses that are each about eighteen meters high, and to the left of the temple, next to the grain-sunning ground, stands another new house that is about the same height.

The administrative center of Cheng Village, the offices of the village party branch and the village committee (known colloquially as "the brigade[9] headquarters"), was originally based in Beitang Hamlet's Great Cheng Clan Temple, but now has been relocated to Jiangbei along the road to the market town of Duqiao. That hamlet falls within the town's layout, where the road straightens out and widens to eight meters, with houses lined up on either side, but their size still varies considerably. I later learned that this was because at the time of land allotment, villagers could choose plots of 120, 150, or 200 square meters based on their economic situation. For this reason, the height of the houses also varied from two stories to three or even five.

In sum, the new houses of Cheng Village appear as a jumbled mess from whatever angle you look at them—"as if a dog had chewed them up," in the words of Cheng Shouyi. I asked why he said that, and he replied, "Isn't there a saying 'as crooked as a dog's teeth'? If a dog chewed them up, of course they would be so uneven."

If the layout of the new houses looks like "a dog's teeth," the water drainage system is even more of a mess. Most of the houses are surrounded by ditches paved with concrete or red brick, but they are not connected to any larger network of channels. Those houses located in clearings between the fields let their waste water drain straight into vegetable gardens or grain fields. Those along the roadside often let it drain into random spots next to the road. Since, for the most part, there are no channels on either side of the road, when it rains, the road itself becomes an enormous ditch. In addition, there is no

Figure 1.5 Cheng Shouyi's compound (middle), its gate facing the village road, with house, pavilions, swimming pool, and tearoom inside.

unified garbage collection system in the village. Trash such as paper packaging, plastic bags, etc., that cannot be burned floats downstream through the fields and roads until it reaches the Wutong River in town, some of the debris remaining in fields, roads, ponds, and riverbanks.

For individual households, however, there is no doubt that the new houses are much better than the "ancestral buildings" in the old section of the village. Many villagers have told me that the latter are too close to other rows of houses, so they are stuffy and the airflow is poor, and the windows are too small, so the rooms are dark inside. Moreover, the compounds lie right up next to neighboring houses, with no courtyards, so as soon as you open the door you are facing someone else's house.

Other than a few houses built in the 1970s that still used blue brick (their architectural style already being "modern"), the new houses of Cheng Village generally have red-brick walls, concrete floors reinforced with steel bars, and horizontal roofs also made of concrete and steel (rather than the sloped red-tile roofs of the past). Most of the outer walls are made of unsealed red brick, but many of the more well-off villagers have also decorated them with white tiles or blue and red marble. Some of the less well-off villagers have simply painted their front walls white. One big difference in the appearance of the new houses from the "ancestral" ones is the addition of balconies with guard rails, increasingly decorated with white or green ceramic gourd-shaped columns.

Figure 1.6 New houses next to Cheng Clan Temple from Beitang pond. The middle house (facing temple gate) is eighteen meters high.

It is hard to enter one of these new residential compounds without being invited by someone familiar with the owners. This is because the houses are all separated from the gates by courtyards. Wealthy villagers have courtyards as large as two *mu* surrounded by high walls, while the poorer villagers, or those with more limited residential allotments, have smaller courtyards of at least a dozen square meters. From the road you can see the gates but cannot enter unless the owner comes out to open it for you. Why did they build these courtyards? Many villagers say they are meant to prevent theft. In addition, some of the more educated residents say the courtyards block negative energy and compensate for the poor *fengshui* of certain residential plots. Nowadays it is harder and harder to find a geomantically auspicious site to build a house, the only spaces available being along the road or even on farmland, so it is necessary to add a courtyard. However, some villagers also say this addition's main purpose is for privacy. For example, Cheng Shouyi insists that he is an atheist, but he also built a courtyard of about one *mu* with a swimming pool, artificial hills, a pavilion and so on, with the drainage ditches running into a public pond only slightly lower than the residential plot (i.e., the pond to the left of the eastward-facing temple's entrance in Beitang). He says its main purpose is to "create the sense of having a gated family compound so random people can't just come over and hang out" there.

In contrast, most villagers, even if they have few options regarding the location and orientation of their compounds, still hire a geomancer (*fengshui xiansheng*) to calculate their position and make all kinds of adjustments in keeping with the theory of *fengshui*. For example, if the courtyard is too small, they might dig a little "fish pond" one or two square meters across, or place stone lions to the left and right of the gateway, in order to protect against negative energy. One villager named Cheng Pengcheng, who owns a quarry, has a courtyard of two *mu*, its entrance facing the old riverbed of the Wutong River and, beyond that, the highway. In order to block negative energy from the highway, in addition to building artificial hills and fountains and hanging a round mirror from the gatepost, he also planted a row of fern pines, cypress, and citrus trees within the courtyard. (Some villagers comment sarcastically that such compounds "lie amid the pines and cypress," a metaphor for death.)

For the gates of these compounds, poorer villagers still use wooden doors, while more well-off residents often install stainless steel security doors. (Since the standard type of security doors used in the city are too small, villagers usually have their doors made to order.) Several of the wealthier villagers such as Cheng Pengcheng have also installed Roman columns as a doorframe. Commonly seen couplets hanging in the doorway include:

> May we settle down while working hard so our business prospers; now that our little house has been built, may our lives flourish (*anju fenfa, shiye xinglong*).
> May our good fortune and wealth last a thousand autumns; may our family be harmonious, our business successful, and all things thrive (*fudao cailai qianqiu fu, jiahe yewang wanshi xing*).

(Cheng Shoude, a village expert on writing couplets, says that these verses are vulgar and lacking in literary grace.) The few Christians in the village adorn their doorways with couplets honoring "the Lord." As with the doors, the new houses' windows also exhibit a clear hierarchy in quality. Ordinary villagers use basic glass panels mounted in wooden frames. More "modern" villagers use thicker green glass panels mounted in aluminum alloy frames behind stainless steel security bars.

As for interior finishing, the differences among the new houses are even more apparent (the only similarity being that all strive to be "modern"). Some of the nicer examples include the homes of Cheng Pengcheng, Cheng Shouyi, and the former village party branch secretary Cheng Chengxin, whose first-story floor is covered in marble, the upper levels floored in tile, and the walls painted white with environmentally friendly material. A more modest example is the home of Cheng Qianjin, whose first and second-story floors are tiled, with only unsealed concrete on the third story and ordinary white paint on the walls. More common is for only the first-story floor to be tiled, with unsealed concrete floors on the upper levels and the walls painted only with lime water. The lower-quality homes, such as that of Cheng Shoude's friend Cheng Shoukuan, have only unpainted blue-brick walls and unsealed concrete floors, while his eldest son Cheng Jingzu has unpainted red-brick walls.

14 *An Ancient Confucian Village*

There is generally a positive correlation between the level of quality in finishing materials and the way the living rooms (*keting*) are furnished. For example, the living rooms of Cheng Pengcheng, Cheng Shouyi, and Cheng Chengxin are all furnished with liquid-crystal-display (LCD) televisions, sound systems, high-end clocks on the walls, leather sofas, and large marble tea tables decorated with exquisite carvings. Cheng Shouyi estimates that at least one hundred homes in the village are furnished in this way. He personally is regarded as someone who particularly "knows how to enjoy life," with a separate one-story tea pavilion in his courtyard next to the swimming pool (aside from the living room in his house), itself furnished with an LCD television, speakers, and a large eye-catching tea table carved from tree roots—worth over 500,000 yuan, by his estimate.

In short, zooming in to observe individual compounds, most of the new houses in Cheng Village are already quite "modernized." At the same time, villagers are still cognizant of *fengshui*, so aside from making their residential compounds spacious, bright, and tidy with regard to the "hardware" of construction materials, they also try as much as possible to arrange the geomantic "software" appropriately. However, there is no longer any sense that these compounds are connected to one another in any way that could cohere into a village. Homes lie scattered among filthy and poorly maintained

Figure 1.7 New residential compounds of various sizes along the road in Beitang, with high walls and gates.

roads, drainage ditches, and public ponds. While residents strive to perfect the *fengshui* within their compounds through detailed attention to their layout and furnishings, the village's disorderly condition has made it impossible to maintain good *fengshui* for the community as a whole.

Of course, this does not mean that the villagers no longer care about the *fengshui* of the village as a whole. It is just that no one is willing to take action to rectify the situation, beyond merely complaining about it over the dinner table. For example, from 2008 to 2012, a series of unnatural deaths occurred in Jiangbei, and many villagers believed this was related to the degradation of the hamlet's overall *fengshui*. The proof they provided for this included:

(a) The archway (*paifang*) at the entrance to Jiangbei had previously blocked the road from the view of the wide-open fields and, beyond that, the river and hills, thus creating good *fengshui*. In 1997, however, the land on either side of the road was occupied by the township government and sold to villagers for the construction of houses as part of a unified plan for the road (so this strip became known as "Brigade Street"). Some of these new houses separated the archway from the road, thus rendering it a "dead gateway," destroying its geomantic function.

(b) At the front entrance to Jiangbei's ancestral temple, there is a grain-sunning ground (which doubles as a basketball court) separating the Wutong River's old riverbed from the open fields and the hills beyond

Figure 1.8 Standard furnishings in an ordinary new house, with Earth God shrine to the left of the entertainment system.

them. In 2007, however, two families built houses on the riverbank. They were taller than the temple and blocked its *fengshui*.
(c) Next to the temple, a *bajiao* banana tree grew to be even taller than the temple, further damaging its *fengshui* and filling the village with "heavy, dead energy." The tree belonged to a "druggie" (Ct: *fanjai*)[10] who was in prison at the time, but no one dared to cut it down.

Township Officials

After a year of intermittent research in Cheng Village and Duqiao Township, I learned that the idea of developing the ancestral buildings of Beitang and Nantang as an ancient village had been proposed by Fang Lizheng, the secretary of the township's party committee, and that this plan had been endorsed by the mayor He Ping and vice-mayor Wen Zhibin.

Toward the end of 2008 on the traditional calendar, Wen became willing to narrate the planning process in detail, but this narration opened with a "chronicle of officialdom" (*guanchang jing*) that I had not expected. By that time, we were already on quite familiar terms with one another. More importantly, perhaps, he had already categorized me as "harmless." He said:

> Brother, I can see that your research is just for fun, to satisfy readers' curiosity, dressed up as "cultural research." You're from the ivory tower, so we could say you're a "harmless product," nothing to worry about. At

Figure 1.9 View of Jiangbei archway from "Brigade Street."

An Ancient Confucian Village 17

Figure 1.10 View of grain-sunning ground and houses from main entrance to Jiangbei Ancestral Temple.

> first, to be honest, I was a little worried that you were something like a journalist. I have a love-hate relationship with journalists, when it comes to what I do (my work). I depend on them to attract attention to Cheng Village, but I'm afraid that they'll report something negative. They're like a virus that could break out at any time .... Journalists never stay in the village for such a long time as you have.[11]

I replied, "We're friends, like brothers." Wen waved his hand and added:

> The condition is that, if you were a journalist, we could not really become true friends, much less brothers. In my line of work, it's as if you are "thrown into an arena, where you have no choice but to fight" (*ren zai jianghu, shen bu you ji*). People in relationships based on potentially conflicting interests (*lihai guanxi*) can find ways to cooperate, but they can't let that get mixed up with too many emotions. As you Northerners (Ct: *loujai*)[12] put it: if feelings get too warm, it's hard to coolly consider problems and weigh up the pros and cons of a situation.

This statement was clearly meant to prove that Wen's words bore a great deal of veracity, but I intentionally coaxed him by responding, "How do you know what the secretary and mayor really think? It's not like you're all brothers." Wen defended his position:

> We're all playing this game on the same chessboard, in the same situation, so of course I know what they think. Otherwise, there would be no point in serving as such a "hayseed official" (*zhimaguan*).... Besides, of course, there are no real conflicts of interest among the three of us, especially for me, so they speak pretty openly with me. After this is completed, Fang (Lizheng) will either be promoted or go serve in the county (as the head of a county-level office of some state agency). He (Ping) will probably take his place as secretary. I'm not a party member, but I have my own connections, so my advancement will follow a different path. They know (this).

According to Wen, Fang's initial decision to package and publicize Cheng as an ancient village was mainly aimed as "making some kind of achievement," which we can understand as political capital (*zhengji*). From beginning to end, the plan was meant to "kill two eagles with one arrow."

At a meeting of township officials, Fang had emphasized the material basis for developing the village as a tourist site: all they had to do was to increase their efforts to attract investment, and the project was likely to succeed. He requested that all township cadres publicize Cheng Village's "advantages" whenever they attended events for attracting investment or otherwise communicating with the outside world. His analysis of these advantages was attractive.

I too had experienced this publicity about Cheng's advantages directly. When I first began visiting Duqiao with friends, coming from Guangzhou "down" to the countryside, we did not notice anything special about this place. If you look at a map of Guangdong from the top downward, it is hard to see what is remarkable about this location in the vast basin of the Xi River. But when township cadres, including Fang, kept saying how hard it must have been for us to come "up" from Guangzhou, it became clear that they had a different sense of space than us. Inquiring about this, it turned out that they were using the river as a reference point, and Guangzhou is downstream from Duqiao.

They gestured toward the map, saying how important a location Duqiao and Cheng Village occupied. For example, Wutong—an important branch of the Xi—flows north past the village, with Duqiao's market town sitting across the old riverbed, though now that the river has been diverted, the town has been basically merged together with the village. Looking outwards from Cheng Village, it appears even more to be an important hub for western Guangdong: Thirty kilometers to the west along the national highway lies Wucheng, the seat of Wu County which overlaps with the urban core of Qi Prefecture. Thirty kilometers to the south along the Wutong River and a provincial highway is Fancheng, the seat of Fan County, which houses a famous Buddhist temple, along with many hot springs. To the southwest is Zhanjiang.

Thirty kilometers to the north along the Wutong and a national highway is Tongcheng, the urban core of Tong Prefecture. Tong lies at the confluence of the Wutong and Xi rivers, a provincial tourist attraction. And Guangzhou is two hours to the east after getting on the expressway in a neighboring township.

Fang Lizheng believed that "it's better to be born opportunely (*qiao*) than to be born well," and Cheng Village's chief asset is that it lies in such a "central" location. He sketched a blueprint of how this "advantage" would be converted into an actual resource for tourism: When tourists finish visiting Tong and set out for Fan to pray at the temple or relax at a hot spring, they could stop in Duqiao to see the ancient village. Or when customers go shopping for stone materials in Wucheng, they could take a break in Duqiao to visit the ancient village. For Guangzhou residents who want to spend the weekend at an agro-tourism resort, Cheng Village could become an option. These blueprints could be partly achieved simply by cooperating with a few travel agencies, on the technical level, but they also required investors for the restoration of Cheng's old buildings, the construction of entertainment infrastructure, food and beverage services, and advertising.

However, this was only one of Fang's goals. According to Wen Zhibin, in that meeting with township officials, Fang mentioned another idea: As part of this development project, the township government would take over the land where the Wutong River used to flow between the market down and Cheng Village, using it to set up a commercial street with shops, hotels, and restaurants. While chatting with Wen on a less formal occasion, Fang said that although it would be good if the ancient village project worked out, it did not really matter whether it failed, because in any case the government would benefit by obtaining several hundred *mu* of land in one fell swoop, and the villagers would benefit by making better use of this low-quality land (now mainly used for raising fish and growing vegetables).

In Wen's assessment, it should be acknowledged that Fang did agonize a bit over this matter. He admired Fang's "talent, fastidiousness, ability to come up with ways to kill two birds with one stone, as one hand washes the other with mutual support, concern for both offense and defense, and ability to always win and never lose." I asked, "Was this just a feigned attack? Should it be called 'a combination of the fictional with the real,' or 'inconsistency between surface and content'?" Wen disagreed, saying that if investment could be obtained, then the former goal of developing the old section of the village as a tourist attraction could come to fruition, so it was hard to call it completely fictional. He said that Fang had considered leasing out some of the land from the old riverbed after taking it over in exchange for investment, rather than relying on the ancient village alone, so the "real" goal could be used to make the "fictional" one become real. In this game, however, the underlying "hand to be played," was actually the land that the township would take over from Cheng Village.

From an individual perspective, Wen thought that a third goal of the plan was, of course, to garner political capital toward Fang's own career advancement.

I believe that Wen's analysis of this relationship between "fiction" and "reality" was accurate. Before ever visiting Duqiao, I had met Fang Lizheng and He Ping in Guangzhou. At the time, the provincial government of Guangdong was launching a comprehensive plan for land use at the county level, trying to establish its legal basis by the year 2020, but it had not yet proposed clear guidelines for land-use planning at the township level. (Later it decided that the county-level offices of land management would be responsible for organizing township-level planning.) Fang and He wanted to take advantage of the opportunity to create a plan for Duqiao's land use, and so went to Guangzhou looking for experts qualified to develop such a plan. At the time, they had proposed that the plan's foremost concern was to legally redefine that strip of land in Cheng Village as permissible for construction. (This meant that later, when agricultural land would be converted to construction land, there would be a basis in the plan that would facilitate the obtainment of permission and the completion of land-use documentation.)

After proposing the plan to develop Cheng Village's old section as a tourist attraction, Fang invited journalists from the *Qi Prefecture Daily* to come investigate. They published four brief stories with excellent prose and photographs, reporting on their "surprising discovery" of buildings from the Ming and Qing dynasties and "unveiling the mysteries of an ancient village." Besides introducing the architecture, wells, and *fengshui* in elegant language, they also described a few local customs and legends in an effort to create the "sense of mystery," "rustic atmosphere," and "old-fashioned flavor" requested by the township leaders.

Shortly thereafter, He Ping had a friend track down four specialists in cultural research from a couple universities. After they had come to Cheng Village and observed the old buildings one morning, they participated in a brief "conference" in the township government office. They said that the old village could be called "Lingnan's First Village of the School of Principle," and that it embodied "Five Unities":

(1) The Unity of Nature (*tian*) and People: the village layout had the flavor of the Eight Trigrams, and the architecture formed a pleasing contrast with the landscape;
(2) The Unity of Buddhism and the School of Principle: the villagers were descended from Cheng Hao, and the famous Buddhist temple of Fan County was only about fifty kilometers away, so many villagers practiced Buddhism;
(3) The Unity of Guangdong and Anhui: the architecture (mainly the pot-shaped gables) had features of the Hui style (from Huizhou, Anhui), but it was combined with Cantonese characteristics;
(4) The Unity of Farming and Scholarship: the villagers had been influenced by the School of Principle, so valued both agricultural work and education;

(5) The Unity of Roots and Branches: there was both a Great Cheng Clan Temple and smaller temples for each branch of the clan.

In addition to the Five Unities, the village also embodied "Two Evocations": it evoked the Chan Buddhist Sixth Patriarch Hui Neng's notion that "the flower blooms with five petals," and its external appearance evoked the shape of a lotus blossom. Wen Zhibin later told me, "Those experts were so observant (Ct: *singmuk*).[13] They knew exactly what we were looking for." Henceforth in its publicity work, the township government directly adopted the phrases "Lingnan's First Village of the School of Principle," "the Five Unities," and "the Two Evocations."

In order to attract investment, the township utilized funds from the central government's project to "Construct a New Socialist Countryside" to pave all the public roads in Cheng Village. However, since the value of the land from the old riverbed was too low, it still failed to attract sufficient investors to develop the village as a tourist attraction. Wen, Fang, and He visited many places seeking investment, but to no avail, so "for a while, everyone felt frustrated."

After the Spring Festival of 2008, Guangdong's provincial government began to implement the development strategy of "emptying the cages to change the birds,"[14] beginning to push high-energy, highly polluting industries outward from the Pearl River Delta. Duqiao seized the opportunity to import two ceramics factories worth several hundred million yuan from the delta city of Foshan, and the ancient village plan was quickly cast aside "to cool off." In 2010, Fang Lizheng was promoted to head the office of a state agency in Wu County, He Ping replaced him as secretary of Duqiao's party committee, and soon Wen Zhibin was promoted to head the office of a state agency in Qi Prefecture. In 2011, He Ping went ahead with the preparation of materials and applied to have Cheng Village added to a list of "ancient villages" certified by an office of the provincial government. Asked about this, he said it could not hurt to go ahead and obtain certification, and maybe it would be useful later on. Wen believed that one of the goals here was prestige, and another was that maybe in the future the certification could be used to finally develop the land from the old riverbed.

Village Cadres

As for the plan to develop the village as a tourist attraction, Wen Zhibin repeatedly expressed that the village cadres "were a little frustrated that 'the iron still hadn't become steel'." Among those cadres, not one of them had graduated high school. The party branch secretary, Liang Shengli, belonged to Xixi Hamlet and was not very familiar with the Cheng clan's "ancestral buildings," nor was he the best public speaker. As for the village committee director, Cheng Qianjin, although he was an "authentic" descendant of the Cheng clan from Beitang, unfortunately his speaking skills were even worse, especially when it came to communicating with outsiders in Mandarin, and he knew very little about the clan's history. It especially disappointed Wen that even after the township government had compiled a written account of the ancient village and its story, Cheng Qianjin never managed to memorize it, and as soon as he got off script, he could not discuss the topic coherently. Whenever anyone came to visit, it was often left up to Wen to introduce the village by himself. None of the other cadres were of much help in the matter either.

This being the case, why were more talented people not selected to join the team of village cadres? Wen's answer was that, first of all, more capable people often chose to leave the village to do business and make money rather than stay there long-term and "do politics." Secondly, rural affairs were complicated, especially when it came to the two key positions of party branch secretary and village committee director, and not just anyone could do the job. For the past few years, Liang Shengli and Cheng Qianjin had done a good job overall.

Thus, when outsiders came to see the ancient village, I often observed Cheng Qianjin leading the way, opening the doors of the temple and reciting the prologue to the story of his ancestors: "Our great-grandfather was a descendant of Cheng Hao who migrated here from Henan due to war and then married our great-grandmother... ."[15] At that point, the township cadre would step in to "add a few details" to the story. On many occasions, after the visitors had left, Wen would coach Cheng Qianjin about how to improve upon his narrative the next time, but whenever the next time came, Qianjin never managed to get it right. In August 2010, Wen told me privately of his "final judgment":

> There may be no way to change (Cheng Qianjin). Now I finally understand that this is not just a matter of speaking skills. More important may be the problem of his level (*shuiping*) and perspective. It would be hard to raise his level—he gets nervous as soon as he sees a superior. Same goes for perspective: He hasn't seen the outside world, so he can't interpret people's words and body language. He doesn't know what outsiders want to hear, so he can't grasp the main points and always focuses on unimportant things... . This doesn't mean that he's stupid: He's pretty observant (*singmuk*) at taking care of the village affairs that he's familiar with.

Wen said this "observant" quality of Cheng Qianjin was expressed in two ways: First, Qianjin was good at "grasping" the intentions of township leaders and willing to diligently help out with their work, actively "running around" for them. Secondly, while completing this kind of work, he was also good at "seizing the opportunity" to get something out of it for himself.

In the first half of 2007, the first time Wen mentioned the tourism development plan to Liang Shengli and Cheng Qianjin, Liang's response was,

"You township leaders really have a breadth of vision, we'll do all we can to help. But this mainly concerns Beitang and Nantang, so Qianjin might need to run around a little more." Qianjin discussed the plans with Wen in detail, mentioning the proposal to develop the land from the old riverbed. Afterwards, he conveyed his hope that the township would give preferential treatment to Cheng Village when using the state fund to "Construct a New Socialist Countryside," at least by paving the roads. Qianjin also asked Wen to help him out personally by including his own hundred-meter driveway within the paving plan, saying that it was inconvenient for leaders to come visit his house on a dirt road, and it damaged the reputation of Cheng Village, but he lacked the money to pave it himself. When Wen recounted this later, he noted that he could not turn down Qianjin's modest request for a little personal benefit in the face of his accurate grasping of the township leaders' thinking about the riverbed in particular, and his willingness to "run around" in order to help out.

Once Liang came to see the benefits that the tourism development plan could bring, he grew more enthusiastic about it as well. In December 2007, he approached Qianjin (also asking Wen for guidance) with a plan to organize about three hundred villagers, including cadres, primary school students, and teachers, to clean up the old section of the village. They cleared out some of the garbage and scrubbed the remnants of advertisements off some of the walls and electric poles. When discussing the activity later on, Liang and Qianjin considered it to be a "work achievement" for the township. The township's work report on the activity stated:

> The township party committee and government highly value the work to preserve and promote the ancient village. In order to transform the village's backward appearance due to its unsanitary environment, and in order to truly embody the characteristics of "Lingnan's First Village of the School of Principle," the township party committee and government launched a patriotic sanitation campaign called "Beautify the Ancient Village of the School of Principle, Strive to Be Civilized Villagers," centered on thoroughly rectifying the village's appearance, clearing out the garbage and standing water, and removing the "four pests" (flies, mosquitos, rats, and cockroaches) …. In all, the campaign cleared out three tractor loads of garbage and eliminated sixteen unsanitary spaces.

By the end of 2007, still no progress had been made toward attracting investment. As the local township and village cadres often put it, however, they had at least "prized open" a few things. Although they had not accomplished any substantial "achievements" regarding the tourism plan itself, "there were always more solutions than problems," they had "planted beans and harvested melons," and "when it's dark in the east it's light in the west." The tourism plan had become an opportunity for the township and village authorities to acquire several important business deals.

That winter, Fang Lizheng, feeling a little frustrated that things were not working out smoothly, brought up an old topic that had been discussed before among the township cadres. (On that previous occasion, Fang had been serving the dual positions of vice-mayor and vice-secretary of the Duqiao party committee. In 1999 he had been promoted to mayor of another township, then in 2005 transferred back to Duqiao as secretary.) The courtyard of Duqiao's office building for the government and party committee had bad *fengshui*: the road was at a higher elevation than the entrance to the courtyard, so every day the cadres had to walk downhill from the road to their offices, symbolizing that they were "going downhill," so of course they were having trouble making "achievements." Although plenty of cadres, including Fang, had obtained promotions, those present at the meeting agreed with Fang's point. He even blamed the previous cadres, saying "When I was serving here as vice-mayor, I pointed out this problem repeatedly, but they never did anything about it. Those 'elder brothers' (*laodamen*) lacked the will."[16] In August 2010, when Wen Zhibin mentioned this incident, he laughed, saying "You thought our meetings would be more serious than that? Brother, the township is just that countryfied (*shanzhai*), not like your meetings in the city.... Yes our meetings really do discuss problems with *fengshui*."

After Fang brought this up, the cadres agreed that the township's Central Primary School would be the best place to build their new compound. However, according to Wu County's plan for the distribution of education resources, that school could not be closed. Moreover, the market town had many school-age children who actually needed a school.

This time, it was not only Wen Zhibin but also Fang Lizheng and He Ping who invited Liang Shengli and Cheng Qianjin to dinner, nominally as an informal holiday gathering among friends. Over dinner, Fang again analyzed the prospects for the tourism project, this time inserting some pessimism within the optimistic analysis normally shared on public occasions meant to attract investors. Then he proposed converting the Cheng Village Primary School into the township's Central Primary School as a way to encourage parents to build or buy houses on the village's former riverbed. Qianjin later recounted:

> It was Secretary Fang who brought this up first. He said that tourism could bring restaurants and hotels, but during the initial phase of development, it would be hard to attract investment. Our location was close to Fancheng, Tongcheng, and Wucheng, and that was both a blessing and a curse. Tourists may just come here to have a look but then go on to one of those cities to eat and stay in a hotel. So at first it might be best to attract locals to come buy land and build houses. To that end, using the school might be a good solution. Our village is close to the street (i.e. the market town), so it made sense to locate the Central Primary School here. A lot of parents might send their kids to school here and then come and rent houses, or build their own. The mayors He and Wen added a few

comments supporting this proposal. Liang (Shengli) and I felt this made sense, so we agreed.

Converting the village school to a township school meant that there would not be enough space for all the students, so the township cadres offered to allocate resources for the construction of new classrooms within the existing schoolyard. Liang and Cheng then proposed to invite village "bosses" (i.e., entrepreneurs) and former villagers (*qiaobao*) to "practice generosity" (*huayuan*) in the name of "developing ancestral buildings" and "supporting education," using the donations to build the classrooms, so a portion of the township government's allocation could go toward renovating the offices of the Cheng Village party branch and village committee. The township cadres agreed. After the Spring Festival in early 2008, Cheng Village spent about 100,000 yuan renovating its dilapidated two-story office building (with four offices and two meeting rooms). The township government gave the village a set of educational equipment (one computer, one color TV, and one digital satellite TV receiver) that had been donated by a work unit in Guangzhou. For a while, the "brigade headquarters" looked as good as new. Cheng Qianjin often told people that the office renovation and new classrooms were merely a prelude to the development of the ancient village, that much more was to come, and that "although our salary is only 800 yuan (a month), we're doing a lot of service."

Many villagers took exception to such statements, pointing out that the "bosses" funding the new classrooms had connections with the cadres, and those funding the office renovation were friends or relatives of Cheng Qianjin and Liang Shengli. As they saw it, the cadres were not doing anything for the village based on the "ancestral buildings," but merely taking advantage of an opportunity for personal benefit. As Cheng Shouyi put it, Qianjin was a typical case of "eating the grass closest to the nest": "In the village he knew how to compete for small personal gains, but as soon as higher-ranking authorities came, he suddenly grew too nervous to speak, let alone to take advantage of opportunities to benefit the village as a whole."

Over the next few years, I discovered, Liang Shengli never commented on the villagers, and was regarded by them as "low key," so people rarely gossiped about him. They were more likely to complain about Cheng Qianjin. On the one hand he would often defend himself, saying he felt "wronged," but on the other he did not really care. As for the ancient village, during the 2011 National Day holiday, he told me:

> I know it would not be easy to actually develop tourism here. But as long as the township leaders are interested in our ancestral buildings, of course I'll support that. Besides, as a village cadre, I have to do whatever they've decided, whether I like it or not, and whether or not there's something in it for me. In any case, surely this will benefit our village to some degree.

As for the office renovation, he said, "I asked several bosses, but no one was willing to do it because there was no profit to be had, considering the project's costs and quality specifications," so he had no choice but to find relatives to do it. He sighed:

> Although everyone came from the ancient village, now people's hearts and mouths have grown complicated. If you do something for the good of the tourism project, they don't see it, and as soon as you obtain any small advantage from it, their eyes get red.

Clan Elders

As for the history of the ancient village, I always felt that Cheng Qianjin had trouble explaining it clearly, and the narrative of township cadres like Wen Zhibin had too many traces of commercial "packaging." I therefore asked Qianjin to introduce me to an elder who was more familiar with the history, then maybe I could stay at his house. At first, Qianjin just said "There aren't really any others. None of the old people know any more than me." He took me to meet two old men in Beitang and Nantang who were responsible for painting couplets for the temples during holidays, but when I brought up clan affairs they were not sure about them. As for lodging, although I kept emphasizing that "we rural researchers need to live and eat together with the peasants," Qianjin said that would not be convenient according to "Cantonese customs." He and Wen Zhibin wanted me to stay at the township government compound because it was more hygienic and convenient, equipped with air conditioning in the summertime. When I insisted on staying in the village, Qianjin arranged for me to sleep in an office on the second floor of the brigade headquarters, fashioning a simple bed out of benches and boards and telling me to eat at restaurants in the market town.[17]

From those two old men in Beitang and Nantang, I learned that Cheng Shoude in Jiangbei was "the most educated person" and "a clan elder" (*zulao*). Considering that they had also called Cheng Qianjin a "clan elder," by this term they seemed to mean someone who knew more about clan affairs. Actually, there were at least ten people still registered as residents of Cheng Village who had attended vocational secondary school, and Shoude had only attended high school. When I requested to meet him by name, Qianjin finally introduced me.

From the brigade headquarters to the township government compound, it was only a ten-minute walk across the bridge over a stream next to the Wutong River's former bed, and then across an old street and two new streets. Cheng Shoude had two homes: a blue-brick house in Jiangbei and an old shopfront on the old street. He normally stayed on the old street, where he ran a shop for repairing wristwatches. Nowadays, customers rarely came to repair watches, but old and middle-aged people often gathered in groups of three or five to drink tea and chat. Prior to being introduced, I had walked by the shop several times every day on my way to and from dining in town, and he already knew about my research.

Shoude had taught school, so everyone called him Teacher Cheng. When Qianjin introduced us, he said something like "Teacher Cheng is very well-read" before leaving us to talk in private.

From Shoude and the people drinking tea there I learned that it was right to insist upon staying in the brigade headquarters, or at least that it was better than staying in the township government compound. Although the two places were separated by only a short distance, they had "a very different feeling." Shoude put it bluntly, "Behind those walls (of the compound) are officials (*guan*). We're commoners (*min*). It's hard for the two sides to communicate on friendly terms."

Later Shoude mentioned that back when the township government and village committee first proposed the tourism project, Qianjin had approached him and two other elders from Nantang and Beitang. The three of them just happened to be the representatives of the three Cheng-surnamed hamlets, and were also more concerned about clan affairs, so sometimes they were considered to be "clan elders." Qianjin had asked them to compile a set of stories about their "great-grandfathers." Shoude looked through some related documents and wrote a few couplets for Qianjin, but before long he discovered that the plans for the ancient village were completely different from what he had expected, so he stopped participating. In addition, the actual tourism development work never saw any progress, so Qianjin stopped approaching Shoude about it. When it came time to change the couplets for the temples and public buildings, Qianjin asked the two "elders" from Nantang and Beitang to write them. Their calligraphy was fine, but they were not so skilled at composing couplets, so they just kept reproducing those composed by Shoude, or copying from standard collections of couplets. (The latter were not specific to Cheng Village so incapable of embodying features of the School of Principle.) Eventually, they too began to feel that the tourism project was more of a government affair than a clan one, so they also stopped participating in such activities as much.

What particularly bothered Shoude was that the project essentially excluded his hamlet of Jiangbei. He said:

> As the name implies, an ancient village is defined by its age. Their publicity says that Cheng Village was settled by descendants of Cheng Hao who migrated here, but where exactly did they settle first? Jiangbei! Our great-grandfathers migrated from Henan to Nanhai (in Foshan), then when that settlement grew strong and populous, some of them migrated along the Xi River to Tongcheng. When Tongcheng too grew strong and populous, one of our great-grandfathers migrated along the Wutong River to Jiangbei. Later, when Jiangbei grew crowded, a few brothers finally moved to Beitang and Nantang.
>
> If you want to talk about Cheng's ancient village, of course you have to start with Jiangbei. Jiangbei's clan temple was the earliest one to be built

in the village, and Jiangbei's old houses were also built earlier. But as they tell the story, it sounds like our great-grandfathers migrated directly to Beitang and Nantang, and they say the Minghuici ("Ming Dynasty Hui-style temple") was the earliest clan temple to be built. But it wasn't. At best it's just an ordinary building. Back in the day, for major ceremonies, they would come over here to worship the ancestors. Minor ceremonies could be performed in Beitang, that's why it's called a "temple," but strictly speaking, the Minghuici is not a clan temple. To claim the Minghuici was the earliest clan temple to be built, isn't that just a barefaced lie? To put it bluntly, if the goal is just to make money, even the ancestors don't want it. They even call it an "Ancient Village of the School of Principle," but if you don't even correctly identify who is the father and who is the son, distinguishing between elder and junior, how can that be called the School of Principle?

Shoude had explicitly requested that if Cheng Village was to open to the public as a tourist attraction, Jiangbei should be included in the "ancient village" section. Otherwise, he would not cooperate. Not only would that be unreasonable, he believed, but it would also be energy wasted on a thankless job, "getting mixed up in the affairs of somebody else's village, after all." Shoude's brother Cheng Shouzhi and a few other villagers had echoed this sentiment, approaching He Ping and Wen Zhibin when those cadres had "come down to the village" and asking them about the same thing.

These requests were not satisfied, for one, because the entire tourism project itself was just an illusory "flower in the mirror." Besides, even if investors were to come, it would not be realistic to develop all three hamlets because in both areas the old buildings were surrounded by new houses, and the two areas were about a kilometer away from each other. As Wen Zhibin put it, "If we were to develop them together, demolishing the new houses in between the two old settlements, that area to be demolished would be even bigger than that of the ancient buildings. How could we afford that?"

Therefore, not only did the Duqiao government avoid mentioning Jiangbei's old buildings in their publicity, but it also included only Nantang and Beitang in its use of the New Socialist Countryside Construction fund for the paving of Cheng Village roads. Jiangbei had previously been richer than Nantang and Beitang, so in 1993 the hamlet had raised money internally to pave the 500-meter road from its clan temple to the brigade headquarters. By 2008, the road had become damaged in some places, so residents requested that the township government allocate some of the road-paving fund to repairing those portions. That request was denied.

In order to illustrate Cheng Village's origination in Jiangbei, and the hamlet's age and importance, Shoude and Shouzhi told me over and over again how special their temple was and how outstanding their ancestors were. Instead of pot-shaped gables, as on the Great Cheng Clan Temple in Beitang, the Jiangbei temple's sidewalls had sharply angular eaves, like so many red flags inserted to the left and right of the outer walls. Shoude pointed out that these outer walls resembled the caps worn by imperial officials, a symbol that only high-ranking officials could use, and that the eaves' three layers indicated that Jiangbei's ancestor must have been an official of the third rank (*sanpinguan*). As evidence, Shoude pointed out that the base and steps of the temple's front well were all made of red stone. He believed that this color also showed that the person who built this temple had received an edict from the emperor. Shouzhi also provided another piece of evidence: In 1981, when the San-Mao Railway Line (from Sanshui to Maoming) was planned to pass through Cheng Village, this temple was used as the headquarters for a nearby section of the line, and one engineer noticed that the temple was shaped like an official's cap, saying that the ancestor must have been a high-ranking official. In addition, several old people, including "clan elders" from Nantang and Beitang, mentioned that "Before Liberation (1949), Jiangbei was much richer than Nantang and Beitang. (During Land Reform,) over ten people (in Jiangbei) were classified as landlords, many more than those in Nantang and Beitang combined."

In sum, when clan elders discussed the ancient village, they were mainly interested in talking about the stories of their ancestors, and as soon as these stories came up, their continuity and the ancestors' location seemed particularly important. The problem, however, was that the villagers had already partitioned the legacy of their ancestors into different hamlets. The township officials, who were more concerned with economic affairs, were not willing to pay the costs of developing those ancestors' legacies as a whole. And it was because of such contradictions that clan elders such as Shoude discontinued any substantial participation in the tourism project.

Of course, it is not that the elders do not understand how to revise or omit portions of their ancestors' stories according to certain needs, it is just that there is a huge difference between their standards and those of the Duqiao officials. For example, the elders rarely mention that the first ancestor to settle in Jiangbei was probably the child of a concubine belonging to one of the Tongcheng ancestors. During one casual conversation, Shoude described a 1940s Grave-Sweeping Day ceremony where Cheng villagers "paid homage to our great-grandfather" (Ct: *bai taigung*):

> First a boat team had to be organized, with one boat in the front steered by the person in charge, called the "chief minister" (*zongli*). Several hundred people paraded in mighty contingents along the (Wutong) River all the way to Tongcheng. Our great-grandfather also had other sons and grandsons who were buried there. After paying homage to our great-grandfather, we came back (to Jiangbei) to pay homage to our great-grandmother, who brought her son—our first great-grandfather here—to live in Jiangbei, where she was buried.

30 *An Ancient Confucian Village*

Figure 1.11a&b Typical couplets in the entrances of temples in Nantang and Beitang.

Figure 1.12 External view of the Cheng Clan Temple in Jiangbei.

From this it appears that the mother of the first "great-grandfather" to settle in Jiangbei was probably not her husband's formal wife (*diqi*). Otherwise, it would be hard to explain why she migrated to Jiangbei with one son while her husband and his other sons and grandsons remained in Tongcheng, thirty kilometers away. Elders such as Shoude of course understood this. When we discussed historical stories about Jiangbei's ancestors, he acknowledged, "That's what they say, but we normally don't talk about it.... It's a feudal manner of speaking used to discriminate against us. We stopped speaking in those feudal terms long ago." Of course, logical deduction points to another possibility: These stories from the clan elders themselves retain traces of revisions to the narrative that were collectively forgotten, consciously or not, in the past. As Shoude put it:

> So many years have gone by that it is hard to be sure exactly what happened. But the ancient village is real and still present. Only thirty or forty years ago, people were still living in almost all of these houses.

The Masses

Most of the villagers have neither experience of serving as cadres nor experience of taking major roles in clan affairs. Nor are their families particularly wealthy. The township officials often call them "the masses" (*qunzhong*). In certain formal contexts, this term has the political sense indicating the people whom the cadres are meant to serve. More commonly, as Wen Zhibin put it, "It just means ordinary people, the majority, without any special status, nothing particularly admirable."

On this point, Wen said, "This term is obviously a bit arrogant, as if these people don't have any important individual characteristics. In reality everyone is different." Since, however, the term is still used in both the cadres' work and everyday village life, there should be some logic to it. What logic? When pressed, Wen figured that policy requirements and behavioral habits were basically the same because "the masses" did not have any special characteristics.

At least with regard to the tourism project, Wen's delineation of "the masses" seemed to be convincing. Throughout several years of interaction with many villagers, I discovered that they were also interested in the stories of their ancestors, but not as serious about it as clan elders such as Cheng Shoude.

At the entrance to the Great Cheng Clan Temple in Beitang, I often heard villagers say that the paintings on the temple walls were so lifelike, and that the wooden carvings on the screen in the temple's foyer were so beautiful, that their ancestors must have been rich, otherwise how could the temple have been crafted so elegantly? Similarly, at the entrance to the Nantang temple, multiple villagers have pulled me over to admire the exquisite carvings under the eaves, commenting on the meaning of their subject matter, along with the beautiful ceramic on the windows. Several of them seemed to have completely forgotten that they had already shown these to me more than once. When discussing these things, often the conclusion would be, "What a pity that so much was destroyed in the 1960s!" For example, some of the murals had been covered up with lime, and quotations from Mao Zedong or revolutionary slogans had been written on top. Also, in the shrines of several temples and public buildings, statues of the bodhisattva Guanyin and the deified general Guan Gong had been smashed. However, other villagers would lament that even more were destroyed in the 1980s and 1990s. At least the destruction in the 1960s–1970s was part of a national policy, so "there was no way around it," or "it was done for ideals," but in the 1980s–1990s, members of the same clans had taken the initiative themselves to do it for "one word: money." For instance, several villagers pointed out places where brick carvings, ceramic figurines, or stucco had been secretly removed in the dead of night and sold in the last two decades of the twentieth century. They concluded:

VILLAGER A: This had to have been done by someone from the village. What outsider would dare to sneak in at night?
VILLAGER B: Plus they would have had to climb up on the roof, prize it off, and then transport it out.
VILLAGER C: At that time there were lots of dogs in the village, too. They would have barked if strangers had come in. If the dogs didn't bark and

nobody noticed, it must have been done by someone familiar from the village.

VILLAGER D: Yeah. The point is that if it wasn't a local, how would they have even known there was anything of value on the rooftop of this particular building, especially in the dark? It had to be a public building. If it was a stranger, I can't believe they could have managed to climb up on the right one.

On several occasions, saying, "Well, I don't have anything else to do," villagers would get a ladder, climb up with me onto a rooftop, and show me the traces of where something had been stolen. They explained that these places could only have been accessed in this way, and then they had to get the object down without anyone noticing. Puzzled, they would wonder, "I don't understand how they could avoid making loud noises while doing that." Their goal in showing me all this was obviously not to solve the mystery, but just to show that these ancestral temples and public buildings used to be nice, and what a pity it was that they had been destroyed by relatives from the same village.

Of course, occasionally villagers would tell some unusual stories. For example, one villager mentioned something strange about the well next to Nantang. He said that after Cheng Village was founded, for the first five generations, people got their water from the fishpond in front of the village.

Figure 1.13 Window with decorative pane missing.

34 *An Ancient Confucian Village*

Figure 1.14 Brick carving with centerpiece missing.

Figure 1.15 Old village schoolbuilding, slumping.

The fifth generation "great-grandfather" understood *fengshui*, and one year the fishpond dried up in a drought. The ancestor chose several geomantically auspicious sites and gathered his relatives to dig wells there. After digging over ten wells on every side of the village, however, none of them yielded any water.

Figure 1.16 Wooden eave carvings with pieces missing.

As the drought became more serious, the ancestor grew worried. Suddenly one evening, he dreamed that a god came and told him to go to the flat land in front of the village at noon the next day and dig down three *zhang* (9.6 meters). He did that, and sure enough the new well yielded plenty of water. The young villagers who had been listening to the story were not convinced. Two pointed out that this completely contradicted both logic and the local conditions. First, if the great-grandfather knew so much about *fengshui*, why could he not find the right place to dig a well, requiring a god to come help? Secondly, the area was surrounded by streams and rivers on all sides, and anywhere you dug down a few meters you could find groundwater, so why would people drink from the fishpond for several generations? For many villagers, however, the point was not whether these stories about the ancestors made logical sense, but whether the knowledge underlying them was consistent with their own "common sense." The elderly storyteller retorted, "Even the journalists at the *Qi Prefecture Daily* think this story is good, so why don't you agree?" Some of the other listeners replied that they had never heard the story before, but "It's not important whether the specific details are true or not. Things like gods and *fengshui* are worth believing in, at least a little."

Some younger villagers believe that when it comes to the age of the ancient village, the older the better, but if that age cannot be converted into money, then it is useless. When the cadres called on some of "the masses" to move back into the ancestral houses to live (reasoning that if no one lived in the "ancient village," it would not be appropriate for tourism), every one of the younger villagers refused. One after another, they said that those houses were not fit for inhabitation: The rooms were too small, the ceilings were too low, the wooden floors accumulated dust and dirt, the roofs made of traditional tile shingles tended to leak, and so on. Some of the younger villagers directly retorted:

> You've got to be crazy! In the past we only lived there because we were poor, unskilled, and had no other options. It took a lot of effort for us to build new houses. Who would want to go back to those old things?

Often when discussing the tourism plan, villagers would gradually redirect the conversation toward the current economic situation. For example, under the banyan tree next to Nantang's grain-sunning ground, a villager named Cheng Nanshan launched into a detailed calculation of an "ordinary peasant's" income in Cheng Village.

Nanshan said that the area of his household's farmland was just above average for the village:[18] one *mu* of wet-rice fields (*shuitian*) and 0.4 *mu* of dry-crop land (*hantu*). He plants about 0.4 *mu* of rice, basically enough for him and his wife to eat. (Their children moved to Guangzhou and Shenzhen to work after completing vocational secondary school.) The remaining 0.6 *mu* of wet-fields and 0.4 *mu* of dry-crop land are used for growing vegetables, which they sell at the Duqiao market, other than a small portion for personal consumption. When prices are good, they can net 10,000 yuan per year (including the agricultural subsidy from the government) from vegetable sales. When prices are low, they can only earn about 4,000 yuan. In addition, they have about five *mu* of hilly woodland planted with tangerines, and when prices are good they can net 5,000 yuan per year from this, 1,000 yuan when prices are low. As for expenses, Nanshan said that his household was more frugal than most in the village, except for a few of the older people. Even so, they still spent over 12,000 yuan per year on daily expenses. (He did not smoke, whereas male villagers who smoked spent about five yuan per day on cigarettes.) In addition, they spent about 10,000 yuan per year on gifts (*renqing*) and 1,000 to 2,000 yuan on medical costs. According to this calculation, even when agricultural prices were good, agricultural income was not even sufficient to cover half of the household's annual expenses. Between Nanshan and his wife, therefore, it was necessary for at least one of them to leave Cheng Village and work for about half the year. (In the Pearl River Delta, monthly wages for "common workers" were about 2,500 yuan.) Prior to this, before their children had begun to work, the household's expenses were even higher. Nanshan asked, "If it weren't for the help of relatives, how could a rural family such as ours afford for our kids to attend school on such a meager income?"

The idea of developing Cheng Village's old section as a tourist attraction was, therefore, attractive to "the masses." I often met villagers who would ask, "Didn't the township cadres say they would develop tourism? How come they've been saying that for so long but we still haven't seen any activity?" On the other hand, it was also clear to them that such a plan would not be easy to implement. Some villagers even "blew cold wind" (as Cheng Qianjin put it):

VILLAGER E: You think money will just rain down from Heaven? That those old houses left behind by the ancestors will be enough for us to eat two meals a day (i.e. to cover basic living expenses)?

VILLAGER F: Yeah, if there's no money to be made, what boss would be willing to come invest? How could they be like Lei Feng (altruistic), investing just to help *us* make money?

VILLAGER G: I bet those officials are just talking. It's probably a project for their own prestige (*mianzi*). Do you really think these old houses can be turned into a big load of cash?

Other villagers proposed that, if it were really possible to develop the ancient village as a tourist attraction, the investment problem could be solved if members of the Cheng clan pooled their resources, but this proposal was immediately countered by a series of doubts expressed by other villagers:

VILLAGER H: That would just be a small amount of money to play around with. How could we mobilize enough people to raise all that would be needed?

VILLAGER I: Yeah, it wouldn't be easy to organize. And even if we could raise the money, how to use it would become another problem. You say we should do this, I say we should do that, then he proposes his own idea, and in the end nothing is done. It's hard to do anything involving a lot of people.

VILLAGER J: This would have been possible before Liberation: the clan elders would decide what to do, and everyone else would follow suit. It could also have been done in the days of Chairman Mao: The cadres would make a pronouncement, then everybody would act accordingly. Even if a few people were unwilling, would you dare to say no? But nowadays it's hard: Everyone has their own ideas, every household has its own plans. Even if we wanted to do something, we couldn't afford it. Those with money, like (Cheng) Shouyi, aren't very enthusiastic about clan affairs.

VILLAGER H: Even if he were enthusiastic that wouldn't make a difference. It's not like he (Cheng Shouyi) just found his money on the ground— he couldn't just invest it indiscriminately. If it were you, you would also have to do things according to the laws of market economy. Unprofitable business, even if you say it's for the Cheng clan—would you be willing to invest a bunch of money in it? That's not investment, you can only call that "donation," treating it as a charity. If it were you, maybe you'd give a few hundred yuan, but would you be willing to throw away more than that?

38 *An Ancient Confucian Village*

The villagers' discussions about the ancestors' stories and the tourism project are still far from over, but these are not very important as far as the township and village cadres are concerned—they are just some "opinions of the masses," common and lacking in judgment. "Otherwise they would not be called 'the masses'," as Wen Zhibin put it.

For me, however, it was precisely because of the "ancient village" project that I met all kinds of people in Duqiao and Cheng Village. Their faces often float to the surface of my mind, where they sometimes appear unnatural but extraordinarily lifelike in this era of dramatic changes. In donning the tinted spectacles of academia to sketch these faces, is it possible to approach their minds?

Notes

1 In order to protect the privacy of informants, the names of all people and fieldwork sites mentioned in this book have been changed, according to academic convention. (*Translator's note*: This includes the names of cities, prefectures, and counties such as "Qi," "Wu," etc., except for major cities such as Guangzhou.)
2 In Duqiao, one to two township cadres were assigned responsibility for the Chinese Communist Party affairs and social governance work of each village or residential committee. In everyday work, these grassroots (i.e., township) cadres were called *baocun*, or those "in charge of the village."
3 *Translator's* note: The School of Principle (*Lixue*) was a Neo-Confucian school of philosophy associated with the Song Dynasty scholar Zhu Xi (1130–1200) and his predecessors, the brothers Cheng Hao and Cheng Yi. It had far-reaching impacts on imperial institutions and culture throughout East Asia. See Peter Bol (2008).
4 Actually, there were many other surnames in the village. For example, most of the people in Hedong hamlet were surnamed Chen, those in Xixi were surnamed Liang, and of course most of the women who married into the village had other surnames.
5 *Translator's note*: Cheng Hao (1032–1085) and his brother Cheng Yi (1033–1107) were students of Zhou Dunyi (1017–1073) from Luoyang, located at the confluence of the Luo and Yellow rivers in present-day Henan. Together with Zhu Xi, these scholars are credited with founding the Song Neo-Confucian School of Principle.
6 Judging by their external form, Nantang and Beitang appeared to be one big hamlet, but the villagers divided it into two based on factors such as kinship and villager teams (*cunmin xiaozu*).
7 *Translator's note*: The Cheng brothers' home is believed to have lain within a forest of Chinese parasol trees (*wutong*) along the Luo River in Luoyang, present-day Henan.
8 *Translator's note*: Mount Ni was the birthplace of Confucius in present-day Shandong.
9 *Translator's note*: During the collective era from the late 1950s until the early 1980s, villages were called "brigades" (*dadui*), subdivided into "production teams" (*shengchandui*), and townships were called "communes" (*gongshe*). After decollectivization in the early 1980s, these administrative units officially reverted to their earlier nomenclature, with "production teams" now known as "villager teams" (*cunmin xiaozu*), the size of each unit often changing (with multiple

brigades merging into one "administrative village," for example). It is common throughout China for villagers to continue using these collective-era terms (brigade, production team, commune) into the present, as in the case of "Cheng Brigade"—along with pre-socialist terms for "natural villages" (translated in this book as "hamlets") such as Beitang, which are usually smaller than an administrative village but larger than a villager team.

10 *Fanjai* (Cantonese pronunciation of 粉仔, Mandarin: *fenzai*; literally "powder boy") is the villagers' general term for people who use any kind of illegal drugs. This can be specified depending on the drug as "K powder boy" (for ketamine users), "white power boy" (for heroin users), etc. (*Translator's note*: "Ct" indicates Cantonese pronunciation throughout. Other transliterations are according to Mandarin pronunciation.)

11 Here and below, words in parentheses have been added to clarify the meaning. Since my Cantonese is not very good, I used Mandarin when I could (with young and middle-aged people who could communicate effectively in that language) or had someone interpret for me (only occasionally communicating directly in Cantonese), so these transcriptions were mainly written in Mandarin with a small number of special Cantonese words retained for flavor.

12 *Loujai* (捞仔, Mandarin: *laozai*) is a Cantonese term for people from northern China in general but is often used specifically referring to men who speak Mandarin.

13 In Cantonese, this term *singmuk* (醒目, Mandarin: *xingmu*; literally "eye-awakening," normally translated as "eye-catching") implies that someone is observant, intelligent, and understanding.

14 This policy of "dual transfer"—of industries and labor-power—aimed to direct labor-intensive industries away from the Pearl River Delta out to the eastern, western, and northern parts of Guangdong and other provinces, and to upgrade the region's industrial structure.

15 In Cantonese, *taigung* 太公 and *taipo* 太婆 (literally great-grandfather and great-grandmother) are used as general terms for ancestors, but may also refer to specific generations of ancestors, depending on the context.

16 "Elder brother" was the local cadres' general term for the person in charge of any work unit, referring here to the township party committee secretary.

17 Later I discovered that Cheng villagers truly are hesitant to host outsiders in their homes. In late 2008, over a year after I had begun research in the village, I finally managed to obtain lodging at the home of Cheng Shoude's brother Cheng Shouzhi. However, many villagers expressed that if the cadres had introduced me and made arrangements at the beginning, it would have been easy to find villagers willing to host me.

18 At the end of 2013, Cheng Village had a total area of 9,580.5 *mu*, including 584.4 *mu* of wet-rice fields and 366.75 *mu* of dry-crop land. The population was just over 3,100, so the average per capita allotment was 0.2 *mu* of wet-rice fields and 0.1 *mu* of dry-crop land, but there was a great deal of variation in the area of wet-rice fields actually allotted to each household, for three reasons: First, the 1982 decollectivization of land (*fen tian dao hu*) was organized on the basis of production teams (now known as "villager teams"), using the land area per team delineated in 1962, with considerable variation in the per capita area of wet-rice fields among the teams. Secondly, prior to 2000, each team adjusted land allotments every five years to account for deaths and relocations due to marriage, people leaving for

school, etc., with some households losing land and others gaining land in order to make sure the allotments were about equal per capita. Since 2000, the policy of "keeping the land allotments the same despite changes in the number of people" has been implemented more and more strictly, so the teams stopped adjusting the land, and the area of wet-rice fields per household has become less equal as the number of people per household has increased or decreased. Thirdly, some of the teams in Donghe Hamlet lost all of their wet-rice fields to confiscation by the township government.

2 A Centralist Cadre

Rising to Prominence

During the 2013 Spring Festival, while conducting research in Cheng Village, I joked with Cheng Shoude, "Your village has so many people with so many things going on, it's enough to write another *Records of the Grand Historian*." Shoude replied, "In that case, you should write 'Basic Annals'[1] about Chengren and Shouyi." I believe that Shoude, who had attended high school and served as a primary school teacher, was particularly perceptive in this regard. At least in the eyes of older and middle-aged villagers, the life stories of Chengren and Shouyi truly possessed a certain symbolic significance.

Cheng Chengren was born in 1922, the beginning of an age of warfare: first between the Guangxi and Guangdong warlords, then the Japanese invasion, and finally the Liberation War (i.e., the civil war between the Nationalist Kuomintang and the Chinese Communist Party). In the phraseology of Cheng villagers today, the Liberation War was the "revolutionary" era, and some of them tell stories about a "revolutionary martyr." Later I learned, however, that this "martyr" was the head of the local peasants association who died in 1927, being named a "martyr" in July 1950. Old villagers seem to recall only one "struggle" with Nationalist soldiers, in 1948 when a "Central Army" unit was stationed in Cheng Village. One night, a soldier accidentally fell into a pond and drowned, and the unit detained several villagers, preparing to execute them as "underground Communists." The clan elders contacted a man born in the village who was serving as a university professor of law and working at the Guangdong Provincial Court under the Nationalist Government. He came out to mediate, and finally the villagers were released.

Cheng Chengren himself acknowledged, "Before Liberation, I didn't participate in revolutionary activities." As for the details, he wasn't willing to say.

Other old villagers, however, say that although Chengren was not "revolutionary" before Liberation, his family was actually quite poor. They recall that he used to work as a clerk at the Duqiao market town's Reciprocity Gambling House, serving tea and minding the door. He worked there with three other villagers, and the four of them were bound together in an "Oath of the Peach Garden" (as in the *Romance of the Three Kingdoms*), calling each other

DOI: 10.4324/9781003353072-3

"brother." One of them, named Cheng Liguo, was also from Jiangbei Hamlet, but within the clan hierarchy, their relationship was technically avunculate (*shu-zhi*). The main reason the four of them went to work in the gambling den was that their families had no land to farm. Some of the old villagers think, however, that laziness also had a role to play, "Otherwise why didn't they just rent someone else's land?" They said this later came up during the Cultural Revolution, "but he lucked out: He was a V.I.P., so no one could touch him."

In 1950, the political protagonists of Cheng Village were no longer the clan elders, and the clan-style heads of the ten-household tithings (*jia*) and the hundred-household security groups (*bao*) also fell by the wayside. Under the new state policies, Duqiao's township government began to support the village's poor people and minority-surname families. Chen [*not Cheng*] Xin of Jiangbei Hamlet became head of the Cheng Village Peasants Association, went to Tongcheng for rudimentary training, and then joined the party. The first task assigned to Chen was "redistributing the fruits of labor": confiscating buildings and other property (excluding land) that had been owned individually by landlords and collectively by clans, and distributing them to be used by poor families. One summer evening in 1951, a few Jiangbei villagers were resting in the shade of a banyan tree next to the Wutong River. A villager named Cheng Chengliu was talking with the others, expressing suspicion that Chen had been secretly benefiting personally from the redistribution, when Chen just happened to overhear. (In their recollections, some villagers suspect that Chengliu and others had intended for Chen to overhear them.) After Chen argued with them, yelling, "I've been falsely accused," that night he went and hanged himself in order to prove his innocence. Chengliu and the others were also from poor households themselves, so the township cadres just criticized them but did not do anything substantial about the incident.

Working at the gambling den gave Chengren an opportunity to come into contact with numbers. Although he had only attended two years of school, he knew some basic mathematics and writing. He had been one of the people Chen Xin had relied upon in his redistribution work to help keep records. After the suicide, Chengren was pushed to the center stage of Cheng Village politics. He became the most central figure in the village's Land Reform campaign, other than the work team sent down from Wu County. According to the recollections of several elderly villagers, Chengren truly had a certain knack for management: Although he had not attended much schooling, every job he did turned out pretty well. Later the campaign to form cooperatives again put his talents into play, garnering praise from the township leaders. He joined the party in 1955, then in 1956 he was appointed brigade chief, and in 1957 secretary of the brigade party branch.

After officially becoming the person in charge of Cheng Village, he appointed Chen Xin's brother Chen Lin to serve as the head of Jiangbei's production team, and Cheng Liguo to serve as bookkeeper. Since Chen Lin came from a poor family, and since many team members felt regretful about his brother's suicide, there were no objections to his appointment as head. But some members did comment that Chengren's appointment of his sworn brother Liguo as bookkeeper amounted to favoritism. At a team assembly, Chengren publicly criticized those members who had been "speaking ill," defending the appointment by saying: First, the concepts of "sworn brothers" and "avunculate clan relations" belonged to feudal society, and he did not indulge in such things. Second, his good relationship with and trust for Liguo derived from class sentiment, because they both came from poor peasant families. Third, his recommendation of Liguo derived from public-mindedness, where "virtue should be recognized regardless of kinship." After this, Chengren's two other sworn brothers were appointed as team bookkeepers in Nantang and Beitang.

It was also at this time that ordinary team members began to "keep a respectful distance" from Chengren: "He had risen in prominence (*chutou*), as if he belonged to a higher rank," as Shoude put it. They had no objections to his authority as a cadre, but their habit of addressing people according to their relationship in the clan quietly began to change with regard to Chengren. "Everyone began to call him 'Secretary' instead of 'Ah-Seven,' 'Senior Uncle,' or 'Junior Uncle.' On the surface this was respectful, but in reality it expressed fear."[2]

After this, the estrangement between Chengren and ordinary team members kept growing deeper. In the 1957 Anti-Rightist campaign, he announced that Chengliu and several other villagers had driven Chen Xin to suicide by saying bad things about him, and he labeled them as "bad elements." Chengliu and the others were immediately "overthrown," first being subjected to self-criticism at the team assembly, that being "struggled against" at the brigade assembly. In everyday work, Chengliu began to be treated as inferior to everyone else. For example, when obtaining tools from the team, he had to wait until everyone else had finished picking their tools before he could get one for himself. In addition, Shoude's wife Cheng Ju was also discriminated against in the team on the grounds that Shoude worked as a substitute teacher at Shantang Secondary School in a neighboring commune (i.e., township), so he "associated with rightists all day." As Shoude later told it himself, "According to the policies of the time," he should not have become a "target of the campaign" because he had not been classified as a "rightist," but Chengren insisted on this point, so Cheng Ju—who had graduated from high school—lost any opportunity to be commended as "advanced" or to serve as a cadre.

In 1958, Cheng Village was blessed with a bumper harvest. At the same time, the Duqiao People's Commune began promoting the policy of "people's canteens." Due to his outstanding achievements in political work, Chengren was promoted to the level of "state cadre," so began "eating state grain" and was put in charge of the Duqiao Goose Farm. His replacement as Cheng Brigade Party Branch Secretary was the former brigade chief, Cheng Lifang (from Nantang), and a villager from Xixi surnamed Liang replaced Lifang as brigade chief.

44   *A Centralist Cadre*

After Cheng Lifang and Chief Liang had taken the reins, in addition to taking care of agriculture, they also needed to carry out Great Leap Forward policies such as the "mass production of iron and steel." The trees covering the hills around Cheng Brigade were felled without restraint, their timber transported nonstop to support construction elsewhere via the newly built highway. At the same time, the "winds of exaggeration" blew through the village, the rice yields reported to the commune and the county growing ever higher. Wu County sent cadres down to inspect. According to Chengren's recollection, Lifang and Liang approached him for advice, worried about how to deal with the situation. Chengren recommended that they report the truth, but they wavered. Later, under the "guidance" of cadres from Duqiao, they mobilized villagers to transplant rice stalks from more remote fields to those closer to the village and the road. They also moved windmills from throughout the brigade to blow on those densely planted fields, saying this would help to aerate the rice. In addition, they installed lamps there, saying this would improve their photosynthesis. After the inspection team had left, a villager from Beitang came and told the commune cadres that the rice plants did not have enough air, that they would become "steamed dumplings" (Ct: *cha siu bau*).[3] As a result, that villager was immediately chastised for "saying bad things about socialism, beating a retreat from socialism (*da tuitanggu*), and supporting the 'landlords, rich peasants, reactionaries, bad elements, and rightists,'" and was reclassified as a "bad element." As Chengren told this story, he sighed: Thank goodness he did not step up and tell the truth, otherwise he too would have been labeled a "bad element."

These exaggerated reports led to horrific consequences. Although the brigade's agricultural output did not fall over the following two years, the government took away so much grain that famine struck anyway. The canteens disbanded.

During the famine, Chen Lin (the head of Jiangbei's production team) angered his team members by "eating and taking more than his share." By the time of my research, still many villagers would suddenly become furious as soon as this topic came up. For example, Cheng Shouzhi said, at that time he was still in primary school with Chen Lin's son, and once when he went to their house to play, he saw Chen feeding leftover sweet potatoes to the dog. When Shouzhi tried to snatch one of the sweet potatoes to eat, Chen ran him out of the house. As he ran away, he could hear the man scolding and beating his son. Another villager asked Chen on multiple occasions to help him get a ration ticket so he could go buy half a *jin* (0.25 liter) of cooking oil at the Duqiao Supply and Marketing Co-op, but Chen kept saying "the tickets have all been distributed." The villager suspected that Chen must have embezzled many of his team members' tickets (and this was later proven in the 1964 Four Cleanups campaign), because his family remained healthy while most of the villagers were growing emaciated and even bloated from severe malnourishment. In recalling this experience, the villager said wistfully:

It was our poverty that was to blame. If something like that happened today, we all have plenty of food, so it doesn't matter if the cadres take a little more than their share. At the time, no one had enough, so if they took more than their share, even if it was just a little, that meant we were stuck with even less—you could see the consequences immediately. It was as if you were so hungry that your eyes were blurry, but then your rice was directly dumped into their bowls. Can you imagine that feeling?

The famine did not let up until the early rice harvest of 1962. That winter, the production teams were adjusted to be smaller, with Jiangbei splitting into three teams.

From 1958 to 1964, Chengren did not work in the village, and it is said that he had little connection to village affairs. Although some villagers say that "his family was better nourished than ordinary villagers," that could only be attributed to his position at the goose farm. I discovered a strange phenomenon, however: Villagers would comment on other people only when specific incidents were mentioned (for example, details about Chen Lin taking more than his share), but when the famine was discussed in general terms, many of them would blame everything on Chengren, saying things like, "When he served as party branch secretary, we were starving"—as if he had become a symbol and general representative of all the brigade cadres throughout the collective era.

Returning to the Village

In Cheng Chengren's own recollection, "1964 was an important turning point in my life." This was not because of the Four Cleanups campaign often mentioned by other villagers (which targeted work-points, bookkeeping records, storage, and collective property), but because that was the year he was sent back to Cheng Brigade to serve as party branch secretary. "Otherwise," he said, "I would have continued to work at the goose farm, and when it closed, I would have transferred to another post, continuing to eat state grain rather than being a peasant."

That year, Cheng Lifang was bitten by a dog and soon died from rabies, and Chief Liang fell ill for a long time. Duqiao Commune therefore sent Chengren back to Cheng Brigade to take charge of the work there, with Cheng Shouyi (who had come to prominence during the Four Cleanups) to serve as vice-secretary and a villager named Cheng Chenggong as security director (*zhibao zhuren*). At the same time, a Four Cleanups Work Team, comprised of two professors from a university in Guangzhou and one cadre from Wu County, were stationed in Cheng Brigade.

As Chengren saw it, Shouyi was a young person who had risen to prominence through the good graces of the Four Cleanups Work Team, without as much mass support as himself. On multiple occasions, Chengren had Chenggong tell Shouyi to do his work more responsibly. Shouyi, on the other hand, felt that Chengren was not professional enough. Several of "the masses," for their part, believed that Chengren was somehow connected to the cadres targeted by the Four Cleanups campaign.[4] Chengren suspected this view was caused by Shouyi making mischief behind his back. Years later, when recalling this period of cooperation with Shouyi, Chengren said:

> At that time, he (Shouyi) was young and impetuous, very "Marxist-Leninist,"[5] and several cadres in Cheng Brigade were targeted in the Four Cleanups campaign... . One time, during a team meeting in Jiangbei, Shoukuan said, "Wasn't Chen Lin initially promoted by Cheng Chengren?" I think it was (Shouyi) who had Shoukuan make mischief. I said, "I also promoted Liguo, so why is there nothing wrong with *him*?
> *(I asked: "Was it really Shouyi who had Shoukuan say that?")*
> He has never admitted it—neither at the time nor to this day. He said "no," as did Shoukuan. But Shoukuan was sure that the two of them stood together ideologically.

Chen Lin, the former head of Jiangbei's production team, had been investigated and was found to have colluded with the team's storekeeper in taking over 500 kilograms more than their share of the grain. What angered the villagers even more was that he not only kept some of his team members' cooking oil ration tickets for himself, but —unable to use them all and afraid people would find out—he also went so far as to take the rest and burn them. When recounting this years later, Shoukuan and Shouzhi sighed, "Ultimately you can understand why someone would take more than their share: because they were hungry. But it's just beyond the pale to burn the leftovers rather than sharing with us!" Chen Lin was dismissed from his post and forced to pay compensation for the grain he had embezzled, but not stripped of his party membership as requested by Shoukuan and Shouzhi.

After Chen Lin's investigation, then, Chengren had returned to serve as Cheng Brigade's Party Branch Secretary. The new policy he had brought along with him was, "The problems lie with the cadres, but the roots of those problems lie with the enemies, the key is to guard against and attack (the efforts of) 'landlords, rich peasants, reactionaries, bad elements, and rightists' to sabotage socialism." Of course, Chengren had no power to formulate policies, and the Four Cleanups Work Team implemented the new policy together with him, but many villagers saw the change as the result of Chengren's return to the brigade as secretary. For instance, Shouzhi believed that "As soon as he returned to serve as secretary, he rehabilitated Chen Lin. He (Chen Lin) was someone he had promoted. When it came to other people, he was (more) 'leftist' (i.e., unforgiving)."

Regarding Chengren's "leftism" in the Four Cleanups, several villagers mentioned the story of "blowing black the lamp" (*chui hei deng*). "Blowing black the lamp" was a method of giving someone a beating. It is said that the people who invented this method were cadres from Duqiao Commune. Three to five cadres would meet to have a talk with someone labeled as belonging to one of the "landlord, rich peasant, reactionary, bad element, and rightist" categories, then one of the cadres would blow out the oil lamp and beat the person up, so they would not know specifically who had done it. As villagers explained, if they had known who had beaten them, they could have defended themselves in the future, to some extent, so this method was meant to prevent that. Chengren was probably the first person to use "the black lamp" in Cheng Brigade's Four Cleanups work, according to many villagers, because he had worked at the commune level and learned their methods. He did not admit this, however, telling me in conversation that it was the security director Cheng Chenggong who had first thought up the method. In any case, the villagers were terrified of the black lamp, especially those I interviewed in Jiangbei who had been beaten themselves—all said they were afraid. One said:

> How could you not be afraid? After being beaten a few times, as soon as you ran into a cadre you would get scared and try to run and hide. In everyday work you would try to be as careful as possible to avoid giving them any kind of excuse.

In their recollections today, Shouyi was probably the only brigade cadre who did not participate in this practice, whereas Chenggong participated often. Whenever Chenggong is mentioned, however, alongside Chengren's denial of his own participation, villagers all place the blame squarely on Chengren's "leftism" as party branch secretary, with Chenggong serving merely as his underling.

Chenggong had two brothers, but at the time they were on bad terms with one another. According to his oldest nephew's account:

> (During those years) Uncle (Chenggong) looked down on our family. He thought my dad was too naïve, that he was useless. He wasn't nice to my elder uncle either. He was talented, he served as security director—don't you think that was impressive enough?
>
> At first my dad and uncle were still nice to him anyway, because "a great man does not bear petty grudges," right? They were brothers, after all, so they still had to show concern for his affairs. When it came to marriage, a lot of people were willing to act as matchmaker, and a lot of women wanted to marry him, but he wasn't willing. He was too picky, and in the end he missed his chances. Their backgrounds weren't good enough, and he looked down on the others. He thought that being an official would always make him better than everyone else.

Starting with the Four Cleanups, Chenggong became Chengren's "good partner and helper" (as Chengren put it). In the eyes of ordinary villagers, however, especially those who suffered "the black lamp," he was Chengren's "lackey" and "thug."

After the Chen Lin affair, Chengren no longer dared to make use of people who were too close to him personally. For example, Cheng Liguo had been the bookkeeper for Jiangbei's production team, but when the team split into three, he became the bookkeeper for just one of the three smaller teams. He complained about this to Chengren, but the latter told him that they were in the public eye, so there was no way around it. Similarly, his two sworn brothers had been bookkeepers in Nantang and Beitang, but they were not good at the job, so when the teams were adjusted in 1962, they were voted out of office, and Chengren did not voice any objections. In his account, "At the time I was at the goose farm and had no influence over (Cheng) Brigade affairs... . We had been close when we were younger, but had grown apart. It was a different era."

In 1965, however, Chengren did give special treatment to Liguo again. When the armed forces recruited soldiers that year, Liguo's son Cheng Chengheng passed the physical exam, but only five villagers were allowed to join out of the twenty applicants, and in the selection process, political background became the deciding factor. After excluding a dozen children of "middle peasants," there was still competition among the remaining candidates. At this point, the opinions of the brigade party branch became crucial, and Chengren obtained the position for Chengheng.

That same year, the content of the Four Cleanups underwent a major change, from "cleaning up work-points, bookkeeping records, storage, and collective property" to "cleaning up ideology, politics, organization, and economy." As Chengren understood it, the focus was to be placed on ideology and politics, because "There was nothing left to clean up economically. The 'Four Unclean Cadres' had already been cleaned up, and there wouldn't be anyone else with economic problems." The Four Cleanups Work Team was still stationed in Cheng Brigade, but they no longer "caught" anyone, only occasionally organizing meetings for political study, or dragging out the same "landlords, rich peasants, reactionaries, bad elements, and rightists" who had already been attacked to "criticize and struggle against" them again. Throughout the course of my research, only a minority of villagers still recalled that one time someone else was almost detained.

This incident started with a piece of hilly woodland (including dry-crop land) belonging to Production Team One. Prior to 1949, this was an "ancestral hill" belonging to a branch of the Cheng clan, whose members included some of the residents of Jiangbei. (They lived in Team One, but that team also included people from other branches of the clan.) However, no ancestors had been buried on the hill. During the Great Leap Forward, members of the Jiangbei Production Team (later split into teams One, Two, and Three) opened up two *mu* of dry-crop land on the hill to plant sweet potatoes. In 1965, Chengren, who lived in Team Three, recommended that the hill be reallocated to Team Ten (located in Nantang) because it was "outlying land" within the boundaries of Team Ten's woodland, and therefore hard to manage. This decision irritated the members of Team One, including Shoukuan, who went to the entrance of the Jiangbei Clan Temple (functioning as the office and storehouse for teams One, Two, and Three) and loudly cursed Chengren, saying he was "deranged." He demanded to know (as recounted from memory), "Why would you give Team One's land to Team Ten? You don't belong to Team One, on what basis can you do that? How could you do that without discussing it with us first?" After an intense quarrel, Chengren declared that Shoukuan was a "bad element" with ideological and political problems who needed to be detained. He also brought up some "old business," saying that a year earlier during the "cleanup" of Chen Lin, Shoukuan had "said bad things about the organization (i.e., the brigade party branch)."

However, at the Cheng Brigade Party Branch meeting, Chengren's proposal to "criticize and struggle against" Shoukuan as a "bad element" was opposed by Shouyi, and nothing came of it in the end. Shouyi recalled:

> At the time he (Chengren) said that Shoukuan needed to be dealt with. I said, "I know Shoukuan pretty well. He's got a bit of a temper, but even when it's directed at cadres, he's still reliable politically — he's not a bad element. Besides, nowadays isn't policy saying the production team is the foundation for the three tiers of rural ownership (commune, brigade, and team)"? He was fighting for his production team, not for his own individual interests, and it was not unfounded, not something he just cooked up. Of course, the brigade should have the authority on this matter. I'm not opposed to small adjustments (of hilly woodland use rights). After all, it's still "three tiers of ownership," and the brigade is one of those tiers.

Regarding this matter, Shoukuan told me the following:

> He (Chengren) should not have come back from the commune (goose farm). He used to enjoy a great deal of popular trust, and it would have been a small matter if he offended anyone—no one was keeping score. But in the Four Cleanups he started truly offending people, and then it was no longer a small matter, because now it was backed by the real force of "criticism and struggle." Some people were more tolerant and still didn't keep score, but others were less tolerant and refused to accept it lying down... . It's not that (he) was really a bad person, he was just too obedient, too leftist: If his superiors said something, he did it. In this Four Cleanups campaign, what was the point of taking out his frustrations on us ordinary villagers, instead of attacking the "unclean" cadres? He didn't know how to be a person (i.e., to live in the social world).

In Power

In 1966, the Four Cleanups Work Team withdrew from Cheng Brigade, but political conflicts only escalated as more and more "revolutionary militants" began announcing their own "revolutions," labeling everyone else as "conservative" or "royalist." In the environs of Duqiao Commune, most people were divided into the "East Wind" faction and the "Red Flag" faction. The former derived its name from the revolutionary slogan, "If the east wind does not prevail over the West, then the west wind will prevail over the East." Most of the villagers of Cheng Brigade declared themselves members of the Red Flag faction, including cadres such as Chengren. Duqiao's market town, just across the river, belonged to the Duqiao Residents Brigade, whose members held urban household registrations (*hukou*), although rural women who married into the brigade after 1956 retained their rural registrations. Most of them declared themselves members of the East Wind faction during the Cultural Revolution, along with most of the Duqiao Commune cadres.

Chengren rarely made statements related to the conflict between these two factions, and he never participated in their public activities. This led some Red Flag members to believe that he was only making a pretense of supporting their faction, that he had "two faces and three knives." For example, Shouyi, who later became the head of Duqiao Commune's branch of Red Flag, still believes to this day:

> At that time, Chengren just wanted to serve as an official. He was the most pragmatic: he took whatever position his superiors took. Since the commune cadres were East Wind, of course he followed suit. But then in Cheng Brigade, he had no choice but to say he belonged to Red Flag.

Chengren's own memory of this period was that he was not interested in factional disputes, but "when cast into the arena, one has no choice but to fight." He said:

> I was the brigade secretary, and everyone in the brigade was saying they were Red Flag. How could I say otherwise? (If I said otherwise) how could I do my work as a leader? The commune leaders were all saying they were East Wind, and how could I go against my leaders at work?... Production couldn't stop, it still had to be carried out. All I could do was try to not say anything (not participate in factional struggles) and focus on my production work.

On July 16, 1967, an armed conflict erupted between the factions in Duqiao's market town, where one villager from Cheng Brigade was shot and killed. Several militants from Red Flag collected ration tickets for oil and cloth to give the family as "revolutionary compensation." Chengren did not make any statements or take any actions about this.

Shortly thereafter, under the banner of "revolutionary linking-up," Shouyi was transferred to work at the Wu County Revolutionary Committee, keeping his post as vice-secretary of Cheng Brigade Party branch, but only as a part-time post without actual involvement in the brigade's work. At the same time, Chen Weihua from Donghe Hamlet became the new brigade chief, but he was inexperienced and not very good at the job. In the villagers' eyes, then, "After Shouyi went to Wucheng, Cheng Brigade became the kingdom of Chengren and Chenggong."

However, Chengren discovered that it was now even harder than before to manage the villagers. Before the Great Leap Forward, he said, very few villagers would question the cadres. This second time he served as brigade secretary, however, many more villagers said "bad" or "strange" things about him behind his back. This was especially true of the young students who returned to the brigade to work, "suspending school to make revolution"— they said a lot of strange things. Chengren recalled:

> Now that they had some education, they looked down on us old cadres. They had read a few books and learned a few things, so now they liked to say strange things and chastise you every time you turned around. With some people it wasn't because they'd read too many books, but just because they liked to say strange things. At that time, everyone had to obey (the cadres') management (instructions), so how could it work if everyone was saying strange things every day? It undermined morale.

Therefore, as elderly and middle-aged villagers recount today, a new method of "fixing people" (giving them a hard time) was devised in those days, called "ascending the longan tree." This referred to a big longan tree and two banyans next to the grain-sunning ground on the south side of Nantang, where "thousand-person assemblies" (plenary assemblies for the entire brigade) would "criticize and struggle against" the people who had said "bad things" and "strange things." The place where the enormous tree roots covered the ground was elevated, like a stage. Often Chengren, Chenggong, and other brigade cadres would sit under the banyan trees and have the troublemakers stand under the longan, where they would be criticized.

I learned from the mouths of several villagers about one "rather interesting" man, named Cheng Nanshan, who was "criticized and struggled against" multiple times by Chengren and Chenggong, but who still "proved unteachable and refused to change." I talked to Nanshan specifically about this on several occasions. Regarding that year's "history of struggles," he said:

> I was pretty troublesome at that time, constantly causing small problems but never serious ones, and there was nothing they (Chengren and Chenggong) could do about it. The first time I "ascended the longan tree" was because I'd said "strange things." And it was true.... Normally people "get bored and cause problems after eating their fill," but I caused problems even though I was still hungry. While taking a break under the banyans, I composed a rhyme: "The Cultural Revolution is pretty neat, yes it's neat, we don't have enough food to eat." When Chenggong heard it, he informed Chengren, and the next evening I had to ascend the longan tree. They told me to admit that I'd attacked (the Cultural Revolution),

but I just said, "No, I didn't." They told me to admit that I'd made a mistake, but I said, "It's true that I don't have enough food to eat. Have you been eating enough? When standing under someone else's eaves, one has no choice but to lower one's head. I'm willing to admit mistakes, it won't happen again."

Later I composed a few more rhymes. One of them mentioned that Chenggong was uneducated. Once, looking at a newspaper in the brigade headquarters, he exclaimed, "Wow, why is this train flying?" He was holding the newspaper upside down and couldn't read a word of it. Lots of people made jokes about that. So my rhyme said, "Illiteracy puffs up faces (with imagined abilities) so trains can fly." He made me ascend the longan tree again, saying my uncle was a rightist and he had miseducated me, that my words were weird and confusing. I pointed out, "Aren't *you* my uncle?" Lots of people were laughing. He got angry and said, "I'm not qualified to be your uncle."

Indeed, in terms of clan relations, Chenggong was Nanshan's uncle within "the five degrees" (*wufu*),[6] and villagers considered this close enough to address someone as "Uncle." But when Chenggong said "your rightist uncle," he was referring to a man named Cheng Chengbang.

Nanshan's father was Cheng Chengyou, born in 1912. His brother Chengbang was born in 1925, and their relationship became a model of fraternal affection in the villager's memories. In 1932, both their parents died and the family fell into destitution. Chengyou became a long-term farmhand (*changgong*, a kind of servile status) to help raise his brother. Later he learned how to sew and opened a tailor shop in Duqiao's market town, paying Chengbang's school expenses with the shop's meager income. When Chengbang graduated from Duqiao Primary School at age 13, Chengyou was 26. At the time, this was considered to be approaching the deadline for marital age, after which it would be hard to find a spouse. All their friends and relatives felt that Chengbang had already gotten enough education (at the time most boys could attend school for only about three years), so they urged him to stop financing Chengbang's schooling and instead save money to prepare for marriage. But Chengyou rejected all their matchmaking offers and persisted in financing Chengbang's education through middle school and high school, waiting until Chengbang had found a job before beginning to prepare for marriage. As his relatives had expected, it was extremely difficult for Chengyou to find a spouse, and it was not until age 34 that he finally managed to get married. Then his wife got sick and died, so he had to live alone for several years. In 1949, he remarried, his wife giving birth to Nanshan the next year.

During the period of Japanese occupation, Chengyou was forced to work as head of the Cheng Village Committee for Maintaining Order. In 1954, hearing rumors that the government would investigate this background, Chengyou fled to Hong Kong. Chengbang, his family already living in hardship, adopted

Nanshan and provided financial assistance to the boy's sick mother. In 1957, Chengbang and his wife were labeled "rightists" in the Tongcheng railway office where they had been working, so they were transferred to Guangzhou, where they had trouble supporting themselves. Nevertheless, they continued raising Nanshan and paying for his education until he graduated from primary school. In 1963, Nanshan's mother went to Guangzhou to see the doctor, but died in Chengbang's home. Chengyou went to Guangzhou to organize the funeral but did not return to Cheng Village (finally returning to Hong Kong and dying there from illness in 1972).

In 1964, Nanshan graduated from primary school and began working in the production team. When he became an adult, Chengbang and his wife asked multiple people to help find a spouse for him, but they had no luck because his family was poor, their political background was not very good, and Nanshan keep having to "ascend the longan tree." One villager recalled:

> Nanshan was a bit frivolous in the way he talked. To put it positive, he was humorous but had no ill intent. Chenggong was his relative, yet he was the one who kept making him ascend the longan tree. They belonged to a different production team than us, but even we couldn't bear to watch. At the time, lots of people said, maybe Chenggong was "impotent" (Ct: *m dat*) and unable to marry, so wanted to prevent other men from marrying as well. Think about it: (Nanshan's) family was already poor, and then he kept getting sent to the longan tree—in that era, who would be willing to marry him?... You can't be so "absolute" about things, especially toward an unfortunate person like (Nanshan). If the problem was really that he "said strange things," lots of people were complaining in those days, why would you choose *this* kind of person to pick on? It's "bullying the weak and fearing the strong." Unconscionable.

Of course, other villagers felt that this informant was biased. According to their description, Chengren and Chenggong did not specifically target Nanshan, but became hostile whenever they encountered obstacles in their work. For instance, several villagers mentioned incidents starting in 1977, when those two cadres began to implement the Family Planning policy. They were unusually heavy-handed about it, stricter than other brigades in the area—especially in 1979. That year, Chengren and Chenggong would get a rope, kick open villagers' doors, and say unacceptable things to the effect of, "If you don't go on your own to get your tubes tied, we'll tie you up and drag you there. If you keep refusing to cooperate, we'll string you up—here's the rope. If you prefer to drink pesticide, we'll prepare it for you." Also in two brigade assemblies, Chengren announced that if people resisted Family Planning, "you may choose between the knife, the rope, or pesticide." Under this sort of "work intensity," by the end of 1980 Cheng Brigade's Family Planning work had progressed so rapidly that it took the lead in Duqiao Commune and was commended as an "advanced model."

In addition, several villagers felt that the Cultural Revolution should affect everyone alike, but cadres like Chengren and Chenggong were not affected at all—in fact, it even strengthened their authority, which they used for private gain. One example they mentioned was the time when Chengren helped Liguo's second son Cheng Chengxin to join the army. In 1968, when Chengxin took the physical exam, the number of people who passed the exam far outnumbered the recruitment quota. Chengren talked to Liguo and Chengxin, saying that a few years before he had helped Chengheng join the military, so he could not do the same for Chengxin. At the end of 1969, however, when the number of qualified candidates again outstripped the quota, this time Chengren did help Chengxin obtain a spot. About this, Shoude commented:

> He (Chengren) took good care of his sworn brothers. It was only because he opened back doors for Chengheng and Chengxin that they were able to join the military. He also tried to care of his other two sworn brothers, but they turned out to be lame ducks, so nothing came of it. At the time, everyone was talking about it.

Chengren denied the claim that he had "opened back doors" for anyone. He said, "What I did was permitted within the scope of policy." Moreover, he felt that Chengxin normally made a positive impression and was politically reliable. Once he had given an example to prove that he was not corrupt: His own son had not attended enough school, so he did not open a back door for him, because that would have fallen outside the scope of policy and violated the rules. Not long thereafter, however, people found out that in 1972 Chengren's son Shouwang had somehow obtained a post as sales clerk at the Duqiao Supply and Marketing Co-op. Although the post was not a permanent position on the state payroll (*bianzhi*), it was still something that was highly sought-after by villagers at the time.

Regarding the marriage of his children, Chengren combined the strictness of a traditional father with "revolutionary" characteristics. His two sons-in-law and his daughter-in-law were all chosen on the basis that they "had proper stems and red roots, were honest in their affairs, and were loyal and reliable." As a result, all three came from poor families, but their personal abilities were mediocre.

Hard Times

In 1981, Chengren stepped down from his post as brigade party branch secretary. Villagers said this was because the commune cadres felt that he could no longer keep up with the times. Chenggong stepped down at the same time. According Chengren, however, it was himself who no longer willing to work as a cadre. He said:

Earlier I had been the one to lead the village's collectivization, and now they were telling me to decollectivize it. I didn't want to do so many things anymore, first this way then that. It was the state's business, but I was the one who got blamed if anyone was unhappy about it. If they wanted us to "work alone" (as households in farming the land), then I would work alone. Let the young people take care of the state's business. Later they appointed Chen Weihua as party branch secretary. He was enthusiastic about decollectivization. I recommended Chengxin as vice-secretary and security director. He started working for the brigade when he returned from the army.

In 1982, the Household Responsibility System was implemented in Cheng Brigade. In early 1983, the brigade was renamed "village committee," and the production teams were renamed "villager teams."

Like the other villagers, after decollectivization Chengren began to focus on the 0.5 *mu* of wet-rice fields and 0.3 *mu* of dry-crop land that was allocated to his household. For the first few years, Chengren managed to fare a little better than his neighbors just by farming this land. As he recounted:

> At that time there was no official who could just take it easy. I focused my energy on agricultural production, and I did pretty well economically. Every year I could sell some rice, and in between I could sell vegetables at the Duqiao market. The price of rice and vegetables kept rising every year, so I could make a little money. In '85 I had a grandson over the (Family Planning) quota, and my son was poor, so I paid the 200 yuan fine for the over-quota birth. For my grandson's first birthday, I spent 500 yuan buying them a 14-inch Gold Star black-and-white television. At that time, very few people had a TV, and most of them were only 12-inch—very few were 14-inch. Everyone would gather around to watch it.... Things started going downhill in 1988. The price of rice fell, and the Duqiao grain station wasn't even willing to buy our rice.

In the analysis of other villagers, however, Chengren's "path to prosperity" was a little more complicated. As one summarized:

> At first (right after decollectivization), he (Chengren) was doing well. For one thing, the two of them (husband and wife) actually worked pretty hard, in the fields from dawn to dusk every day. For another, (their son) Shouwang had already married, as had their two daughters, so they didn't have to worry about family expenses. The two of them had enough food to eat, their health was pretty good, and there wasn't much they had to spend money on—unlike us, who had to spend a lot money on our children's school and our parents' medical expenses. In addition, Shouwang worked at the co-op, so he could get them "within-plan" fertilizer at the low price set by the state, whereas people like us, without

connections, rarely had access to that, so we mainly relied on market-priced fertilizer (outside the plan).⁷ At that time, the same kind of fertilizer could cost over twice as much (at market price)—it was too expensive for us to afford. Not only did he have plenty of fertilizer for rice farming, he would even use it for growing vegetables. What a luxury!

From 1990 to 1991, Chengren also tried to raise a breeding sow. He reasoned that with the price of rice falling, it would be more economical to feed the rice to pigs, and in that case it would be more profitable to raise a sow and then sell the piglets. What he failed to realize was that higher profit means greater risk. Before the end of the first year, after the sow gave birth, both mother and piglets came down with foot-and-mouth disease. The township government required that he bury the pigs that had died. He recounted:

> I was someone who did what he was told, so I just buried them. Besides, I wouldn't have been able to sell them—anyone could see they were sick. Some people cheat and sell their (diseased) pigs at the market, and no one notices... . It's hard to make an honest buck.

This loss had a major impact on Chengren, costing him all of his savings. He believed, however, that disease would not strike every year, so if he tried again the next year, he could probably recoup his losses. So in 1991, he borrowed small amounts of money from multiple relatives until he had put together enough to buy another sow. This time he took extra precautions, first having a technician from the township veterinarian station come and disinfect the pig pen, and then having them come back several times to have the animal tested. That winter, the sow gave birth without any problems—but Chengren still ended up losing money, this time because the prices of pork and piglets had fallen precipitously. After that, Chengren never dared to raise breeding sows again, instead just raising ordinary pigs for meat every year. In Cheng Village, raising breeding sows is considered a form of investment, to make money, but raising a pork pig every year is more like a "piggy bank," something to do with leftover rice and vegetables throughout the year until it is killed and eaten, but not a way to make money.

In 1992, Duqiao Supply and Marketing Co-op underwent a personnel change. Since Shouwang did not have a permanent position on the state payroll there, he was laid off and sent home to farm. Chengren was extremely disappointed, regretting that he had chosen to have his son work there. In sharp contrast, after the Wutong River diversion project was completed, a neighbor's son had gone to work at the water conservancy station in 1979. Although he did not have a permanent position either, he was not sent home to farm, and his salary kept rising steadily. However, Chengren believed this could also be attributed to Shouwang's unwillingness to study when he was a child, so his grades were poor and he did not finish middle school, whereas the neighbor's son had graduated, and water conservancy required some education, after all. Shouwang saw it differently: First, his low grades as a child were a result of the way his father raised him. Secondly, he could have gotten a job at the water conservation station even without completing middle school. The main problem was that his father was uneducated and so did not have enough foresight, Shouwang believed.

After this, Chengren no longer had special access to low-priced fertilizer, and at the same time, since Shouwang had lost his steady salary, now he began to ask his father for money on a regular basis. Chengren said:

> It feels like all of a sudden the pressures have increased. He (Shouwang) isn't good at farming, he hasn't done it in many years. Both my grandsons need money for school and he can't afford it. My granddaughter's grades weren't very good, she's not willing to study, and now she's gone to Guangzhou to sling dishes (work as a server in a restaurant).

Chengren discovered that it became harder and harder to make a living from farming rice and vegetables. The prices of seed, fertilizer, and agro-chemicals kept rising, and money kept losing its value. Although the prices of rice and vegetables also rose, they could not keep up with the rapid rise of farm supply prices and the falling value of currency. By the mid-1990s, it had become impossible to make money from planting. At the same time, the Duqiao Township government kept demanding more and more payments of all kinds: fundraising for the construction of classrooms for primary and secondary schools, for the payment of *daike* teachers (part-time rural teachers not on the state payroll), for the repair of irrigation ditches, and so on. Technically, these fees were all "supplementary," in addition to the agricultural tax but collected together with it. Chengren began to complain more and more about these changes. He believed that it was right to raise money for education, but that only villagers with children in school should have to pay that. For instance, he thought it was reasonable to ask his son and daughter-in-law for money, but not elderly couples like himself and his wife. As for repairing irrigation ditches, he believed that the government should provide the money while "the masses" provided the labor, that way the costs would be lower, since peasants had free time but little cash income. Chengren's complaints did not change anything, but some villagers would joke, "How come even the old secretary is now 'saying strange things'?" In response, Chengren would make somber statements to this effect:

> The current situation is completely different from before. Now these young officials are thoroughly rotten. Look at these township cadres, where is their communist spirit (*dangxing*)? The village cadres are even worse. The "scriptures" sent down from above are good, but these "monks" down below read them wrong. They've completely forgotten where they came from, selling their grandfathers' legacy without remorse and ruining the country. They don't know how hard it was to build all this.

Sometimes some of the less well-off villagers would express agreement with what Chengren said, but in most cases, any villagers standing around would just regard him as someone who "likes to prattle on." Once his neighbor described him in this way: "After things went downhill for his family, he became like Xiang Lin's widow (from Lu Xun's story "New Year's Sacrifice").[8] He always thinks he's the smartest, as if he were still the party branch secretary, not realizing that the world has changed."

Chengren also tried to do business, but since he did not have any money, he could only operate on a very small scale. In the 1980s, he saw several neighbors become "10,000-yuan households" by doing business, so he applied for a loan from the Duqiao Credit Union in order to set up a tobacco stall in Guilin, but was turned down on the grounds that "the authorities were strict (about offering loans)." In the mid-1990s, he approached the credit union again, saying, "Now authority has devolved to the local level, so you can lend me a few thousand yuan," but this time he was told, "Too many people have been defaulting on their loans, so you can only deposit money—we're not offering any more loans." The director of the credit union was a member of the Duqiao Residents Committee surnamed Wang. In formal settings, the villagers called him "Director Wang," but informally they called him "the God of Wealth." One villager explained:

> The (term) "God of Wealth" meant two things: One, that he had plenty of cash on hand, and two, business was good: If you had the capital to start with, you could make a profit with any kind of investment. Wasn't that just like the God of Wealth? If only he'd lend you money, you'd make a profit.... Having money alone didn't make you a God of Wealth. That term only applied to people who could profit from money they already had.

No one was surprised that the God of Wealth was unwilling to lend money to Chengren. For example, Shouzhi said:

> For one thing, this was because he (Chengren) had offended too many people back when he served as party branch secretary. Although he had not directly offended the God of Wealth, he had a bad reputation. No one wanted to cooperate with him. For another, he didn't know how to give gifts. If you went to ask for a loan and all you brought was "a couple bunches of bananas,"[9] or offered a Coconut Tree (brand) cigarette,[10] something on that level, who would even give you the time of day?

Chengren also tried borrowing money from relatives, but he had few relatives to begin with, and those he had were not very well-off economically, so that came to nothing as well.

In the end, therefore, the only business Chengren could do was to hawk goods at a few rural markets in the area. The most profitable venture he can recall was hawking loose tobacco. In the 1980s tobacco wholesaled for about one yuan per *jin* and retailed for 1.2 yuan, about the same price as pork, with a profit of 20 percent. In the 1990s, however, this became less profitable: while the price of pork rose by ten-fold throughout the decade (despite several major dips along the way), the retail price of tobacco rose by only three- or four-fold. It was also at that time that more and more smokers (except for a few older people) began switching from smoking pipes to buying cigarettes. Selling cigarettes required a business license, and Chengren felt it would be a waste to get a business license just to sell cigarettes, so he gave up.

In addition to farming and hawking, another important source of Chengren's income was working as a day-laborer. Of course, he could not make much money from this, especially in Duqiao before the year 2000, when the daily wage was low: about 4 yuan in the 1980s, increasing only to 35 yuan by the late 1990s. Since he had no technical skills, most of the work Chengren did was basic, unskilled manual labor. One example he recalled plaintively was that in 1988–1989, Cheng Chengxin contracted for several service-road projects on the Duqiao section of the San-Mao Railway Line, hiring several stoneworkers and bricklayers to cut stone and lay foundations, but Chengren could only do purely manual jobs such as digging and carrying gravel. Not only was it tiring, but the pay was also much lower than that of the stoneworkers and bricklayers.

Living Out His Days

At the dawn of the new century, the Tax and Fees Reform was carried out, ending the collection of all rural levies other than the agricultural tax. A few years later, the government abolished the agricultural tax as well, in addition to providing a number of rural benefits including grain-farming subsidies. All this delighted Chengren, who often said, "Nothing this good has happened since Pangu first parted Heaven and Earth." The changes decreased his household expenditures by nearly a thousand yuan and increased their income by about 200 yuan. For most villagers, the subsidies were just a little "spending money," but for Chengren it was hugely important.

This was because Chengren's health had been declining since the mid-1990s, so he had to spend several hundred yuan at the village clinic every year. By now the clinic was completely different than it had been under "cooperative healthcare" when he had served as party branch secretary. Now the doctor was an "individual entrepreneur" (*getihu*) whose goal was to make money, increasingly using the method of intravenous drips to treat patients, so the fees had increased fifty-fold since the early 1980s. In order to reduce expenses, in the late 1990s, Chengren had quit smoking, although he still occasionally hawked tobacco at the Duqiao market.

After 2000, it became more economical to farm rice and vegetables, but Chengren had lost the ability to work due to his declining health. Other than a little land kept for his wife to grow vegetables for household consumption, he let his son Shouwang farm the rest. But Shouwang's own household was also doing poorly economically, with almost no money leftover after providing rice and oil for their parents. Meanwhile, Chengren's medical expenses kept growing every year, so he often had to visit the clinic on credit, keeping a tab there. He rarely dared to visit Duqiao's small health center, let alone an actual hospital in the city. On holidays, Chengren's children would give him "a handful of tens" (no more than 100 yuan), which he would use to pay off his debt at the clinic. This contrasted sharply with the situation of most villagers, who could afford to eat meat almost every day.

In 2005, Duqiao Township began to implement Guangdong's policy of establishing a "New Rural Cooperative Healthcare" system. This policy did not provide much direct help for Chengren, however, because it focused on major illnesses, whereas his main problems were chronic issues such as low blood pressure, a long-term cough, and joint pain, for which the system provided only a small partial reimbursement whenever he went to Duqiao Health Center. In 2010, the village clinic refused to continue treating Chengren on credit. The doctor called Shouwang in to ask for his agreement, in front of several other villagers being treated there, that in the future Chengren's treatments could be charged under Shouwang's name. Only under those conditions could Chengren continue to be treated on credit. Over the subsequent two years, Chengren's medical fees escalated through the roof, and they had to be covered almost entirely on credit. In 2013, the doctor complained to me about it:

> During the two years before the death of (Shouwang's) father (in 2012), he racked up huge medical bills, including about 20,000 yuan at my clinic, nearly half of which still hasn't been paid. His family is so muddleheaded.... I can't escape my own personal obligations (*qingmian*) either: It was only by (Chengren's) recommendation that I could become a doctor. In July 1969, he had a lot of power. Under cooperative healthcare, without his recommendation, I wouldn't have been able to go (to medical training to become a community doctor). Of course, one has to be flexible: If I hadn't studied medicine, I might have gone into business and gotten rich by now. Actually, with him always paying on credit, it was hard for me to cover my expenses. Everyone (in the village) is "uncles and brothers" (members of the same clan), so if everyone tried to pay on credit, I would have had to close my doors long ago. But one has to operate with a conscience. He did help me after all, and at the time he was so pitiful, I had no choice but to make an exception and keep extending credit. Oh me, life is so inscrutable.... Let's just forget (about the troubles caused by Chengren in his later years) so I can get some peace of mind.

As life grew harder by the day, Chengren approached the township cadres on several occasions, hoping to obtain some kind of support, but one after the other, they just said "their hands were tied," there were no relevant policies or funds they could use for that purpose. In 2005, one township cadre agreed to add him to the list of villagers receiving 120 yuan a month in minimum social security benefits (*dibao*)—a policy just introduced at that time. According to Cheng Qianjin, the policy was actually meant only for people with disabilities and seniors without children, but Chengren had both children and grandchildren, so adding him to the list was already an exception. On this point, Chengren was full of complaints about the township cadres:

> If these people just smoked a little less, that would be enough for us to live on for a month, it's just that they aren't willing—they have no compassion. We used to talk about "the three sames" (cadres were supposed to eat the same food, live in the same type of houses, and perform the same type of labor as ordinary peasants), but now they don't even have "one same." …I devoted my life to the party, but now that I'm old, no one will take care of me.

Qianjin did not deny such statements, saying, "Now we have a market economy, so the party can't do anything but waive (Chengren's) party membership dues, using a little money from the village budget to pay it for him."

Besides economic hardships, what Chengren lamented the most was "the fickleness of human relationships," saying no one cared about him anymore. In the past, when he was brigade secretary, lots of people used to fawn on him, smiling whenever they met, but now that he was old, the same people did not even bother to say "hi" anymore, pretending they had not seen him.

Chengren lived in an old-style blue-brick house he had obtained during the "distribution of the fruits of labor," when landlord properties were seized and parceled up among the poor families. Its front door faced the main road in Jiangbei, and there always used to be people coming and going, stepping inside to visit or drinking tea in the doorway when they had nothing else to do, so Chengren had to keep a lot of benches on hand. After he got older, however, hardly anyone came to drink tea anymore. In the winter of 2009, when he had no money to buy coal and no energy to go collect firewood in the hills, and Shouwang had not gotten around to bringing his parents any firewood, Chengren asked his wife to chop up those benches and burn them.

Perhaps thinking that too many people had "changed their faces" too quickly, when chatting with me about this topic, Chengren rarely specified anyone's names, but the two brothers Chengheng and Chengxin were exceptions. About them, he complained:

> According to the party's principles, it would be inappropriate for me to speak of loyalty among sworn brothers (*jianghu yiqi*), but I still value such loyalty. When I was in office, I never treated Liguo's family unfairly. How could his two sons have both become soldiers if I hadn't helped them? Just look around, where else can you find a family where two brothers would both have the chance to join the army, one after the other? Nowhere… .

Liguo himself is fine, but those two sons are no good—no conscience at all. The older one (Chengheng) got a job at the Water Conservancy Office (in Wu County), but whenever he comes home and drives by my house, all he leaves is dust. The younger one started out serving as party branch secretary, but after he went to work at the Duqiao Land Office, he started ignoring people as well… . Back in the day, the two of us called each other "brother." We were as close as could be.

Oh me, I just blame my own short-sightedness. Back then someone warned me, "Be careful doing people favors, you might not get reimbursed." I thought he was just trying to stir up discord… . Now that I already have one foot in the grave, I no longer believe that people get what they deserve. Look at Chengxin's selfishness, yet didn't he get promoted to an official position? He's just a crude, uneducated peasant, but now he's on the state payroll. Where's the justice in that?

After he lost the ability to work, whenever the weather was nice, Chengren would be sitting in his doorway under the eaves. Villagers would walk by—some in a hurry, others taking their time—on the road only a dozen meters from the house, but very few of them would say "hi." Looking from the outside, he had become a completely unremarkable old man, quietly gazing at the road every day "with nothing in the world to do." It took a long time for me to even notice this key figure who had made such an impact on the history of Cheng Village. It was only after conducting research for a while that I discovered that this old man, whom I had often walked by, was the same Cheng Chengren that villagers kept mentioning when discussing historical events.

According to Shoude, on several occasions in the 1990s, he had invited Chengren to participate in clan events such as updating the genealogical records, organizing ceremonies to honor the ancestors, linking up with other villages from the same clan, and officiating weddings and funerals. However, as Chengren could not write couplets, knew little about clan history, and was not well-liked among the villagers, he stopped participating after a few times. Chengren said this was mainly because he did not like "that old feudal stuff." Secondly, events such as linking up with other villages required him to pay for transportation, and at the time he did not make enough from hawking to afford such expenses. Thirdly, since he did not know much about wedding and funeral ceremonies, even if he attended, all he could do was odds and ends like sweeping the floor, and he felt that people like Shoude looked down on him, so "it was no fun." With the addition of those last two reasons, he was even less willing to participate in such events.

In our conversations, there were two people he praised by name:

I'm old and can barely move around. "As waves push waves on the Yangzi River, the younger generation surpasses the old." Nowadays few people have a conscience, but there are two people who do—time reveals a person's heart. One is Dr. Cheng at the brigade (i.e., village) clinic: If you go there, he'll give you a cup of tea, and if you don't have enough money, he'll treat you on credit. The other is one you wouldn't think of: Shouyi. We used to be partners, but our views were always different. He headed a rebel faction (in the Cultural Revolution), whereas I never participated in those things. Later he withdrew from the party.... Every year he comes over to drink tea at my place, before holidays. Whenever he comes he gives me two or three hundred yuan, more than my children give. The first few times, I told him to keep it, but he insisted. Later I stopped declining, and now I just accept however much he gives. His heart is wider, more concerned with loyalty. He's someone who got what he deserved: He made a lot of money, as did his children. We used to not get along, but now I can see he was right—he was smarter than me, and I'm ashamed.

In the eyes of ordinary villagers, if you chatted with Chengren in his later years, what you would hear the most would be lamentation about the impermanence of things in his life. Many villagers described him as "loving to prattle on and on." My own impression, however, at least since I began talking to him in 2008, was that he had already stopped doing that. Often, after he had said "there's no value into dredging up the past" or "there's nothing to say about that," I had to sit with him for a long time, discussing unrelated topics, before he became willing to talk about his own past, along with complaints about life in general. At the end of 2011, during my last conversation with him, Chengren seemed to have seen through it all: "In this life, that's just how it is: We're born with nothing, and we leave with nothing, just passing through this world. What's the point of lamenting or worrying so much?"

A few months later, in late spring, Chengren left this world. When I received the phone call from his landlord Shouzhi, I was busy with teaching duties and could not go to Cheng Village right away. Later, villagers said that Chengren's funeral was simple. The only township cadre to attend was the Duqiao Party Committee's head of organization, who briefly visited the Jiangbei temple and gave a short speech, honoring Chengren for "living for the Communist Party, forever young (in our hearts)," suggesting that he truly was a bit different from ordinary villagers.

Closing the Casket

After Chengren died, if he came up in conversation, villagers' opinions were even more diverse than when he was still alive. This was obviously a classic case of inability to "reach a final verdict" about a man even though his "casket is closed."[11]

The first topic villagers debated was whether Chengren was clever or not.

Many villagers would say that he was a smart man.

Some villagers believed that he was good at speaking. Although his education level was lower than that of Shouyi, his speaking ability was far superior.

Regardless of the topic, he could come up with one set of reasons after another "that could be placed on the table" (i.e., suitable for public discussion). In addition, they said, Chengren was also smarter than other cadres when it came to power struggles. They mentioned several examples, showing that in order to prevent other brigade cadres from replacing him as party branch secretary, he would take precautions against those with more education—especially those with a stronger ability to get things done—and if he could "grab a hold of their pigtails" (i.e., find some mistake they had made as an excuse), he could figure out a way to elbow them out of the group.

One example they mentioned was the time that Chengren had "dropped stones into the well after Chen Xi had fallen in" (i.e., attacked him when he was already down). Chen Xi had been committing an extramarital affair with the wife of Cheng Shouli. Shouli was Shoude's older brother who had moved to Hong Kong in 1949, where he had remarried. Meanwhile his first wife back in Cheng Village had raised their child as a single mother for over ten years. Chen Xi had served as brigade chief and was also married with three sons and one daughter. After the affair was discovered, both parties divorced their spouses and remarried to form a new family. Current party branch members, including vice-secretary Shouyi, urged Chengren to limit their punishment of Chen Xi to an "internal warning" or "probation," but Chengren insisted on expelling him from the party. That marked the end of Chen Xi's political career in Cheng Village.

A second example of Chengren's intelligence in power struggles that villagers mentioned regarded another man from Jiangbei who had served as brigade bookkeeper. During the 1965 Four Cleanups, Chengren expelled him from the party for embezzling 100 yuan. It was said that 100 yuan was considered a large sum at the time, but the punishment was too severe for that type of crime. One villager commented:

> It's like when (the legendary) Wu Dalang ran his shop and refused to hire anyone taller than him.[12] Chen Lin was also a cadre (targeted by) the Four Cleanups, but (Chengren) protected him rather than expelling him from the party. (Chengren) said this wasn't because he had given (Chen Lin) the job, and maybe this had some truth to it, but the main reason may not have been what (Chengren) had said—that "the policies sent down from higher levels had changed"—but because Chen Lin was not (as much of) a threat to him (as the bookkeeper he had expelled).

Villagers participating in such discussions would also mention a third example from 1979, when Chengren expelled Shouyi from the party. His logic in doing this was the same as above, "Because Shouyi was better than him in many ways." They seemed to have forgotten that a few minutes earlier they had praised Chengren as a more capable cadre than Shouyi.

However, some of these same villagers would also say that Chengren was not clever at all.

First, although he was good at public speaking and could articulate a set of reasons for anything he was doing, he was always doing "leftist" things, and this tendency became more pronounced over time. "Leftist" was bad, so it was as if Chengren's intelligence was "helping the tyrant King Zhou to oppress the people." Some villagers believed that Chengren was only smart on the surface and stupid underneath, being "too naïve" and knowing only a few petty tricks. When policies coming down from superiors were clearly problematic, his brain was not flexible enough to resist or adjust them to local conditions, and instead he would implement them in an even more extreme manner than intended. One villager commented, "He was smart, but he only used his intelligence to do stupid things."

Secondly, although he had cleverly pushed more capable cadres out of the team, those people actually managed to benefit from the situation, whereas Chengren just ended up with a miserable retirement. For instance, after Chen Xi was expelled from the party, he enjoyed a pretty good life with his new wife (Shouli's ex-wife), making some money in the 1980s, building a new-style blue-brick house at the entrance to Jiangbei, tearing it down in the late 1990s and building a red-brick flat-roofed house with modern furnishings. The former bookkeeper targeted in the Four Cleanups was also good at "doing economy" (*gao jingji*) after decollectivization, so he built a shopfront in Duqiao market town and ran a restaurant there that served breakfast and afternoon tea, making a respectable income. As for Shouyi, he had already grown rich by the end of the 1980s, becoming a major "boss" over the next decade. Since Chengren had neither the ability to make money nor a reliable network of connections, he could not obtain funding, so in the 1980s he did not make money, and in the 1990s things got worse by the day. One villager said, "If he weren't so clever, he wouldn't have pushed out so many people, stupidly offending so many people and isolating himself."

The second topic villagers debated about Chengren was whether he demonstrated "loyalty and righteousness" (*yiqi*).

Many villagers, including Shoude and Shoukuan, believed that Chengren was a loyal and righteous man. They mentioned that, as Chengren himself admitted, it was entirely out of loyalty to Liguo that he had helped out the two brothers Chengheng and Chengxin. Also out of loyalty to Liguo, Chengren went so far as to sidestep "revolutionary principles."

However, Shoude and Shoukuan both believed that Chengren could be said only to have practiced "petty loyalty" (*xiaoyi*) rather than "great righteousness" (*dayi*). On the level of "personal" affairs, Chengren was loyal only to sworn brothers such as Liguo, but not to other uncles and cousins within the clan, which would have been an expression of "great righteousness." On the "public" level, by refusing to make exceptions for fellow members of his clan, he appeared on the surface to be "placing righteousness above kinship" in order to complete "revolutionary tasks," but the policies he was carrying out were clearly wrong-headed. Shoukuan said, therefore, "He cared only about completing tasks in a mechanical way, ignoring the great righteousness of Chairman Mao's call to 'serve the people wholeheartedly'."

The third topic villagers debated about Chengren was whether he should be considered selfish or altruistic.

Several villagers believed that "Everyone is selfish, and Chengren was not cut from a different cloth, so how could he have been any different?" There was, of course, strong evidence for this. For instance, Chengren helped his son obtain a post at the Supply and Marketing Co-op, and then used this to purchase discounted fertilizer. Or again, when evaluating his wife's work-points in the production team, she received one or two more points than other women, even though her labor output was clearly the same. Pushing other cadres out of the leadership team was also mentioned as an example of Chengren's selfishness.

After discussing this topic for a while, however, some of the same villagers would often turn the conversation toward comparing Chengren with other cadres in Cheng Village and Duqiao Township. In that context, one villager after the other would express that Chengren was not really that selfish, or even that he was not selfish at all. One asked, "Who cares about that kind of small-scale selfishness? His efforts to benefit a little were so pitiful they can be simply overlooked. Look at these cadres today... ."

The fourth topic villagers would debate about Chengren was whether his life could be considered "worthwhile" or not.

Several younger villagers felt that Chengren's life was not worthwhile at all. Although Chengren had once been arrogant, with a commanding presence, he never got a chance to enjoy the good life. During the collective era, at best he managed to perform a little less manual labor than ordinary villagers, but even then he still had to work together with them (as long as he was not in a meeting), living in conditions only slightly more tolerable than the others, but still unable to eat meat more than a few times a year. Another villager said, "If today's cadres had that much power, there's no telling how corrupt they would become." After decollectivization, Chengren's life got even worse than other villagers. He was especially miserable in his late years, showing that his life was really "not worthwhile."

However, many of the older villagers and a few of the middle-aged ones believed that Chengren's life was worthwhile. They said that although during the collective era his material conditions were not much better than ordinary villagers, at least his livelihood was secure, and more importantly, "he enjoyed several decades of grandeur (*fengguang*)." Some people said wistfully, "How many moments of grandeur can one experience in a lifetime? (For him it was) several decades, plenty!" Another important reason they gave was that, although Chengren's health suffered in his later years, he never fell so ill that he could not get out of bed: He could sit, walk, eat, and sleep, finally dying peacefully at age ninety. They say, "long illness erodes filial piety," especially when the son's family is poor. Even Shoude sighed, "With or without grandeur, you only live once.[13] With or without good karma, in the end, the best and most important reward is to die well."

In sum, whenever Chengren was mentioned, many of the villagers' views were contradictory. What was strange, moreover, was not that contradictions existed among the views of different villagers, but that they often existed among the comments made by the same person. One phrase many villagers kept repeating was, "It's really hard to say." Compared with 2008, when Chengren was still around, during my research in October 2013, people's narratives about his life had begun to blur the details, but their contradictory image and appraisals of him had become clearer. Regarding this situation, Nanshan's assessment appeared particularly cogent among the villagers standing around:

> None of us has "clairvoyant eyes" (*houyan*) so who can see events several decades in the future? The contrast between Chengren's early glory and his later misfortune appears so striking because, for one thing, he made some mistakes, and for another, the world changed so fast. Otherwise, he would not have become so miserable in his old age.... But when has the world ever remained the same? It will always change, and people can only meet that change by remaining constant themselves. However the world changes, if one can treat it with a steady heart, then one could set out without so much arrogance or overreach, and later one would not be so isolated and miserable.

As Nanshan was saying this, he was smoking and chatting with me and a few other villagers at the entrance to the shop next to the pond on the right-hand side of the Nantang temple. Chenggong walked over, his face emaciated, his hair thin and white, his mouth missing a few teeth, and his movement languid. Since he had never married and he had lost the ability to work, his fields were being farmed by two nephews. Every month they provided him with rice, cooking oil, and coal, but basically no spending money. Since he had been unable to quit smoking, he often had to ask other villagers for cigarettes. I handed him a few, and then he silently listened to Nanshan's monologue as he smoked. Nanshan pointed to him, saying, "(Chenggong) was close to (Chengren) at that time. You can ask him if I've got it right." Then he directly spoke to him in a loud voice (as Chenggong was already growing hard of hearing):

> Is that how it was, Uncle? At that time, you and Chengren used to pick on me a lot, now you tell me according to your conscience, have I got it right? Did either of you expect it would come to this? Now hardly anyone is willing to give you cigarettes, I'm one of the more generous ones, right? If you'd known it would come to this, you would have acted differently in the past, right? So in life, one's heart should be constant, thinking of lacking when you have, and thinking of having when you lack. That way you won't forget who you are when you have, and then become miserable when you lack.

Chenggong seemed to have become accustomed to such questioning, so he took a few quick puffs on his cigarette and then, without any discernable expression on his face, replied: "You're right. There's no cure for regret in this world.... Every era has its own affairs. 'When cast into the arena, one has no choice but to fight.'"

Chengren's wife had long stopped caring about how to "decide on a final verdict" about him "now that the casket was closed." In the mid-1990s she had become a Buddhist. After Chengren had fallen into long-term illness, she became even more convinced that it was a "fated calamity." She often revealed her sadness in the presence of others, but she rarely complained that this fate was unfair. If the course of everything had already been decided, then the most important thing was just to live out the rest of her days in good order, making offerings of incense, chanting mantras, and accumulating merit for the next life. Chengren did not think she was right, often accusing her of "pretending to be mystical." About this, Chengde once said:

> It would have been better if Chengren had believed in fate or karma, then when he encountered hardships, at least he would've had an explanation. Unfortunately, he didn't believe in those things, so he felt miserable. How could his heart have achieved a sense of balance?

Notes

1 The "Basic Annals" (*benji* 本纪) are the first twelve chapters of the *Records of the Grand Historian*, seven of which are biographies of specific rulers.
2 When the residents of Cheng Village address people according to their relationship within the same generation of a clan, they assign a number to all the men within "the five degrees" (*wufu*), calling them "Ah+number," for example, "Ah-Two." Sometimes in order to differentiate, they call them "Landmark + Ah + number," as in "West-of-the-Big-Banyan-Tree Ah-Two." Even so, only relatives on close speaking terms know exactly whom these addresses refer to.
3 *Cha siu bau* is a Cantonese snack. In the local dialect, this term is used to describe things that go bad due to heat, humidity, or lack of air. Here it means that the rice plants would rot due to lack of air.
4 This (literally "Four Cleanups cadres") refers to those singled out for having problems regarding work-points, bookkeeping, storage, or collective property.
5 Here, "Marxist-Leninist" is used in a similar way as "left," but "left" is more explicitly derogatory.
6 *Translator's note*: The five degrees originally referred to the different types of mourning clothes to be worn by relatives, and the amount of time they should be worn, according to degree of closeness to the deceased (first cousin vs. second cousin vs. third, etc.), as well as their generation within the family tree. Now this term refers mainly to one's degree of closeness to a living relative, which may determine appropriate terms of address and familial obligations.
7 *Translator's note*: During the transition to market economy in the 1980s, China had a dual-track pricing system, where the state continued to set quotas and prices for certain important commodities (including agricultural inputs such as chemical

fertilizer). Commodities produced under quota were sold at prices set by the state, then anything produced beyond quota was sold at market prices, which tended to be higher, and the revenue could be kept by the producers and sellers.
8 *Translator's note*: In Lu Xun's 1924 short story "New Year's Sacrifice" (祝福), Xiang Lin's widow endures numerous hardships and is treated as a second-class citizen. The reference here just means that Chengren kept complaining to everyone that he had been wronged.
9 "A couple bunches of bananas" means empty hands, with the idea that bananas resemble fingers.
10 Coconut Tree is a cheap brand of cigarettes, a pack retailing for only 2.5 yuan at shops in Duqiao as of 2015.
11 *Translator's note*: This is an inversion of the saying "after the casket is closed, a final verdict may be reached" (盖棺定论), meaning that you cannot decide how to judge a person until after they have died. In this case it was not until after Chengren had passed away that villagers began to debate his strengths and weaknesses.
12 *Translator's note*: Wu Dalang was a character in the classic novels *The Plum in the Golden Vase* and *The Water Margin*. This saying refers to the legend that Wu, who was short, refused to employ anyone taller than himself at his pancake stall, and that this was a bad business decision based on personal insecurity. It is now used to describe someone who refuses to employ more talented people. Here the idea is that Chengren pushed more talented cadres out of the brigade leadership due to fear of competition for his position.
13 *Translator's note*: It may appear contradictory that villagers talk about reincarnation and then say things such as "you only live once." Such contradictions in villagers' cosmology are explored in chapter six.

3 A Peasant Boss

Participating in Politics

In Cheng Village, Cheng Shouyi is often called "Boss" or "Big Boss." Nowadays there are quite a few other entrepreneurs richer than him, but he was one of the earliest to get rich, so the name stuck. When I first came in contact with him, it surprised me to learn that Big Boss Shouyi had been the highly "revolutionary" head of a rebel faction during the Cultural Revolution.

Shouyi was born in 1942 as the sixth boy in his generation of paternal cousins (according to the traditional "five degrees" of kinship within the Cheng clan), so he was called "Ah-Six." He was not very close to any of his cousins, however. Neither he nor his father had any brothers. His father had two sisters, and Shouyi had an older sister, all of whom treated him well. (One of these aunts moved to Hong Kong to live with her husband before 1949.)

In 1962, Shouyi—classified as a "middle peasant"—graduated from middle school at Duqiao Secondary and became the secretary for Cheng Brigade's branch of the Communist Youth League. In those days, although this was an important political post, it was not a central one, being mainly responsible for occasional public events and the "Youth (Labor) Commandos."[1]

In 1964, the Four Cleanups work team came to Cheng Brigade. Two of its members were young university instructors from Guangzhou. Shortly after arriving, they noticed that it was easy to talk to Shouyi. The three of them discussed everything from local agriculture to the nation's revolutionary politics, from Marxism-Leninism and Mao Zedong Thought to *The Water Margin*, *Romance of the Three Kingdoms*, *Investiture of the Gods*, *Journey to the West*, and *Xue Dingshan's Expedition to the West*. Shouyi recounted:

> They were surprised that someone from this kind of village had read such books and knew so many things. They praised my theoretical sophistication. This was mainly because in those days I used to read a lot, borrowing books from all kinds of people. Since we had interests in common, we would hang out together whenever we had the chance.... In the 1980s, I went to visit them at (a certain) university in Guangzhou, and they were so friendly!

Due to this experience, and the personal relationships it established, in early 1966 one of the instructors helped Shouyi to begin the procedure for joining the party. Within a year, he had become a full member and assumed the post of vice-secretary for Cheng Brigade's party branch.

After Cheng Chengren returned to work in Cheng Brigade, his ideas differed from those of Shouyi. As Shouyi saw it, Chengren's low level of education made him inclined to follow conventions inflexibly, without challenging the commune authorities for the benefit of Cheng Brigade. At first, however, Shouyi did not express any clear opposition until it came to the matter of Chen Xi's extramarital affair, when he openly disagreed with Chengren. Various details led him to believe that Chengren was unprofessional in his work, even incompetent in some respects, merely implementing the commune's orders and, during political campaigns, shouting revolutionary slogans as a "cudgel with which to beat people."

At the height of the Cultural Revolution, the Duqiao area was roughly divided into the Red Flag and East Wind factions. The peasants of Cheng Brigade aligned themselves with Red Flag, with about one hundred young villagers participating actively in the conflict. Following Shouyi's suggestion, they named the brigade's Red Flag group "Sunrise" (*taiyang sheng*), after the revolutionary song lyrics "The east is red, the sun is rising." Starting in May 1967, they declared that East Wind, to which the commune cadres belonged, was "royalist" and insufficiently revolutionary. The residents of Duqiao's market town also aligned themselves with East Wind and denounced Red Flag as the real royalists, "waving a red flag against the red flag." Duqiao Residential Brigade's East Wind group had about fifty young militants, mostly workers from the lumber mill and the brick factory. They belonged to a different organization than the Duqiao cadres' East Wind group, but they were close. At the Duqiao Secondary School, however, the teachers and students aligned themselves with Red Flag, naming their group "Rising Sun" (*xuri sheng*).

These factional groups were just names without any clear organizational structure. Strictly speaking, they had no formal leaders, but there were always militants who stood out from the crowd and became known as "heads." For example, in Sunrise, Shouyi had a special status. He was a young brigade cadre with a certain charisma, and whenever he did something there were always people willing to go along with it. The other militants, then, just happened to regard Shouyi as the head of Sunrise. Other cadres such as Chengren would say they belonged to that faction but never participated in its activities, so militants considered them "merely nominal members, actually having nothing to do with it." Within Sunrise, Cheng Shoude and Cheng Shoukuan were both a year older than Shouyi. In the second half of 1966, Shoude was transferred from Shantang Secondary School to teach at Cheng Brigade Primary School. He rarely showed his face in public factional activities, but often made suggestions from behind the scenes, so became known as "the dark counselor" (*hei canmou*). Shoukuan, by contrast, stood out as a militant but rarely took part in planning, so became known as a "commando" (*tujishou*).

On July 16, 1967, a serious armed conflict took place between Sunrise and Duqiao Residential Brigade's East Wind group. (This became known as a "the July 16th Incident.") In this battle, Shouyi assumed the role of his group's leader without any formal decision being made, and henceforth everyone considered him to be the head of Red Flag as a whole in the Duqiao area.

The direct cause of the July 16th Incident was that several days before, as the Duqiao Secondary School's Rising Sun members were demonstrating in the market town, they were assaulted by East Wind militants from the lumber mill, injuring one of the students. When I interviewed formers members of both factions (including Shouyi and Shoude from Red Flag as well as members of East Wind), everyone agreed that the lumber mill workers were in the wrong, because middle school students are no match for strong adults. Cheng Brigade's Sunrise militants decided to support their Rising Sun comrades in full force. This was during the agricultural slack season, so there was a large turn out from both groups when they organized a mass demonstration, demanding that the commune authorities arrest the "thugs" who had beaten the students. Since the Duqiao cadres also belonged to East Wind, however, not only did they reject this demand, but they also went so far as to equip the workers with a dozen rifles and a machine gun "in order to protect production and state property."

On July 16th, under the leadership of Shouyi, Sunrise brought weapons such as homemade grenades, dynamite, and knives to another demonstration in the market town. When they reached the entrance to the commune headquarters, East Wind militants surrounded them and attacked. Shouyi had some Rising Sun members take the old people, women, and children, who had accompanied them in the demonstration, and hide in the school compound while Sunrise militants charged in the opposite direction. Shoukuan threw a grenade and broke out of the encirclement, and most of the Sunrise members withdrew to Cheng Brigade. One person from East Wind tried to take advantage of the smoke from the explosion to attack Sunrise as they withdrew but was shot and killed by a rifle from his own ranks. (In the ensuing investigation, the bullet would serve as evidence.) At the time, East Wind members believed he had been killed by the grenade explosion, so they fired directly into the crowd as a deterrent. A Sunrise member was hit and fell into the Wutong River from the wooden bridge between Cheng Brigade and the market town.

Shouyi and a few other militants could not make it across the bridge in time, and so chose to flee upstream to Fancheng. There the factional struggle was less intense, without armed conflict, and although there were two different rebel groups, both belonged to Red Flag (each accusing the other of being fake). As core members of Duqiao's Red Flag groups, Shouyi and the others were met with a warm welcome and hospitality by both of the groups in Fancheng, which provided them food and lodging. A few days later, the

Fancheng groups transferred them to a commune in Wu County also controlled by Red Flag. Once the situation had settled down, some of the Wu comrades escorted Shouyi and the others back to Cheng Brigade.

At first, this experience led Shouyi to believe that his political career had come to an end. Before long, however, the central authorities' order to relinquish armed conflict made it down to the local level. The Wu County Revolutionary Committee called for "revolutionary unity." Shouyi recalled, "At the time, maybe the Revolutionary Committee felt it would no longer be appropriate for East Wind to control the government alone, now that 'unity' was the order of the day." Shouyi thus joined the Wu County Revolutionary Committee as a representative of Duqiao's Red Flag groups. At the same time, the principal and party branch secretary of Cheng Brigade Primary School was promoted to vice-secretary of Duqiao Commune as a representative of Rising Sun.

In the Revolutionary Committee, Shouyi possessed no real power, but he actually enjoyed this situation. He recalled:

> For a peasant in those days, joining the County Revolutionary Committee was an outstanding honor. I was happy. At least I didn't have to do so much manual labor, and I could read all kinds of documents. Otherwise, a peasant wouldn't have the opportunity to read such documents in his whole life. But actually I wasn't interested in reading them. I didn't want to compete for power, so what was the point? So I often went to the county library to check out books. In those days, many books were impossible for others to read (i.e. they were banned), but I had permission to borrow them, even *The Plum in the Golden Vase*.[2] Besides that I would just wander around the city. When (the Committee) held routine meetings, I would often take leave, saying I was sick. During important meetings, I would read illustrated books (*lianhuanhua*) and traditional stories (*pingshu*). In the mornings we were supposed to do the Loyalty Dance (*zhong zi wu*) together, but I wouldn't participate, saying I had a stomachache. I wasn't competing for power, so they didn't put pressure on me. There were a lot of tensions and conflicts among them, but those had little to do with me. The commune cadres below me knew I was only there for show, so they didn't come pester me, instead just saying hi and giving me a cigarette. There was no pressure in their interactions with me, since there was no real hierarchy in our relationship. Some of those commune cadres became good friends later on.

One time in the presence of Shouyi, Chengxin said to me:

> In those days, he (Shouyi) was just messing around in Wucheng. If you asked him what they had discussed in a meeting, he would have no clue. But if you asked which shop had the best *nanru* peanuts,[3] you could be certain he would tell you exactly where to go.

It therefore seems that Shouyi was telling the truth when he said he said he was not interested in participating in power struggles.

In Cheng Brigade, Shouyi's relationship with Chengren improved. Although Shouyi often looked down on the way Chengren worked, the latter did not really care. On the contrary, Shouyi's wife enjoyed obvious preferential treatment in the production team, just as Chengren's wife did.

Escaping Poverty

In 1978, Shouyi's relationship with Chengren changed dramatically and unexpectedly. That winter, policy changes resulted in Shouyi's return to Cheng Brigade as vice-secretary of the party branch (a position many villagers believed to be temporary, since he was expected to replace Chengren), but then Shouyi embezzled 1,000 yuan meant to be used as remuneration for village labor expended on a reservoir construction project. When this crime was discovered, he sold his two pigs and also borrowed money from his aunt in Hong Kong in order to pay back the money he had stolen. Chengren called for having Shouyi expelled from the party, or at least put on probation, but the Duqiao Commune Party Committee just marked a demerit on his record. Shouyi recollected:

> Although Marx said that manual and mental labor both count as labor, peasants believe that only manual labor counts. As they see it, they work a lot but can't eat meat, while the cadres don't work much but often get to eat meat during their meetings.... After receiving the demerit, the brigade would still invite me to meetings, but I wouldn't go. People would poke fun at me, saying, "Shouyi, why don't you go to the meeting? They'll have meat for you there!" As if the only reason I had served as a cadre was to eat meat on the state's dime.

Shouyi's wife Cheng Xiu interjected:

> (Everyone) was poor in those days, poor to the point of fearfulness. At the time (1973) I had our first daughter, and (Shouyi) bought half a kilo of meat from an old breeding sow, the kind where the sow gets too old to breed so they kill it, but the meat is too tough to chew. When I ate it I just wanted to cry. That's why people made jokes like that.

Shouyi concluded, "I'm someone who strives to outdo others and couldn't stand being the butt of jokes like that, so I refused to attend meetings. I even stopped paying dues for party membership."

In the summer of 1979, after six months of nonpayment, Shouyi met the conditions for "automatic withdrawal from the party." According to organizational work procedure, the brigade party branch was supposed to investigate the reasons for nonpayment and conduct "thought work" (persuasion).

Instead, however, Chengren chose to convene a branch assembly for the expulsion of Shouyi from the party. Shouyi did not say anything at the time, but looking back later on he felt that Chengren, in trying to "grab him by the pigtail" (using Shouyi's past mistake as an excuse) to kick him out of the party, he had actually not been clever enough. Shouyi said:

> He was always worried that I would seize power, even telling others that I had obtained my position through rebellion. In reality I had already become vice-secretary before the Cultural Revolution, so how did that make any sense? Besides, I didn't even contend for power when I was in the County Revolutionary Committee, so why would I care about his little post in the brigade?

In early 1980, changes in rural policy again seemed to demonstrate the importance of "reading plenty of books and newspapers to keep up with the times," as Shouyi had mentioned. He said:

> Judging by information in the newspaper, I could tell that central policy seemed to be changing, so I felt it would be important to "undertake economic vitalization" (*gaohuo jingji*). My own household also really needed to make some money, otherwise we would be in trouble: We already had three daughters and one son, and my parents' health was declining. If I relied on (doing farmwork and other activities for work-points in) the production team alone, I would definitely fall deeper and deeper into debt. So I took an oath that I would make a lot of money, and then more money, and then still more.

Farmland had not yet been decollectivized in 1980, but the government had already begun to relax its restrictions on market-oriented activities. Shouyi began to practice carpentry at night, producing furniture for sale, often skipping the farm work he was supposed to be doing for the production team. After decollectivization, carpentry became his main profession while farming was reduced to a sideline. Other than transplanting rice seedlings and harvesting, he basically left the rest of the farm work to his wife.

In the first few years after decollectivization, lumber was still a scarce resource regulated by the state. Hilly woodland was still controlled by village collectives, and there was no privately-owned timber. If a collective wanted to cut timber, it had to obtain approval from the Ministry of Forestry, and that was no easy feat. For people who made a living from carpentry, the scarcity of lumber was a "curse" (*jinguzhou*). Objectively, however, this scarcity also meant it was easy for carpenters to sell the goods they produced. If they could obtain materials, they could have all the work they wanted to do and plenty of opportunities to make money.

As far as Shouyi was concerned, not only did this "curse" of lumber scarcity constitute no limitation to his business, it also even helped him. According to his analysis, in the late 1970s and early 1980s, his turn to carpentry took full advantage of the "opportunities of time, place, and people." Since Cheng Brigade was located next to Duqiao's market town, transportation was convenient by both water and land, providing outstanding advantages for the transport of materials and products, as well as for marketing. More importantly, since Shouyi had worked at the Wu County Revolutionary Committee, he was already on familiar terms with many cadres at the county and commune levels. The relationships and connections he had accumulated over the years could now come into play. With these connections, Shouyi could easily purchase scarce resources that were unavailable to other people, including lumber. Up until he abandoned carpentry in the late 1980s, he never had to worry about how to obtain wood. Needless to say, this sharpened his edge in competition with other carpenters.

Other villagers who practiced carpentry also had problems obtaining money to use as capital, even if they had the connections necessary to purchase lumber. It was a universal phenomenon in Cheng Brigade that the villagers had just begun to have enough food to eat and still lacked any reserve of cash. However, Shouyi managed to obtain wood on credit from many brigades and tree farms on the strength of his verbal promises alone. The ability to "do business without capital," therefore, was one of Shouyi's competitive advantages and secrets to making money, and the foundation underlying this ability was his connections. He recalled:

> What kind of capital did we have for doing business back then? None! Lots of people didn't have any money for business. Business requires capital, and carpentry is no different. But I could do it without capital. At the time, lumber was mainly purchased at tree farms, so I would tell the cadre in charge of a farm, "I don't have any cash for you," and they would say, "You're from Cheng Brigade, you think I don't know you? That I'm afraid you'll run away without paying me back? If I don't show you respect (*gei mianzi*), then who else would I show respect to? Besides, you used to be a cadre too, and I know you're reliable. Go ahead and take the wood, then just pay me back once you've sold the products." The people selling lumber would have this kind of attitude, as would the (drivers) transporting it—all would say "just pay me back after you've sold the products." That way, I didn't need cash to buy wood or transport it. Other (carpenters) couldn't do this, so of course they couldn't do business at a large scale.

Good quality and far-reaching connections also played a major role in the production process. In 1983, after Shouyi began using electrical equipment to process the wood, access to electricity became a key factor determining whether production would go smoothly. At the time, the Ministry of Electric Power prioritized making sure that cities had enough power. There were separate grids for urban and rural areas, and rural access to electricity was extremely limited. Rural residents mainly used electricity for lighting, with few other uses. In order to decrease wastage, transformers were often switched off during the day, until electricians came at sunset to switch them back on. (Moreover, this was limited to two-phase power—it was impossible to use machines requiring three-phase power.) If ordinary villagers wanted to use electricity in the daytime, there was simply no power supply they could access. In order to help Shouyi, however, the Duqiao Township Power Station made an oral agreement with him for the Cheng Village electrician to run a three-phase dynamic power cable from the transformer just for Shouyi to use, and to ensure he could use it in the daytime. In addition, although villagers were normally required to install electricity usage meters on the outside of their houses in order to prevent theft of power, Shouyi installed his meter inside his house (so other villagers could not see how much he was using), and neither the village electrician nor the township power station said anything about it.

As for marketing, although wooden products were already easy to sell at the time, overall, Shouyi's connections also gave him an advantage in this respect as well. Since he knew a lot of people, there were more potential buyers for his products, as long as the price and quality were acceptable. And it was not just the quantity of this contacts—their quality was also superior to those of other villagers, being better-off economically than the "poor relatives and indigent friends" of most villagers, with much stronger demand and purchasing power when it came to upgrading furniture. For example, among Shouyi's acquaintances, many of them were current or former cadres from Duqiao Township or the villages and residential committees under its jurisdiction. Among these people, many of them were relatively well-off at the time. In the wave of new house construction and furniture additions from the late 1970s to the 1980s, when it came to household consumption, these people's demand for wooden products was the most robust. Since they were on friendly terms with Shouyi, these customers were willing to wait in line for his products instead of buying those already made by other carpenters.

Orders from work-units created an even larger, more reliable, and more profitable market for Shouyi's products, and this became an opportunity for making money that other carpenters in Cheng Village could only dream of. For instance, prior to decollectivization, Duqiao Commune's health center needed to install a large number of office tables and chairs, hospital beds, and medicine cabinets. Many carpenters wanted to seize this opportunity, but since several of the center's main leaders were on good terms with Shouyi, they gave him the entire order. When the commune reverted to the administrative structure of a "township," the number of party and state cadres increased and the office facilities were upgraded, so the government needed to install dozens of sets of desks, chairs, filing cabinets, and wooden beds. The township party committee's secretary at the time was the same Red Flag representative who had been promoted from Cheng Brigade Primary School to serve as vice-secretary of the commune in 1968, so of course the entire order was commissioned to Shouyi. Such large orders are rarely seen in the countryside, so it is hard for ordinary carpenters to obtain these opportunities on their own, but it was nothing special for Shouyi. For example, he mentioned:

> About two years after (completing the order from the township government, 1985–1986), the Furong Village Primary School was renovated. They asked me to make all the windows and doors, blackboards, and over 200 sets of desks and benches for the classrooms. I made a lot of money from that. According to my calculation at the time, I netted over 100 yuan per day. And money was worth more then, so 100 a day was pretty impressive.... It took over a month to complete (that order).

Similarly, Shouyi received orders for desks and benches for several other villages' primary schools and the Duqiao Secondary School.

Of course, Shouyi was not just a carpenter who relied on connections to eat. In fact, his own abilities and the advanced equipment he used became the secret weapons that ensured he would hold the lead in the woodworking industry for many years. After the introduction of electric motors as a source of energy, the superior efficiency of tools such as chainsaws, electric planers, and power drills became clear for all to see. For instance, it took ordinary carpenters at the time an average of ten days to make a bed, but it took Shouyi less than one day using power tools. When customers bought a bed from other carpenters, they had to order in advance, but with Shouyi, they could receive the finished product the same day. Sometimes, Shouyi would make twenty-some beds or thirty to forty doors and windows in one batch, and then wait for customers to come buy them. Compared with making things one at a time, this sort of batch production (similar to an assembly line) could save a lot of labor time.

All these factors combined to help Shouyi rapidly accumulate more wealth than ordinary villagers could even imagine. In 1985, besides having four children in school, he also tore down his old house and built a new one with red-brick walls and steel-reinforced concrete floors.

Getting Rich

1991 was not a special year for Cheng Village as a whole, but for Shouyi, it seemed particularly important. That year opened a new chapter in his "business chronicles" (*shengyi jing*). Prior to that, one could not say that he had not accumulated a lot of wealth. Although even he could not put a specific number on the amount, almost everyone in the village agreed that he was the first to get rich. At a time when most villagers were worried about how they could afford to send their children to primary and secondary school, Shouyi never lost any sleep over tuition for his four children. When other villagers still built traditional houses with wooden frames covered in clay tiles (*wafang*), Shouyi was building a modern house with reinforced concrete (*loufang*). In the late 1980s, moreover, he increased his house to four stories (five if you count the scenery-viewing structure added to the rooftop), enclosed the courtyard with walls, and built a brick barn with clay roofing tiles for livestock inside them. In addition, he planted trees and grapes in the courtyard, turning it into a dignified garden.

After all these expenditures, however, Shouyi said he was already running out of cash. At first his plan was just to accumulate a little wealth, settle down, and enjoy his life. On this point, he recounted his "business chronicles":

> The chronicles of business are hard to recite. Nothing is unchanging: Something that made money yesterday won't necessarily work today. It's also easy for people to become lazy, thinking it's enough just to get by. That was my thinking at the time: Once I get my house fixed up, just forget about the rest. But later when I looked at my neighbors and started comparing, I couldn't stand it anymore. When boating upstream, if you don't move forward then you move backwards. If you just pause for a moment, everyone comes and laughs at you, saying you're useless. By then I wasn't young anymore, but I still had plenty of energy. I was determined to make money. A little advantage wasn't acceptable—I would accept nothing less than an absolute advantage. It's like in war, where Chairman Mao said, "Let us gather our strength and vanquish the broken foe."[4] Victory alone is not enough—one must win by a large margin. After achieving an absolute advantage, as I have today, no one can catch up with me, they can't even harbor the idea that they might catch up, they wouldn't dare. They "accept their fate," as we often say. Only that can really be considered creating distance (between myself and the others).

As more and more villagers became carpenters, most adopting the use of mechanized or semi-mechanized production, the profession of wood processing became less profitable. Although Shouyi had built himself through this trade and still maintained a certain advantage there, his edge was becoming less clear. At the same time, local governments were relaxing their control over the felling of trees and the marketing of products, so even carpenters without any special connections could purchase all the lumber they needed. The advantages Shouyi had enjoyed with regard to materials, based on his connections, gradually evaporated.

Now that he was moderately well-off, then, Shouyi had to make a decision whether to continue making a little money through carpentry for his family to get by, or to abandon that trade and invest in something else. From the perspective of livelihood among ordinary villagers, the former would doubtless be the safe option, while the latter might create new opportunities, but might also involve unpredictable risks. Shouyi chose the entirely new option of investing in the purchase of live water buffalo and the sale of their meat.

At the time in Cheng Village and its environs, tractors had already basically replaced the use of water buffalo for plowing, so it had become rare for villagers to raise this type of livestock. Much less did anyone specialize in raising bovines of any sort, so the supply of beef and buffalo meat was extremely limited. In addition, the use of industrial feed to raise pigs was still rare in Duqiao, so villagers preferred the taste of pork from traditionally raised pigs to that of pork from pigs raised on industrial feed. Besides, pork was much cheaper than buffalo meat, so pork remained the main type of meat that most villagers would buy, with few ever buying buffalo. Under these conditions, investing in the buffalo meat business presented both opportunities and risks. On the one hand, since there was little existing supply of buffalo, none of the Duqiao butchers specialized in it, with only a few pork butchers selling a little buffalo on the side, so there would be little competition if Shouyi were to enter this trade. On the other hand, since villagers had not yet formed a habit of eating buffalo, it might be hard to expand the market.

Looking back years later, Shouyi explained his decision:

> I never gamble, but I have a bit of a gambler's mentality, a resistance to following conventions. To put it more positively, I have a pioneering spirit, but to put it negatively I like to take risks. In any case I had already built a house, my older kids were about to graduate from middle school, and the younger ones about to finish primary school. Even if I failed (at business), I would still be able to get by. So I had a little capital to risk on a gamble. Another (factor) was that, I believed that my earlier connections would still be useful. I never lost them after making money. I'm the sort of person who "doesn't forget his friends after getting rich." Loyalty is important if you want to be a person in society, and even more so in business. They say "kindness brings wealth": First you have to be kind to others before you can get rich. After making money, I continued to visit those old friends on holidays, maintaining our relationship. If anyone else wanted to get on good terms with them, they wouldn't have a way in. Relationships are the more important thing—without them, even if you tried to give gifts, nobody would accept them. Of course, personal capability is necessary too. If you were a lame duck (*adou*), you wouldn't succeed either way.

Based on those considerations, in 1991, Shouyi began rebuilding himself with 5,000 yuan in cash, entering the business of slaughtering buffalo and selling their meat. Before long, he had again accumulated a large sum of wealth.

On the production side, Shouyi used his connections to purchase live buffalo in neighboring counties and even Guangxi, the transport fees often not being paid to the drivers until after the meat had been sold. When it came to purchasing livestock, since he knew how to utilize local cadres and the interpersonal networks they possessed, he was able to find sources quickly, never being scammed while out on the road. At the time, social order was not well maintained in many areas. When some other people in this industry went to buy buffalo, they often had to pay tribute to local gangsters (i.e., small gifts showing respect) in order to avoid extortion (having to pay them large sums of cash). In addition, with regard to marketing, since some of Shouyi's former colleagues from the Wu County Revolutionary Committee were now serving as party or state authorities in Wu County and even Qi Prefecture, he was able to acquire two buffalo meat distribution points at excellent locations in the county seat, Wucheng, soon establishing a firm foothold in the market. He also set up a distribution point at the market in Duqiao. Only rarely did any of those shops meet with harassment or extortion from gangsters from the street or officials from the Bureau of Industry and Commerce.

What surprised Shouyi was that, in the first few years starting in 1992, some broader societal changes took place that created more opportunities for his business. For example, with the Pearl River Delta's rapid and dramatic economic development, peasants from neighboring parts of Guangdong (including Cheng Village) began entering the ranks of migrant workers (*dagongzu*), one after the other. Since they spoke the same Cantonese language as delta locals, although with different accents, it was easier for them to obtain labor management positions, such as foreman, in factories and construction sites, in comparison with migrants from elsewhere. As the people of Duqiao saw their income rise, in addition to renovating their houses, their effective demand for meat also rose—including for higher-end types such as buffalo. At the same time, pork from pigs raised entirely on industrial feed was beginning to flood both urban and rural markets, including the one in Duqiao, reducing consumers' interest in that type of meat—whose quality they felt inferior to traditionally produced pork. (In my research, I often heard villagers complain that the taste of pork was getting worse and worse.) Under these conditions, the markets in Wucheng and Duqiao saw the demand for buffalo meat go up.

Shouyi's investment occurred right in the midst of this process. During my research, he flipped through old account books and noted that, when profits reached their peak, each buffalo could fetch 1,000 yuan in net profit, or 700 to 800 even in normal times. In the busy season, Shouyi's family members all worked in the three distribution points. Shouyi and his wife were each in charge of one of the shops in Wucheng, while their son Fudao (who had just graduated from middle school) ran the shop in Duqiao. For a while they also opened a shop in Tongcheng run by their two daughters, but later they insisted on leaving to work in a garment factory, and the shop closed. In 1994, they set Duqiao's record for the most bovine meat to ever be sold in one day: the meat from eight whole large buffaloes. Normally they would sell the meat from two to three buffaloes each day. Due to insufficient investment or lack of connections, Shouyi's competitors limited their sales to Duqiao's market days (once every three days), selling no more than one buffalo's meat each of those days. Moreover, since no one raised buffalo in the vicinity of Duqiao, many butchers had to buy the animals from Shouyi if they wanted to sell buffalo meat. This situation continued until 1998, when more people entered the industry, so Shouyi got out and began raising fish.

Raising fish is one of the traditional industries in Duqiao. By 1999, villagers had already become adept at modern aquaculture, including the use of industrial feed and fishponds with oxygen pumps. If Shouyi had merely followed the same business model as other villagers, it is certain that such a newcomer to the trade would not have been able to make more money than experienced fish farmers. But Shouyi sought out a different model, contacting his friends and acquaintances who worked in the government, enterprises, or public services, along with former business partners who had gotten rich, and informing them of the fishpond he had built (on the gardening plot his household contracted from the village, about one *mu* in area). He told them they could come fish at the pond he was operating for 50 yuan per half-day, and they could keep all the fish they caught at no extra charge. According to Shouyi, 50 yuan was basically equivalent to the price of 7.5 kilograms of carp, but the customers who came rarely caught that much fish in half a day of fishing. Unlike other fish farmers in the village, moreover, it was unnecessary for Shouyi to hire workers for catching fish or to spend most of the day selling fish at the market (or wholesaling them to retailers, splitting the profit with them), so his pond was more profitable than theirs. More importantly, as Shouyi saw it, this was a process combining business with the development of personal connections: While existing connections helped the business to grow, the business also provided opportunities for officials and friends from all walks of life to fish together with him, "deepening relationships with old friends and creating new relationships."

As Shouyi recounted these "chronicles of business experience," he seemed quite pleased with himself, saying:

> I made money while also making friends. How could anything be more perfect? This was my advantage over other people. How much money could you make just by raising fish alone, and how much hard work would it take? ... . China is still a Confucian country, so relationships are the most important thing. If you want your business to grow, you have to understand how to operate (*jingying*) relationships. To operate a business is to operate relationships, and *vice versa*, but relationships are the primary thing. Without relationships, you have nothing. You can do a little vending at the market, but if you want to make the big money, it's impossible.

Before long, these relationships began reeling in immense profits. During a flood in the summer of 2000, when a road near the pond was blocked in a landslide from a neighboring hill, the Duqiao Township Party Committee secretary and a cadre who had come from Wu County to direct the disaster-relief work decided to commandeer Shouyi's pond for use in storing the soil and debris removed from the road, paying nearly 100,000 yuan in remuneration. As he put it candidly, that one-*mu* pond netted him at least 300,000 yuan in less than half a year (including another 200,000 from business).

In the 1990s, when Shouyi was buying buffalo in Qi Prefecture and Guangxi, he also dabbled in the antique business. I asked, "Do you know how to appraise antiques?" He answered:

> That question shows that you have the business mindset of an honest person. It's hard to make money with that kind of mindset. The antique trade is highly unregulated—how could so many antiques be bought and sold right and left at their real prices? Even if I knew how to appraise them, how much time would it take to do it accurately? No one can tell whether they're real or fake, so I don't really differentiate. The secret lies in acting as if everything is fake when you buy it. I'd say, "Look, I'm just a butcher who buys and slaughters buffalo for a living, I don't depend on these antiques." I would say I just happened upon these antiques while traveling to pick up livestock and was just buying a few to take home and decorate my house. The places I visited were all remote villages. Nowadays, buffalo are only raised in remote places, and also peasants selling antiques can only be found in remote places. In that sort of place, everyone is more honest, so when I said this sort of thing, nine times out of ten they would believe me. Of course most of what I bought was fake, but sometimes they were real. Then when I sold them, I would act as if everything were real. Some of the buyers were experts, and they would find something real in the pile and pay a high price for it. Others weren't experts, and they would pay high prices for both real and fake things. With whatever was leftover, I would lower the price until someone bought it. This is called a "double scam" (scamming both sellers and buyers), haha! This couldn't be done with other things, like food, alcohol, or clothes, but it could be done with antiques. As the saying goes, "playing around with ancient toys" (*guwan, guwan*)—because antiques were meant to be played with in the first place.

According to Shouyi, he made at least as much money from antiques as he did from buffalo meat and re-selling livestock.

However, what Shouyi and other villagers felt was his most successful undertaking was not any of these business ventures, but the wedding of his son Fudao. Since Shouyi's family as a whole was well-off and Fudao himself was doing pretty well, they received plenty of matchmaking offers. In 1998, Shouyi rejected multiple proposals (including two girls with whom Fudao was rather satisfied), finally choosing the daughter of the former party branch secretary of Xujiao Village, which sat next to the Duqiao Residential Committee compound. This secretary was even better off than Shouyi, his two sons having opened stone processing plants in the mid-1990s, another daughter working at the Qi Prefecture Health Bureau, and the daughter who was offered to marry Fudao often helping out with her brothers' stone plant, being skilled at doing business herself. Through this arrangement, it could be said that Shouyi found a capable pillar for "the joining of forces between two powerful families."

In 2000, Shouyi converted most of his assets to about eight million yuan in cash and had Fudao use it to open a stone processing plant in Wucheng, withdrawing from the business world himself.

Enjoying the Pleasures of Life

After turning his business over to his son, Shouyi still had 300,000 yuan left over for his own use. At that time, his two daughters were each running their own garment factories in Tongcheng with a considerable income. He made a rule that each year Fudao must give him at least 50,000 yuan in "spending money," "suggesting" that his daughters also give "a few thousand"— although he made no definite request from them. That way, Shouyi had plenty of money to spend every year.

Shouyi said he could have continued doing business for a few years but decided to begin "wholeheartedly enjoying his life" out of two considerations: One, he believed his son should start his own business as soon as he got married, otherwise "the family's wealth would not last more than three generations." Secondly, in 1998 he was found to have high blood pressure. Although it was not serious, this gave him an entirely new perspective regarding the question, "What's the point of living?"

After 1998, it was as if Shouyi had become a different person. Prior to this, he had smoked four packs of cigarettes a day. After discovering he had high blood pressure, the next day he quit cold turkey and gave all the cigarettes in his house to Shoude and Shoukuan. In Cheng Village, many villagers say half in jest, half in earnest, "He's a demigod." They do not know how Shouyi made so much money, but they witnessed his resolution to quit smoking with their own eyes and cannot help feeling admiration. One middle-aged long-term smoker joked:

> Quitting smoking is no easy feat, and his addiction was so serious, yet he just stopped as soon as he said it. At first we thought it was just talk, so were astonished when he truly never smoked again. This was harder than "castrating oneself in order to achieve superhuman powers."[5]

Prior to this, in the eyes of villagers, although Shouyi had always been generous to others, he did not know how to enjoy life, but after discovering his health problem, he embarked on an entirely new way of spending money.

On this, Shouyi recounted:

> At that time I had a sudden awakening: of course making money was the most important thing, but after making money one needs to know how to spend it. Only if you're willing to spend money does it really belong to you. If you just save it in the bank, it's just a pile of numbers, so how could it really be yours? You can't take it into the coffin with you.... My wife couldn't change her old habits of unwillingness to spend. I used to

think this was good, but later I started scolding her, "Do you want to take it into the coffin with you?" You only live once. If you've taken care of your kids and saved enough to eat two meals a day, why not enjoy the rest? Otherwise what's the point of living?

Henceforth, Shouyi began furnishing his house with appliances such a liquid-crystal display TV set (which was not cheap at the time), a refrigerator, a camera, and high-end speakers, spending his free time at home drinking iced beverages and singing karaoke. In the courtyard he built a small swimming pool, where he went swimming every few days. In addition, he bought a horse, which he rode along the riverside most mornings and evenings. All of this consumption struck other villagers as extravagant, or even absurd, but Shouyi just said, "Actually they were the shortsighted ones. Just look, before long didn't everyone want a color TV and a VCD or DVD player?" When other villagers began enjoying such appliances, however, in 2004 Shouyi made another upgrade: He bought a personal computer, connecting an internet cable from Duqiao's market town to his home (and later installing wireless internet equipment). Before long he could proficiently use the computer and internet. In 2009, next to the swimming pool he built three structures for drinking tea, listening to music, and singing karaoke. His son Fudao spent 500,000 yuan furnishing them with large tea tables, carved from tree roots, and a high-end sound system.

Shouyi said the key to enjoying one's life was one's own feelings rather than what other people valued. For example, Shouyi never spent over 50 yuan on a pair of shoes, and he would wear them until they were falling apart without ever polishing or repairing them, just buying a new pair when they got old. He rarely spent over 100 yuan on shirts or trousers, never choosing famous brands. Once while chatting, his grandson said, "(These clothes) you always wear around are so creased and wrinkled, they're obviously fake." Shouyi sternly criticized him on the spot:

> That's right, they *are* fake. Clothes are good enough if you can wear them, what's the point of showing off? Are you worried people won't know you're rich? If you're really rich, why do you care? If you're poor, what's the point of puffing up your face (putting on airs)? I've always told you not to look down on the poor, you know? Your aunt earned her money (by selling) this sort of "fake clothes." If you want high-end clothes, why don't you show me you can earn a few bucks?

Similarly, out of concern for remaining "low-key," Shouyi always rode public buses whenever he went anywhere, or he drove an old, run-down motorcycle designed for women. In Duqiao, this sort of motorcycle cost about 2,000 yuan, whereas young male villagers would normally buy larger motorcycles for over 5,000 yuan. Shouyi explained that he did not need to drive on dirt roads or work in the hills and mountains, and the women's motorcycle was

86   *A Peasant Boss*

good enough for paved roads. He was not only frugal but also warned his son Fudao not to buy fancy vehicles.

If Shouyi's pursuit of luxury at home contrasted sharply with the low profile he maintained in public, even more surprising was his extravagant spending on extramarital sex.

Shouyi told many people, including me, about his first experience "looking for ladies" (i.e., hiring sex workers) while visiting Guangxi on livestock business in 1994. Each time he told the story, he would vividly describe the "debonair" manner in which he pulled a roll of hundred-yuan bills from his pocket, emphasizing how this move served to humiliate a lobby boy who had looked down upon Shouyi because of his rustic appearance—at a time when it was still unusual for people to carry around bills worth more than 10 yuan each. Prior to 1998, however, he did not do this sort of thing often, and he rarely mentioned such experiences to other villagers.

According to Shouyi's own memory, after he discovered that he had high blood pressure and quit smoking in 1998, due to the major changes in his attitude toward money and the meaning of life, he quickly began doing this sort of thing more often. Henceforth he believed that money was meant to be spent on enjoying life's pleasures. As for how to enjoy those pleasures, besides material pleasures such as eating well and living comfortably, "messing around with women" (Ct. *kau neui*) was indispensable. Up until the end of 2012, Shouyi went out to "look for ladies" at least twice a month. Sometimes he felt that was too direct and a bit boring, so he was willing to spend more money to take the women out on dates, as if they were a couple: having dinner and going for walks before conducting the transaction. Including expenses such as transportation, these activities cost up to 30,000 yuan a year. In 1998 he also began dating a twenty-seven-year-old married woman in Tongcheng on a regular basis. One day in the summer of 2013, Shouyi estimated that he had spent about 100,000 yuan on that girlfriend over the years. From 2000 to 2004, he also covered the living expenses (*baoyang*) of a young mistress from northern Hunan, eventually paying for her to open a flower shop. (That relationship changed, but they stayed in touch.) Shouyi said that although this "Hunanese little sister" had feelings for him, it was mainly a monetary relationship, so he spent more money on her than on the married girlfriend.

After 1998, another important change in this respect was that he began to enjoy bragging in front of acquaintances. On one occasion with a lot of people around, he proclaimed that he had superior luck with women and was a "lady killer."[6] Many villagers flattered him about this, but men close to him such as Shoude, Shoukuan, and Shouzhi often expressed disapproval, pointing out half-jokingly but half-seriously that this was just an illusion created by money, and that they were surprised Shouyi would mistake it for reality. One day in 2008, for example, he made this proclamation again, and Shouzhi, who had been chatting together in the same group, made a gesture of counting money, implying that all this "luck with women" had been bought with money. Sure enough, Shouyi defended himself, saying that his strong constitution was at least a contributing factor, and that it was not just about the money. What shocked some of his friends even more was that on several occasions Shouyi had secretly made video recordings of the process of "messing around with ladies," which he carried around on a flash drive so he could show the videos to friends on certain occasions.

Shouyi had a set of his own unique "theories" about this hobby. He believed, for example, that in the phrase "prostitution, gambling, and drugs" (*huang du du*),[7] prostitution could delight the body and relax the mind, whereas gambling and drugs were bad because they hurt the body and agitated the nerves. One day in September 2011, as Shouyi was explaining such theories to me in his courtyard tearoom, his wife Cheng Xiu happened to walk in. (Cheng Xiu rarely enters Shouyi's tearoom or music room except to clean them.) She chastised him, "Damn you! Always saying indecent things and justifying them with ridiculous theories. These feudal things will bring you to a bad end." On the one hand, Shouyi responded that he was "just talking nonsense" in his own home, but on the other, he still tried to defend himself rationally: "Even the Sage Confucius said this (sex) was as important as eating. Later our ancestor (Cheng Hao) got it twisted with ideas like 'maintain the Heavenly principles and extinguish the human desires'."

Later, this statement came up in a conversation I was having with Shoude, who was more educated and familiar with clan history than Shouyi. Shoude said:

> If I haven't heard that type of reasoning a hundred times, I've heard it eighty. This man is fine in other respects, but when it comes to this he has no self-control, and you could say he lacks moral integrity, and then tries to justify it with fancy words. He's uneducated, distorting Confucius and insulting our ancestor (Cheng Hao). As they used to say, his is "a life of bourgeois decadence," or "decadent feudal thinking." ... Nowadays everyone lives in their own way, and he just puts hedonism before everything else. But he has plenty of money, so he can afford to enjoy himself. Compared with a lot of other rich people, he's not that bad. Out of "eating, drinking, whoring, gambling, and smoking," he just sticks to that one thing.

For many younger villagers, what Shouyi said was appealing. As they saw it, he was a "carefree man who knows how to enjoy life." Once at the entrance to the Beitang temple I ran into a dozen young people gathered to watch a card game, and when they mentioned Shouyi's "legendary adventures," basically all of them expressed this sort of sentiment. One of them said with admiration, "Don't they say, 'men go bad as soon as they get rich'? He's a classic example. Even if a man is handsome, without money it's no use—he can't afford to be bad!" Even older male villagers like Shoukuan, who often criticized this sort of behavior, would occasionally sigh, "That's not 'enjoying life's pleasures'—it's 'enjoyment to the extreme'." In other words, Shoukuan felt that Shouyi *was* enjoying himself, but just a little too much.

Only once did I hear a more thoroughly negative statement, during the National Day break in 2012, while several people were discussing the topic at Shoude's watch repair shop. Shoude's wife Cheng Ju said, "Always doing improper things, he's completely lost the dignity that an old man should cherish." This could probably be considered the attitude of middle-aged and older women.[8]

Settling Down at Home

With so many people aware of Shouyi's complicated extramarital sex relations, of course his children knew as well. He said that his children had insinuated that they would not interfere as long as he "still wanted to keep this family" (i.e., did not initiate a divorce) and their mother did not become too upset, but if he could not ensure that, they would disown him and only recognize their mother as family. "That's my principle as well," he said. "How could I abandon my family?"

Of course, it would have been impossible for Cheng Xiu to remain unaware of what was going on, but she never publicly acknowledged that there was any evidence. Shouyi acknowledged it in front of everyone else but her, in whose presence he categorically denied everything. Considering the possibility that Cheng Xiu might actually know the truth in her heart and just be feigning confusion with a last layer of "window paper," I did not take the risk of directly asking her what she thought of Shouyi's behavior, lest that paper be broken and the two of them fall into an awkward situation from which it might be hard to recover. With respect to this sensitive topic, as an outsider I just observed from the sidelines, listening to whatever she said voluntarily, to whatever degree she said it. However, various signals indicated that she was actually well aware of what was going on.

According to Shouyi, when he began dating his girlfriend, sometimes Cheng Xiu would yell and scream, but he would not utter a word except to "deny everything even if she beat him to death," and eventually it became impossible for them to quarrel. Later, the focus of Cheng Xiu's fury turned toward the Hunanese mistress. Shouyi said this might have been because several years had passed, so Cheng Xiu felt the girlfriend was no longer much of a threat, whereas the mistress did seem threatening. I believe Shouyi's conjecture about Cheng Xiu's thinking was probably reliable. As an example, he mentioned that Cheng Xiu did not really interfere when it came to purely "monetary transactions of the flesh" such as "looking for ladies" in "bathhouses." Although in quarrels she would denounce this sort of behavior, more often she would say, "Why doesn't Heaven open its eyes and have those degenerate roadside wildflowers infect you with venereal disease? I can't be bothered to warn you, at least I'm old so you won't infect me."

In 1998, Cheng Xiu went sobbing to the home of Ah-Two (Shouyi's older paternal male cousin), denouncing Shouyi for being "unconscionable and ungrateful" and saying that she had endured a lifetime of hardships together with him but now he wanted to cast her aside. She asked Ah-Two to intervene, but Ah-Two said, "Nowadays it's hard to intervene in the private affairs of other households." He repeatedly tried to comfort her, saying, "I don't believe he would want to leave the family (i.e. initiate a divorce). Go on home, don't run around causing a fuss. Just look, your daughter-in-law only recently joined the family. Fussing like this won't be good for anyone." After that, even if Cheng Xiu felt upset, she restricted her lamentation to the home, no longer "seeking reinforcements" from other households. She once described this predicament was "asking for help from Heaven and Earth but receiving no answer."

Shouyi's method of dealing with these complaints was twofold: He would deny everything, and then "show concern for the family" in both word and deed. Once when we were chatting in 2008, he explained:

> When it comes to "messing around with ladies," it's not like this is something strange or unusual. This sort of thing is common nowadays, and I'm not the only one doing it. Her complaints are just verbal—she won't actually do anything to me. As for my girlfriend, (Cheng Xiu) seems to have guessed a few things, but she has no proof. I haven't admitted it, so there's nothing she can do about it... . Another thing is that I'm not saying I no longer want (a wife) at home just because I have (a girlfriend) outside. I'm still good to (Cheng Xiu). She's been suffering from stomach problems, and I've been willing to spend as much money as it takes to take her to different doctors. After two years it's finally almost better. As long as I have time at home, I do all the housework like cooking and laundry. I do a better job of it than her. I'm also kind to everyone on her side of the family, giving her face with them. That's no easy feat... . In short, outside "the multicolored flag blows in the wind," but at home "the red flag never falters" (i.e., despite having many lovers, I keep the marriage stable).

Starting in 2005, Shouyi's relationship with his Hunanese mistress began to change. They spent less time together, and Shouyi started giving her "holiday money" on holidays instead of a "living allowance" every month. This new arrangement continued until the end. Shouyi believed that prior to this, she had seemed something like what people normally mean by the term "second wife" (*ernai*), but this was no longer the case. For one thing, he explained, "Her flower shop had begun to make plenty of money, so she could support herself." More importantly, she no longer objected to him seeing other women, and this suggested she was preparing to move back home and get married.

The same year, Cheng Xiu basically stopped quarreling with Shouyi and began to formally practice Buddhism. Previously, she had already been more or less interested in that religion. Starting in the early 1980s, she would burn incense and pray to an image of the bodhisattva Guanyin at home during holidays, and sometimes she would go with others to make offerings at temples nearby. On major Buddhist holidays once or twice a year, she would even visit a certain temple in Fan County, making large monetary donations on each trip. She used to tell others that people should worship "the Buddhist ancestors," but she was not a pious follower herself, more frequently praying to Guan Gong.[9] Around 1994, she had Shouyi buy a very modern Guan Gong altar. Although this altar came equipped with electric "incense" and "spirit money" that would light up as long as the power was switched on, Cheng Xiu still burned real incense and spirit money every day.

Starting in 2005, according to other villagers, Cheng Xiu finally became a pious Buddhist and stopped praying to Guan Gong. Her account of this in 2011 (after having converted to Christianity in 2008) was as follows:

> What's the use of praying to Guan Gong so much? What's the use of having so much money? What people need is not money but good fortune. When you're poor, it's fortunate to have money, but when you're rich, that's no longer the case.... Of course money is still important, and my children worship Guan Gong, because they're the ones making money now. I'm old and no longer need to make money, so I don't worship him anymore. Now that I'm old, I worship karma, like it says in the *Sutra on Past and Present Causes and Effects*, you know? I'm not educated, so I don't understand much of it.

Not only did Cheng Xiu begin to worship Buddhist entities as diligently as she had worshipped Guan Gong, her trips to the temple in Fan County were also more zealous than before. Besides growing vegetables for her own consumption and watching television, she spent much of her time chanting mantras. She told me that although Cheng villagers were still not as distant from their neighbors as urbanites, who did not even know their neighbors, it was less common than before to visit other villagers. Now when nothing else was going on, people closed their courtyard gates and watched TV at home or played cards or mah-jong with a few people they were close to. She did not play such games, so there were far fewer opportunities for her to visit people. For a while, chanting mantras became an important part of her life, "as if the sun could not set if I didn't chant at some point during the day." In the summer of 2010, Shouyi took me to his rooftop to photograph the old section of the village. On the second floor, he showed me Cheng Xiu's bedroom, saying they had "slept separately for over ten years, only sleeping together when we visit our son in Wucheng." Although Cheng Xiu had converted to Christianity two years before that, all kinds of Buddhist prayer beads hung from her walls, and the desk was covered in Buddhist literature such as the *Sutra of Past and Present Causes and Effects* and the *Platform Sutra of the*

Sixth Patriarch (along with the Bible, of course, and there was also a cross hanging on the wall).

However, Cheng Xiu had some difficulty making progress in reading these texts. She had only attended primary school, so could not really understand what they said. During one of my research visits shortly before the end of the lunar year in 2008, it was only after multiple, stuttering attempts that she finally managed to recite those famous lines from the *Platform Sutra*: "Bodhi originally has no tree, no stand has the mirror bright; ultimately there is not a thing, so where could the dust alight?" Then she said, "Oh me, I'm so uneducated, it's no use. Never mind, now I follow the Lord anyway."

Cheng Xiu's conversion to Christianity was closely related to the influence of Cheng Ju and Shoukuan's wife Feng Lan. Feng Lan had begun practicing Christianity in 1991 as a result of her mother-in-law Ms. Mai's evangelism. Henceforth, Feng Lan became an active missionary in Duqiao. Cheng Ju's conversion in 1998 was also related to Feng Lan's influence. Since Cheng Ju had attended high school, she was good at organizing activities and communicating with others, plus she lived right next to Duqiao Church of the Gospel, so around the year 2000 the church designated her as the "parish director" for Cheng Village.

Cheng Ju and Feng Lan had already tried to convert Cheng Xiu many times, but the latter had always said she was too busy raising her grandchildren, so did not become their "priority target of development." Finally in 2008, their appeals became more attractive as Cheng Xiu experienced frustration at her difficulty in reading Buddhist texts due to her low level of education. One Sunday, she finally went to church with Cheng Ju and Fang Lan. She discovered that "the Lord's" ideas were easy to understand because the "teacher" (i.e., the pastor) at the pulpit spoke in the local dialect, explaining the Bible with examples from real life, and the ideas he talked about seemed to make sense. "Also," she added, "everyone sang songs together, like the performing arts activities during the collective era." Therefore, she soon came to accept Christianity.

In comparison with Cheng Ju, although Cheng Xiu had not attended much school, she could speak fluent Mandarin due to her experience talking to people from other parts of China while doing business in Wucheng. In addition, when it came to interacting with others, she was better at communicating and planning events. In 2009, therefore, she replaced Cheng Ju as parish director.

Over the next few years, I noticed that when Cheng Xiu spoke highly of Jesus, it was often combined with nostalgia for hardships. In conversation, her expression of nostalgia for the hard days of the past was almost as frequent as her complaints that the past was difficult. One day in 2010, for example, after inveighing against a Cantonese soap opera about a love triangle, she sighed:

> Nowadays the world is a mess. Would you say things aren't going well now? They seem to be going well enough. Would you say they're going

well? Everything seems to be meaningless. Back when we used to be poor, we wanted to make money, but after we became rich, it felt like money wasn't satisfying... . Jesus is different. He tells you that life still has meaning, after all.

In any case, it could be said that things settled down in Shouyi's household. He actively supported Cheng Xiu's religious activities, whether they were Buddhist or Christian. One Sunday in 2011, I visited Shouyi while he was at home cooking and cleaning, and he explained, "My old lady is busy at the church, so has no time to do the housework." In addition, he joked:

> A classic line on TV is, "I'd like to thank the people, the central government, the party, the viewers, Central Chinese TV, and all the TVs." For me it's like, "I'd like to thank the bodhisattvas, the gods, the Lord, the monks, the believers in Jesus, and all the believers." ... After all, now our household seems to have settled down peacefully. This project of settling down hasn't been easy.

Soon, however, a new destabilizing factor emerged: When Shouyi's grandson began attending middle school, he became uninterested in school and often indulged in computer games, and several times when he went gaming at an internet café, he got into fist fights. Since both Fudao and his wife were busy with their business, Shouyi had no choice but to take up the task of looking after his grandson. Shouyi had preferred to live in the village, never staying in Wucheng for more than three days at a time, but at this time he had to start basing himself in Wucheng in order to take care of his grandson, returning to the city the same day even if he visited the village. On many of my trips to Cheng Village he told me on the phone that I needed to go to Wucheng if I wanted to see him. When we met up on National Day in 2012, he said:

> Now I'm just like those government personnel responsible for "maintaining stability," taking care of (my grandson) every day. There's no way around it, in one's lifetime one can't always focus only on one's own enjoyment. I can't just let him go unattended, otherwise if he goes bad, wouldn't all that money I made through so much hard work go to waste? ... Nowadays this society is so out of control, it's hard for families to relax.

True Self

In the eyes of villagers from Shouyi's generation, between the rebel of the Cultural Revolution and the businessman he later became, there were both continuities and ways in which Shouyi seemed to have been two entirely different people.

When villagers emphasized the continuities, they often said, "that's just how he is." In a positive sense, they praised him for getting rich even when times were rough, for his ability to make friends and to refrain from harming them out of self-interest, for treating his friends as equals even after getting rich, and for "upholding the red flag" at home even though he "flew colored flags" elsewhere. At the same time, they disparaged him for being lazy both during the collective era and after he had become a boss, for being sloppy about his work and failing to behave properly, and for remaining a country bumpkin even though he had gotten rich, "always dressing like a pile of pickled vegetables."

When people emphasized how he had changed, they often said that he was good at "changing with the times." In this respect, they praised him for understanding what was necessary during different eras: during the collective era talking about Marxism-Leninism until he was "so red that he was almost purple," then in the market era reciting "the mantras of business" until he was "so rich he was greasy"; living simply and frugally when things were rough, then after getting rich throwing himself into the enjoyment of life's pleasures. At the same time, they criticized his capriciousness when it came to how he has treated relatives, first daring to resist wrong-headed policies from above during the collective era and taking care of his uncles and cousins, but then forgetting about them after he had started doing business; first working together with his wife to make a living back when they were poor, but then running around cheating on her after they had become rich.

In the eyes of many younger villagers, however, their image of Shouyi was unusually consistent: that of a "capable man," "a successful person," "amazing." One day in the summer of 2010, for example, I was standing outside a shop with a few young people who were chatting and smoking as they prepared to go fishing. When the conversation turned to comparing Shouyi with Chengren, one of them said something particularly representative:

> How can you compare them? One is up in the sky and the other is down under the ground. One is rich, the other sits in his doorway every day and no one talks to him. There's no way to compare them. As the saying goes, "He who succeeds is a king, he who fails is a bandit." If Chengren were really capable, how would he have fallen so low? Shouyi is different. We youngsters aren't clear about what happened in the past, those stories may as well be legends. But when it comes to doing business, he's really been the best—that much we've seen with our own eyes. You can't help but admiring the man's ability.... Not just in business, even when it comes to quitting smoking, who can just quit like that as soon as they say it? *He* can. He's so good at controlling himself. Like Sun Wukong (the monkey king from *Journey to the West*), he can immediately change into any shape he wants. Why was Sun Wukong more powerful than Zhu Bajie (the pig-man in the novel)? Because he could change. Chengren's inferiority comes from his inability to change. Already in the past he was inflexible: If his

superiors said something then he did it, even if it didn't make any sense, and even if it was bad. Later the times changed, but he didn't change. Inability to change means inability to be "flexible or unblocked" (*tong*), and that means "pain" (*tong*). As they say (in traditional Chinese medicine), "Unblocked means there's no pain; pain means there's a blockage." So now Chengren is so miserable because his mind is stuck and his brain won't change—it's his own fault. And Shouyi is so successful and impressive because of his ability to be unblocked and flexible.

Shouyi said he knew some villagers' opinion of him "had a disparaging flavor," even admitting that "actually there's some basis for this," but he did not care. He was willing to continue "walking my own path, let them say what they will." Regarding the claims that he was "lazy," for example, or that he was "sloppy about his work" and "failed to behave properly," he said, "They're right, but the problem is: What intelligent person doesn't try to slack off? Why not cut corners, if it's possible? Only incapable people are completely honest and well-behaved." At the same time, he said, "Sometimes I actually did take advantage of loopholes and make some shady deals. They're right to criticize me." As for calling him a "country bumpkin," on the one hand Shouyi acknowledged that he was "country," but he also claimed that he always stood at the forefront of the times, including his proclivity for extramarital sex. He admitted that it was wrong to do that behind his wife's back, but he also commented that "people who can't eat grapes say they're too sour," and that at least he was not as bad as "people who abandon their wives for mistresses." Regarding the claim that he neglected obligations to uncles and cousins after he got rich, he admitted this was true to some extent, but he had never been interested in clan affairs, he said, and besides, if he had tried to mix that kind of relationship with business, it probably would have hurt both his business and the feelings of his relatives.

As for other villagers' words of praise, Shouyi said, "I've heard it so many times, but you can't take it too seriously." It was just by chance that he got that job in the County Revolutionary Committee, he pointed out, and one cannot deny that his later success in business was partly due to luck. "Living frugally" was the only option possible when he was poor, and it was true that he enjoyed his life after getting rich, but he admitted that he overindulged in sex. The only comment that he completely agreed with and took pride in was that he treated his friends well both before and after he became rich.

Shouyi's appraisal of himself was often extremely contradictory as well. Every time we chatted, he would speak highly of his attentiveness to interpersonal obligations, his talent in business, and his adaptability to changing circumstances, but then he would also say that he was not a "good person." On National Day in 2011, during a long conversation in Wucheng, he said wistfully:

I used to be very Marxist-Leninist, but now I've become the man you see today. Truly like stepping from one era into another. This world changes so fast, life feels simply like a dream. The problem is, this dream is actually real, believe it or not. Sometimes when I think about it, I'm not even sure myself which of my "selves" is the real one.

Furthermore, Shouyi recalled, when he was young, he sincerely wanted "revolution," feeling genuine anger toward those corrupt cadres, such as Chengren and Chenggong, and toward their bureaucratic attitude. But it was also during that era that Shouyi, after acquiring some power, had embezzled public funds himself. He clearly acknowledged that if things had continued in that way, he might have become an "unclean cadre" himself, becoming a target of other revolutionaries. Shouyi believed, therefore, that his wholehearted turn toward making money was due in part to being "pushed" by people such as Chengren, in part to being "pulled" by the overall trend of the times, and in part to his own decision.

Right after decollectivization, Shouyi said, he just wanted to make a little money to improve his family's living conditions—it never occurred to him that one day he would become a rich boss. So family was important to him. In addition to familial harmony, he especially cared about his children's education. In contrast with most villagers, however, he did not care so much what kind of grades his children got in school, being more concerned with their character, habits, and ability to do things. The emphasis, then, was on preventing his children from becoming "bad." This educational philosophy has continued into the way he looks after his grandsons now: He does not care much about what kind of grades they make in school, but he strictly forbids them from getting into fights, watching pornography on the internet, wasting money, etc. The facts demonstrate that this approach has been relatively successful: All four of his children have avoided the sort of problems common among "the second generation of rich people" (children of the *nouveau riche*), and three of them have become successful at running businesses themselves.

After becoming truly rich, however, Shouyi discovered that a destabilizing factor had emerged within his family. He said:

> My habits are generally good. I don't eat or drink too much, and I don't gamble or use drugs, unlike many bosses with their debauchery. It's just that one area where my desire is too strong—I can't keep it in my pants!

Shouyi had once figured that if he could quit smoking cold turkey like that, then he could do the same with his sex addiction. But every time he raised the idea of quitting, he would soon be defeated by his theories about sex "delighting the body and relaxing the mind." At this point, Shouyi said that some "theoretical clarity" could be gained by mixing in his former "attainments in revolutionary theory"[22]:

Marxism-Leninism's critique of commodity fetishism is powerful, but at the time I was poor and just reading about it in books, without understanding it from experience. Now I've begun to understand, and sometimes I feel that in my bones I still truly believe in Marxism-Leninism. What was that term he (Marx) coined? ... "Alienation." You must be familiar with that, right? Alienation means that because of money, people become objects, things without life. And sometimes I feel that I've become an object. For example, after doing it with a "pretty girl" (Ct. *leng neui*), I'll be watching the video (of himself having sex with her), and sometimes I'll ask myself, "Is that person me?" It seems to be, but then again it doesn't—I'm not even sure, it might just be an image.... There are some areas where Marx didn't go into enough depth. As far as I see it, he never really experienced the life of a rich man, so it was hard for him to discuss it in depth. For instance, money isn't yours if you save it in the bank, or if you change it into gold or silver and hide it under your bed. How could it be yours unless you spend it? Of course, it's not yours after you spend it either. It's only yours during the moment when you're spending it, you know? Look at all these reports about corrupt officials trying all kinds of ways to hide their money, but is it really theirs? It's not. That kind of money is nothing but something that causes fear and makes your heart itchy. And those pretty girls also seem to be a case of alienation, when you think about it: They've become objects that you can use if you pay money. But the really mysterious thing about pretty girls is precisely the fact that they're *both* objects you can use if you pay *and* actual living beings. When it comes to objects, have you ever seen pots and pans, or beer and cigarettes that voluntarily do all they can to satisfy your desires? No. If you don't like them, first you have to tell the boss who produced those things, and then the boss will have to come and improve them—the things themselves are dead. But pretty girls are different because they're alive and will voluntarily do all they can to make you feel so good that you're ready to die. So this is alienation but it's also not. It's not that they become an object, but that they become another "self." When they're doing it with you they become another person, not the person they normally are. I'm serious—this is what (the Hunanese mistress) told me.

When saying this, Shouyi's facial expression kept switching between an irreverent grin and a look of extreme gravity. He used topsy-turvy language to demonstrate to me that his life was real, but he was unsure as to which of his "selves" was real.

Especially when it came to extramarital sex, at first he said it was good, but later he said, "It's not good for one's children and grandchildren. Thank goodness I carry those recordings around with me in a flash drive—if my grandson found them in the computer, that would be harmful."

I said, "Nowadays it's easy for kids to run across that sort of thing on the internet." Shouyi replied:

> That's why I need to keep an eye on him when he's using the internet. If he found (my) videos, he might turn against me saying, 'Even you do these things, so what right do you have to discipline me?' ... Sometimes I think I need to quit this (habit) for the good of my grandson.

After a while, however, he played it down again, saying:

> Nowadays there are so many stories like this (about love and lust).... . Just go online and you'll see, if you change the name of the protagonist, I guarantee most of the stories are basically the same.... . Back when I was in Wucheng (at the Wu County Revolutionary Committee) reading novels every day, I had already noticed that the plots of love stories were all basically the same, whether ancient or modern, Chinese or foreign—they never changed. So I never watch those romantic serials they show on TV nowadays—they're too poorly made. (Paying for sex) is the same: Even if you switch girls, in the end they all feel the same. The basic movements never change.

Similarly, it was at the end of this conversation that Shouyi said:

> I've indulged in too much pleasure during this lifetime. I know I'll end up dying prematurely. With so much (extramarital sex), although I paid money for it, I still feel a little guilty. Besides, according to science this will shorten one's lifespan. Whether it's traditional Chinese medicine or Western medicine, both say that too much sexual activity is bad for your health... . On the upside, I've already enjoyed everything I could in this lifetime. That's about enough, and now I'm ready to die.

I knew that these words did not mean Shouyi was about to go commit suicide. At most they expressed that sometimes he felt that life had already lost any meaning, and he only felt this way occasionally. Several minutes earlier, he had been talking about how important it was for him to educate his grandchildren properly—more important than money or his own corporeal pleasures.

Notes

1 *Translator's note*: During the socialist era, Communist Party cadres often applied the military term "commando units" (*tujidui*) to groups of the "strong and healthy workforce" (*qiangzhuang laodongli*) that were mobilized to complete special tasks, often urgent ones during an emergency. When these commandos were young, agrarian production teams sometimes called them "Youth Commandos" (*qingnian tujidui*).

2 *Translator's note: The Plum in the Golden Vase (Jin Ping Mei)* is one of the six classic novels of Chinese literature, published in the late Ming dynasty (first print edition 1610) by an unknown author with the pen name "The Scoffing Scholar of Lanling." It has been banned as pornographic under multiple regimes, with permission to borrow it from libraries granted only to readers meeting certain requirements, such as university professors specializing in Chinese literature.
3 *Nanru* peanuts is a Cantonese snack made with peanuts and fermented tofu roasted with other seasonings.
4 *Translator's note*: From Mao Zedong's 1949 poem "On the Occasion of the Liberation of Nanking by the People's Liberation Army." Translation from Ma 1986: 88.
5 This (欲练神功，挥刀自宫) is a line from martial romance (*wuxia*) television serials, meaning that in order to achieve otherworldly fighting abilities, one must first castrate oneself and cut off all sexual desire.
6 Literally "master's old lady killer." "The master's old lady" (Ct. *si naai* 师奶) is a Cantonese term for a married woman.
7 *Translator's note*: This phrase is used by the Chinese state to denote three types of crimes associated with entertainment venues such as dance clubs and karaoke bars, so the words often appear on the walls of such venues as a reminder that such activities are prohibited. The term translated here as "prostitution" literally means "yellow" and also includes other types of sexual products outlawed in China, such as pornography.
8 As for younger women, I never had occasion to inquire into their views about this, but Shouyi's daughters-in-law had a slightly different view (introduced below).
9 *Translator's note*: Guan Gong ("Lord Guan") is a god derived from the historical figure Guan Yu (d. 220 BCE), who served as general under the warlord Liu Bei in the Eastern Han through Liu's founding of Shu Han (one of the Three Kingdoms). He has been worshipped as a god since the seventh century and is still widely worshipped throughout the Chinese-speaking world. He is usually considered to be a martial deity, so has been associated with members of the military, police, and criminal organizations (either as part of either the Daoist religion or within less clearly defined folk beliefs) but is also worshipped by Buddhists as the Sangharama Bodhisattva. So it would not have been contradictory for Cheng Xiu to worship him while calling herself a Buddhist. However, the quotation below shows that she equated Guan Gong with Caishen (the God of Wealth), although these two gods have different histories, associations, and conventional depictions—Guan Gong generally being depicted with a red face and Caishen with a light flesh-toned face, among other distinctions. The author confirms that in this and other regions of China, Guan Gong is widely regarded as the "Martial God of Wealth" (*Wu Cai Shen*), so is worshipped not only for martial success or protection, but also for economic prosperity.

4 Two Intellectuals

Heading the Household

The two brothers Cheng Shoude and Cheng Shouzhi graduated from high school at Duqiao Secondary, as did their wives. When I first arrived in Cheng Village and began inquiring about its "ancient" section, I asked several people, "Who in the village is relatively well-educated?" I soon learned that Shoude and Shouzhi were widely considered to be emblematic of "intellectuals," or that "their whole family is full of intellectuals." Sometimes, other villagers would say that the brothers were "old-fashioned intellectuals," because "what kind of modern intellectual would continue living in the countryside? Anyone else would have left to make money long ago." Clearly this term "intellectual" was rather vague in its significance. In photographs from the high school class reunions both brothers had organized, quite a few residents of Cheng Village could be found among their classmates. When I pointed this out, villagers would explain that "intellectual" does not simply refer to one's level of education. I also pointed out that Shoude and Shouzhi's elder brother Shouli had not attended much school at all, while their younger brother Shoucai had only graduated from middle school. The villagers would explain that the phrase "their whole family" really just meant those two middle brothers and excluded their elder and younger brothers. It was only after about two years of research that I gradually began to understand that this description of Shoude and Shouzhi as "intellectuals," and this exclusion of Shouli and Shoucai from "their whole family," were both related to a whole series of details about their life histories.

Shouli was born in 1933 and attended three years of primary school. In 1945, because the family was poor, his father sent Shouli to apprentice with a cousin who worked in Guangzhou as a barber. After three years of apprenticeship, Shouli left with the intention of starting his own barbershop. But first, at his father's request, Shouli returned to Cheng Village for betrothal at the end of 1948, getting married a few months later. Shortly thereafter, since Shouli lacked the capital to open a barbershop, he returned to work at his cousin's shop in Guangzhou. In 1949, before the People's Liberation Army entered Guangzhou, Shouli and his cousin moved to Hong Kong and lost touch with the family for about two years.

When Shouli left Cheng Village, his wife was already pregnant, giving birth to a daughter the next year. According to the policies of the Land Reform Work Team, she was allowed to remarry, but she decided not to, since it would have been hard for a mother to find a new husband, and she was still waiting for news from Shouli. Shouli did not return, however, instead marrying another woman in Hong Kong several years later, who bore him two daughters and a son.

Shoude was born in 1939. Due to poverty, he did not have a chance to begin school until 1950. He therefore cherished the opportunity, devoting himself to his studies. Later Shoude recalled that his dream as a child was to become an engineer or a mechanic. He became especially fascinated with physics and mathematics. In 1959, he failed the entrance exam for vocational secondary school (*zhongzhuan*). If he had passed, according to national policy he could have "eaten state grain" (gotten onto the state's payroll) after graduation, but according to Wu County's local policy, graduates of academic high school (*gaozhong*) could also be assigned jobs at state-owned enterprises or public service institutions. Shoude therefore decided to attend academic high school until graduating in 1962. Just as he graduated, however, the policy changed such that he could no longer obtain a state job. Meanwhile his classmate Yang Xianzong, who belonged to the Duqiao Residential Brigade and therefore had an urban household registration, was assigned a job at the Duqiao Commune Lumber Mill and began "eating state grain."

Shoude was particularly close to another classmate from middle school and high school, surnamed Mai. Mai came from a neighboring commune called Shantang. His uncle was the leader of a certain department at a farm in Zhuhai. The farm was a state-owned enterprise originally set up to employ overseas Chinese people who had returned from Southeast Asia, but it also employed some peasants from China as agricultural workers without permanent positions (*bianzhi*). In 1962, after Shoude failed to find local employment, Mai helped him obtain a job on the farm. Shoude soon discovered, however, that the work was even more strenuous than that in his production team at home. Besides, most of the people he worked with had no experience with agriculture prior to returning to China, and many were not even Cantonese, so they did not know how to arrange their farm work according to the climate and soil quality of Zhuhai. Although the government tried many methods to help the farm improve its productivity, the results were disappointing. Shoude was regarded as a local person, so he had to take the lead in everything and had a more arduous workload. Moreover, he recalled:

> Besides those objective reasons I mentioned, I had my own subjective reasons. I was basically an intellectual. Ah-Tan,[1] think about it: as a student who had just left school, how could I endure such hard work? Also I didn't have a permanent position, so I had to work more but got paid

less than half of what they received—10.50 yuan a month, basically just enough to survive on, with hardly anything to take home. My dad had it really rough: Ah-Zhi (Shouzhi), Ah-Cai (Shoucai), and my big brother's (Shouli's) daughter all had to attend school, so my family had a lot of expenses. With wages so low, it didn't make sense to continue. So after working for just over a year, I resolved to quit, packed my backpack, and came home.

It was the winter of 1963 when Shoude returned to Cheng Village. Shortly thereafter, under pressure from his parents and the introduction of a matchmaker, he married Cheng Ju, who was three years his junior, from Nantang. The next year, they had a son. A few months later, they moved out of Shoude's parents' house. Since his father was in poor health, however, Shoude still had to support his parents and brothers. To make matters worse, due to postpartum complications, Cheng Ju was unable to work in the production team for a long period of time, so the family fell on hard times.

In the Fourth Month of the traditional calendar in 1965, as Shoude's family was running out of food, he wrote a letter to Mai explaining his predicament and asking for help. After completing the letter, her searched every corner of the house but could not find the 8 cents necessary to buy a stamp and an envelope. Out of options, he went to the bus stop in Duqiao every day asking if anyone was going to Shantang. Every day there was a bus that would pass through Shantang on the way to Wucheng, and finally on the third day he met a commune-level cadre on his way to Shantang for work. The cadre delivered the letter to Mai, and two days later, Mai rode a bicycle in the rain for 30 kilometers to bring Shoude a package of waxed paper containing 12 yuan and ration tickets for 10 *jin* of grain. After eating a sweet potato at Shoude's home, Mai rode back to Shantang.

Shoude told me this story many times in order to illustrate the hardship he had endured. Upon completing the story, he would sigh something like, "loyalty is so important," "hardship reveals true friendship," or "it's not easy to head a household." On countless occasions, Shoude expressed that these feelings came from the bottom of his heart, since this classmate had really helped him so much. Shortly after lending that money and those grain ration tickets, for example, Mai had helped him to inquire and make the connections necessary for Shoude to apply for a position as teacher at Shantang Secondary School. In that time of extreme difficulty, Shoude went to Shantang, took the employment examination, and successfully acquired the position. Prior to this, Shoude had detested the idea of working as a teacher, since he had dreamed of becoming an engineer or a mechanic. Ruminating on those days, Shoude said, "Me becoming a teacher was like Lin Chong (in *The Water Margin*) being forced to join the outlaws on Mount Liang (i.e., only because of poverty)."

In addition to poverty, there was another important thing that came up when Shoude was lamenting the difficulties he encountered in "heading a household": a conflict that had emerged with his brother Shouli in 1965, regarding the affair between Shouli's wife and Chen Xi.

After the affair had become known and the brigade secretary Chengren had urged him repeatedly, Shoude mailed several letters to Hong Kong requesting Shouli to return to Cheng Village and handle the matter. When Shouli finally overcame all kinds of pressures and arrived, before formally meeting with Chen Xi or Chengren, a serious dispute had occurred with Shoude. (Since their father was in poor health and felt that Shoude was the most educated of his sons, he had placed Shoude in charge of the family.)

Shouli was inclined to affirm that the relationship with this wife had already dissolved long ago. In addition, he said that he could not take his daughter with him back to Hong Kong. He hoped, therefore, that his parents or Shoude could take care of the girl until her mother remarried. Shoude felt, however, that Shouli's marriage in Cheng Village was a historical fact, so even though he had remarried and had children in Hong Kong, he should uphold his image as a husband at home. Shoude also felt that Shouli should carry out formal divorce proceedings with his wife in Cheng Village, taking his daughter with him back to Hong Kong or paying child support, since their parents were in poor health and the family was having trouble making ends meet. Shouli responded that his life in Hong Kong was also quite hard, so there was really no way he could take care of things in Cheng Village on top of that. In addition, Shoude said that Shouli should firmly oppose his wife marrying Chen Xi, lest conflicts arise in the future if everyone continued living in Jiangbei, where they would often run into each other. But Shouli was not concerned about this and did not bring it up in his formal meeting with Chen Xi and Chengren.

The conflict's ultimate resolution was satisfactory to Shouli but diverged significantly from Shoude's thinking on the matter. The couple had never obtained a marriage license in the first place, so they just carried out the divorce proceedings orally. Chen Xi was expelled from the Communist Party, but he chose to divorce his wife, maintain custody over his daughter and three sons, marry Shouli's ex-wife, and adopt her daughter into his household.

With Shoude already unhappy about all this, some of Shouli's statements enraged him and led to further conflict. One was that Shouli kept commenting about how nice Hong Kong was and how poor Cheng Village was, and another was that he blamed the poor health of their parents and two younger brothers on Shoude's alleged failure to head the family properly. Later, Shoude recounted:

> My older brother had no conscience at all. He was completely incapable of grasping how hard it was for me to head the family. At the time my salary was only just over 10 yuan a month, I had a son of my own, most of the time I had to teach school in Shantang, and on the weekends I still had to come home and do farm work in the production team. I only ate the worst food and wore the worst clothes. You think that was easy for me?

It wasn't, it was so hard. You (i.e., Shouli) keep saying how great Hong Kong is. If so, then why don't you give mom and dad a little money? And how can you give your daughter away for someone else to raise? The way (he) talked was like an imperial official returning home in ancient times, it made me angry just to hear it. Especially when he went so far as to accuse me of failing to head the household properly—you're not the one whose back hurts when you stand there criticizing from the sidelines! ... At the time I was young and impetuous, so I shouted back at him. I think I was too harsh and disrespectful, and we parted on bad terms.

After that occasion, Shouli did not return to Cheng Village again until the early 1980s. Their parents placed a high value on education, so although the family was poor, they insisted that Shouzhi attend high school at Duqiao Secondary. At least on the weekends and during the winter and summer breaks Shouzhi could help the family earn a few work-points. In 1966 the parents' health gradually started to improve, as did the family's living situation to some degree. Two years later, Shouzhi graduated from high school, but due to the new policy of selecting college applicants according to class background and personal recommendations by cadres, he—belonging to a "middle peasant" family rather than a "poor" background—had no choice but to do begin doing farm work for the production team. In 1972, their father passed away, and the two middle brothers Shoude and Shouzhi organized a simple funeral. Shouli did not come back from Hong Kong to attend. Thinking back to the reasons for this, Shoude explained:

In those days, long-distance communication was difficult, and it would have taken too long if we had waited for a letter to reach him, and for him to come up here. So I just had my little brother (Shouzhi) write him a letter after the funeral. I couldn't be bothered to write, and he just wrote back saying he was sad that he couldn't fulfill his filial duty, that it was hard to complete the paperwork necessary for him to come home, blah blah blah. I told Ah-Zhi (Shouzhi) not to reply, that it would be pointless. Neither of us had any feelings for him.

The Dark Counselor

In the eyes of many villagers, Shoude was not only educated, but also possessed a surprising political sensibility and ability to analyze and predict political trends, but unfortunately, he never participated in politics by serving as a leader.

Shoude's outstanding ability to analyze politics was first seen during the Four Cleanups campaign. At the end of 1964, the Four Cleanups Work Team determined that Cheng Shoulu, bookkeeper for Production Team Three, had embezzled ("eaten and taken more than his share") a certain amount of cassava (*mushu*). (Team Three was one of the three into which the Jiangbei

Team was divided in 1962.) In everyday work, Shoulu had often reprimanded ordinary members of his team, with Chengren supporting him from behind the scenes, so many villagers were angry but did not dare to speak up about it. According to the recollections of several villagers, because of Shoulu, his wife also often spoke in "an extremely arrogant manner," as if she were better than them. They were unhappy about this too, calling it "the fox borrowing the tiger's roar." After Shoulu was investigated, rumors circulated among villagers that he would be sent to prison or even executed. Needless to say, Shoulu's whole family grew worried. At the time, in conducting such investigations, the Four Cleanups Work Team had to work together with several villagers who had not served as cadres, calling them "secretary personnel" (*shujiyuan*). Due to Shoude's higher degree of education, villagers recommended him to serve in this capacity as secretary personnel for a while. Shoude later recounted:

> One evening (after Shoulu had been investigated), my family had just finished dinner, and (Shoulu's) wife came (to my house) with (her) two children. (She) said, "Your cousin (Shoulu) wants to die," that he was preparing to "walk the short path" (commit suicide) by hanging himself that evening, and thank goodness she had found out in time. She asked me to help save him. I tried to comfort her saying, "Tell him not to do it. No matter how they handle this thing, I understand the policy, and they won't execute him." When I got to their house, I told him my analysis: "(The policy calls for) leniency for those who confess, severity for those who resist. You've already confessed, so they won't execute you. Besides, 'the bullet hits the bird that sticks its head out,' but your case (of embezzlement) is a minor one, so they won't execute you. That's the second reason. Thirdly, to put it bluntly, they say 'officials protect each other,' but you haven't offended any leaders at the commune or brigade level, so as soon as they let you go, there's no way they'll execute you. That's the third reason." After hearing this, his heart seemed to be more at ease.

Later, it turned out as Shoude had predicted: Shoulu was merely required to pay back the cassava he had embezzled and could keep his post. Shoulu praised Shoude saying, "(You people with) more education really are different, with more insight and a brilliant intelligence—such a waste that you don't go into politics." But Shoude did not try to finesse his connections with the Four Cleanups Work Team members as Shouyi did. For this reason, although Shoude had helped the team with its work, its members did not take it to heart or recommend him for a political post. As Shouyi saw it, this demonstrated that Shoude did not understand how to make use of connections.

However, Shouyi also expressed admiration for Shoude's intelligence in political matters. This was referring to his performance in political conflicts.

In the early summer of 1966, Shoude was teaching at Shantang Secondary School. Since several of the teachers had been classified as "rightists" in

1957, now the school was covered in big-character posters criticizing them. Some of these posters targeted Shoude, calling him a "rightist dark counselor" (*youpai hei canmou*). This may have been because he treated everyone kindly, including those labeled as "rightists." When some of those teachers were treated unfairly, he would privately say words of comfort to them, as he had done with Shoulu. Some of the "rebels" therefore believed that he was always supporting the rightists and secretly conspiring with them. Shoude recalled:

> I was truly wronged. Ah-Tan, think about it: Who would dare to conspire with the rightists in those days? All I did was to say a few words of comfort as a colleague. For that they attacked me with big-character posters. As soon as I saw what was going on, I decided to figure out a way to transfer back to Cheng Village to teach at the primary school there. There (in Shantang) I was an outsider, and as soon as the struggle escalated, outsiders would easily become scapegoats. Think about it: If they really wanted to get someone, they would surely target outsiders first. Besides, the principal of Cheng Village Primary belonged to Red Flag, and that's the faction I identified with more ideologically. So I thought it would be safer here both as a local villager, and as a member of the same faction. Also that would make it easier for me to help out with the farmwork and take care of my family.

After Shoude returned to Cheng Village, the poster attacks on him in Shantang gradually dissipated. In later struggles, Shantang Secondary School became one of that commune's most intense battlegrounds, with his "rightist" colleagues suffering fierce criticism.

However, Shoude soon found himself at the heart of factional conflict in Cheng Village as well. In terms of political views, Shoude belonged to Red Flag. He was both a local villager and a teacher at the primary school, plus he got along well privately with the principal and Shouyi, so shortly after returning, the Duqiao Residential Brigade's branch of East Wind labeled him the top "dark counselor" of the commune's Red Flag faction. And indeed, Shoude had played an important role in the July 16th Incident.

During the days of that incident, Shoude met with his former classmate Yang Xianzong in the Duqiao Residential Brigade on several occasions to parley. Since Yang was local, he enjoyed a certain degree of influence within the Duqiao Commune Lumber Mill's branch of East Wind. After they had obtained weapons from the county's armed police unit (*wuzhuangbu*), Yang had become one of the people in charge of guarding them. With great anxiety, he conveyed this information to Shoude, telling him that if they heard East Wind's gongs sounding during a demonstration, they should retreat at once, as this meant they were preparing to fire. When Shoude learned that the enemy had real guns with ammunition, he grew concerned. As he recalled, at the time he had told Yang:

> We all need to withdraw from this political game if possible. You especially need to be careful, being responsible for the guns. Many of our classmates (belong to Red Flag)—don't end up shooting them! Besides, when we march, don't forget there are secondary school students from Rising Sun marching with us. Some are from Cheng Brigade, others from Duqiao (Residential Brigade), and all are the sons and daughters of our uncles and cousins. No matter who gets hurt, it would be sinful (*zaonie*). And many of the people on both sides are relatives. Politics is politics, eventually this movement will pass. How many events like this have happened before? Didn't they all pass? But we still have to live the rest of our lives here. How will we be able to face our elders?

At that point, Yang offered to switch sides, bringing some weapons with him over to Red Flag, but Shoude rejected this proposal, saying:

> Of course I'd welcome you if you came over, but it would be better if you didn't. We'll protect you from our side while you protect us from yours. Politics is cruel. This is called 'having a foot in two boats,' there's no way around it.

Henceforth, in Shoude's own words, he truly became a "dark counselor," drawing back from ordinary factional activities but attending all the important meetings and making suggestions from behind the scenes.

On July 16th, Cheng Village's Sunrise group and Duqiao Secondary School's Rising Sun marched together. What still stands out to this day in Shoude's memory was the moment his sexagenarian father handed him a sharpened chisel, telling him to use it for self-defense. After recalling this, he said wistfully, "Even old people like him supported (armed struggle)—how crazy was that? Everyone was really out of their minds."

After Shouyi fled to Fancheng, Shoude and Shoukuan retreated to Cheng Village with the others, demolishing the wooden bridge into town. From the opposite riverbank, East Wind besieged them in the village for a week. Shoukuan continued trying to transport weapons for defense, but Shoude admonished him, saying "Don't mess with that stuff anymore, come and help me punt this boat up the river." They took up their production team's duty helping the Duqiao Supply and Marketing Co-op to transport local products, punting a boat up the river to Tongcheng and then staying there a few days, thus sidestepping the storm of events. Later, Shouyi was detained and investigated, but Shoude managed to avoid that because he had merely been a "dark counselor" rather than leading his faction publicly. When it came time for "the great linking-up of revolutionaries," however, this same factor also denied him the opportunity to be promoted, which Shouyi and the village school principal enjoyed.

Henceforth, Shoude recalled, he became cautious in his everyday speech and conduct, striving to keep a low profile lest he get caught up in another political conflict. When he was not teaching, in his free time he worked alongside the other members of his production team. However, it was still hard to avoid minor frictions with the cadres. Normally his response was just to endure these jabs, but when that became impossible, sometimes he would openly erupt into hostility. In 1968, for instance, Production Team Three's head, Shoulu, often assigned Shoude's wife Cheng Ju to work in the labor group supervised by Chengren's wife. He had intended this as an act of reciprocity, since Shoude had helped Shoulu back during the Four Cleanups, so Shoulu asked Chengren's wife to take it easy on Cheng Ju, but this move ended up backfiring. Cheng Ju had graduated from high school, whereas Chengren's wife was illiterate. The latter was suspected of taking advantage of her power to bully people under her supervision, and Cheng Ju expressed discontent with this behavior, so it was hard to avoid conflict between them. Later, during several public events, both Chengren and his wife accused Cheng Ju of "entering the canteen before the bell rang." On the surface, this sounds as if they were accusing her of violating labor discipline by eating before the designated mealtime, but in the local dialect, this expression contained a deeper metaphorical implication: that Cheng Ju had committed pre-marital sex, so she had not been a virgin when she got married. Upon hearing this accusation, Shoude openly erupted into hostility toward Chengren's wife. He later recalled:

> During one team assembly, I walked in front of her and loudly asked, "Are you standing behind me?" She replied, "Oh yeah, that just happens to be where I'm standing." So I asked, "Do you always follow me around, even when I'm asleep?" She noticed there was something wrong with my tone, so she said, "Don't talk nonsense!" By that point, lots of people had gathered around to rubberneck. That's just what I was aiming for, so then I seized the opportunity to yell, "In that case, how do you and your husband know whether my wife entered the canteen before the bell rang? And you're telling me not to talk nonsense! Who's the one talking nonsense?" She was speechless. Later when Chengren found out, he told everyone that I was truly a "dark counselor," normally keeping silent but then suddenly erupting with a mouthful of spleen. (He said) I was like a dog: Those that bark the least are the most likely to bite. I just ignored such talk. Everyone could see who was right and who was wrong, and that's all that mattered.

Shoude's reputation as a "dark counselor" was also related to his persuasion of Shouzhi to quit his post as head of the production team. Shouzhi had begun working for the team in 1968, becoming the team's bookkeeper two years later, and then assuming the post of team head in 1975. The following year, Shouzhi's wife had a child, but it died before it was three months old. In 1977, Chengren began making a big stir about implementing the Family Planning Policy. Shoude felt that if Shouzhi helped Chengren to enforce the policy, he would offend his uncles and cousins by preventing some of them from having a son or grandson, but if he *refused* to help enforce it, he would be accused of violating discipline. Shoude recommended that Shouzhi request to resign on the grounds that he needed to help take care of his wife when she got pregnant again. Chengren was already discontent with Shouzhi's lax attitude toward implementing the policy, so he approved his resignation, as well as annulling his status as a "key target for development as a potential party member." At first, Shouzhi felt that the latter annulment was unfortunate, but Shoude comforted him, saying:

> Don't take it too hard if you can't join the party, it's not that important. No one can predict how long political things will last without changing. Even if you did join, how high-ranking of an official do you think you could become? So many people become major officials with great fanfare, but what have they got in the end? Look at the Gang of Four. ... If you offend someone over a small matter, it's no big deal—after a while it'll be forgotten. But if you offended someone over this (Family Planning Policy), now that's a whole different matter. It's a matter of cutting off the family line so they don't have any descendants! People would resent you for the rest of your life.

Warm and Full (Just Getting By)

In the late 1970s, remuneration for work (*gongjia*) in Cheng Village's production teams gradually rose. In Team Three, to which Shoude belonged, ten work-points (the standard remuneration men received for a day of work) were worth about 1.5 yuan, so with the addition of bonuses for extra work, a man would make 50 to 60 yuan a month. For Shoude's work as a teacher at Cheng Village Primary School, however, his salary was not adjusted upwards. He had already been receiving the highest salary for *minban* teachers (i.e., those outside the system of public services with permanent positions on the state payroll): 35 yuan a month. With the addition of 1.5 days of work for the production team on weekends, he received a total of only 45 yuan each month. Shoude's family therefore felt a little more economic pressure than ordinary villagers. Cheng Ju often complained that her husband made even less as a teacher than she did working for the production team.

All along, however, Shoude felt, as a man of letters, that it was not right for manual laborers to enjoy an advantage over him. He therefore began to sympathize with what Shouli had said—that going to live in Hong Kong (or "fleeing" as villagers put it) might actually be a good solution. It was said that the daily wage there for a man was over 60 Hong Kong dollars. In the winter of 1976, shortly after Chairman Mao had died, a fellow villager invited Shoude to flee with him to Hong Kong. At the time, Shoude really felt determined to do it. Besides, Cheng Ju supported the plan, saying she could stay behind in the village and take care of their child by herself, as long as Shoude could send some money home every now and then (as other people who had already fled to Hong Kong were doing). On the afternoon before they had planned to set out (the villagers usually flee under cover of darkness), Shoude changed his mind. The students he taught had not yet taken their final exams, and he worried they would perform poorly if he left suddenly, so he decided to wait. The villager who had invited him managed to arrive in Hong Kong safely, but due to increased border restrictions, Shoude ended up waiting for several years.

In 1980, he decided it was time to finally go. This time, what directly stimulated him to make up his mind was his family's house. At the time, the cadres of Cheng Brigade received orders from above to implement the Overseas Nationals Policy: Anyone who had fled to Hong Kong prior to the mid-1950s would be counted as an overseas national (*qiaobao*), and their former residential property should be returned to them. The house that Shoude's family lived in belonged to this category, having been redistributed to his father during Land Reform in the early 1950s. After Shoude emptied out the house and returned it to its original owner, the government of Wu County compensated him 100 yuan, but this was obviously far from enough money to build a new house. That year, Shoude's son was already 16 years old, and according to local custom, it was time for the parents to consider the resources necessary for seeking out a fiancée—including a house. After much consideration, the only solution to the family's economic problems seemed to be for him to flee to Hong Kong.

To observers, however, Shoude was still as naïve as could be. He originally planned to flee in May, but just as had happened the last time, he waited until his students had completed their final exams in July, and then he followed the formal procedure, completing the paperwork for a *minban* teacher to resign from the job. He did not set out until August, and during those few months, major changes had taken place in the outside world, with the border control becoming stricter than ever. Shoude and several other villagers spent over ten days climbing hills in order to avoid roads on the way to the Shekou border (in present-day Shenzhen), only to be promptly detained by soldiers there. Cheng Ju sent her brother to bring them back to Cheng Village. Shortly thereafter, Hong Kong replaced its "Touch Base Policy"[2] with the "immediate arrest and release" policy. Shoude's dream of fleeing to Hong Kong thus went up in smoke.

When these major life changes came up in our conversation, Shoude seemed surprisingly magnanimous about them. As he put it:

> At the time, my father-in-law was opposed to my resignation from the teaching position. I told him, "35 yuan is simply an insult to all the studying I've done." 35 was the highest possible monthly salary for a *minban* teacher. I had taught for 16 years, but there was no way I could make any more than that…. If I hadn't (resigned), I'm sure eventually I would have been promoted to become a formal teacher (with a permanent position

on the state payroll). Many friends asked whether I regretted my decision, but I just said, "There's nothing to regret." If I hadn't resigned, by now I would surely be doing well, with a retirement pension, but at the time my whole family was desperate... . By resigning I sacrificed myself but saved the family. Living in this world, sometimes you just have to make a decision. So there's nothing to regret. Life consists of doing this for a while and then doing that for a while. You can't evaluate past decisions on the basis of later changes.

After the unsuccessful flight to Hong Kong, Shoude began to consider new ways to make a living. Noting that wristwatches were becoming a symbol of fashion, he recalled his previous interest in mechanics and came up with the idea of learning to repair watches as a way to make money. He contacted an old high school classmate who was working in Guangzhou, and through him found an opportunity to apprentice at a watch factory there. Within two months, Shoude had already learned the components and structure of the common types of watches, and how to repair them. Looking back with the hindsight of a "Zhuge Liang (strategic genius) in retrospect," if Shoude had stayed at the factory, his opportunities for development would doubtless have been a bit better. At the time, however, he believed that doing so would limit him to the position of a temporary worker—that he could not become a formal employee with a permanent position. Besides, with his wife at home in the village raising their two sons and two daughters, he did not dare to invest wild expectations in the prospect of remaining in the factory long-term as an apprentice, instead aiming merely to learn a few skills "through the back door" that he could use at home to supplement their meager income from agriculture.

After returning to Cheng Village, Shoude visited the party committee secretary of Duqiao Commune (the former principal of Cheng Village Primary School and leader of the local Red Flag rebels), asking him for help in finding a spot to open a watch repair shop. Shoude recalled:

> I asked him to help me get a business license, and at first he said, "Why don't you just go talk to them (the staff of the relevant state offices) yourself?" I said, "Think about it: wouldn't it be different if you went there with me?" He said, "Actually it would be." So he went with me to the Tax Bureau, the Bureau of Industry and Commerce, etc., and the people there were polite and offered me cigarettes. If I had gone by myself, how could I have been treated so well? Of course *I* would have been the one offering *them* cigarettes. More importantly, they would have dragged out the procedure for a long time, and at the time I was eager to go ahead and open the shop at once.

After Shoude obtained the business license for 3 yuan, the commune secretary also asked the party branch secretary of Duqiao Residential Brigade to help them acquire a shopfront. The secretary agreed, finding one at a good location in the market town. Until Shoude finally moved out of that space many years later, the brigade (which later changed its name to the Duqiao Residential Committee) never even asked for rent. Not only that, but the Tax Bureau and the Bureau of Industry and Commerce never asked Shoude to pay business tax or a management fee.

A year later, Shoude used the money he had earned from the shop to take out a loan for building a new-style blue-brick house, about 200 square meters in area. Throughout this process, however, neither of his brothers Shouli or Shoucai offered to provide any help whatsoever. This was because when Shouli came to visit Cheng Village at the end of 1981, there was another dispute between him and the two middle brothers, Shoude and Shouzhi. By that time, Shoude and Shouzhi had already moved out and Shoucai had just gotten married, but as the youngest son, he and his wife lived and ate together in the same house with the mother. Shouli had brought a new tape recorder and an old one with him back from Hong Kong. Shouzhi, who had previously been active in the production team's performing arts, wanted the new recorder, but Shouli said Shoucai should keep it since he lived with their mother, and she should be prioritized. Shoude was not interested in the gifts himself, but he said the new recorder should be given to Shouzhi, since the mother did not even want it. As they argued about this, Shouli used harsh words against his two middle brothers, and, refusing to be bullied, they responded "We may be poor but we're not poor in dignity," telling him to keep both of the recorders. While they were quarreling, the new recorder was broken, so in the end Shoucai was left with only the old one anyway—another cause for discontent.

So again, they parted on bad terms after years without seeing each other. The conflict was only magnified with regard to the construction of Shoude's new house. Over the course of two years (1981–1982), he and Shouzhi built the house under difficult conditions without any help from their other two brothers. The following year, Shouli paid to have a red-brick modern house with a reinforced concrete structure built in the village, installing a sign on the courtyard wall reading "Residence of Cheng Shouli," although the use-right belonged to Shoucai. The two middle brothers did not provide any assistance to Shouli or Shoucai throughout this process, either. Afterwards, they never communicated again, except when their mother died in 1987. The following year, Shouli bought Shoucai a small truck for him to use in transporting goods as a business, then in 1994 he had the house remodeled.

Regarding all this, Shoude and Shouzhi said that Shouli was partial toward their baby brother, and that Shoucai was also a calculating person, knowing how to curry favor with his older brother in order to get what he wanted. By contrast, Shoucai said that it was only natural for the eldest brother to take care of the youngest. The middle brothers were not only unable to do that, but even tried to compete with him for Shouli's resources, and that was wrong in any case. Other villagers felt that Shouli was "too hot-headed," but the two middle brothers were too "intellectual," being both "pedantic" and "aloof," whereas Shoucai was the only brother who was "observant" (Ct. *singmuk*) enough to humble himself in order to cultivate relationships that would prove useful. For example, Cheng Shouyi once commented:

> The two of them (Shoude and Shouzhi) may think that they're highly educated, that they've been to high school, so they don't take the initiative to contact Shouli, instead waiting for *him* to contact *them*. Shoucai understands how to be flexible, often finding some pretext to interact with Shouli, talking about his own difficulties, then Shouli naturally feels compelled to help him out. Otherwise, I can't think of any explanation for it.... I think the main thing is that they're not flexible enough, so they can't even maintain their existing relationships (with kin), to say nothing of creating relationships with other people (they're not related to) or doing business with them.

In 1994, the Duqiao Supply and Marketing Co-op entered the stage of "responsibility for its own profits and losses" (a stage in China's marketization process), and all of its storefronts were closed and put up for auction. For a low price, Shoude managed to purchase one of the four-room properties (with two main rooms on the ground floor and two upstairs), located on the market town's busiest strip. He was able to do this with the help of his friend Yang Xianzong. (In 1975, Yang transferred from his post at the lumber mill to the co-op, where he achieved a leadership position in 1982.) After Shoude had acquired the storefront, he did some minor remodeling, setting up the front room for his watch repair business, the inner room as a kitchen and dining room, and the second floor as a bedroom. Even so, the business made only enough money to supplement the family income, not enough to make them rich. Later, as the town began to develop a new shopping area, the location of Shoude's shop came to seem a little remote. And as cell phones became more popular, fewer and fewer villagers used wristwatches, so Shoude's craft grew outmoded, and his income plummeted.

Over the past few years, other than an exceedingly small amount of watch repair work, Shoude has also done business selling farm supplies such as rat poison, making about 5,000 yuan a year from both sources combined—barely covering his expenses, including 2,000 yuan for utilities (water, electricity, phone service) and 2,000 for social obligations such as gifts. On this, he said:

> Wristwatches are being phased out, but the good part is that we old fogeys in our seventies and eighties are being phased out too! ... Normally, besides farming rice and vegetables (for my household's consumption, we don't have any source of livelihood, except when) friends and classmates sometimes give us small gifts (of money or meat), but I don't go asking them for it.... At least we still have some land we can farm, enough for us to get by, otherwise we wouldn't even be able to eat.

In the slack season, Shoude can always be found sitting in his shop drinking tea, smoking, and chatting with friends and others from the neighborhood and Cheng Village who come to visit. In the eyes of Shouyi, however, such relationships have no practical value.

Kin

Since 1996, other than trying to come up with ways to make a little money to survive, Shoude has devoted most of his energy to clan affairs. Previously, he had not been especially interested in clan affairs, believing that his energy should be focused on solving the problems of his own household. However, the elderly villagers who initiated the project to update the genealogical records kept seeking out Shoude for help. They praised his superior level of education, and his knowledge and talent, while also saying that they could not find any young people willing to help with the project, so they hoped that he could devote some energy for the sake of his kin by taking on the role of coordinating clan affairs. Otherwise, no one would be able to do it in the future.

Shoude thus began to participate and learn how to update the records. The work progressed smoothly, in under two months completing an investigation into the births, deaths, and survival of villagers since the previous update of genealogical records in 1946. At the same time, they raised over 200,000 yuan in funds for this purpose. This mainly came from three sources: First, each man in the clan was asked to donate 50 yuan; second, each villager team donated 2,000 yuan from its collective budget; third, each individual member of the clan (male or female) was invited to donate as much as they wanted. This fundraising event had caused Fang Lizheng—the township deputy secretary and *baocun* cadre assigned to Cheng Village—to sigh loudly. While chatting with me once in 2008, Fang commented:

> In those days it was harder to collect agricultural taxes than it was to climb up to Heaven. But when it came to updating the genealogical records, they managed to come up with so much money in such a short period of time. The township (cadres) said they wanted to hire these people as "tax assistance personnel" (to help the government collect taxes, but they) refused, one after the other. You want to know what Chinese peasants are? These are a prime example. Deeply rooted feudal thinking! Can these be called modern people? Modern citizens? Is this a "New Socialist Countryside"? As soon as there's some kind of problem, if you tell them to go ask their kin (for help), they won't do it. They'll only come looking for the government.

I conveyed these words to a few villagers, and they had their own interpretations. For example, Shoude's analysis was:

> When they collected (agricultural taxes), that money wasn't for us common people to use. We weren't even sure where it went, likely into the pockets of these officials. If it were really given to the state, "from the people, for the people," why would we be unwilling to pay? But our money is different: Every transaction is posted on red-paper honor boards (*hongbang*) at the entrance to every temple, clearly indicating where every penny came from and what it was spent on. Everyone can see whether there are any problems with the accounting. Besides, we're all uncles and cousins. This is our own business, so of course we're more enthusiastic about it.

While participating in updating the genealogical records, Shoude also encouraged villagers to get back in touch with kin living outside the village. Shoude and the elders of hamlets such as Nantang and Beitang contacted clan members living in Tongcheng, Nanhai (in Foshan), and Yangchun (in Yangjiang—all three places in Guangdong), and as far away as Zhangzhou in Fujian province, going to visit them and formally pay respects. Prior to 1949, those people in Tongcheng had often interacted with their kin in Cheng Village, so after establishing contact this time, they invited the village to send representatives to participate in the Tongcheng ceremony for "paying homage to the great-grandfather" on Grave-Sweeping Day, themselves sending representatives to Cheng Village to participate in the ceremony, unsealing and distributing the new genealogical records in book form among the households. When Shoude and others went to Nanhai, their kin there, whose collective enterprises made them particularly well-off, entertained the visitors lavishly. Shoude showed me photographs of their visits to kin in various places on multiple occasions, once saying:

> Look, when doing things we can take both "public" (i.e., clan) and private interests into consideration. We pay transport ourselves, and our kin (outside of Cheng Village) take care of our room and board. In this way, we've visited many places in the past few years. (Back in the late 1990s,) Chengxin and the other village cadres used our public funds to take trips to Hong Kong and Beijing just for fun, showing off their photos of the Great Wall when they got back. No one said anything to their faces, but there were some harsh words behind their backs. This thing that we're doing, on the other hand, no one's said anything (bad), but only expressed respect for us. I'm old and content with enough (money) for two meals (i.e., to survive), not striving for much else, so I was just glad to have the opportunity to travel a little. Later I started to like it, plus I had more and more free time, so whenever there was any kind of clan event, I tried to devote as much energy as I could to it.

Out of such considerations, in the late 1990s Shoude began to focus on accumulating knowledge related to the coordination of clan affairs. For example, he brushed up on his calligraphy skills, learned how to compose couplets, and studied the ritual knowledge for officiating weddings and funerals. He recalled that, although he had graduated high school, he had previously been interested only in science and mathematics, hoping to become an engineer or a mechanic, and as a teacher he mainly taught mathematics, so he found these new skills a little hard to learn. In a book that an old villager had left for him, the Ming dynasty *Treasury of Allusions for Children* (*Youxue Qionglin*), I noticed that Shoude had filled the margins with notes and comments in various colors, demonstrating more effort than your average reader. According to the other clan elders, within less than two years, Shoude had already become one of the best composers of couplets, his ritual knowledge of weddings and funerals was quite mature, and only his calligraphy was improving a little slowly. Shoude's own explanation was that as soon as he discovered something was valuable, it would become fun to learn and he would do so diligently, making progress more quickly.

After 2000, when the residents of Jiangbei conducted weddings or funerals, Shoude was usually the indispensable "master of ceremonies." When organizing such events, Shoude had a clear set of procedures. Before a wedding began, for example, he was well-versed at finding the right type of people with whom to consult about determining the event's specific format, procedures, allocation of personnel, and division of labor, as well calculating how much it would cost. The work he did himself consisted mainly of arranging the division of labor, calculating the expenses, composing couplets, and controlling the timing of key parts of the ceremony. These were the essential tasks, as far as ordinary villagers and other people who helped him officiate saw it. In the past couple years, as Shoude's declining health has made it harder for him to stay up late at night, he has gradually begun to step back to less important roles in wedding planning. When these things are mentioned, villagers express that what makes people respect Shoude even more is that he does all this work basically as a volunteer, "earning only a few packs of cigarettes and a few meals." When he organizes a wedding or a funeral, normally the host family gives Shoude a red envelope with one or two hundred yuan, but then he turns around and uses the same amount of money as a gift for the family, as if he were just an ordinary guest attending the event. If the host family is closely related to him, Shoude even adds another hundred yuan to the gift.

In addition to weddings and funerals, some years Shoude also helps other residents of Jiangbei to renovate the incense halls (*xianghuotang*) and pay homage to ancestors on Grave-Sweeping Day. In Cheng Village, the term "incense hall" refers to the ancestral shrines in temples and public buildings, including altars and tables used for burning incense, candles, and spirit money, and for placing other offerings. Due to ashes from the burnt offerings and moisture from the humid climate, the halls need to be renovated every four or five years. This involves fundraising, hiring people to carry out the

Figure 4.1 Shoude showing me the couplets he wrote for an incense hall.

renovation work, and hiring a ritual specialist (*yinyang xiansheng*) to re-install the altars and tables after they have been removed, repaired, and cleaned. Shoude and most other villagers believe rather strongly in the efficacy of renovating incense halls. He told me about one example many times. In the spring of 2004, he took the lead with Shouzhi and others in organizing the villagers to renovate the Jiangbei temple's incense hall, and "as a result," four students from the hamlet tested into university that year. Shoude and many other villagers believe there are causal relationships between these coincidental events. Once I intentionally "debated" with him, asking why there were no "effects" when Cheng Ah-Seven and others took the lead in renovating the same hall six years later. Shoude replied earnestly, "There are multiple factors involved here, and maybe some of the other factors limited the effects. In mathematics, this is called a necessary but insufficient condition." Shouzhi, Shoukuan, Yang Xianzong, and others participating in the conversation all expressed agreement with this statement.

Figure 4.2 Shoude showing me the ancestral tablets inside an incense hall.

Paying homage to the ancestors on Grave-Sweeping Day is also voluntary with regard to fundraising and direct participation. Normally, the organizers are led by Shoude, Ah-Seven and other old men, while middle-aged men and children form the main contingent ascending the hill to sweep the graves, and women are in charge of "rear services" such as cooking and cleaning. In recent years, about a dozen young men have been returning to Jiangbei from their jobs in the Pearl River Delta to participate in these ceremonial activities. Surprisingly, young people who stay at home farming throughout the year, or who work or do business in Duqiao's market town, rarely participate directly or even show up for the activities, instead just donating money. Shoude explained that this depends entirely on the individual: Of course, it is better if people donate *and* show up for the ceremony, but they are also welcome to donate without attending, and they are not reprimanded even if they do neither. Prior to 1949, however, he said that all married men were required to attend, and the funds were taken from the grain that the clan collected as rent from farmers who worked its collective land.[3] Now the expenses are paid by one-off fundraising drives, and all the money is spent at each event.

On Grave-Sweeping Day in 2012, I went to Cheng Village and participated in the ceremony organized by Shoude, Ah-Seven, and others. That time, they had raised over 2,000 yuan. On the day before the ceremony, Shoude arranged

Figure 4.3 Cheng-surnamed Jiangbei residents paying homage to ancestors on Grave-Sweeping Day.

for people to buy food and rice wine, and to clean the temple, cook, and ascend the hill to sweep the graves the next day. During this process, Chengxin (the former village party branch secretary and current director of Duqiao Township's Office of Urban-Rural Planning) stated some opinions about how things should be done, some of which were adopted while others were ignored, as the villagers did not respect him very much. They respected Shoude more, so it was his plan that was adopted in the end. The bridge over the Wutong River from Cheng Village to Jiangbei's ancestral hill had been destroyed in a flood two years before, so in order to reach the graves it was necessary to ride motorcycles about forty minutes through another township and then walk uphill for an hour. Since Shoude was already quite old at that point, he could not accompany me on this trek. For this he apologized profusely, repeatedly asking Shouzhi to make sure to tell me about various geomantic phenomena as we ascended the hill, such as "the roc spreading its wings" and "the beautiful woman tossing aside her comb."

Sometimes, Shoude would get into a little trouble because of clan affairs. In 2008, Duqiao Township purchased two ceramics factories from Foshan. One of them was located on a plot that encroached upon a two-*mu* "dry-crop field," which had actually been abandoned and overgrown with bushes. The township's occupation of this land raised its economic value to nearly 20,000

Figure 4.4 Records of donations received and spent for Grave-Sweeping Day, announced on honor boards at the temple entrance.

yuan, with the factory planning to occupy the surrounding wooded hills in its second phase of development. This led to a conflict between the hamlets of Jiangbei and Nantang.

When the policy of "three rights and four fixed (factors of production)" (*san quan si guding*) was implemented in 1962,[4] this plot of dry-crop land and the surrounding hills belonged to Production Team One (present-day Villager Team One, located in Jiangbei). In 1965, Chengren proposed that the land be transferred to Team Ten (in Nantang). Members of Team One such as Shoukuan opposed this, so the Cheng Brigade cadres came up with an ambiguous compromise (without any written record) that "since this 'outlying land' was located too far from Team One, it would be temporarily managed by Team Ten." For the next forty-plus years, Team One never requested that the land be returned to their management. Since it was so far away, no one in Team Ten was willing to take it on as household-contracted farmland during decollectivization, so it was treated as part of Nantang's collective woodland (meaning that each of that hamlet's three villager teams controlled a share of it). According to Shoude's analysis, the main reason Team One never asked for that land to be returned throughout so many years, including during the key moment of decollectivization, was that it was both remote and small in area, with little economic value.

After the land suddenly rose in value, Team One's members announced one after the other that they were its rightful owners. When they discovered that their opponents were not just one but all three of Nantang's teams, they changed strategies. Now they said the land was Jiangbei's ancestral hill, and they wanted to use it as a graveyard in the future, so outsiders could not occupy it. (This meant that all three of Jiangbei's teams should participate in the dispute.) Since it became a struggle over an "ancestral hill," this was now clearly a matter of clan affairs, so Shoude was dragged over to Nantang for negotiations. Even relatives who had moved to Hong Kong before 1949 were pulled into the dispute.

Shortly thereafter, Shoude discovered that the land under contention was not an ancestral hill after all, and that it was not meant to be used as a graveyard, but that the dispute was about compensation payment for the factory's occupation of the land, and that the residents of Jiangbei were not unified on that matter. He therefore refused to participate. Prior to this, Shoukuan had urged him to stay out of the matter, like himself. Shoukuan said, "If it were really a matter of uniting together to fight, I already tried that back in 1965, and it didn't work." At the time, Shoude had thought that although Shoukuan lived in Jiangbei, he actually belonged to the same clan branch as the people in Nantang, and that was why he was unwilling to participate. Now he finally realized that his motivation stemmed not from kinship, but from disappointment in Jiangbei residents' lack of solidarity.

Village Affairs

Like Shoude, Shouzhi was enthusiastic about public service. What interested him, however, was not clan affairs but the official business of the village. As he explained:

> Ever since decollectivization, very few people have any genuine clan sentiment—all everyone cares about is how their individual household can make money. In our hamlet of Jiangbei, it's only children of the same parents that are as close as relatives were in the past, willing to help each other unconditionally. And some brothers aren't even that close—just look at mine! I often say I only have one older brother: Ah-De (Shoude).... In the same hamlet, for example, I'm probably closer to Chen Erdong (from a different clan) than I am to Cheng Hecheng. So it doesn't really make a difference whether you belong to the same clan: "Close neighbors are better than distant relatives." If I become "chief" (i.e., director of public affairs for the hamlet), I want to make improvements to Jiangbei—I don't have anything to do with Nantang or Beitang (even though my kin live there). This is where my views differ from those of my brother (Shoude).

Shoude and Shouzhi once explained to me why, although they both cared about public affairs, one cared more about the clan and the other about the hamlet. They both agreed that this was probably related to Shouzhi's experiences.

After Shouzhi resigned from his post as production team head in the late 1970s, his wife gave birth to a son and a daughter. In 1981, like Shoude, he used his small savings and loans from various sources to build a new-style blue-brick house. Over the next few years, he was unable to repay his loans, so the main concern on his mind was how to make a little money.

In 1986, Shouzhi happened to run across some information: The periodical *World of Birds and Flowers* was organizing a correspondence course about how to raise squab pigeons. He felt that this trade should be profitable, and that he was educated enough to learn the requisite skills, but he lacked the funds not only for starting a business, but even for the course's tuition. He therefore seized the opportunity of an upcoming holiday to ask for a loan of 500 yuan at the Duqiao Township Credit Union, bringing two bottles of liquor as a gift to the union clerk stationed in Cheng Village. This clerk was a resident of Beitang and a member of the same branch of the Cheng clan as Shouzhi.

Shouzhi's gift has been selected carefully. At the time, two bottles of liquor together cost about 30 yuan, so this would be considered a high-end gift between relatives, but not a bribe. I checked this with other villagers, and they said that at the time many credit union clerks accepted bribes in the form of kickbacks, for example 10 percent of the loan (later rising to 30 percent in the mid-1990s). In that case, if Shouzhi had wanted to bribe the clerk, he should have given him 50 to 80 yuan in cash. If he had given a gift worth that much money, someone else might have seen the gift and put the clerk in an awkward position as a target of gossip. A couple bottles of liquor worth only 30 yuan, however, would be more ambiguous: It appeared as a token of affection between relatives, but could also convey the message of "asking for help" while actually benefiting the clerk. The villagers I talked to, then, felt that this gift was the most appropriate and intelligent way to approach the situation.

After the clerk received Shouzhi's gift, however, he refused his request for a loan, claiming that funds were tight that year, so he should try again in a year or two. A few days later, however, several other villagers obtained loans from the same clerk.

When Shoude heard about this, he fetched Shouzhi and the two of them brought another two bottles of liquor (also worth 30 yuan) to the credit union's director. This director was also a member of the Duqiao Residential Committee who was on good terms with Shouyi, and he also liked to raise poultry. At the director's home, the three of them talked at length about their experiences related to the June 16th Incident. When Shouzhi raised the thorny issue of applying for a loan, the director gladly agreed to lend him 1,500 yuan. This was enough money not only to cover the tuition but also to launch Shouzhi's business raising pigeons.

Several months later, Shouzhi received his certificate of course completion from the editorial board of *World of Birds and Flowers* and began raising pigeons. At first, he purchased four pigeons, each four months old, and then he sold the squabs that they hatched. He sold them at the rate of 50 yuan for a pair of hatchlings, 60 yuan for a pair of ten-day old squabs, and 80 yuan for a pair of month-old pigeons. If no one bought them by then, three months later they would become adults and sell for 200 yuan a pair. According to Shouzhi, this turned out to be rather profitable, and once he had grasped the skills, he could begin farming pigeons on a larger scale. Although the income was modest, he made at least as much money as farmers who specialized in raising chickens. After doing this for a year, however, as soon as he had recuperated the expenses for the training course and the purchase of pigeons and feed, he abandoned this project, although it could have made him some money.

There were three main reasons that Shouzhi abandoned pigeon farming. First, he suffered from hyperthyroidism and his health was always subpar, so "I wasn't in the mood to focus on making lots of money." Second, it was not very profitable to raise only a small number of pigeons, and his family lacked the funds that would have been necessary to expand the business, with all their meager savings going toward tuition for their two children. Third, the pigeons' coo sounded like a sick person burping, so some people felt it was inauspicious and urged Shouzhi not to raise such creatures in his yard. (At the time, there was still no precedent for villagers going out into the woods and clearing an area for raising livestock, as they do nowadays.) Shouzhi countered that we should believe in science rather than such superstitions, telling his wife Li Jing, "In the past, landlords raised pigeons in the yards, and isn't it best for us to follow their example? I've never heard of this being unlucky." But Li Jing was not interested in this talk about "scientific reasoning," insisting that the idea that "raising pigeons was inauspicious" was more credible and logical, providing counterevidence: "What ended up happening to those landlords? Those who weren't executed were criticized and struggled against. This shows that it's reasonable for people to say (that raising pigeons is inauspicious)." Considering that his family already had plenty of problems, and that it would be better to have one less thing to worry about, Shouzhi finally caved in and gave up raising pigeons.

From then onwards, whenever anyone in the vicinity of Cheng Village encountered difficulties in raising pigeons, they would often come to Shouzhi for help. This made him feel rather respected. Even so, he had already missed the opportunity to get rich as a pigeon farmer himself. He summed up this experience (especially the part about obtaining a loan) with the adage: "Close neighbors are better than distant relatives, and good friends are better than kin."

In 2007, when I first began my research in Cheng Village, every time I ran into Shouzhi chatting with others in his watch repair shop, I would notice him commenting on the public affairs of Jiangbei. At the end of 2008, after I had begun staying at his house, I discovered that at home, too, he specifically criticized the hamlet's current "chief" and several other people in charge.

Actually, Shouzhi had served as Jiangbei's chief for only three years. Prior to that, in 1996, since his two children had already graduated from middle school, he had prepared to participate in public affairs at the village level. However, when the construction of Cheng Village's "Brigade Street" occupied a portion of Jiangbei's land, a conflict emerged between Shouzhi and several township and village cadres, including Chengxin. In order to protect the villagers' interests, Shouzhi questioned the township party committee secretary to his face: "We can afford 50,000 yuan per *mu*. How about we buy *your* land for 50,000 yuan per *mu*? Why can you buy a *mu* for 50,000 but we can't?" The township government had no choice but to raise the price to 70,000 per *mu*. Shouzhi was still not content, since the government planned to turn around and auction the land for construction to buyers throughout the township, receiving between 20,000 and 40,000 yuan for every 120 square meters. (One *mu* = 666.7 square meters.) The Jiangbei residents whose land was to be sold were not unified, however, so finally they accepted the offer of 70,000 yuan per *mu*. Shortly thereafter, in the village committee election, Shouzhi ran against another villager for committee member, and the result was a tie. According to the rules, there should have been a second vote, but the township leaders had Fang Lizheng—vice-mayor of Duqiao and the *baocun* cadre assigned to Cheng Village, who was on good terms with Shouzhi—come out and "conduct thought work" on Shouzhi, encouraging him to withdraw from the race and stand down from the election for hamlet chief of Jiangbei. Shouzhi refused to withdraw, but Fang said, "Give me a little face, don't be so stubborn!" Shouzhi sought out the previous party branch secretary of Cheng Village, asking him to come out and arbitrate. The township secretary then accused Shouzhi of "sabotaging the election" and claimed that this disqualified him from running for office. Fang then went back to Shouzhi and tried to console him, but the latter just said, "I've lost all faith in the village committee's games."

In 2000, Shouzhi was elected hamlet chief of Jiangbei, truly making a deep impression on the residents. Once in office, he immediately began raising money to channel spring water two kilometers to Jiangbei from the Dongshan valley across the river. First, he collected a portion of the money from the residents themselves, encouraging the more well-off households to donate 200 yuan each, exempting elderly residents who lacked support from children. The next year, Shouzhi obtained a 10,000-yuan construction grant for "Safe Drinking Water Projects in the Countryside" from the new township secretary, who had just been transferred into the position from another region. In addition, by patiently and repeatedly pestering a couple factories in Foshan, he managed to purchase a shipment of plastic hoses for half price, and a shipment of stainless-steel pipes for two-thirds of the market price. (In return for the favor, he presented each factory with a plaque thanking them for "supporting safe drinking water projects in impoverished mountain regions.") By that winter, the residents of Jiangbei were drinking safe spring water. To this day, many villagers still say this was the biggest public work Jiangbei has seen since the roads were paved in the early 1990s.

In the winter of 2003, Shouzhi learned that his blood pressure was a little higher than it should have been. With advice from his children, he resigned from the post as chief of Jiangbei. But he still likes to talk about public affairs. Most villagers praise him as public-minded, saying he takes care of things in a skillful and meticulous way. Occasionally, however, someone criticizes him for being overzealous. In the dog days of 2012, for example, Shouzhi noticed that some villagers were spraying the drinking water on their rooftops in order to keep the top floor cool. This would lead to shortages in the evening, when water was needed the most. He went to the home of these people to make them pull the hoses down from the rooftops, but two families complained, saying, "I've never seen anyone so nosey about other people's business! It's not your family's water. We also contributed money to have these pipes installed."

Shouzhi did not really care that other villagers called him "nosey," but he often expressed disappointment when their concern for the petty interests of their individual households prevented them from uniting to fight for collective interests. Between 2005 and 2008, for instance, Shouzhi tried on multiple occasions to push residents to fight for compensation that they had never received. The background was the Wutong River diversion project of 1975–1978, carried out jointly by Wu County and Tong Prefecture, when the new channel occupied land belonging to the Wu production teams of Jiangbei, Xixi, and Donghe, and a brigade in Tong called Jiangwei. According to the policy at the time, the government was required to compensate these places with grain every year. In 1992, this changed to monetary compensation, but after 1998, those hamlets in Wu County stopped receiving any compensation at all, while Jiangwei Village continued receiving theirs from the government of Tong Prefecture. Shouzhi discussed this with Duqiao's township secretary Fang Lizheng and the vice-mayor Wen Zhibin on several occasions, also writing numerous "reports," "explanations," "requests," and "petitions" to relevant offices at the township and county levels—delivered by himself or by the hamlet chief—but still received no response. Many residents expressed support for these efforts, but very few were willing to cooperate when it came to the key steps of signing documents with their fingerprints, providing documents, or petitioning higher authorities for help. This caused Shouzhi to lose heart, and finally he gave up.

After telling this story, Shouzhi grumbled, "Nowadays you need power. Without power, you just get bullied right and left." Shoude was also present, and although normally opposed to serving as an official, on this occasion he said wistfully:

> Ah-Tan, of course it's good that you're so highly educated, but it's a waste if you don't convert that education into political power. What's the point of reading so many books? Besides, since ancient times our nation has

emphasized this Confucian tradition, "a good scholar will become an official." Take our (clan's ancestor) Cheng Hao, for example.

In recent years, Shouzhi has mainly been farming vegetables at home with his wife, selling them to cover everyday living expenses. Occasionally, he works odd jobs in the surrounding area, but there are not many opportunities for work there, so the income is only enough to supplement their household budget. Their main other responsibility is taking care of their grandchildren. In his free time, Shouzhi goes to his brother's shop to drink tea and chat. When the couple have any expenses they cannot afford, their son Cheng Jingshan helps them out.

Body and Mind

When Shouzhi was young, the impression he gave other villagers was that he was "hot-headed," and his wife Li Jing often complained that he was moody and quick to anger. In 1988, he was examined at the Tong Prefecture People's Hospital and diagnosed with hyperthyroidism. The doctor said that this was the cause of his irritability and moodiness, along with his insomnia and the inability to put on sufficient weight no matter how much he ate. This could be treated with surgery, but the more conservative treatment was to take medication. Considering the risks of surgery and the ability to pay gradually for the more conservative treatment, he opted for the latter. After a little over a year of pharmaceutical treatment, his condition improved, including the insomnia, but he remained irritable. To treat this part, a friend introduced him to a doctor of traditional Chinese medicine (TCM). The TCM doctor diagnosed him with "dampness" due to "excessive fire," saying that herbal medicine would produce more long-lasting results than Western medication, plus it would be cheaper and have fewer side effects, although the treatment would be slower. The doctor also told him to pay attention to "the nourishment of life" (*yangsheng*), saying he could not work at all or do any kind of strenuous activity, and advising him to eat only mild, "warm-tempered" food, avoiding too much meat or fish but not going completely vegetarian, and completely abstaining from foods that were "extremely cold" or "dry and hot."

Shouzhi asked Shoude for his opinion. In general, Shoude approved of what the TCM doctor had said. If it became necessary for Shouzhi to have surgery, he would figure out a way to lend him the money, but he felt that it made more sense to take herbal medicine and adjust his lifestyle. He said that Western medicine was for emergencies, whereas TCM was for long-term care. In contrast with both the doctors, however, Shoude believed that the root of Shouzhi's ailment was in his "mind" or "heart-mind" (*xin*): that he was thinking too much about too many different things that he could not achieve, and that this was what had caused his "excessive fire," giving rise to physiological changes. Shoude therefore advised Shouzhi to "adjust" (*tiaoli*) his mind in order to adjust his body, saying that would be more fundamental and long-lasting than the TCM treatment.

Shoude explained this abstract concept of "mind" by saying Shouzhi should not obsess over external objects or compare himself with others. To put it positively, he urged him to "always be content and happy with what he already had," and then his "excessive fire" would naturally dissipate, and his health could improve. As Shoude saw it, Shouzhi had already taken Western medication for over a year and his blood tests at the hospital showed that the thyroid was now functioning normally, yet he still remained irritable. This could not be explained physiologically, so Shoude believed it was a result of Shouzhi's excessive ambition: He saw others less talented than him making more money or getting positions as cadres, so his belly was full of anger. When people got too angry and could not deal with "the ways of the world," they looked for people around them to vent their discontentment on trivial things like "chicken feathers and garlic skin." Ultimately, this anger was generated by the mind's lack of serenity.

Shoude repeatedly expressed frustration with Shouzhi's indecisiveness toward his advice. For years, Shouzhi would listen to his brother for a while and then ignore him for a while, and Shoude had pestered him about this his whole life. On several occasions I personally witnessed while the brothers were drinking tea in the watch repair shop, Shouzhi would sharply criticize the township, party, and hamlet cadres, and Shoude would respond (roughly):

> How many times do I have to tell you? You've got to curb your anger and relax your mind. What's the point of getting so upset? When this damages your health, will they pay your medical bills? There are so many unfair things in the world, can you fix them all?

Yang Xianzong was another one of the people who would come to drink tea in the watch repair shop almost every day, without fail. His views were always in line with those of Shouzhi, but he would grow even more strident about them. He had worked at the Duqiao Supply and Marketing Co-op for years until he retired, plus his son and two daughters were all civil servants, so he was quite familiar with the workings of grassroots (i.e., township-level) officialdom and, when criticizing corruption, could also provide all kinds of specific details as examples. Often, he would compare these examples with ancient and modern cases from China and abroad, concluding wistfully that if something were not done about this corruption, we would all be doomed. Normally this topic would be brought up by Shouzhi, while Yang would silently smoke cigarettes and drink tea. After Shouzhi had finished and the others had chatted for a while, Yang would finally speak, expressing that the cases they had mentioned were nothing special, that he knew many cases of corruption that were even worse and more unjust. Just when Yang had gotten to the story's climax (often accompanied by gesticulations, groaning, and a face red with anger), Shoude would interrupt him by offering a cigarette or filling his teacup, telling him to relax.

During Dragon Boat Festival in 2012, I happened upon another of these conversations. When Yang grew excited, Shoude interrupted him and said earnestly:

> You're really something. Your blood pressure is already high, and so is Shouzhi's. You're always so negative about everything, so extreme. Why do you keep talking about these things so much? Can't you say something positive about how everything is getting better? Your life is better than it used to be, no matter how you look at it. This is called "eating the meat, setting down the chopsticks, and then berating the cook." … Be more accepting, your health his important. Only our bodies truly belong to us, the rest will be lost when we die. Too much anger is bad for one's health. Think more about pleasant things, positive things.

Yang retorted, "But why (Ct. *dimgaai*) am I so angry? Isn't it because I feel the world is unfair?" Shoude consoled him, saying, "Don't 'push up the roof' (Ct. *dinggoi*)[5]—my ceiling is only made of wood, I don't want you to bust a hole in it." … "You should be content. If people like you (i.e., those who are better off economically, with higher social status) think the world is unfair, then isn't it even more unfair for people like us (who are worse off)? But don't people like us survive?" The other people present agreed one after the other that health was truly important. Then they switched topics and began discussing which ingredients made the best *zongzi* (sticky rice dumplings eaten on this holiday), as if nothing had happened. After Yang and Shouzhi had left, however, Shoude said, "Typical intellectuals. Books make people angry."

Shoude often criticized Shouzhi for continually failing to control his mind despite beginning to understand that the mind is an important factor affecting one's physical health. For over the past ten years, for example, Shouzhi had been obsessed with buying underground lottery tickets (villagers called them "numbers," the odds being one in forty), and Shoude considered this "possession by (the desire for) wealth" even scarier than possession by a ghost. Every Tuesday, Thursday, and Saturday, Shouzhi would spend at least 4 yuan buying "numbers." The highest jackpot he won was 4,000 yuan in March 2012, for which he had spent 100 yuan buying tickets. That day, Shouzhi happily celebrated at home and spent 50 yuan buying a carton of Baisha brand cigarettes as a gift for Shoude. (Normal middle-aged and older villagers smoked loose tobacco or cigarettes that cost only 20–25 yuan per carton.) Shoude not only refused to congratulate Shouzhi, he even criticized him, saying (roughly): "Your mind is always craving what other people have, but in the end, they took more from you. In losing you win, and in winning you lose. Always so agitated, how can your health not deteriorate?" Needless to say, this comment was both a reflection on Shouzhi's past actions buying

Figure 4.5 Lottery paraphernalia often seen in villagers' homes.

lottery tickets and a prediction of what he would do in the future. In that year alone, he spent over 6,000 yuan on this obsession.

Like many other villagers, Shoude still believed that *fengshui* affected people's health, and that a house with geomantic problems would hurt the health of its occupants. In 2004, Cheng Ah-Three and Cheng Ah-Four built houses across from the grain-sunning ground next to the entrance of the temple in Jiangbei. That year, Ah-Three's youngest son died of cardiovascular disease due to obesity. Two years later, his eldest son also died of disease after using drugs for many years. In February 2007, his second daughter died of a sudden illness. Only his second son was left, but although he had long been old enough to get married, no one has dared to marry him to this day. In 2008, Ah-Four's mother died of disease. In addition, the wife of the drug user whose banana tree blocked the temple's side wall (mentioned in Chapter One) died of bone cancer in 2007, and villagers believed this was related to *fengshui* as well. In 2010, Shoukuan's younger brother Shoushu drowned in the Wutong River, and many villagers said this was because his family's new house had bad *fengshui*.

Shoude's wife Cheng Ju also believed that the mind was closely related to health, but not because of thinking too much or building up too much anger, but because of thinking too *little*. From her perspective as a Christian, everyone was guilty of original sin, but if they learned this and could muster the determination to turn their minds over to God, then God would protect their health. If, on the other hand, one did not know about original sin, or knew but could not turn the mind over to God, then one's health would inevitably deteriorate. As for the relationship between *fengshui* and health, she believed it was utter superstition, saying that people imagined nonsensical connections with external object due to fear in their minds. Cheng Ju often urged her sister-in-law Li Jing to convert to Christianity rather than believing in "superstition." This was because Li Jing had been praying to Guanyin and other entities for over ten years, partly out of concern for Shouzhi's health. On holidays and the first and fifteenth days of every month, she would make offerings of food, incense, and spirit money to the bodhisattva. In addition, she also often prayed to her ancestors and to deities such as Taishang Laojun, tree gods, and water gods.

Of course, Cheng Ju had not always been a Christian. In terms of beliefs, she had previously been similar to Li Jing. In 1998, however, she and Shoude had both suffered from a serious illness. The same year, their daughter Cheng Jingsi, who had married into a town near Wucheng, returned to Duqiao to open a restaurant, but it soon fell into debt and closed down when customers from work-units such as the police station kept eating at the restaurant on credit and failing to pay off their tabs. Shortly thereafter, the Wucheng Family Planning Office searched for Cheng Jingsi and her husband to charge a fine for over-quota births but could not find them, so instead detained Shoude instead. Cheng Ju and her son Cheng Jingxiu had no choice but to borrow 50,000 yuan from friends and relatives to pay the fine, and only then could

Figure 4.6 Cheng Ju praying at the church 30 meters from her family's shop.

Shoude come home. Meanwhile, over the previous few years, Shoukuan's wife Feng Lan had begun to urge Cheng Ju to believe in God. Therefore, she converted to Christianity. The only small change that occurred after this was in 2009, when the Duqiao Church of the Gospel appointed Cheng Xiu to replace her as "parish director" for Cheng Village. After this, Cheng Ju stopped going to church, believing that the church director valued Cheng Xiu's family's money, which could often be donated to fund activities. She decided that it was enough to have the Lord in one's own heart, and it was unnecessary to go to church.

Regarding Cheng Ju's belief in Christianity, Shoude's attitude has always been neutral, neither supporting nor opposing it, and describing the situation as "one family, two systems." After Cheng Ju stopped going to church on Sundays, Shoude said:

> It doesn't matter whether you go, the most important thing is that you have no anger in your mind. Otherwise, it would be bad for your health, and wouldn't you have lost more than gained? She's also an intellectual: well-educated with a good sense of judgment.

Indeed, after this comment, Cheng Ju stopped holding a grudge about the issue.

Notes

1 It was common among many villagers to refer to people by the moniker "Ah" followed by their family name. So, I was often called Ah-Tan.
2 This policy had stipulated that anyone who arrived in urban Hong Kong and was able to work would be allowed to stay and issued a local identity card.
3 *Translator's note*: Prior to Land Reform in the early 1950s, the clan and its main branches owned a certain amount of farmland collectively, known as "clan fields" (族田). Usually this was purchased with money donated voluntarily by members, but sometimes the money came from the clan's collective commercial activities. The land was leased out to landless or land-poor peasants, who farmed it and then paid a portion of the grain to the clan (or branch) as rent. During clan events such as ceremonies, this rent would be used (either directly as grain or by selling it and using the money) to cover expenses such as banquets, rice wine, cigarettes, and firecrackers. Clan members contributed labor to these events voluntarily, but sometimes outsiders were hired as performers, for example.
4 This refers to a specific policy under the institution of "three levels of ownership with the production team as the foundation." This affirmed that the team level controlled the basic rights of production and operation, along with the right to allocate the factors of production and the fruits of labor. The "three rights" included planting rights, the right to allocate labor-power, and the right to control technical measures. The "four fixed (factors)" referred to oxen, farm implements, land, and labor-power—so-called because their ownership and use was fixed at the level of the

production team. (This policy was announced by the central government in 1960 but not implemented locally until 1962.)

5 *Translator's note*: The Cantonese term for "why" (点解) sounds similar the phrase "push up the roof" (顶盖), so Shoude is making a pun on Yang's use of this word in an effort to defuse his hostility.

5 An Authoritarian Official

Village Enterprises

The average area of farmland per capita in Cheng Village was extremely low, so villagers could only obtain enough income through farming for mere survival at best. This reality was understood even by Cheng Chengren, whom other villagers regarded as simple-minded and rigid. In the mid-1970s, after building a water conservancy network and adopting the use of chemical fertilizer and hybrid rice, the residents of Cheng Brigade had completely solved the problems of basic subsistence. This was when Chengren proposed that they develop "commune and brigade enterprises." Cheng Brigade launched its first enterprise in 1976: the Cheng Brigade Red Brick Factory. In 1977, a precast concrete plant was added, and together the two were called the Cheng Brigade Building Materials Factory. Cheng Chengxin was appointed as the cadre specifically in charge of factory.

Chengxin was born in 1950, graduating from middle school at Duqiao Secondary in 1965. In 1968, he wanted to join the army, but since his brother Chengheng had joined in 1965 and not yet been transferred to civilian work, and the number of villagers who could join was limited, Chengren refused to grant approval. In the summer of 1969, Chengheng was transferred to work on the Wu County water conservancy system. At the end of the year, Chengxin again applied for the army and, with the help of Chengren amid an even more limited quota, obtained permission to join as a new recruit in 1970. For the next four years, Chengxin served in Guangdong's Hailufeng region. At the end of 1973, when his period of service ended, he expected to be transferred to civilian work as Chengheng had been. Instead, however, he was notified that, due to the Lin Biao Incident, his unit would conduct rectification work, and everyone would be transferred to civilian work in their places of birth. Since prior to joining the army his household registration had been rural, Chengxin was transferred back to Cheng Village. One of his fellows in the unit, being previously registered as an urban resident of Wucheng (the county seat), was transferred to work in a state office of Wu County.

Due to his experience in the army, where he had also joined the Communist Party, in 1974 Chengxin was appointed commander of the Cheng Brigade

Militia. (He also got married that year.) At the end of 1976, he replaced Cheng Chenggong as security director for the brigade. According to Chengxin's own recollection, at the time he was rather discontent with this outcome. When asked, he said this was because when he had first applied for the army, Chengren could not help him, otherwise he would have already been transferred to "eating state grain" back in 1972. Now, however, he was already back in Cheng Village and had no better options, so he did not dare to express this discontent to Chengren.

Chengren was still clearly taking good care of Chengxin. Many villagers said that Chengren treated Chengxin better than he would have treated his own cousins. They believed this was primarily because of Chengren's "sworn brother" relationship with Chengxin's father, Cheng Liguo. From the perspective of this relationship, Chengxin should have called Chengren "uncle." Times had changed, however, and Chengren accepted it when Chengxin called him "cousin" (according to their relationship by blood within the clan) in informal settings, and "(party) branch secretary" in formal ones. As some villagers recalled, Chengxin was a cadre who "followed right behind Chengren, always praising him and showing respect through his actions."

For these reasons, as soon as the Cheng Brigade factory was established, Chengren appointed Chengxin as "general manager." First, he was "Commander of the Brigade Militia and Manager of the Red Brick Factory," then he became "Brigade Security Director and Manager of the Building Materials Factory."

When it came to how he ran the factory, many villagers expressed admiration for his talent. Even a "capable person" like Shouyi, for example, acknowledged that Chengxin was rather "observant" and good at managing. Chengxin gave Shouyi's wife, Cheng Xiu, a job at the brick factory, raising her income about 50 percent over that from farmwork for the production team. Because of this, Shouyi actively used his status at the Wu County Revolutionary Committee to cozy up to leaders of the Coal Bureau, ensuring that the brick factory never had to stop production due to lack of coal. (Meanwhile, Xujiao Brigade's brick factory, also in Duqiao Commune, often had to stop production for this reason.) Later in the precast concrete plant, materials such as concrete and steel bars were all provided by the state under "unified purchase and marketing," with only sand and labor-power under the control of Cheng Brigade. Those state-provided materials were controlled by too many different agencies that it was hard for Shouyi to influence, and this was why the plant closed after less than a year of operation, leaving only brick production as the sole activity of Cheng Brigade Building Materials Factory.

Shouyi pointed out that Chengxin's ability to run an enterprise was also demonstrated by his refusal to dismiss Cheng Xiu from the factory even after Chengren had expelled Shouyi from the party. Later when Shouyi built a new house, the cost of the bricks was simply deducted from Cheng Xiu's wages for a year. Shouyi commented, "At that time, he was a person of conscience who was principled in his actions."

The factory generated considerable income. In addition to giving the workers wages higher than what other villagers received from farmwork, it made enough profit from brick sales in the first year to expand into precast concrete production. In 1978, the brigade used the factory's profit to purchase two hand-held tractors—one for transport and another for both transport and plowing. In 1980, the brigade used the factory's income to buy another two tractors. At first, those villagers unable to obtain jobs at the factory expressed a little veiled discontent, but after they saw how the tractors made their farmwork easier, they began to acknowledge that the enterprise was actually beneficial to them as well. Besides, working at the factory was as hard all year long as farmwork was during the busy season alone, so those excluded from factory jobs gradually accepted the situation. Shoude, for example, acknowledged that even if he were offered a job there, he would not have been able to handle it.

After decollectivization, the factory did not disband, remaining a collective enterprise of Cheng Village. Other than one of the tractors used by the factory, however, the other three were sold at a discount to individuals: one purchased by a villager from the hamlet of Donghe (within Cheng Village), the other two by residents of Duqiao's market town. After the money from these sales was split up among the production teams, not much was left, but the villagers were happy to receive any cash at all. When it came time to transport things, however, some villagers lamented, "How did they end up being the ones to profit?" In 1984, after the person in Donghe had made money driving the tractor for other villagers (who paid him to transport goods and plow fields), he started a pig farm. Within a few years, when people were still talking about "10,000-yuan households," his output value had already reached about 80,000, for which he was publicized as a model farmer.

In 1984, competition between Cheng Village's brick factory and several others in the area (including Xujiao Village's as well as several new ones) was growing ever more intense. Cheng Chengxin (serving as village committee director and party branch vice-secretary at the time) proposed that they close the factory and open two new ones producing steel wire and "honeycomb" coal briquettes. This idea met with approval from the secretary and other village cadres, and later they believed that Chengxin had been gifted with foresight and management ability.

At the time, people in the area were beginning to use coal instead of firewood as an everyday source of fuel, but many of them just used regular coal briquettes (which burned more slowly than honeycomb briquettes, with a lower rate of combustion). Only a few households had begun to make their own honeycomb briquettes by hand, but this could be done only once or twice every couple months (requiring a lot of space and a period of time without rain). Factory production was many times more labor-efficient than household production. Most importantly, it was free from the constraints of weather, since the briquettes were dried on racks within a large shed. Villagers soon discovered that purchasing readymade briquettes was not only convenient, but also affordable and could conserve labor. Since Cheng Village started producing these first, although other villages later began following suit, for a long time it was able to corner the market, with over half the briquettes sold in Duqiao produced there. As late as 1994, although the factory had downsized, it was still able to control the village's market and maintain a small profit.

The steel wire factory also did well. Although its profit was lower than that of the coal briquette factory, it maintained profitability all the way up until 1992. In the second half of that year, Chengxin became secretary of the village party branch. According to his calculation at the end of that year, the factory had netted just over 10,000 yuan. At the time, that was a large amount of money. In early 1993, next to the bridge crossing from Jiangbei over the river to Duqiao's market town, Cheng Village built a two-story office with a structure of reinforced concrete.

According to Chengxin, between 1985 and 1992, the two factories had paid levies to the village and township authorities on behalf of the residents of Cheng Village, so the villagers had not been paying. Villagers I spoke to confirmed that during those years they had only paid the agricultural tax, although in principle they had been required to pay 10–20 yuan per capital each year for the "three deductions and five charges."[1]

In 1993, the price of raw materials began to rise and put pressure on the two factories, and the village committee was unable to obtain a loan, so it ran into difficulties operating them. That year, the coal briquette factory earned a small profit, but the steel wire factory encountered competition with products from the Pearl River Delta and its profit fell to zero. By the end of 1994, inflation had nearly doubled the cost of materials. Chengxin announced that the briquette factory was no longer earning money and the wire factory was operating at a loss. Early the next year, the wire factory halted production. Over the following two years, Chengxin announced that the briquette factory was losing money, and, at the end of 1996, he sold it to a private investor (who ran it for another five years before finally closing down). In 1997, the wire factory was also sold to a private investor, who sold most of its equipment at the price of scrap metal. Over the next five years, Wu County carried out a township-and-village enterprise campaign with the slogan "every village lights the fire," forcing Cheng Village to open a rice noodle factory and a rice liquor distillery, but all of them failed to earn money and ended up closing.

However, many villagers blamed the failure of the village enterprises on alleged conniving by Chengxin and others. They said that in the 1980s, cadres including Chengxin would at most use the enterprise's name to eat in Duqiao's teahouses, with limited expenditure. One villager, who had served as a member of the village committee from 1988 to 1990, said that at the time they had worried that if the masses audited them later on, it would be hard to explain these payments. After Chengxin became "the man in charge" in 1992, however, in addition to eating and drinking in Duqiao, the cadres also began to organize sightseeing trips every year, first to Tong Prefecture in 1993, then to Hong Kong in 1996, and to Beijing in 1997. In Chengxin's home in

Duqiao's market town, I saw him in a group photo touring the Great Wall at Badaling together with several other village cadres, his wife, and the vice-mayor of Duqiao at the time. Several villagers I talked to knew about this photo and were not happy about it. Chengxin said, however, that public funds had not been used on that trip, and that the cadres had pooled their own money to pay for it. Ordinary villagers did not believe this, just as they did not believe cadres' claims that their private medical insurance and pensions had been purchased with their own money.

In addition, many villagers suspected that when Chengxin and the others had sold the enterprises, they had conducted some kind of "shady" business. They suspected that the reason the coal briquette factory had been sold at such a low price was that either the buyer was related by blood to one of the township leaders, or the cadres had received a kickback. Otherwise, if the factory really had to be sold because it had been operating at a loss, then how did the new boss manage to make a profit while running it for the next few years? Another piece of "evidence" these villagers provided was that the wire factory's equipment was sold at low prices approaching that of scrap metal. Later, the accounting books for both the factories and the village committee could not be found, and when asked about it, all the cadres would just say "I don't remember clearly." All of this generated suspicion among the villagers.

Urban Construction

In 1996, another of Chengxin's "great works" was the planning and implementation of "Brigade Street." This street linked Cheng Village Primary School on the west side of Beitang, the archway of Jiangbei, and the "brigade headquarters" of Cheng Village with Duqiao's old market street on the opposite side of a seven-meter-wide waterway, forming a "T" shape.

The basic idea for the plan was fairly simple: to repurpose 20 meters of land on each side of the road running by the brigade headquarters so they could be used for construction, and then to divide that land into housing plots of 8 by 15 meters, with 5 meters separating their entrances from the road. The houses could not encroach beyond those parameters, but there was no limit set for their height.

Although the plan was simple, its implementation was not easy. First, from a bureaucratic standpoint, it was hard to repurpose land.[2] The road itself was a product of the collective era and therefore classified as construction land, but the land on both sides of the road was either farmland or the former bed of the Wutong River (officially classified as "horticultural land" but regarded as "dry-crop land" by the villagers). When the brigade headquarters was built in 1992, it occupied 300 square meters (including the courtyard and pond) of horticultural land in the old riverbed. This constituted conversion of agricultural land to construction land, and later (with the help of township leaders), the village committee paid a nominal fee to complete the paperwork for land conversion at the Wu County Bureau of Land Management. This time, however, the Brigade Street project involved 4 *mu* of horticultural land and 4 *mu* of farmland. The Bureau of Land Management could not grant the quotas to repurpose so much land, and even if they could, the regulations stipulated that the village committee would have to pay over 200,000 yuan in taxes and fees. After the bureau rejected the project proposal, Chengxin and others decided to "act first and report later," going ahead with the plan. Other cadres hesitated, but Chengxin insisted that as long as the villagers built houses in sufficient number (they aimed for fifty), it would be impossible for the bureau to demolish them, so they should just take the gamble.

Subsequent facts demonstrated that Chengxin had won this bet. After Brigade Street had been built, there was nothing the Bureau of Land Management could easily do about it, plus the township leaders did "thought work" to persuade the bureau officials, and Chengxin asked several natives of Cheng Village who worked in related offices in Wu County to help smooth things out. Finally, the village committee paid 50,000 yuan to seal the deal. Actually, the county authorities never formally granted permission for the land conversion, but only recognized the fact that the land was already being used for construction. It was unclear, therefore, whether that 50,000 yuan was a fee or a fine, according to Chengxin, but afterwards the village committee never encountered any problems related to the matter.

The village cadres also ran into problems regarding the occupation of the land itself. In order to avoid direct conflicts with the villagers, Chengxin convinced the main leaders of Duqiao to announce that this was a project for the "Development of Small Towns and Cities" (*xiao chengzhen jianshe*), so the village committee could occupy the land in the township's name. In return, Chengxin promised the village cadres would cooperate with the township government's plan to build a street that would run by its own headquarters, to be called Fuqian Road (literally "In-Front-of-the-Government Road," although residents called it "Government Street" or "Yamen Street"). When the government offered to buy the land from the villagers at 50,000 yuan per *mu* of wet-rice fields and 20,000 yuan per *mu* of dry-crop land, however, the residents of Jiangbei resisted. The government organized several rounds of negotiations, two of which were attended by the secretary of the township party committee, leading to a squabble with Shouzhi on one occasion. In the end, both parties came to an agreement that the government would pay 70,000 yuan per *mu* of wet-rice fields and 30,000 for dry-crop land.

Afterwards, the cadres began selling residential plots, based on the blueprints, for 20,000 to 40,000 yuan (depending on the exact location) for each plot along the road, taking 50 percent of the payment in advance and the rest after the land was handed over. At the same time, they also signed agreements with the people who bought the plots stipulating that they had to complete construction of the first floors of their houses by the end of 1997. As Chengxin had anticipated, there was plenty of demand for new residential land among the villagers, and since these plots were close to the market town and convenient for transportation, every last one of them had been snatched up in less than ten days. Quite a few households even bought two plots. After the initial payments were received, Chengxin hired a construction team to level the land and raise it to about twenty centimeters higher than the street, build ditches running behind the plots, and use steel pipes to divert tap water from the market town to each plot.

By the summer of 1997, the infrastructure was basically completed for Cheng Village's Brigade Street. Throughout the entire process, the village committee did not have to pay a penny and even earned over 100,000 yuan. As for specific numbers, all of the village officials who participated later said that they could not remember clearly. Chengxin said that some of the money was later used to renovate the brigade headquarters, and the rest was spent on subsidizing a portion of the agricultural tax (including add-ons)[3] on behalf of the villagers. The latter was necessary because, at the time, some of the villagers refused to pay or delayed payment as add-ons grew more and more onerous, but the county government still required the township governments to pay everything that was owed each year, classifying this together with Family Planning as a non-negotiable policy. Many villagers suspected that Chengxin and other village cadres embezzled some of the money, but at the same time they expressed sentiments to the effect of, "We can't be sure of what happened exactly, and we couldn't be bothered to do anything about it in any case."

In the first half of the same year, the township government launched its thousand-meter Fuqian Road construction project. Its model of construction was identical to that of Cheng Village's Brigade Street, except that a portion of the land belonged to the Duqiao Residential Committee, and two shopfronts to the left and right of the entrance to the government headquarters already belonged to the government. First, the government requisitioned land from residents of Duqiao's market town, Cheng Village, and Xujiao Village (but mainly from Cheng Village). Then it sold residential plots on the basis of blueprints, using the advance portion of the payments to level the land and connect the plots to the water system and the power grid, finally receiving the rest of the land payments when the plots were handed over to the buyers.

Since they could use the land requisition prices from the Brigade Street project as a reference, and also since Chengxin and other cadres from Cheng Village had agreed to help out, the land requisition work was soon completed without any complications. Shortly thereafter, a small area of land in Xujiao was also requisitioned at the same rate of compensation. Disputation emerged, however, when it came to the land under the jurisdiction of Duqiao Residential Committee. At first, the township government announced that they would take the land at the same rate as wet-rice fields in Cheng Village, but the residents rejected this offer one after the other on the grounds that their land was already classified as urban construction land. This meant that the government did not need to pay taxes and fees to the Wu County Bureau of Land Management in order to convert it from agricultural land into construction land, and it could also obtain permits for land use (*tudi shiyong zheng*). In the end, the Duqiao Residential Committee received 110,000 yuan for about 1.2 *mu* of its land (of which a portion was distributed to the residents).

Township cadres and also many village cadres were well aware of the difference between agricultural land and construction land, so more than ten of them were the first to select plots located on the Duqiao Residential Committee's land, and after building houses there they had deeds (*fangchanzheng*) written up. Other buyers, and those who had bought plots on Brigade Street, did not even know that it was necessary to obtain a deed for their own houses. At the end of 1998, Wu County carried out the first round of comprehensive land-use planning (according to orders from above), and the Duqiao Township Government seized the opportunity to reclassify these two illegally built streets, and the land it planned to use for building several streets nearby, as construction land. In this way, the houses built on the residential plots could obtain land-use documentation, and in order for the Bureau of Land Management to get all the townships to support its planning work (or as the township cadres put it, "to scheme together") while complying with the needs of investigations from above, it granted land-use documentation to all the completed buildings without collecting any taxes or fees.

From 1998 to 2000, the township government followed this same model in building two more streets about 700 meters long (with three rows of houses) to the left of the headquarters between Fuqian Road and the old market street, along with a new market area with a structure of reinforced concrete covered in canopies. The land requisition price was similar to that of the wet-rice fields in Cheng Village, but since it was already classified as construction land, it was easier for the people who bought these new residential plots to obtain deeds. Duqiao's "Small Town Development" rapidly underwent a qualitative leap, in 2000 receiving a commendation from the Wu County Bureau of Urban-Rural Planning as an "Advanced Unit of the Development of Small Towns and Cities." One township cadre commented that they should thank the Bureau of Land Management for making full use of policy to "play edge-ball" (*da cabianqiu*, i.e., to exploit legal loopholes) in ways that benefitted Duqiao: "If you want to acquire political capital, then you need to make unexpected moves (*jian zou pian feng*)."

In the township cadre examinations organized by Wu County in 1998, Chengxin tested into the Duqiao Township Office for Urban-Rural Planning (known as "the Planning Office" and sharing a space with the Township Office of Land Management). Wu County treated this as that year's work on "the three rural problems" (agriculture, rural institutions, and rural people): recruiting outstanding village cadres to serve as township cadres and model personnel at enterprises and public service units. The Planning Office was a permanent public service position on the state payroll with a salary of about 2,000 yuan per month. Chengxin's responsibilities there were identical to what he had done as the party branch secretary of Cheng Village—mainly requisitioning land for "Development of Small Towns and Cities" projects and then supervising the work. In addition, Chengxin and his colleague in the Office of Land Management participated in the township's first round of "Comprehensive Planning on Land Use" in 1998. As Chengxin once explained, the main reason the township leaders recruited him into the Planning Office was that they had been impressed at his ability to requisition land for the government in Small Town Development work. As for Chengxin, he had always dreamed of "eating state grain," so he gladly accepted the position.

While Cheng Village's Brigade Street was being built, Chengxin already knew the township was about to launch its Fuqian Road project. When he was helping the township government "do thought work" to persuade the residents of Jiangbei to sell their land, therefore, he repeatedly claimed that he was just "making a bridal gown for someone else" (i.e., that he would not benefit directly). Later, during the Fuqian Road project, however, Chengxin and some of the other township cadres took advantage of the opportunity to be the first to buy plots that had been requisitioned from the Duqiao Residential Committee, in a good location almost right across the street from the township headquarters. Later, Chengxin built a three-story house, renting out the first floor as a shopfront and moving into the second and third floors as his own residence. The house's interior was finished with the finest materials available in Duqiao at the time. His four-story house in Jiangbei was basically left vacant.

Many villagers and residents of the town claimed that the main leaders of Duqiao at the time must have embezzled from these construction projects, but they could not provide any evidence. They also felt certain that the director of the township credit union had earned a lot of money through his connections with these leaders. As it turned out, although the government did make some money by selling the plots along Fuqian Road in 1998, all of this was soon spent on paving the road, which actually cost more than they had made. (Chengxin believed that the township leaders had profited from the paving, nevertheless, since it generated political capital as an "achievement.") In addition, when several villages were unable to subsidize their residents' payment of agricultural taxes and add-ons, the credit union office of Wu County prohibited its township branches from making any more loans to village committees. The government of Duqiao had no choice but to scrape together money on their own to pay the taxes. In 2000, therefore, when it came time to pave two newly built streets, the government could only pay the contractor 30 percent in advance and had to pay the rest over the course of three years. The director of the Duqiao Credit Union carried out this project in his own name.

Digging

As Chengxin saw it, Duqiao's township government and Cheng Village's committee were no different from ordinary peasants: All depended on the land to "make a living" (Ct. *wansik* 搵食). Of course, the government also derived revenue from industry, commerce, and local taxes, but many of its larger business deals were based on land. In a relatively backward place such as Duqiao, this was the government's basis for survival. While Chengxin worked at the Planning Office, several rounds of township leaders came and went, but all of them liked to say things to the effect of, "We'll do whatever's necessary, even if we have to dig down three feet (*chi*) into the soil."

According to Chengxin's recollection, prior to about 1993, the government could still acquire enough revenue from the "three deductions and five charges" and tax remittances to basically cover its everyday operations. Another important factor, he said, was:

> In those days the government didn't have many expenses, it just had one small car. Other cadres didn't even have motorcycles to ride to work—they just walked or rode bicycles. Most cadres lived in the headquarters. It wasn't like later: Even though cadres are assigned housing in the compound, now they basically only stay there if they're working the night shift. Normally they live in the city and commute to work every day. (As with a school,) we call the former "residential students" and the latter "day students." By the time I started working at the Planning Office, the government already had five or six cars: The secretary (of the township party committee) and the mayor each had his own personal vehicle, the Family Planning Office had one, and the deputies shared one. Our office, the Joint Offices of Planning and Land Management, also had a car, but it was always being used by the township leaders and we couldn't use it. Back when I was working in the village, I had ridden a motorcycle to work and only had to be reimbursed 50 yuan a month for gas.

Chengxin also mentioned that over the course of the 1990s, the number of personnel employed by township agencies such as the Water Conservancy Station, the Financial Affairs Office, and the Family Planning Office nearly tripled. The vast majority of the salary for these employees had to be financed by the township government itself (as opposed to higher levels of the state). By the time Chengxin had begun working there, this number amounted to about 800,000 yuan per year. This dramatic increase in expenses formed a sharp contradiction with the shrinking income from the "three deductions and five charges." At the same time, after the development of township-and-village enterprises had been pushed so vigorously, almost all the village committees were now in the red, and the township government was also deeply in debt. To make matters worse, starting in 1995, Duqiao began to face the "top-down calculation of tax responsibilities." This meant that the amount of tax to be collected each year would be determined not by the actual situation, but by a number proposed by Wu County, and the township had to submit that amount as a non-negotiable policy. The numbers proposed by the county government kept rising each year, but Duqiao's economy did not grow at the same rate, so it became harder and harder to pay the stipulated amount of tax.

At one point, Chengxin actually felt a bit regretful about trusting the secretary and mayor about getting a job in government. This was because in 1998, Duqiao's government encountered unprecedented difficulties: Besides all the cadres being required to work overtime in an effort to collect taxes, they also hired several "tax assistance personnel." As Chengxin saw it, most of these personnel were simply "gangsters" (Ct. *laanjai* 烂仔). Through such a "diversity of tactics," the township managed to slightly accelerate its tax collection. They were required to complete half of the year's collection before the end of June, however, but by mid-June they were still nearly one million yuan short. At a meeting of the township party committee leadership, therefore, it was decided that all cadres should "take the initiative to launch an attack," visiting Wucheng and townships such as Chengjiao that were better endowed with tax sources and, there, to "pull taxes" (*lashui*), "digging down three feet into the soil" until they had come up with enough tax sources to complete their assignment. As Chengxin explained, the main method of "pulling taxes" was to convince enterprises to pay their local tax to the Duqiao Township Office of Local Taxation by offering discounts. Originally, they had said every township cadre had to help out, but later this proved impossible, and there was nothing the leaders could do about it. In the end, the mayor and the township party committee secretary had no choice but to set off on their own and try to "buy taxes" from the leaders of Chengjiao Township. Chengjiao had already completed its tax collection responsibilities with plenty to spare, so it could afford to transfer 600,000 yuan in tax revenue to be reported under the name of Duqiao Township. In return, Duqiao paid Chengjiao 50,000 yuan in "work expenses." Chengxin said it was only because the secretaries of the two townships already had a relationship "as firm as iron" that this transaction could be achieved at all, let alone for so little money—otherwise it would have been much more expensive, if it were even possible.

In the second half of 1998, Duqiao augmented its efforts to attract investment by requisitioning land, carrying out the "three connections and one leveling" (leveling the land and connecting the new plots to water, electricity, and road access), and offering plots for rent much lower than that in Chengjiao—in some cases free of charge. Soon over twenty stone-processing enterprises had come to set up shop in Duqiao. In order to lower costs, the government located these enterprises along the national highway, so all it had to pay for was obtaining the land, leveling it, and connecting it to water and electricity. Throughout all this, Chengxin was called in for multiple talks with the township leaders, asking him to "make full use of local cadres' strengths" in helping the township to obtain land "by any means necessary." He recalled:

> That first year working there was really stressful. First, we had to "pull taxes." The second half of the year we rushed around trying to requisition land, but only half of it was in Cheng Village, the other half in Xujiao.

I had to go coordinate, negotiating with the villagers from dawn to dusk, talking until I was blue in the face. The hardest part was that we couldn't choose which piece of land to requisition and then give it to the boss (i.e., the investor). Instead, the bosses came first and looked at the land, and whichever piece they wanted, we had to requisition it. Of course, the bosses all liked the leveled farmland along the road, it was convenient (to use). But farmland was the most trouble, hard to negotiate with the villagers, who wanted a high price for it that the (township) leaders weren't willing to pay. It wasn't like land that was already (classified as) residential, like "wool growing on a sheep's back." The government wanted to "catch a wolf with empty hands" (i.e., get something for nothing). Neither the bosses nor the government were offering any money, so it was up to us to convince (the villagers), to the point that sometimes we had to trick or threaten them. I wronged a lot of people. Besides, land-use documentation couldn't be done for basically any of this land, so strictly speaking it was all illegal, and those of us doing the coordination were a little worried we'd be investigated by the Bureau of Land Management, but there was no way around it. Nowadays rich bosses are bigger than Heaven, so we had to serve them wholeheartedly.

After those twenty-some stone-processing enterprises had moved into Duqiao, the taxes and fees collected for the second half of the year were finally sufficient for the township to complete its responsibilities. From 1999 to 2001, the township attracted another twenty-plus stone-processing enterprises. Later, when the price of land rose in Wucheng and Chengjiao Township, several small-scale stone-processing enterprises began moving from there to Duqiao of their own accord. The Duqiao government began collecting a certain amount of rent—as the later vice-mayor Wen Zhibin put it, they had finally achieved the "glorious transition" from using land to complete tax collection responsibilities to using land "to eat." With the eventual reform of agricultural taxes and fees and the streamlining of administration, the government's financial situation improved dramatically. "Previously (our salary was) 2,000 yuan a month, and often we didn't receive it, but now it's increased to 2,500, and we can get it on time." Even the key village cadres (secretary, director, and bookkeeper) received 1,200 yuan a month.

In Cheng Village, Liang Shengli, who had replaced Chengxin as party branch secretary, also found it to be a major headache trying to collect agricultural taxes and add-ons from the villagers. Although Chengxin had already gone to work for the township, he was also assigned to Cheng Village as *baogan* cadre and so found it hard to separate himself from village work. At one point, Liang approached Chengxin requesting to resign from his position as secretary, since not only did he never receive his monthly stipend of 200 yuan, but he had also lost hope in the possibility of completing his tax collection responsibilities. Chengxin advised him that the village committee still had about 800 *mu* of collective woodland. Although all the trees had been cut down and sold to help the village enterprise pay off its debt, the land itself was still valuable. With Chengxin acting as a go-between, then, a boss from Wucheng contracted the right to manage (*jingyingquan*) Cheng Village's collective woodland for thirty years at the rate of 10 yuan per *mu*, paying half of the rent upfront after signing the contract and agreeing to pay the rest in installments every five years. Soon this boss had hired people to clear the land and plant fast-growing eucalyptus trees (which mature in five to seven years). By 2005 they had matured, and he planted a second crop. According to the estimate of Chengxin and Shouyi, the boss had already recouped his thirty-year investment in 2005.

What bothered ordinary villagers even more was their discovery that, after this type of eucalyptus trees grew for a few years, they acted like a pump sucking up much of the spring water. This especially affected the residents of Jiangbei, many of whose fields lay in the hills below the eucalyptus farm, and whose drinking water came from a spring in a nearby valley. After the eucalyptus was planted, these fields often failed to get enough water. The spring had been estimated to be capable of providing enough water for everyone in Jiangbei and Duqiao's market town to drink, but when Shouzhi began diverting it in 2001, he discovered that it now provided only enough for Jiangbei residents alone.[4] In addition, villagers also discovered that the water in the irrigation channels and fields was often black and emitted a strong smell of eucalyptus oil. This was caused by rain washing fallen leaves and bark into the channels. Villagers therefore often complained that the farm had polluted their fields. Several of the more well-off villagers such as Shouyi, on the other hand, criticized the cadres for renting out the land to an outsider when they could have afforded to rent it themselves, in which case they would have planted less destructive crops such as cypress or pine instead of eucalyptus.

From 2009 to 2010, responding to orders from above, Duqiao implemented the reform of woodland rights aimed as "clarifying property rights." According to relevant policies, all the collective woodland for Cheng Village as a whole and for each of its villager teams must be contracted out to individual households (a process the villagers called "distributing the hills among the households"). This included the woodland planted with eucalyptus. The boss who had rented that land felt that his contract with the village committee was still valid and refused to give up his right to use the land. The committee had no choice but to contract the eucalyptus farm's 800-*mu* of woodland to villager households, but then convince them to turn around and subcontract its use-rights back to the boss for fifty years at 12 yuan per *mu* each year. He paid half of the rent upfront and the rest in installments every five years. The old contract was annulled, and the committee returned the unused twenty years of rent to the boss.

After each villager team's collective woodland was "distributed among the households," all of it was then subcontracted to bosses in the same way as the eucalyptus farm—with arrangements for thirty to fifty years at rents of

15 to 25 yuan per *mu* each year. In order to make himself look more legitimate, Chengxin contrasted himself with these bosses, saying many of them were corrupt township-and-village cadres or their relatives, and that they sometimes even collaborated with "gangsters." When a few villagers refused to subcontract their land, cadres came out in person to persuade them, and sometimes the "gangsters" would come and threaten them, until the problem was resolved. I asked some villagers who had been threatened and found that Chengxin's account was accurate. They said they had yielded because they wanted "one less problem to worry about," but often they also lamented that their "hearts hurt" or that they still felt bitter about it. One villager, for example, said:

> Although the hills (the woodland) were only "contracted" rather than "privatized," how many thirty or fifty years can a person live through? Who knows what things will be like several decades later? By that time I'll have gone to meet my great-grandparents. There's no way we'll get the (use-rights to the) hills back, so we may as well say they belong to them and their descendants, that they've been converted into money for healthcare or caskets. People like us have no rights and no power. We don't want much, just that Heaven will bless us with good health.

In Duqiao's search for a path to prosperity through "digging down three feet into the soil," the most significant deal was the construction of the ceramics factory, without a doubt. For this, village cadres such as Qianjin nearly came to blows with the heads of several villager teams. In the presence of other villagers, two of those team heads pulled out 2,000 yuan and threw it at Qianjin, saying "We don't want your money! We're not helping you take any more land!" The villagers' observation of Qianjin attempting to "buy off" the team heads confirmed that "shady deals" were taking place in the process of land requisition. Later, Chengxin intervened with a combination of carrot and stick tactics, on the one hand slightly raising the compensation for land, but on the other asserting that villagers who claimed use-rights for a piece of land but could not produce documentation to prove it would not find support in the legal system—stating, moreover, that he was sure about this as an old cadre of Cheng Village. In 2008, the township government helped the ceramics factory set up there by offering 2,000 *mu* of extremely cheap land, henceforth receiving over three million yuan in tax refunds from Wu County each year. Chengxin said that after this "leap," his salary rose to about 3,500 yuan per month, and that of civil servants with permanent positions on the state payroll rose from 4,500 to 5,000 yuan.

What bothered local people, including Chengxin, was that Duqiao's air quality suddenly declined precipitously. In October 2013, I came to conduct research in Cheng Village. Autumn had previously been the most pleasant season here: The temperature would drop from scorching to warm, the rain would fall less frequently, and the humidity would be just right. But now it was also the time of year when the wind's direction would blow from the ceramics factory toward Cheng Village and the market town: The sky had become gray, you could see large particles of soot floating by, and the air reeked of burning coal. Chengxin once grumbled that, according to experts from the Wu County Bureau of Environmental Protection, that smell came from sulfur dioxide in the air. One villager who had been chatting with us interjected, "Don't you township cadres always say you're doing everything possible to promote development for the good of our grandchildren? The way I see it, this (air pollution) is going to cut off the family line!"

Governmental Businesspeople

After Chengxin began working for the township government, he never completely abandoned the village. He and his wife no longer participated in manual farmwork, except for a little gardening that his wife did for their own consumption, and they gave the rest of their farmland to relatives. In 1998, however, Chengxin rented about 200 *mu* of woodland, combined that with his own 50-plus *mu*, and hired people to plant tangerine trees and look after them. When he went to rent this land, several of the villagers who rented it to him had asked for his help in the past, or planned to ask in the future, in order to obtain residential land-use permits for building houses. They therefore gave him a good deal on the woodland, asking for only 10 yuan per *mu* each year over the course of fifteen years, half to be paid upfront and the rest in installments every five years. These were also the main people Chengxin hired to plant and look after the tangerine trees. Their wages were determined by the market, but during busy times when it was hard to find people to apply fertilizer or pick fruit, these villagers would make sure to work for Chengxin before they worked for anyone else. In 2009, one villager told me:

> A few years ago, (Chengxin) planted tangerine trees. Tangerines have to be picked fast at just the right time. If you pick them too early, the fruit is unripe and sour, it doesn't taste good. If you're too late, it'll rot on the tree... . He works for the government, and there's no telling when we might need to trouble him for help. Whenever his family needs anything, no matter what it is, we all try to find ways to help out. Call it mutual aid if you like. Otherwise, there's no way we would have rented that hill (woodland) to him so cheap and then work for him every year. He and his wife don't do anything themselves; they just wait to sell the tangerines and collect the money. You tell me, on what basis can they do that? Right?

In addition, the boss of farm supply shop in Duqiao's market town said that when Chengxin's family buys large amounts of chemical fertilizer and pesticide from the shop every year, he sells everything at the price of purchase (not even accounting for the cost of shipping). The boss explained that the reason for this was that his brother worked at the Duqiao Township Water

Conservancy Station, and Chengxin's brother Cheng Chengheng worked at the Wu County Water Conservancy Bureau. "His brother 'covers' (*zhao*) my brother, and my brother covers me. How can I not show him some respect?"

As Chengxin put it himself, with regard to tangerine farming, he had "taken full advantage of the appropriate land (*di li*) and people (*ren he*), so even if the weather (*tian shi*) wasn't perfect, there shouldn't be any major problems." Indeed, from 2001 when the trees started bearing fruit until 2010, during normal years, Chengxin netted between 800 and 1,000 yuan per *mu*. Even in "small years" (when the yield was low), or when the market price fell particularly low, his orchard never lost money. After 2008, the input costs for tangerine farming throughout the region rose from 0.15 yuan per *jin* to 0.5, plus as the trees aged, some of them became infected with "yellow dragon disease,"[5] so Chengxin stopped operating the orchard in 2011. He took the initiative to return the right to manage the land (along with the trees themselves) to the villagers it belonged to one year in advance. For this he often praised himself as "generous" and "loyal to friends" (*jiang yiqi*).

Chengxin believed that if township cadres wanted to live well, they had to "do business on the side" (*jianye*). At the end of 2012, he calculated the following main expenditures:

(1) On average, each month he would treat people to a meal at least once, paying 500–1,000 yuan per meal, spending at least 10,000 yuan on meals each year;
(2) Each day he would spend 30–50 yuan on 1–2 packs of cigarettes, amounting to about 15,000 yuan each year;
(3) On holidays he would give gifts to leaders, spending between 5,000 and 30,000 yuan each year;
(4) On favors for friends and relatives, he would spend over 30,000 yuan each year;
(5) For everyday household expenses, he would spend over 20,000 yuan each year.

Factoring in other expenses as well, Chengxin estimated that, as an ordinary township cadre, he would require a monthly income of over 8,000 yuan just to get by, to say nothing of savings. He said:

> Of course, there are also a few "iron roosters" who are stingy, "not even plucking one feather," but this sort of person has a bad reputation and is unable to develop good relations with others to get things done. Or they have good family backgrounds and just eat other people's food, rarely treating anyone to meals. Same with gifts: They receive more than they give. I'm not including people like this, but just ordinary people.

Chengxin therefore pointed out that, other than the mayor and the township party committee secretary, who had to devote themselves wholeheartedly to the basic responsibilities of their posts in order to vie for a position at the county level, most of Duqiao's township cadres had "business on the side." There were two types of side business: One consisted of the commercial activities of friends and relatives in which they became shareholders or sole investors. The other type was businesses they ran themselves through family members such as a spouse or a child.

In order to illustrate just how common and normal these side businesses were, on several occasions Chengxin mentioned a few cases to which the people involved admitted openly.

In 1996, the director of Duqiao's credit union provided the capital for his daughter and her husband to open a restaurant that still operates today. It has three big tables on the first floor and five private rooms on the second, and it was the first to install air conditioning in the town. According to the owner, prior to the end of 2008, her restaurant was the main place where township cadres gathered for meals and entertained guests.

In 1999, a certain Mr. Wang, who had formerly served as the chief of Duqiao's police department, used his relationship with the police chief of a neighboring township to obtain the use-rights for about 500 *mu* of woodland there to plant tangerine trees. Wang's brother was put in charge the orchard's regular maintenance. In return, Wang helped him obtain 800 *mu* of woodland in two villages within Duqiao (including Cheng Village) for him to plant eucalyptus trees.

From 2000 to 2012, Wen Zhibin, while serving as Duqiao's vice-mayor, ran two preschools in Wucheng and another county seat in Qi Prefecture, with his wife as their legal representative. Together, the two preschools recruited over 100 students. The one in Wucheng was mainly oriented toward the children of migrant workers, while the one in the other county focused on the children of local rural residents. According to Wen, these schools "only made a little money to help support our family—about 100 or 200 thousand yuan (in profit) per year." According to Chengxin's estimate, however, the two schools must have netted over 400,000 yuan each year.

In 2003, Cheng Jinhua, the head of Duqiao's Land Management Office, got together with Xujiao's village committee director and rented 50 *mu* of pond area there to raise fish. The two partners split the investment and income fifty-fifty, but the director was in charge of the fish farm's everyday management until it closed in 2009.

From 2005 to 2011, Mr. Li, the vice-chief of Duqiao's police department, contracted the use-rights for a large-scale duck farm in one of the township's villages. The farm could raise over 1,000 ducks, selling them at four times throughout the year. Mr. Li paid the village party branch secretary 1,500 yuan a month to manage the farm.

In 2006, Duqiao's vice-mayor Mai Jia got together with a classmate to open a restaurant in the town, running it until 2008. Mai Jia "took care of" rent and initial investment, while his classmate served as legal representative and managed the restaurant. Normally, Mai Jia's main role was to attract customers (especially when the government's various units entertained guests), and then to make sure they eventually paid.

In 2008, the chairperson of Duqiao Township People's Congress, Mai Yi, got together with his brother and opened a "farmhouse-style" (*nongjiale*) restaurant on the roadside between the market town and the national highway, operating in the same way as the vice-mayor's restaurant until 2011. Shortly after this new restaurant opened, the vice-mayor and his classmate chose to close theirs.

In 2009, the only son of Duqiao's former mayor (then serving as vice-chief of a certain office at the county level) set up a stone quarry in the township and ran it for two years. Over the previous decade, the quarry business had flourished due to the demand generated by the large volume of government projects, coupled with the construction of houses by local families in Duqiao and the surrounding region. This was also the cause of frequent conflicts between quarry bosses, as well as among local gangsters. As Chengxin put it, "If you want to run a quarry, you need people on the sides of both darkness and light (i.e., connections with gangsters and the government), or at least you need to control one of them." By the time the province had launched its "Three Strikes, Two Build-ups" campaign in 2012,[6] the quarry was already closed.

As for township cadres who did not publicly acknowledge their involvement in "business on the side," Chengxin expressed that there were many others, but it was "hard to talk about them." Some were actually well known, while others were hidden more successfully, so people did not dare to confirm them. For example, Chengxin suspected that two cadres owned "dry stock" (shares granted to political backers without monetary investment) in two red-brick factories, but he did not have any proof.

While the township cadres were engaged in such "business on the side," their relatives, classmates, and friends ruled the roost economically in Duqiao's market town. In 2011, Chengxin enumerated the "political backers" (*kaoshan*) behind several of the town's most profitable shops.

The motorcycle shop next to the entrance of the township government headquarters was owned by the cousin of Duqiao's former party committee secretary. There were only three motorcycle shops in town, and this one was bigger than the other two combined. Since local people were riding motorcycles more and more instead of walking, its business was always good.

Across from the headquarters, the tenant of Chengxin's shopfloor property ran a construction materials shop there selling steel bars, concrete, and tiles. Its owner was the brother of the party branch secretary of a certain village in Duqiao and the brother-in-law of a certain vice-mayor. There are more than ten other construction materials shops throughout the township, but most were small-scale and had few selections. Chengxin described this shop as "occupying half of Duqiao's battlefield. Now with so many people building houses, his business would prosper even if he didn't want it to."

Duqiao had three large farm supply stores. One of them was owned by the brother of the Water Conservancy Station director, another by a cousin of the Family Planning Office director, and the third by a classmate of the vice-secretary of the township party committee. In the market town, there were a few shops that sold farm supplies among other things, but Chengxin said they could only be considered "retail" while the three big stores were "wholesale."

The township's only rice processing plant oriented toward the market rather than household consumption was owned by the Agrotechnology Station director's son-in-law. Duqiao's only remaining distillery was owned by a relative of the vice-chief of the Agricultural Bureau of a certain county and the classmate of Duqiao's vice-mayor in charge of agriculture. The township's only large hotel (six stories with forty rooms and over sixty beds) was owned by the nephew of the vice-chief of a certain county's Investment Attraction Bureau and the classmate of a Duqiao police officer. This had more beds than all the other hotels in town combined. Plus, it was located at the intersection of the national and provincial highways, its furnishings were relatively modern (with tile flooring, air conditioning, color TV, water heaters, etc.), so the other hotels could not even dream of competing with its business. It also had a large banquet hall on the first floor, where every year it hosted the weddings and birthday parties of many residents of the town and surrounding villages, and it was the only option available when work-units such as the government, the secondary school, or a large-scale stone-processing plant wanted to hold a banquet.

In such an atmosphere of "business on the side" and helping friends and relatives to do business, Chengxin was not about to fall behind the other cadres. After he had abandoned the tangerine orchard in 2011, he rented the courtyard behind the Cheng Village headquarters and opened a preschool there, with his wife working there part-time and his daughter-in-law and her sister working there full-time. In the courtyard, he built three simple rooms, installing a few bunkbeds for the students to take naps, and he filled in a fishpond next to the courtyard, installing some plastic playground facilities for the children play on. For lunch, Chengxin and his wife did the cooking themselves using vegetables from their garden. During the season when green beans were ripe, they often served these to the students for several days in a row, then when the squash ripened, they would serve squash for a week—leading to complaints from many parents. Other than this one and the preschool run by the Central Duqiao Primary School (formerly Cheng Village Primary), the township had only one other preschool to choose from. Central Primary's preschool only recruited 100 students each year, as did the other preschool, while Chengxin's recruited fifty to sixty. In March of 2012, Chengxin retired from his post in the Planning Office and devoted himself to running the preschool full-time together with his wife and daughter-in-law.

As Chengxin saw it, not only was it common for township cadres to run businesses on the side, but the grassroots government was itself a "businessperson" since most of its work consisted of doing business. Fiscally,

Duqiao Township and Wu County "ate from separate kitchens": Township cadres' salaries and benefits were directly linked to the township's revenue, so the entire government was basically just focused on making money. To this end, the cadres had to think of ways to develop the local economy. Looking at this from a positive angle, Chengxin said, the township government ran itself like a business, and he saw that as a good thing. At the same time, however, sometimes this approach went too far and had negative consequences, as when the requisition of land gave rise to conflicts with "the masses," when eucalyptus farming degraded the soil and contaminated the water, and when ceramics production polluted the air.

Only local cadres like Chengxin would think about these consequences, however, since he had to continue living here, and his son eventually had to come back from where he was working to settle down in Cheng Village. Most of the main township leaders were outsiders, so all they thought about was how to develop the economy, accrue political capital, and obtain promotions to posts somewhere higher up the ladder, such as Wucheng. "So," Chengxin said:

> Every one of those leaders acts like he's been injected with chicken blood, using political (means) to promote economic development, and using economic (means) to attain political promotion—just leaving us behind here to breathe the poisoned air.

Joining a Faction

Another thing that made a deep impression on Chengxin regarding this period of experience serving as a township cadre was "choosing which faction to join" (*zhan dui*). Especially when thinking back to the contrast between himself and Chen Jinhua, Chengxin would always sigh, "I joined the wrong faction."

Back in 1998, the reason Chengxin had obtained the Planning Office post was the initiative of Fang Lizheng, the vice-mayor and vice-secretary of Duqiao's township party committee. After the mayor and secretary had agreed to this proposal, Fang was also the first to discuss it with Chengxin on behalf of the township leaders. During the cadre recruitment examination later on, and especially during the interview, Chengxin had passed in no small part due to this man. Chengxin recalled:

> From beginning to end, Secretary Fang helped pull lots of strings for me. Otherwise, with my middle school education followed by years of vegetation, there's no way I could have passed. But that's also exactly the reason that, after I started working there, everyone regarded me as his person, belonging to his faction…. grassroots (governments) are all like this: On the table (formally) what matters is hierarchy, who is in charge of whom, but off the table (privately) what matters is who has allegiance to whom. The subordinates you're directly in charge of won't necessarily

stand together with you when it comes time to join a faction. If you bring it up, no one will admit to this, but everyone knows what's going on. But it's important to put effort into showing respect. There's no way around it, you can't express your allegiance to your faction too openly. You have to make people think you're on good terms with everyone. When you oppose others, you have to do it secretly.

According to Chengxin, after he had started working there formally, as a cadre native to the area, in his land requisition work for the government's construction of the two new streets, he was definitely at an advantage. Regarding this, the mayor and secretary praised him at many joint meetings of the township government and party committee. In private conversation, Fang Lizheng also spoke highly of Chengxin: "He's great. You could say he strengthened my face." At almost the same time, in response to orders from Wu County and the Bureau of Land Management, Duqiao began to create its first comprehensive land-use plan. Since the township's Planning Office and Land Management Office shared a space in the government headquarters, they were seen by others as "one unit of troops with two signs," and this project became part of his core work. In this work, however, Chengxin was basically "illiterate," whereas Chen Jinhua from the Land Management Office, who had graduated from vocational secondary school, was the more "professional" one.

Chengxin recalled that, at the time, Jinhua was close to a lower-ranking vice-mayor surnamed Xiao and could be considered part of his faction. However, "That circle had basically no centripetal force" since Mr. Xiao had no influence whatsoever in the township. In addition, Jinhua had no reliable connections in Wu County. Chengxin, on the other hand, had entered Fang Lizheng's faction, and Fang was the third most powerful official in Duqiao (in terms of actual power) after the "elder brother" (the party committee secretary)—even the mayor had to yield somewhat in the face of Fang. Therefore, although Jinhua looked down on Chengxin's ability to do this work, there was nothing he could do about it. Chengxin said:

> At the time, I felt that (Jinhua) had the air of an intellectual, and I couldn't be bothered to fuss about these things with him. If he was more capable, then just let him do more of the work. I was happy to have the extra time.

In the second half of 1999, the party and government leaders of Duqiao underwent a periodic shuffling of personnel. Chengxin believed that, under normal conditions, Fang Lizheng would become the new mayor without incident. But the outcome was surprising: After the mayor and party committee secretary were transferred away, Fang was transferred to serve as mayor of Shantang Township, and he stayed there for six years. Duqiao's new secretary and mayor were both transferred from elsewhere, and the mayor was

Jinhua's schoolmate. The balance of power in the office suddenly shifted out of Chengxin's favor. On this, Chengxin recalled:

> The new mayor was (Jinhua's) classmate. I reckon they weren't particularly close before—I never saw them interact much. They weren't studying the same major. But now they were working in the same unit, plus they were both outsiders, so maybe they felt they could trust each other more than others since they were classmates. The first time (everyone) met and drank (together), the mayor took the initiative to drink with him. (Jinhua) finally observed (what was going on) and suddenly became friendly, joining his faction. On many occasions, when returning to Wucheng in the afternoon after work, the mayor said, "Ride with me" (in the government car assigned to him). Sometimes they worked the night shift together, not returning to Wucheng but instead drinking together half the night in a restaurant.

While they were working, the new mayor often encouraged Chengxin to strengthen his "studies," implying that his level of education was insufficient. Chengxin did not feel this was really inappropriate, however, since after all he was quite capable when it came to taking care of local matters. Meanwhile, he began trying to get closer to the new secretary of the township party committee, but soon he discovered:

> It's easy to get closer to someone you already know, but it's harder to win the trust of a leader you don't know at all yet. It might take a long time. With the former secretary, Fang, I could confide him, but not the new (secretary)—he was more circumspect. It's not like he would open up if I just gave him a few more gifts. Without trust, if you give too many gifts the person won't accept them. Who knows what kind of ulterior motives you might have?

Chengxin concluded wistfully, "Time doesn't wait for people." Before he had managed to establish himself in the right faction under the new leadership, the key opportunity of his life arrived. In early 2000, the head of the Joint Offices of Planning and Land Management applied for early retirement, so the position was open. This was important to both Chengxin and Chen Jinhua, since it was not only a cadre post at the rank of *zhenggu* ("section head"), but also a permanent civil servant position on the state payroll. The township leaders granted this opportunity to Jinhua. According to Chengxin, at the time there was already a slight difference between such positions classified as "civil service" and those classified as "public services," and this distinction only grew more pronounced in the coming years. Moreover, at this time the Office of Land Management came under direct administration at the county level. As the new office head, Jinhua received the same salary as *zhenggu*-ranking cadres at the Wu County Bureau of Land Management, about twice that of Chengxin.

At this time, Chengxin became closer to Vice-Mayor Xiao when the latter discovered that Jinhua had "become more distant" from him after the new mayor had assumed office, so he sought out Chengxin as an ally. Regarding this development, Chengxin said:

> During the transition, you could say that (Xiao) was promoted: Although his title was still "vice-mayor," previously he had been one of lower ranking vice-mayors, whereas now he was number four or five, right behind the vice-mayor who also served as chair of the (Township) People's Congress. He started calling me into his office to drink tea, whether or not he had business to discuss. Some evenings he invited me to play Chinese chess with him, even though I was terrible at the game. Sometimes when he went out to take care of official business, he would ask me to come along. During meetings he would find opportunities to speak highly of me. In other words, you could say he was inviting me to join his faction.

Eventually Chengxin withdrew from these advances, however, when he learned that Vice-Mayor Xiao belonged to the same faction as the director of the Wu County Government Office, since they had served in the army together. Meanwhile, the mayor of Duqiao was related by blood to the head of the Wu County Party Committee's Organization Department, and they belonged to a different faction. Chengxin became "worried that the water was too deep," so tried not to get too involved, lest a conflict emerge between those two factions, since "when the gods fight, the imps suffer" (that is, when officials quarrel, their subordinates suffer). Besides, Chengxin said, he could never figure out the new township secretary's attitude, so he did not dare to make any rash moves. He sighed:

> Everyone says there are no eternal friends in politics, only eternal interests. Of course this adage is correct, but not entirely. Take us grassroots cadres, for example: In such a small township, or even in a county, everyone knows each other. Of course it's normal to join different factions as interests change, but if you're always switching from one faction to another, you'll ruin your reputation. No one will trust you. Who knows whether one day you'll turn the barrel of the gun against me and become a "reactionary"? So when joining a faction, there actually aren't many choices. If you're always switching sides, it's possible no one will accept you into their circle.

Chengxin also analyzed the factions that other people in his office belonged to. When he started working there in 1998, the joint offices officially had five people: two in Land Management, two in Planning, and one Ms. Xu in charge of both. Besides Chen Jinhua, Land Management also had a 25-year-old man named Li Zhewen, and besides Chengxin in the Planning Office there was a middle-aged woman surnamed Zeng.

Mr. Li had begun working there, with a permanent "public services" position, right after graduating from a famous university, but at the time he had already been "borrowed" by the Township Party and Government Office for three years, where he wrote up paperwork. As Chengxin saw it, Mr. Li's education and abilities should not have been stifled for so long on this job where his status was little better than a contract worker in a printing office. The explanation given was that the young man was rather aloof. It was said that when he arrived in Duqiao, not only did he not know how to join a faction, before long he had also offended the secretary, the mayor, and Fang Lizheng—each representing one of the township's three main factions. Chengxin's evaluation was:

> This sort of thing just won't do. At first it might have been that he had just graduated and was a bit bookish, thinking the others had only attended vocational secondary school or vocational college, whereas he had a bachelor's degree from a famous university. Before he had become accustomed to society, he had already been pinned to the ground. But later, after more interactions, I started to think there was something wrong with his personality, that he wasn't good at navigating interpersonal relations. Intellectually he was mature, but his personality prevented him from getting anywhere. Even after several changes of leadership, he never solved the problem of joining a faction. Everyone else in the office had been promoted, but he always remained a "specialist" in writing up paperwork.

In 2005, Fang Lizheng, He Ping, and Wen Zhibin were transferred (back) to Duqiao to serve as party committee secretary, mayor, and vice-mayor, respectively. According to Wen and Chengxin, stretching a bit you could say that Fang and He belonged to the same faction, since they were both were close friends with certain stone-processing plant bosses in Wucheng. Although they each belonged to different political circles, there was no conflict between them. He Ping and Li Zhewen had attended the same university. Through He's mediation, Li was appointed director of the Township Party and Government Office with the rank of *zhenggu*, but his main job remained that of writing up paperwork. (In 2009, with the help of a classmate who worked as secretarial assistant for a certain leader, Li was finally transferred to work in a certain agency at the county level.)

Ms. Zeng of the Planning Office was already more than forty years old and was not interested in advancement, her husband serving as chief of a certain division of the Wu County Bureau of Agriculture. She did not really belong to any faction in the township government, being "ambiguous" in her interpersonal relations, avoiding conflict and maintaining a distance. She did her work in a perfunctory manner, leaving much of it to Chengxin. However, as her family background was "neither hard nor soft" (moderately well-connected), and she had the image of a "people-pleaser" (*lao haoren*) in Duqiao, all the cadres (including Chengxin) normally tried not to offend her.

As for the office head Ms. Xu, her husband was the People's Congress chairperson of another township in Wu County. Ms. Xu did not belong to any faction in Duqiao. Her work performance was mediocre, but the mayor and party committee secretary were polite toward her. Chengxin said, "Everyone knew she was just waiting to retire, so no one pulled her into their faction, but they wouldn't do anything to offend her either."

Chengxin also mentioned that people often spoke of the phenomenon where someone would get a promotion by bribing officials and joining their faction, and he said this did happen. But usually there was no direct proof of this, unless the case was investigated. (In the 2012 "Three Strikes, Two Build-ups" campaign, one person in the township was convicted of bribery.)

In 2005, Fang Lizheng's return to Duqiao as party committee secretary was naturally important to Chengxin. As Chengxin recalled, when he learned of this he felt, "In the end I had joined the right faction after all." Indeed, after this, things went much better for him in the office. On several occasions, Fang reservedly told Jinhua to take good care of Chengxin as an "old, local cadre" who could do a lot of work that no one else could do. Jinhua had stopped regarding Chengxin as a competitor long ago. When cadres were assigned to work in different villages, then, Chengxin, Jinhua, and Wen Zhibin chose to work in the same group in charge of Cheng Village. As for Chengxin's hope to achieve the formal status of a civil servant, however, Fang clearly refused to grant this, saying, "Nowadays no one can become a civil servant without taking the exam, there's no way around it." Instead, he urged Chengxin to spend more time with his grandchildren.

"Why is it necessary to join a faction," I asked one night in August 2010, while eating supper with Chengxin and Wen Zhibin on the eve of Wen's transfer out of Duqiao. Chengxin replied, "Everyone does it. If you don't it's like trying to clap with one hand (that is, you are isolated). People take advantage of you." Wen's reply was a little more detailed:

> If you don't want to get a promotion, of course it's ok to avoid joining a faction. But doing so gives you more opportunities. Otherwise, even if you do a good job, your superiors may not find out about it. Or even if they do find out, when it comes time for cadre appointments, recommendations for training courses (*jinxiu*), organizing observation trips and so on, people may pretend not to know about your achievements.

After all, you're not the only one who did a good job.

> Of course, leaders also need to pull subordinates into their factions, otherwise it's just wishful thinking and no substantial faction will take shape. This is because it would be impossible for you (a leader) to complete all

of your work by yourself. But if you just rely on formal institutions to ask your subordinates to do things, they won't necessarily put 100 percent of their hearts into it. There's an adage that says, "Only brothers can defeat a tiger, and only fathers and sons can win a war." Only people belonging to the same close-knit circle will go all out to get something done. Another thing, especially in grassroots government, nowadays a lot of work is done by "playing edge-ball," "being flexible," or even using methods against the regulations. If it's not "your own people," do you dare to trust them to do that sort of thing? To say nothing of illegal business, where it's even more necessary to rely on your own private circle.

Officials' Luck

As the conversation with Chengxin and Wen Zhibin continued to unfold, the issue of "officials' luck" (*guan yun*) came up.

Chengxin said that previously he had not really believed in the concept of officials' luck: "When I was young, I thought that the vicissitudes of one's career as an official (*zuo guan*) depended on specific people and things, nothing mystical." Several villagers had also confirmed to me that Chengxin "didn't believe in spirits" when he was younger. As for "one's career as an official," Chengxin often told villagers that success or failure had nothing to do with anything supernatural like "fate" or "luck." He believed it was his superior abilities that enabled him to inch his way up from brigade security director to vice-secretary, along with his understanding of how to manage interpersonal relations. Although he felt discontent with Chengren, for example, he could go over ten years without expressing this, instead finding ways to curry favor and win his trust. As for the most unfavorable event, namely Chengxin's inability to begin "eating state grain" when transferring from the army to a civilian post, he placed the blame squarely on Chengren's political pedantry, naïveté, and lack of loyalty to friends. This had prevented Chengxin from joining the army right after passing his first physical exam, he would say, so that by the time he had finally completed his period of service, the transferal policy had already changed. Almost all the villagers who knew Chengxin well told me that, after Chengren had stepped down, the person who complained about him the most was no one but the very Chengxin he had done so much to help over the years. As for those "landlords, rich peasants, reactionaries, bad elements, and rightists" whom Chengren had persecuted, and the villagers he had forced to comply with Family Planning (through sterilization or abortion), although they felt discontent, they rarely criticized Chengren in public the way Chengxin did. Or if they did criticize him, they rarely blamed all their life's problems on him.

Other villagers' recollections basically tallied with what Chengxin said: It was not when he was still an ordinary peasant, but after he was already "eating state grain" that he had started believing in "mystical things" (contrary to expectations that party-state personnel be scientific and atheist). For instance,

Chengxin had previously been uninterested in renovating the temples' incense halls and paying homage to ancestors, but after becoming a township cadre he grew enthusiastic about such activities. Similarly, it was not until after he had started working for the township government that he began to worship various supernatural entities. About this, he said candidly:

> One reason I gradually began to believe in these ideas (about officials' luck) was that I kept seeing myself just barely missing opportunities for promotion, and I felt that I couldn't change this situation no matter how hard I tried. So I started thinking that it wouldn't do for me to continue refusing to believe in certain things. Another reason was that I discovered that most township cadres actually believed in officials' luck, even more so than ordinary people, and more sincerely. Everyone knew this in their hearts, it's just that they didn't vocalize it. I was from the countryside, after all, and my wife was still a peasant, (so) at home I openly burned incensed and prayed to the Buddha. I could also go to (a certain temple in Fan County) openly. Other (cadres) wouldn't normally dare to do (this sort of thing) openly, even being secretive about going to the temple, saying something like they were just accompanying friends for sightseeing. They would also choose days when fewer people were there to go.

Wen Zhibin said that he rarely prayed, especially after he had become vice-mayor, when he basically stopped praying out of "fear that it would make a bad impression." At the same time, however, he said that he believed in officials' luck. In order to seek out good luck, he would ask his wife to "burn extra incense at home" and pay attention to his house's *fengshui*.

When asked why it was so common for grassroots cadres to believe in officials' luck, Wen said, "The reasons are complex, it's a long story." First:

> This is probably related to our feudalistic traditional culture. This sort of culture is deeply rooted in our marrow. Don't be misled by our refined, modern appearance in Western suits, leather shoes, and eyeglasses. In our bones we're still very feudal.

In addition, Wen believed, "The most important reason may be that there's no direct connection between your work achievements and actually getting promoted. To a certain degree, promotion depends partly on your achievements and partly on luck." He pointed out that, if you want a promotion, achievements are certainly necessary, otherwise no one would go to so much trouble seeking out political capital: "Even if someone wants to promote you, they still need a convincing excuse." However, it was not as if such an investment would necessarily yield the desired outcome. Just as "fair and aboveboard" achievements would not necessarily work, however, neither would "crooked methods" such as bribery necessarily obtain what you wanted, Wen said:

Of course this sort of phenomenon exists, and it's really bad. The cadres also think it's bad—at least the grassroots ones do. You think it's easy to come up with the money for bribes? How could grassroots cadres have that much money on hand? If you try to take it from ordinary people, it might lead to a "contradiction between cadres and the masses," or even an "extreme incident," then wouldn't you be even worse off than before? Not only would you fail to get the promotion, you'd also lose the "black gauze cap" (official post) you already had. Isn't that "breaking the eggs after the chicken runs away" (losing everything)? Besides, the key thing is that the situation just isn't that simple. It's not like you'll necessarily get a promotion if you spend money on bribes. If it were that simple, I could just go borrow money from friends or relatives, pay for the bribe, and then return the loan one day when I can give someone else a promotion. If it were really that simple, rich businesspeople wouldn't need to ask officials for favors, they could just buy an official to do their bidding. Are things that simple? No.

Wen gave several vivid examples he knew about firsthand, illustrating that promotions depended partly on luck, involving all kinds of indeterminate factors. Among these, the most common and frustrating ones were systematic. Wen said the most prominent characteristic of "the culture of Chinese officialdom" was ambiguity. For all documents, policies, and words spoken by leaders, you had to try to "grasp their spirit." In other words, the spirit was not their literal meaning but their "overtone" or implication. He said:

When I told you it was exhausting, you may not have understood. I'm not talking about physical exhaustion but mental. I can only relax when I go home or spend time with real friends. As soon as I'm in work mode, it's no good. When the people around me talk, the truth is always mixed with falsehoods. The more skilled the speaker is, the harder it is to parse: The same sentence is both true and false—true from one angle and false from another, depending on how you interpret it. Put positively, this is called "the art of speech." Put negatively, you could say the everyday language of work is mendacity. This is what people call "official-speak" (*guan qiang*). So you have to try to grasp its spirit, you have to guess the actual meaning the person wants to convey from a big pile of lies. This is called "insight" (*wuxing*). People with a high level of insight are good at both speaking and grasping the spirit of what others say, and even at thinking of things that the speakers themselves were not aware of. Just to be an ordinary cadre, you have to do this with at least 80 or 90 percent (of what leaders say). I you're just pretending to understand, then you'll run into problems. There's no way around it: Fate is in the hands of people, not institutions, so you can't avoid being subjective. So every day my brain has to keep making such sharp turns. How could I not be exhausted?

In Wen's view, then, sometimes it might be just one misspoken sentence, or one misunderstood meaning, that thwarted everyday work for grassroots cadres, or even prevented a promotion. This was actually quite similar to luck.

In addition, Wen also listed several factors that depended "purely on luck." After a big flood in the summer of 2010, the bridge connecting Cheng Village and the hills to the east of the Wutong River (built during the river diversion project in 1978) collapsed. For this, one of Duqiao's vice-mayors was criticized by higher-ups for violating basic safety responsibilities. Shortly thereafter, Wen's friend who had been serving as mayor of Shantang Township was dismissed from office on the same grounds.

Both sides of the national highway running through Shantang were covered in stone-processing plants, with manure pits and methane harvesters behind them. In order to prepare for an inspection and guidance tour by a certain provincial-level agency, the township government hired a group of migrant workers to clean the manure pits and methane harvesters. Time was not allowed for the pits to aerate sufficiently, and after several of the workers went in to clean them, four ended up dying from methane poisoning. This "major safety accident" occurred at a sensitive time, and the next day the mayor was dismissed, and the township party committee secretary was criticized. Wen's analysis was that "If this incident did not completely ruin (the mayor's) political career, at least it seriously damaged it, interrupting the normal path of promotion and possibly closing off many opportunities that may have existed."

Several months later, that mayor was transferred to serve as vice-chief of the County Cultural Bureau at the rank of *zhengke* ("section chief"). He was still depressed about his "bad luck" at the age of thirty-eight, however, uncertain whether he could "muddle" his way to the position of bureau chief before retirement. It was said that according to unwritten conventions, if one had not achieved a *zhengke*-rank "head" position (such as bureau chief or party committee secretary) by the age of forty, there would be very little chance of further promotion after that. Wen said wistfully, "One's career as an official really depends on officials' luck. Sometimes it truly is as they say: 'planning is up to the person, but the outcome is up to Heaven.'"

As for what Chengxin said about his own "officials' luck," many villagers disagreed. In their thinking, Chengxin's luck was already as good as could be. As Shouzhi put it, "Discontentment can make a snake try to swallow an elephant (feeling that nothing is ever enough). With only a middle school education, he started as little more than a mere "stable boy" for the brigade, then managed to become the party branch vice-secretary, secretary, and finally a township cadre. How could this be considered bad luck?"

While Chengxin felt his luck was bad and other villagers felt the opposite, all agreed that officials' luck was not the same thing as one's ultimate fate and whether one's life turned out "satisfactorily" (*yuanman*).

Chengxin once mentioned that the former director of Duqiao Credit Union had enjoyed good officials' luck his whole career, but upon retirement he was diagnosed with cerebral thrombosis. Chengxin believed this was "fate." In that man's fate, he should not have enjoyed such good officials' luck or acquired so much money, but he did, and as a result "his fate doomed him" to have problems in other areas: "After all, fate determines everything, and one's life is a balance sheet, so if you have more in one area, you'll have less in another." Many villagers had similar views with slight variations. One day in September 2008, I went to the restaurant owned by the daughter of that credit union director, along with Shouyi, Shoude, and Shouzhi. The former director, sitting at the entrance clutching a cane, tilted his head and greeted us with a lisp. Later as we ate in a private room, Shouyi and the others mentioned that the road-paving project the director had organized had been done so shoddily that within two years the road was full of potholes. "He ate too much dirty money with a guilty conscience, so now he's suffering karmic retribution—that's why he's become this way." They repeatedly emphasized that this idea of "retribution" was based on "science" rather than "superstition: He had suddenly grown rich through illicit means and then spent the money on too much food and drink, so "naturally" this had led to cardiovascular disease. "Plus he was always getting agitated and angry. Isn't that why he suffered a stroke?"

As for Chengxin's good luck as an official, some villagers believed this too was related to shady dealings, for which he had also suffered karmic retribution. He had openly admitted to many people that he had used his personal connection with the chief of Fancheng's Health Department, along with a gift of 50,000 yuan, to secure his daughter's admittance into Tongcheng Medical School, thus helping her to become a nurse at Tongcheng Hospital. Later, after she had gotten married, she gave birth to a son who was deaf. Chengxin said that when his daughter and her husband had to spend over 40,000 yuan just on hearing aids, he "suddenly felt (himself) being dragged down, (as if) it had started raining all night as soon as the roof had sprung a leak." Several villagers believed that this "all-night rain" was karmic retribution for Chengxin's shady dealings and luck as an official. He disagreed with such claims, saying, "They're just jealous… . These days, if you have power and connections, why wouldn't you make use of them? If they had the opportunity, wouldn't they do the same?"

Similarly, many middle-aged and older villagers said that the misfortunes that Chengren and Chenggong encountered late in life were also retribution for their excessive luck as officials earlier in life.

In addition, during countless conversations after dinner in Cheng Village, I heard all kinds of stories about officials who had made overbearing use of their luck and then fallen victim to some mysterious higher-up or local gang. The details often involved the officials committing crimes or getting involved with criminal organizations, only to offend some high-ranking official (or their relative) conducting an incognito inspection tour, and then being arrested, imprisoned, or even executed. Or after making money together with partners from a "Jiangxi gang," "Hunan gang," or "Northeasterners gang," conflicts of interest would emerge, leading to an official being "silenced" (killed). After further investigation, I finally discovered that all of these stories, without exception, were either just rumors or completely fictitious.

Notes

1 This phrase (三提五统) refers to three "deductions" (提留) at the village level and five "overall planning charges" (统筹) at the township level, the former including deductions for a reserve fund, a charity fund, and management expenses, and the latter including funds for services "run by the people and subsidized by the state" (民办公助): rural education services, Family Planning, special care for those in need, militia training, and the construction and maintenance of rural roads.
2 According to land management regulations at the time, there were three main categories of "land use characteristics": agricultural land, construction land, and unused land. Agricultural land 农用地 was in turn divided into farmland 耕地 (including naturally irrigated wet-rice fields 灌溉水田, upland fields 望天田, artificially irrigated land 水浇地, dry-crop land 旱地, and vegetable farming land 菜地), horticultural land 园地 (used for orchards and gardens), woodland 林地, pastureland 牧地, and other agricultural land. Construction land was divided into residential plots and land used for independent mining operations, transportation infrastructure, and irrigation infrastructure. State policy restricted the conversion of agricultural land (especially irrigated wet-rice fields) and unused land to construction land (especially residential plots) to different degrees. In addition to quotas limiting the amount of land that could be converted, those who used the land had to pay taxes and fees for conversion.
3 *Translator's note*: Here "add-ons" (附加) refers to taxes and fees added to the agricultural tax, including taxes for local educational expenses, for the construction and maintenance of roads, and for the construction and maintenance of irrigation systems.
4 As the market town developed and its population grew, it was forced to build another waterworks next to the Wutong River. When this proved still insufficient for everyone's needs, some residents began digging their own artesian wells to obtain water for everyday use.
5 This disease (known in English as "citrus greening disease") is a bacterial infection that causes tangerine leaves to become yellow and the fruit to become small and sour. Highly contagious, it is called "the cancer of citrus trees.".
6 On January 6, 2012, Guangdong's Provincial Government and Party Committee launched this campaign aimed at "striking" against "monopolization of the market through violence, the making and selling of counterfeit products, and commercial bribery," and at "building up" systems for social credit and market supervision.

6 An Ordinary Peasant

Freedom

To people around him in Cheng Village, Cheng Shoukuan was an unremarkable, "ordinary farmer." As Shouzhi put it, other than having once served as a "commando" for the local branch of the Red Flag faction, Shoukuan had done nothing of any significance his entire life, so there was not much to talk about. To a certain extent, Shoukuan himself agreed with this assessment. But when he actually started talking about his life, it became clear that this was not entirely true. From his perspective, it was precisely these insignificant things that added up to an endless stream of stories about his life.

In 1941, Shoukuan was born into an extremely poor family in Jiangbei. His grandfather had been born in Nantang, but since the family was poor, he went to work in river transport for a rich family, so he built a shack on the riverbank in Jiangbei, eventually settling down there, where Shoukuan's father was born. Besides renting land for farming, Shoukuan's father also worked as a tailor. Shoukuan's mother, Ms. Mai, was born into a landlord family that had fallen on hard times. Her feet were bound. Shortly after marrying into Cheng Village, she converted to Christianity. According to Shoukuan, since his family belonged to the Nantang branch of the Cheng clan rather than the Jiangbei branch, they were often bullied by neighbors over minor, everyday life issues. It was actually such trivial matters that were the hardest to deal with, since they just had to endure the abuse, whereas with bigger matters they could ask the elders of Nantang to come and intervene. Shoukuan said his mother had mentioned this as one of the reasons she had turned to Christianity.

Shoukuan had two younger brothers: Shoushu (b. 1947) and Shouzhong (b. 1949). Because they were hard up economically, it was not until after they received a two-room house in the 1950 "redistribution of the fruits of labor" that his parents sent the children to primary school. Shoukuan became classmates with Shoude, who was two years older, until they both graduated from middle school.

DOI: 10.4324/9781003353072-7

Shoukuan said he used to respect cadres such as Chengren, whom he would address as "Uncle" whenever they met. This gradually changed after Shoukuan began working for the production team, however. He recollected:

> At that time, I was young and energetic. At school I often served on the sports committee. I liked to move. But after I started working for the production team, how could anyone bear such strict management? Everything had to be controlled. That guy Chen Lin, it was like if he couldn't show his power if there was one thing he didn't control. For instance, one time I sat with my legs crossed while eating in the canteen. Now what does this have to do with him? When he saw it, he said I was lazy. It wasn't like I was being lazy at work! Why does it matter if I'm lazy while eating? Later when Chengren came back from the commune, it was even worse. He was the brigade party branch secretary, but sometimes he would manage our production team. He was even stricter, and his attitude was worse. Cheng Lin would just scold you verbally, but Chengren often got physical. One time we were digging up sweet potatoes in the Eastern Hills, and one old man took a break to smoke. When Chengren saw it, he grabbed the man's pipe and said, "Everyone else is digging, so how can you just sit here and relax? Can't you dig and smoke at the same time?"

Shoukuan, feeling severely unfree, began to detest the brigade and team cadres, often expressing discontentment toward them while chatting with Shoude and others around the same age. Shoude, who had always been more stable than Shoukuan, often warned him against speaking too freely lest he become "the bird that was shot after sticking its head out." However, when Shoukuan complained that Chen Lin was not punished properly for corruption during the Four Cleanups, Chengren got wind of it. In 1965, when Chengren took the "outlying land" of Team One (to which Shoukuan belonged) and reallocated it to Team Ten, Shoukuan finally became "the bird that stuck its head out," and Chengren threatened to arrest him (*faban*) as a "bad element" (*huaifenzi*).

Shoukuan said that after hearing the slogan "it's right to rebel," he felt truly happy. He said, "I had already grown tired of watching the Faction in Power (*dangquanpai*). Now even Chairman Mao was saying we could rebel, that it was right to rebel, and that excited us." He therefore quickly became a Red Flag militiaman. When Chengren announced that he too belonged to Red Flag, Shoukuan urged Shouyi and Shoude to criticize and struggle against him. "Chengren was a typical (member of the) Faction in Power, don't fall for their gimmicks." But Shouyi and Shoude felt that Red Flag should also study Mao's theory of "the united front," that it was better to have more allies than enemies. Shoukuan thus had to abandon the idea of attacking Chengren.

On the eve of the July 16th Incident in 1967, Shoukuan learned how to make hand grenades and volunteered to serve as a grenadier. Looking back on his memories, Shoukuan said:

At the time, the production team had some gunpowder leftover from a construction project. I mobilized a few helpers to gather pebbles on the riverbank, and we also smashed a few bottles. I stuffed the gunpowder, glass shards, and pebbles into empty wine bottles, inserted fuses, and we had homemade grenades. We made about a dozen. Looking back, this was actually pretty dangerous. The pebbles were ok, but with glass shards, if you attacked someone at close range, it would be lethal. Thank goodness I didn't hurt anyone, otherwise I would have regretted it for the rest of my life. At the time I didn't really think about it. We were crazy, just thinking about how the Faction in Power always controlled us so strictly and took away our freedom. The East Wind faction supported them (the Faction in Power), so we really wanted to blow them all up.

On July 16th, when Shoukuan discovered that Cheng Village's Red Flag members had become surrounded by the East Wind Faction of Duqiao Residential Committee, he grabbed the grenades and charged. When he reached the wall of the government compound, he was stopped by someone pointing a gun at him. When the gunman and the grenadier saw each other and realized that they had been classmates in middle school, each retreated. In retrospect, Shoukuan said, "Chinese people still cared about emotional bonds. Although we belonged to different factions, we couldn't hurt an old classmate." During the second charge, Shoukuan threw two grenades, smoke rose to the sky, and most of the Red Flag members fled back to Cheng Village. Later, he saw that several members, including Shouyi, had failed to make it back in time, and he prepared to attack the market town again, but Shoude and others stopped him. For a while, they thought that he had killed a member of East Wind, so they detained Shoude until it was confirmed that the man had actually died from a gunshot wound. Decades later, when former Red Flag militants discussed Shoukuan's "heroic feat," they still praised his valor, saying they might have suffered a fatal loss without him.

After the incident, Chengren, Chenggong, and the other brigade cadres continued to govern as strictly as before, although they did not dare to pick on Shoukuan as they had before. Shoukuan said that henceforth he became disillusioned with political struggles, since nothing had changed except that Shouyi ended up becoming an official.

Shoukuan said, "When cadres govern strictly, if it's within reason, everyone might support it. But if it's not reasonable, everyone just acts one way to the cadres' faces and another way behind their backs." By "within reason," he meant that everyone should have enough food to eat. To illustrate the limits of what was reasonable, he gave the example of sweet potato theft. One time in 1970 when Shoukuan was stealing sweet potatoes from the field, he was observed by a villager with whom he had been in conflict, but the latter did not report him to the authorities. On another occasion, Shoukuan and another villager both happened to be stealing sweet potatoes at the same time. When they saw each other, almost simultaneously both said, "You're here too?" While recounting the story, Shoukuan commented, "In order to live, people need to eat. If even farmers can't eat, what kind of society is that? If stealing food is considered theft, what kind of law is that?"

In response to Shoukuan's words, Shoude provided a more detailed explanation:

> It's not theft if you just steal 1 yuan's worth of sweet potatoes, but if you directly steal 1 yuan in cash, then of course it's theft, or if you steal a towel, that's theft too. Even if it's food, you can't steal too much. For instance, if you steal 100 *jin* of sweet potatoes at one time, then that's actually theft, and if you're found out, not only do you have to return the loot, you'll also be punished.

Shoukuan felt, however, that Shoude's explanation was not rigorous enough:

> If it's a situation where no one has enough food to eat, it's not right even just to steal a little food. Like what Chen Lin did was wrong: At that time everyone was on the verge of dying from starvation, so it wouldn't have been right to steal even a little, and he stole so much. By the early '70s, there wasn't that kind of scarcity, but these cadres still insisted on managing everything so strictly—that was unreasonable. They were just "foxes pretending to be tigers," worried that people didn't fear them enough. They made it so that we didn't have an ounce of freedom.

By the mid-1970s, there was no longer any food shortage at all in Cheng Village. The villagers also had a great degree of freedom: They could raise poultry on a household basis, and during the slack farming seasons they could apply to buy their duties to the production team with cash and instead use that time on sidelines. The purchase of team duties was calculated on the basis of ten work-points a day for able-bodied workers (most men and some strong women), with their cash value determined according to the team's budget for the year as a whole. According to Shoukuan, however, it was precisely at this time that villagers' complaints about the cadres proliferated, mainly targeting their strict management.

When I asked if he felt that the cadres were unfair to the other team members, he replied, "Of course this happened, but that wasn't the main problem. The main problem was that we had no freedom." He said the cadres allotted themselves a few extra work-points, and when it came time to work, they would pick favorites. Under the "task-contracting" (*ding'e baogan*)[1] system, they would arrange for their own family members to use the best tools, the newest hoes or sickles. People felt this was unfair, but it was not a big deal. The most unfair behavior was the sort of thing where Chen Lin had taken more than his fair share of sweet potatoes, but that had already been dealt with during the Four Cleanups. Then later, when Shouyi embezzled public funds, that was considered unfair, but he was punished for that, after all.

Shoukuan felt that what ordinary team members wanted the most was more freedom, whereas cadres such as Chengren and Chenggong may have wanted more power. The conflict deepened, therefore, and the trend toward decollectivization (*dan'gan*) became unavoidable. On this, he commented:

> Have you heard of "dawdling on the job" (*mo yanggong*)? That's when everyone works slowly and leisurely, not expending much energy, just riding the clock. At that time, other than the Wutong River diversion, in places like Cheng Village, the water conservancy projects that needed to be built had all been built long ago. But in the winter, they still made us go out and work, digging ditches and whatnot. They didn't need so much labor-power to do little things like that. But if you didn't go, they wouldn't give you work-points. If you had a sideline, you also had to pay the team in cash. So of course everyone dawdled. What I disliked the most was, even if you could dawdle, you still had to show up at work on time, you couldn't oversleep. Why couldn't Chengren just let us get some rest? He just couldn't bear to see us rest. During the busy farming seasons we did "task-contracting," so why couldn't we do that in the slack season? I liked being able to start and start work on my own schedule, wasn't it enough if we just got the work done? But no, he wouldn't let us. You know, if they had been a little more relaxed about management in those days, I bet there wouldn't have been so many people who felt it was unfree and wanted to decollectivize and farm individually.

Shoukuan said that, although he was not very successful at farming on a household basis after decollectivization, during the last years of the People's Commune system he belonged to the group of people who strongly wanted the freedom to farm individually. About this, Shoude urged him several times to keep his mouth shut lest he commit a "mistake of political lines," for which he might get in trouble in some future campaign.

Struggling

In Shoukuan's memory, the 1980s was the most pleasant period of his life. He described it as "like a person who had been in prison for a long time finally being released, and suddenly feeling that the sky and earth were boundless, and that my spirit was at ease."

When the farmland was split up among the households, Shoukuan and his wife had three sons, so they received nearly two *mu* as "responsibility fields." His two younger brothers had both already married and had children. According to local custom, their elderly mother Ms. Mai should live and eat together with Shouzhong, but considering her friction with Shouzhong's wife—who was interested in new ideas and wore bell-bottom trousers—in

1986 the three younger brothers decided she should move in with Shoukuan and merge her fields with his.

Shoukuan was famous in Jiangbei for his farming skills, and he was especially hardworking. In addition to growing enough food for the household to eat, he could also sell about 1,000 *jin* of grain each year. This income, however, was not at all sufficient to cover their expenses.

Shoukuan therefore took the carpentry skills he had learned making boats for the brigade and applied them to manufacturing other types of wooden products. Compared with Shouyi, however, Shoukuan could only make enough money from carpentry to supplement his household budget—not at all enough to save up anything. His biggest problem was obtaining lumber, since he had no acquaintances or strong enough connections at the tree farms nearby, so he was often unable to buy wood. Lack of funds also prevented him from expanding the scale of his production. On many occasions, when he finally managed to find an opportunity to buy wood, he did not have enough money for it. In addition, when it came to selling the products, most of his acquaintances were poor or just middling, so their purchasing power was limited. Sometimes, after he had completed a set of furniture, many days would pass before he managed to sell it. The speed of his sales and cash turnover was thus completely dwarfed by Shouyi's business. As a result, although Shoukuan was one of the first people in Cheng Village to take up carpentry as a profession, his income remained about the same as that of other villagers. It was not until the early 1990s that Shoukuan had finally accumulated enough savings to purchase power tools, such as a chainsaw and a planing machine. By that time, however, many other villagers were already using power tools for carpentry, plus new styles of furniture were growing popular in the Pearl River Delta, rendering his furniture old-fashioned, so it became harder to sell it for a good price. Shoukuan therefore quit the trade before he had even made back all the money he had invested in equipment.

As Shouyi saw it, the fact that Shoukuan was still practicing carpentry in the early 1990s showed that he was too inflexible. His own principle, he said, was that if other people could do something, then he would not do it. During one conversation with Shoukuan, however, the latter rejected this idea:

> Of course what you're saying is right, but the problem is, who doesn't want to do what other people can't? I don't want to do what other people can do, but what other choice do I have? For example, you and I are both carpenters, you use power tools, I want to use them too, but where could I get the money to buy them? Besides, even if I had the money, I don't have connections, so I still couldn't get enough lumber. Same thing with slaughtering buffalo—if you didn't have the money you earned as a carpenter, how could you go into the buffalo business?

Nevertheless, Shoukuan's carpentry skills still helped to improve his life. In those days, when villagers built houses, they needed to set up wooden scaffolding, known as "installing the frame" (*zhuangmo*), and then wrap the scaffolding in steel mesh and pour concrete over it. Since Shoukuan was particularly skilled as a carpenter, and he was especially hardworking and honest, so many villagers would hire him for this kind of work. At the same time, in addition to practicing carpentry, Shoukuan would also do odd jobs for these villagers: wrapping the steel mesh, mixing and pouring the concrete, and so on. He said, "In the '80s, I almost became a '10,000-yuan household'—almost, but not quite."

The new-style blue-brick house his family built in 1973 was already old, and it had only one floor. In 1989, therefore, he began planning to build a new red-brick house to help his eldest son, Jingzu, seek out a marriage partner. In order to save money, Shoukuan and his wife, Feng Lan, decided to perform all the work they could on the house themselves. They molded and fired their own red bricks by hand, going down to the Wutong River to dredge up clay and pebbles and then hauling them back home in a cart. They also dug the foundations, laid the walls, and installed the frame. As a result, by 1991, only one story had been built, but according to the standards of the day in Cheng Village, at least two stories were necessary.

Perhaps due to working too much over the years and not taking sufficient care of her health, in 1991 Feng Lan came down with a severe case of rheumatism. She sought out treatment in both Western medicine and traditional Chinese medicine, spending over 4,000 yuan on medical fees, but still saw no improvement. Due to this illness, they stopped working on the house halfway through. Late one night shortly thereafter, Jingzu rode his bicycle home after drinking alcohol at a friend's house. On the provincial highway, a motorcycle crashed into him and then fled the scene. The accident broke both his legs and his right hand, costing over 6,000 yuan in medical fees. Over the next few years, Feng Lan and Shoukuan's mother, Ms. Mai, took turns falling ill, together costing five or six thousand yuan, and the family's economic situation continued to decline. In 1993, Jingzu got married. He and his wife both went to work in cities such as Zhongshan and Zhuhai, finally completing the second story of their house in 1998.

Like many other villagers, Shoukuan also considered raising pigs as a path to wealth. Due to insufficient funds, and fear that he could not prevent the pigs from getting sick, he was not willing to take the risk at first. In 1993, however, after quitting the carpentry trade, he finally mustered the determination to try raising pigs. He took the little money his family had saved up, borrowed another 500 yuan each from his brothers Shoushu and Shouzhong, and then purchased six piglets. A few months later, they got sick, four of them dying after the Duqiao veterinarian managed to save the other two. When he sold the two pigs at the end of the year, he found that even excluding labor and the feed he had grown himself, he had still lost several hundred yuan. After that he did not dare to raise pigs on a large scale again, instead just raising one a year, as most other villagers did. In 1999, he stopped raising pigs altogether, when he realized that the Duqiao market had been flooded with industrially produced pork (and that traditionally produced pork would only sell for the same price), so it had become completely uneconomical for ordinary peasant farmers to raise pigs at home. No one in Cheng Village was raising pigs in the traditional way anymore.

Shoukuan also raised honeybees, and he still raises them today. On the Duqiao market in 1985, natural honey sold for 5 yuan per *jin*, about the price of 5 *jin* of pork. By 2013, the price had risen to 70 yuan per *jin*. It is said that honey has always fetched a good price, yet Shoukuan never managed to grow rich through this trade. The main reason was that he just raised them at a small scale near his house, so it was impossible to expand the scale or the area where the bees could collect nectar. There were also rice fields nearby, so every year when the rice flowered, many of the bees would die. (Pesticide would be sprayed on the rice, poisoning the bees when they collected nectar from the rice flowers.) In normal years, he collected under 20 *jin* of honey. Some of that would be consumed at home or given to friends and relatives as gifts, and the rest could only be sold for enough money to cover the cost of Shoukuan's tobacco. He reckoned that if he spent a few months each year raising bees deep in the hills, they would easily yield 600 or 700 *jin* of honey. He knew a beekeeper in Fan County who, like Shoukuan, had begun learning the trade in the late 1970s with the help of the *Beekeeping Guide for Workers, Peasants, and Soldiers*. The two of them often communicated, and this friend gradually earned enough money from raising bees deep in the hills to build reinforced concrete houses for each of his four sons, so Shoukuan thought many times about doing the same. These thoughts never came to fruition, however, as he explained:

> The first reason was my family's circumstances. When I was young, I was the main source of labor in the family, since my wife's health was poor. Our three sons had to attend school, so I couldn't give up farming for beekeeping. Although we only had a small amount of farmland, it was that land that held me back. Once the boys had grown up, they weren't willing to farm, instead they either went out to work, or they did a sloppy job when they did help out with the farming. Later, I had to take care of my grandsons. The second reason is that I was afraid of taking risks. Although my experience raising bees at home showed there was no problem with my technique, when it came to turning this into my main source of income, I was still a bit wary that my skills weren't up to that level. Another thing is that, often when farmers leave the land (i.e., stop farming), their minds become unsettled. Farming provides stability.

Shoukuan once mentioned that 2000 was the only year when he might have gotten rich. That year, Shoukuan took his entire savings, borrowed another 3,000 yuan from relatives, and started a chicken farm. In order to reduce costs, he partnered up with a boss who also ran a longan orchard. Shoukuan was put in charge of guarding and managing the 50-some *mu* orchard, and in return, the boss allowed him to raise chickens under the trees, and to keep them in the orchard's barn overnight for free. Half a year later, after Shoukuan had harvested the fruit, he borrowed 5,000 yuan from the boss to expand production by buying another batch of chicks and feed. He promised to pay him back a month later after the first batch of broilers had been sold. At that point, Shoukuan's youngest son Jingye volunteered to take care of buying the chicks and feed. That night, however, Jingye went out to play cards with several "fiends" in the market town, and he ended up losing all 5,000 yuan. Afraid his parents would beat him, he did not even return home, instead going straight to Dongguan to look for a job. After Shoukuan had sold the broilers and repaid the boss, he was almost broke and had no choice but to abandon the farm. Upon telling this story, he said:

> With a prodigal son at home, you can't succeed at anything. I worked so hard raising those chickens for over half a year, but all I had to show for it was over 3,000 yuan in debt to several relatives.

Shoukuan once said wistfully:

> Life is over in a flash, in the end I haven't accomplished anything, still tending these 2 *mu* of wet-rice fields and 0.4 *mu* of dry-crop land, only a little more than "1.3 *mu* of land" (an expression referring to a family's internal affairs, here suggesting the bare minimum of land necessary for survival).

Other than farming a little rice, Shoukuan devoted the great majority of his time to growing vegetables. His three sons were all out working, so all the family's land was available for him to farm. He discovered, however, that although it was often reported on television that vegetable prices were rising, prices in Duqiao never changed significantly. The surrounding cities, such as Wucheng, Tongcheng, and Fancheng, had all developed specialized greenhouse vegetable farms in their suburbs, and vegetables from as far away as Shouguang, Shandong had appeared in those cities' supermarkets. Cheng Village's vegetables were mainly sold on the Duqiao market and to a few stone-processing plants nearby. Since the peasants who stayed behind to farm in Cheng Village, Xujiao, and several other villages in the area focused most of their energy on growing vegetables, Duqiao often experienced gluts. Every year, many of Shoukuan's vegetables rotted in the fields. Vendors from elsewhere occasionally came to buy vegetables in Duqiao, but often the prices they offered were low. One product that gave farmers in Cheng Village a slight advantage was Chinese mustard greens (Ct. *gai choi*), since this regional variety was particularly well-known in Guangzhou, so its price was a little more stable. Unfortunately, output was limited for traditionally grown greens due to their seasonality. Shoukuan therefore earned almost no money from vegetable farming.

172 *An Ordinary Peasant*

Regarding his life since decollectivization, Shoukuan said, "If I had to describe it in one word, I'd say 'struggling' (*zhengzha*)." He complained:

> My wife and I couldn't have worked any harder if we'd tried, but every time the family seems to be doing a little better, one thing happens or another that pushes us back down so we're just gasping for breath.

Fairness

In the process of "struggling," Shoukuan said, "It's true that peasants are free, but now this society isn't very fair to us."

He often said that peasants regularly lost money if they depended on selling vegetables, even without natural disasters. If they did not grow vegetables, instead growing only rice, they would lose out even more severely. Rural vegetable vendors and urban wholesalers and retailers, however, were ensured a stable income without going into debt, regardless of droughts or floods. One day in the summer of 2012, Shoukuan invited me to help him carry a shoulder-pole of greens to sell at the Duqiao market. We and several other vegetable farmers tried to calculate the costs of growing vegetables, but it was hard to come up with answers. First of all, inputs such as pesticide, fertilizer, and seed were not all purchased at one time, and the prices fluctuated, so their costs were hard to calculate. Secondly, the prices of vegetables fluctuated even more from day to day, so the income was scattered and extremely unstable. The vast majority of vegetable farmers could only say in general terms that income from growing vegetables was only sufficient to cover everyday household expenses, so it was something done by "the elderly, young children, the sick, and the disabled"—able-bodied young adults would not stay home in the village to do it. Vendors, however, could calculate costs quite clearly, endlessly coming up with reasons to lower prices when they were buying vegetables. Here is a paraphrased summary of the key information:

> An ordinary vegetable retail stall in Guangzhou was often run by two people, husband and wife. Their monthly gross income was usually over 9,000 yuan. Their costs included wastage of vegetables that went bad, rent for the stall, a management fee for the market, and household expenses (if their children could not be cared for by their grandparents, these expenses would be even higher), leaving about 3,000 yuan in profit. This required making sure that they netted over 300 yuan each day from the differential between the prices of purchase and sale. If they sold 100 *jin* of greens each day on average, they needed to raise the price 3 yuan per *jin* to net 1 yuan. In order to maintain the average retail price for greens, which had been about 6 yuan for the past few years, the wholesale price had to be lower than 3 yuan. The wholesale market normally skimmed off a differential of 30 to 40 percent, paying the vendor about 2 yuan. After subtracting the costs of transport and wastage, and the vendor's

own earnings, the vendor could pay the farmers no more than about 1 yuan per *jin*, or even lower.

One vendor bought Shoukuan's lettuce and Chinese flowering cabbage (Ct. *choi sam*) for 0.5 and 0.65 yuan per *jin*, respectively, picking only the best specimens and leaving several *jin* of subpar greens for Shoukuan to take back home. Just a few days prior to this, at a budget market near Sun Yat-sen University (in Guangzhou), I had observed the same two varieties selling for 4 and 5 yuan, and they would have fetched even higher prices at more upscale markets. Shoukuan took a puff on his pipe and chuckled bitterly that he had long grown accustomed to such experiences, but he still complained:

> This guy makes a buck, that guy makes a buck. What about us who grow the vegetables? We don't even make a dime! Everything they sell to us is expensive: fertilizer, pesticide, seed—which of them isn't expensive? Everything we sell to them is cheap. As soon as we earn just a little bit from selling vegetables, before our pockets are even warm, the prices of fertilizer, pesticide, and seed have gone up, and it's gone. The cost of labor isn't even counted. If you did you'd basically feel you'd worked for nothing at all—even more unfair. Besides all that, these fields are getting worse and worse. You have to add fertilizer and pesticide every day just to keep up the output. It's like with a women: If she keeps taking chemical supplements every day to have more babies, after a while won't her body get weak? That's how it is nowadays with the fields, trying to squeeze every last drop of nutrients and water out of the soil. But the problem is, even high yields are useless: As soon as vegetable prices fall, aren't you back to square one? ... As long as you're a peasant, there's nothing that can be done. If you don't farm, someone else will do it, and they'll do it at a larger scale, pushing the prices down even lower than yours. But what can you do if you don't farm? Even if you see clearly how unjust it all is, you still have to walk this path into the darkness. It really is so unfair.

Regarding the market's unfairness, besides the problem of buying dear and selling cheap, Shoukuan complained even more about the troubling quality of the things he bought. Of these, what he found the most irritating was Sanlu brand powdered milk and baby formula.

In the fall of 2008, Shoukuan saw on television that Sanlu brand dairy products contained the industrial chemical melamine, which was causing major harm to children's health. At the time, Shoukuan's second son Jingzong and his wife were working in Zhuhai. Their second child, a son, was only three years old, and Shoukuan and Feng Lan had been taking care of him at home for over a year. The powdered milk that Jingzong and his wife had bought for the boy turned out to have been produced by Sanlu. Panic-stricken, Shoukuan went to Shoude's house and used his phone to call Jingzong, asking him to come home immediately and take the child to be examined in Guangzhou.

Fortunately, the doctor said there were no apparent problems, maybe because the boy did not drink large amounts of the milk, plus he regularly ate plenty of greens and coarse grain. In telling this story, Shoukuan joked with a hint of sarcasm, "To put it bluntly, it was our poverty that helped us dodge that bullet." But Jingzong corrected him, saying, "You make it sound like poverty is a good thing. Rich people don't even drink domestic milk, they go to Hong Kong and buy (international brands)." After that, Shoukuan no longer gave the boy powdered milk, instead roasting rice, grinding it into flour, and mixing it with water to make a paste for him to eat. Shoukuan blamed Jingzong and his wife for being duped by TV advertisements into thinking powdered milk would be good for the child:

> Why should (we) believe what these fake foreign devils say? That powdered milk will make (children) smart and healthy? In the past no one drank milk, but that didn't make them any less intelligent, and if anything, we were stronger. Look at these children today: Every one of them is stupid and fat. If you want children to be smarter, the main thing is to educate them. Advertisements are just for deceiving idiots. What they say is ridiculous: that if you want your children to be more competitive than others in the future, you have to start when they're babies, or even when they're still in the womb. Rich people feed their children foreign milk; this is already social inequality. Plus their kids' education is better and, when they grow up, their job opportunities, marriage prospects, and living conditions are all better. You idiots believe those people do well in society just because they drank milk when they were kids, that it was nutritious and made them smart. These unscrupulous bosses act with no conscience at all, putting poison in the milk, and then turning around and deceiving you idiots, saying, "Drink this and your children will be smart." ... In an unfair society, how can intelligence help you anyway? Now on TV everyone talks about *pindie* (competition based on one's father's power, wealth, or reputation). Even if you're smart, you still can't outcompete them, so what's the point of poisoning your children with powdered milk?

In Cheng Village, quite a few people expressed that Shoukuan was one of the most good-natured and light-hearted people they had met, but to everyone's surprise, this incident enraged him. Even when the topic came up several years later, in 2012, he was still condemning the people in charge of Sanlu for being "cruel and merciless." He felt that all lives were of equal value, and if a life was taken, a life should be given in return, so those sorts of people should be executed as murderers. Instead, the court just sent them to prison, and that was unfair. He even predicted that "these people will just pay someone off and waltz on out of prison early to continue enjoying their pleasant lives."

In other matters, even if Shoukuan felt they were unfair, his criticism was more restrained. One day in August 2012, while chatting in the watch repair shop, Shoukuan said that Shouyi's buffalo slaughtering business was relatively fair, but his dealings in the furniture and antique businesses were not. Shoukuan's reasoning was that with the furniture he had depended on his connections to purchase lumber on credit, while other carpenters could not buy it even with cash in hand. As for the antiques, he depended on swindling people, and that was dishonest. Shoukuan also felt that Shouyi's sexual exploits were unfair. Pointing to Shouyi, he said to me and Shoude:

> He always says he paid for it, but that's not fair either. How is it fair for a crusty old man like you to (have sex with) a pretty girl in her teens or twenties? Some things just shouldn't be bought and sold. As long as there's money involved, it's not fair.

When asked why, he explained:

> People are people, they're not ordinary things. People shouldn't be bought and sold. You can't just say anything can be bought if you have the money. If so, then what about a person's hands, feet, or head? Wouldn't society collapse into chaos? If you can just do anything as long as you have enough money, how could that be fair?

Shouyi defended himself, saying that what he bought was neither the girls' hearts nor their bodies, but just a kind of service, a kind of labor, and the body was just its external form. Shoukuan, however, persisted in his perspective:

> A body without a heart is not a person, it's an animal, a skeleton that has become a white-boned demon (*baigujing*). What you're buying is neither a service nor labor—it's an animal, a skeleton. You're taking living girls and treating them like animals or skeletons. Of course it's not fair. They're supposed to be humans just like you.

Of course, this argumentation did not have any effect on Shouyi's behavior. Shoukuan actually believed, however, that although such transactions were not fair, at least Shouyi was spending his own money. Although the way he earned his money was somewhat unfair, at least it seemed much less unfair than what Chengxin had done: selling collective wealth, embezzling public funds, using his power to obtain help from others in raising tangerines, and eating the fruits of their labor. Even so, Shoukuan felt that at least Chengxin's way of doing things was more fair than the vice-chief of the police department's domineering and avaricious behavior. And, without a doubt, even township cadres such as the vice-chief of police could not hold a candle to the greed, lust, and bullying of officials such as Chen Shaoji (former chairperson of Guangdong's Provincial Committee of the Chinese People's Political Consultative Conference), or Liu Zhijun (former head of

176   *An Ordinary Peasant*

the Railway Ministry). On the one hand, Shoukuan said, "With people like these, how could this society be fair?" But on the other, he noted:

> At least they're not stealing food directly from my bowl, they're eating their own meat. Ordinary people like me can drink the soup in our own bowls. As long as we can get by, everyone can spend their days as they see fit. The well water doesn't affect the river water.

In the autumn of 2013, during a conversation with me and Shoude about life experiences, Shoukuan said that everything since decollectivization has been good except for social injustice. As he was wont to do, Shoukuan compared examples from the collective era with the present in order to illustrate how society was more fair back then, and how it was unfair today. Shoude interjected, "Society wasn't fair to intellectuals back then," asking Shoukuan, "Could it be that you want to return to that era?" Shoukuan replied:

> No! Who would want to do that? But if you want to talk about unfairness toward intellectuals like you in those days, it wasn't that bad. Every era has something unfair about it, they're just unfair to different people.... Although I don't want to return, I do miss its fairness. Unfortunately, we weren't free then. We peasants want both fairness and freedom. Now it seems hard to have both at the same time. If you can't have it both ways, (I guess I would) prefer freedom. But if it gets to a point where we can't survive anymore, then I believe people will choose fairness.

Shoude replied:

> China has never been fair. As long as peasants can survive, (our) hearts can endure it. Throughout history this has become a habit. But other than the time of the first emperor Qin Shi Huang (in the third century BCE), there has never been as unfree a time as the collective era. The peasants' hearts couldn't endure it.

Shoukuan said Shoude was "being overly dramatic, but it did seem to make a little sense."

The Three Religions

Shoukuan felt that in his late years he had become like Lu Xun's character Runtu, believing in "the Three Religions and the Nine Schools of Thought."[2] When he was younger, however, he had been a "materialist." When asked why, he explained:

> I remember when I was young, my dad didn't really believe in mystical things. I'm not sure if that was due to my mom's influence. My mom was a

Christian, so she didn't believe in any spirits other than "the Lord." Later, during the collective era, everyone said we had to overthrow feudal superstition, so his belief in such things decreased. Even my mom no longer dared to say she believed in God. What I learned in school was materialism, then after leaving school there were (various political movements). So when I was young I really didn't believe in spirits.

The first time Shoukuan began to believe a little in "mystical things" was when he was trying to father a son. When he married in early 1966, he was already 25, an age considered "late youth" in Cheng Village at the time. (His father had passed away in 1962, so Shoukuan had helped raise his two younger brothers, who were still children at the time. That was the main reason his marriage had been postponed.) His mother, Ms. Mai, hoped to have a grandson within a year, but Feng Lan showed no signs of pregnancy. Ms. Mai secretly prayed about it on several occasions, but to no avail. At first, Shoukuan did not care, even criticizing his mother for being impatient. In the summer of 1968, however, he too began to grow anxious. He took Feng Lan to visit two doctors of traditional Chinese medicine that people had recommended, who told Feng Lan to drink herbal medicine to adjust her body. At the same time, old people close to Ms. Mai gave them some suggestions. Shoukuan recalled:

> They said, "If you want to have a son, you need to pray to the great-grandfathers and Guanyin. If you do as your mom does, not even worshipping the great-grandfathers, cutting off the incense fires, then how could they bless your own incense fires?" They also said that Guanyin was in charge of birth, and we could not afford to disbelieve in such things. I thought maybe they were right. I cast all caution to the winds, "trying to cure a dead horse" (resorting to desperate measures) and decided to pray. It's funny now that I think of it—just a year earlier I had been a Red Flag commando.... At the time I couldn't find any religious icons. With the "destruction of the Four Olds," no one dared to keep such things in their homes. So I just got a piece of wood and used an ink brush to write the words "Bodhisattva Guanyin, Savior from Suffering." The writing was all crooked. I thought, "Oh well, that's the best I can do. It's the thought that counts.... Guanyin will understand."

Although Ms. Mai did not approve of Shoukuan praying to the ancestors and Guanyin, she did not stop him. Half a year later, Shoukuan discovered that his piety had moved the ancestors and Guanyin: Feng Lan was finally pregnant. In 1969, she gave birth to Jingzu. Although Shoukuan did not dare to say much about it, he had come to believe in sayings like "the ancestors bless our good fortune" and "there is Buddha in the world." As for Ms. Mai, since she had become a grandmother and received the grandson she had wanted, she was overjoyed and no longer spoke of the contradiction between the Lord and the Buddha, merely sighing, "fate has been good to us."

Whenever Shoukuan thought back to details about that period of his life, he could not suppress a smile. Once when chatting with me in 2009, he happily drew a circle in the air with his pipe, saying that he had followed the same procedure to father two more sons in 1972 and 1975. Although he never received the daughter he had prayed for, he was quite confident in the effectiveness of praying to the ancestors and bodhisattvas.

After decollectivization, like other villagers, Shoukuan began to worship the ancestors and bodhisattvas openly. He was one of the first residents of Jiangbei to make the pilgrimage to the temple in Fan County. He was even earlier and more active than Shoude in helping organize relatives for clan branch activities such as the processions paying homage at their ancestors' graves in Tongcheng. Particularly during the first procession, several of the main organizers felt they should revive the pre-1949 tradition of riding boats into Tongcheng to the sound of gongs and drums. Shoukuan took an active role in the preparation, volunteering his carpentry to repair five or six old wooden boats. When too many people expressed interest in going, he also rented a big iron dredging barge to help carry everyone into the city. In the 1990s, he gradually withdrew from such clan activities due to his family's economic difficulties.

From 1990 to 1991, Feng Lan was often sick. Besides taking her to see doctors of both Western and traditional Chinese medicine, Shoukuan also prayed that the bodhisattvas would help improve her health. At the same time, Daoist monks and mediums (*shenhan, shenpo*) "serving all manner of spirits" were invited to their house, some of them treating Feng Lan directly, others "purifying" the house. Shoukuan said that each visit cost between several tens and over 100 yuan. The couple also suspected their home's *fengshui* was inauspicious, so they sought help from a geomancer. The geomancer said the problem was that the front gate's orientation had too much "negative energy." Following his recommendation, Shoukuan dug a little pond at the entrance of their new house and hung a one-sided mirror from the gate to block the energy. But these measures proved ineffective: Feng Lan remained ill. On Christmas Eve of 1991, Ms. Mai convinced her daughter-in-law Feng Lan to convert to Christianity. Shoukuan's attitude remained, "Let each believe as they will, as long as neither party interferes with the other." In the extended family headed by Ms. Mai, both of Shoukuan's younger brothers and their wives believed, like him, in the "the Three Religions and the Nine Schools of Thought." This attitude was also mainstream throughout Cheng Village.

Shoukuan said that in contrast with many "hypocritical" Buddhists in the village, however, he never sought to achieve wealth through prayer, instead praying only for health, safety, and good fortune. I know that he was referring to villagers who prayed every day to Guan Gong and the Kṣitigarbha Bodhisattva in the hope of winning the lottery. Even one drug dealer in the village prayed to statues of these two entities at home and sometimes visited a famous temple to Longmu (the Dragon Mother) on the upper reaches of the Xi River in order to seek help from that goddess as well.

In 1994, Jingzu and his wife gave birth to a son, and Shoukuan and Feng Lan attached great value to this first grandson. Although they were poor, Shoukuan insisted on conducting a respectable son-adding fireworks (*tianding shaopao*) ceremony.

In the region, the second day of Month Two of the traditional lunisolar calendar is "Son-Adding Day" (*tiandingjie*). All families that gave birth to sons in the previous year are expected to conduct fireworks ceremonies. (Poor families that want to conduct the ceremony in a more dignified manner than they can afford at the time can wait one or two years, but normally it has to be done before the son's third birthday.) The host family organizes a banquet, inviting friends and relatives, and places a specially made "rocket" firework on the grain-sunning ground in front of the temple. A red envelope is attached to the tail of the rocket, and after it is shot into the air, everyone scrambles to catch the envelope as it falls to the ground in the hope that their wishes are granted and they achieve good fortune. Whoever catches the envelope not only gets to keep it but is also fated to become the newborn boy's "distinguished person" (*guiren*), who will attend another banquet for that purpose. The host family also gives the distinguished person a rooster and two bottles of liquor. Even if the person who catches the envelope is on bad terms with the host family, the two parties are expected to set aside their differences. Anyone unwilling to do that is considered "ignorant of social mores" (*bu dong shi*) and contemptuous of all males in the host family's clan branch.

According to Shoukuan, this holiday demonstrates that "adding a son" is a family's most important event. (Shoude confirmed that this understanding was correct.) Shoukuan recalled that during the ceremony organized for his grandson in 1995, Jingzu was out working to repay loans for building their house, and the family had no money. Before the Chinese New Year, therefore, Shoukuan slaughtered the pig he had been raising and sold the meat, except for a small portion the family ate during the holiday. From this they earned over 1,200 yuan. He then enclosed 1,080 yuan in the red envelope for the fireworks ceremony, signifying, "May the distinguished person prosper" (Ct. *yiu yan faat yan*, which sounds similar to 1–0-8–0, Ct. *yiu ling baat ling*). I was told that in those days, that amount of money was considered above average, although the family was rather poor. Jingzu paid for the banquet, and the rooster given to the person who caught the envelope had been raised for this purpose by Shoukuan over the previous eight months.

Later, after several more grandsons and granddaughters had been born, Shoukuan and Feng Lan "became more and more like pre-school managers." Although Jingzu and his wife had their own house, it was basically empty throughout the year, while Jingzong and his wife did not even build a house. When Ms. Mai passed away in 1998, Shoukuan cleared out her room for Jingzong and his wife to use during their visits home. This one-story blue-brick house with four rooms normally housed Shoukuan, Feng Lan, and five grandchildren. Whenever one of the grandchildren fell ill, they would take them to the doctor, but Feng Lan would also pray to her Lord, while

Shoukuan would pray to Buddha and the bodhisattvas, and even to wells, rocks, and trees.

One summer day in 2010, I noticed ashes from incense and spirit money under a banyan tree near Shoukuan's house. On the tree there was a piece of red paper with the words, "Emperor of Heaven, Emperor of Earth, my home has a boy who cries all night, if you happen to walk by, please pray that he sleeps until sunrise." Shoukuan explained, "My youngest grandson hasn't been behaving, so I'm indulging in a little superstition." Several days later, he again hired a medium (*wenxianpo*) to work her magic on the grandson. This woman in her fifties rubbed the boy's hand, seemed to convulse (a young villager told me this showed that she had been possessed by a spirit), and said that half a month earlier she had been in a place with a lot of water, where she had become terrified and lost her soul (*hun*). Shoukuan thought for a moment and then said that two weeks ago he had taken the boy to work in the fields next to the Wutong River. The medium took a little sack of rice, added some tea leaves to it, stepped out of the house, and began sprinkling the mixture on the ground as she walked to the riverside, chanting as she went. Then, continuing to sprinkle the rice and tea leaves, she began to sing loudly, "God and Goddess of the River, your hearts are kind, I sing this song for you, please repay our offering and bring the boy back across the water... ." Finally, Shoukuan gave the medium a red envelope with 68 yuan inside as payment.

At first, Feng Lan disapproved when Shoukuan resorted to such services. After many days of prayer to no avail, she agreed to let him give it a try, while insisting that she still did not believe in such things. I once went to the Cheng Village Clinic and talked to the doctor who had treated the boy. He said that this sort of problem is normally caused by calcium deficiency, but there had been no obvious improvement after the boy had taken calcium supplements for a few days. Instead, he thought it may have been caused by heat and humidity, so he prescribed herbal medicine to adjust the boy's spleen and stomach. If that still failed to solve the problem, he recommended that Shoukuan have Jingzong come home and take the boy to a hospital in the city. About a month later, Shoukuan happily exclaimed that his grandson was doing much better, "the medium worked!" Feng Lan protested, "How do you know it wasn't the doctor that cured him? ... In any case, at least he's better." Shoukuan agreed, "You're right, it doesn't matter. I don't care which of the Three Religions or Nine Schools of Thought it was, as long as it worked."

One God

In Shoukuan's eyes, his mother, Ms. Mai, was the "seed" that initiated the spread of Christianity in Cheng Village. The religion first arrived there in the late Qing dynasty with the construction of the Duqiao Church of the Gospel, but very few peasants converted at the time. According to him and several older villagers, in the late 1940s there were only a few old women in the village who were Christians. In 1951, the chapel was confiscated by the government, and in 1956 it became a warehouse for the Supply and Marketing Co-op. Shoukuan said his mother may have been the only villager who persisted in her beliefs, and even she did not openly practice due to the political circumstances.

In the early 1980s, the local government implemented a religious policy that brought the church under the management of the Wu County Bureau of Religion, allowing it to resume religious functions, with overseas nationals who had returned to the area attending services there. Ms. Mai belonged to the first batch of locals who began participating in activities at the church upon its reopening. Throughout the 1980s, however, very few people participated in those activities, especially among the peasants, Ms. Mai being the only one from Cheng Village. She tried to convert her three sons and their wives to the religion, but none of them agreed. She also proselytized among other villagers, particularly middle-aged and older women, but to no avail.

In 1991, Feng Lan and her son experienced a series of misfortunes. Shoukuan's brothers and cousins were all preoccupied by their own household affairs and did not provide any substantial help. Other villagers felt this was normal "in this new era." Throughout all this, only Ms. Tai "helped" Feng Lan every now and then by saying that if she believed in God, "He" would think of a way to solve her problems. At first, Feng Lan was not convinced, thinking, "God was a foreign (Ct. *gwailou*) deity, so how could he catch Chinese ghosts and cure Chinese people's illnesses?" After trying almost every method of exorcism that local people could think of with no success, however, Feng Lan finally suspended her disbelief and went to church with her mother-in-law. In recalling this event, she said:

> Normally, if you're in good health, you've got endless work to do every day, so it's hard to devote half a day to go to church. At the time I was in poor health and couldn't work anyway, so I went with my mother-in-law a few times. To my surprise, after a while my joints really weren't aching as much. I thought, "This really works (*ling*)," and then I began to believe.

In 1998, Ms. Mai also convinced Shouzhong's wife, Ms. Zhang, to convert. Ms. Zhang's initial motivation was to help her son quit gambling. When Ms. Mai was on her deathbed, she had told Ms. Zhang that it was a family misfortune to have a grandson addicted to gambling, that it was the work (*zuosui*) of Satan, but if they worshipped God then He could stop the devil. Years later, the young man was still gambling, often stealing the family's property and selling it to pay for bets. Not only did Ms. Zhang embrace Christianity, however, she even became active in proselytizing. She explained that she believed her son would quit gambling eventually, but maybe God felt the time was not ripe yet, and until that time, at least her prayers could help decrease his sin. Since the family was poor, Shouzhong got a job as a sanitation worker in Duqiao's market town, but after two years of that he fell ill and died. Once while accompanying Shoukuan on a visit checking in on Ms. Zhang, Shoude asked, "Could it be that he contracted some kind of disease after handling garbage without a facemask for so long? Maybe we could try asking the township government for a little compensation." Ms. Zhang rejected this proposal, however, insisting that her husband's death was "God's will," that He was testing her faith. When her son failed to come up with even enough money to organize a simple funeral for his father, some villagers scoffed at him. At that point he finally summoned the determination to quit gambling. To Ms. Zhang, this could be seen as proof of God's "effectiveness" (*lingyan*), as well as a practical comfort that strengthened her faith.

In 2010, Feng Lan and Ms. Zhang also convinced Shoushu's wife, Ms. Lian, to convert to Christianity. Ms. Lian had often poked fun at her two sisters-in-law for "pretending to be mystical" (*zhuang shen nong gui*), once even leading to an altercation with Feng Lan. In 2010, when the bridge across the Wutong River collapsed, most villagers were unwilling to ride a motorcycle half an hour across the other bridge downstream in order to tend their fields on the other side, so they just abandoned them. Shoushu's family was particularly poor, however, so they continued to farm there. One day on Month Seven of the traditional calendar, as Shoushu was punting a raft across the river, he fell in and drowned. Several villagers felt that some kind of supernatural force must have been at work, since he had been the best swimmer in the village. Others said this was a common natural phenomenon, and although he was a good swimmer, there were other factors involved: First, he had not punted a raft across the river for many years. Second, so many barges had been dredging sand from the river illegally over the past few years that the riverbed as full of deep holes creating whirlpools. Third, that day Shoushu had been drinking, so it would have been likely for his muscles to have become cramped after falling in the water, and the other villagers were taking siesta at the time, so no one was able to save him. Ms. Lian, however, was more attracted to the supernatural explanations, saying that she often had nightmares about her husband wearing clothes that were dripping with water. After her two sisters-in-law urged her to convert, Ms. Lian quickly adopted Christianity, and soon her nightmares ended.

After Feng Lan's conversion, she and Shoukuan began growing apart in various ways. Shoukuan said that he basically had no free days throughout the whole year, yet every Sunday Feng Lan managed to go to church. On Christmas and Easter, she did not do any farmwork or housework, instead going to participate in activities at the church. Sometimes she would suddenly go out for church events at other times as well. When it came to eating, Shoukuan said he always had to eat in a hurry in order to make time for work or taking care of the grandchildren, starting to eat even before the table had been set, but Feng Lan always wanted to wait until she had said grace before slowly starting to eat. Shoukuan said he did not object to any of this, that he could adapt. What he did object to, somewhat, was when Feng Lan would bring ten or twenty women home for events. While we were chatting one day in the summer of 2012, Shoukuan said:

She doesn't always go to the church for events, sometimes they hold them at parishioners' homes. That's why they talk about "parishes" (*pianqu*)—Cheng Village is one of the church's parishes. In villages without so many Christians, several villages are combined within one parish. Some events are not at the church but internal to each parish, usually held at the parish director's house. So they used to go to Shoude's house, since his wife (Cheng Ju) was the director for this parish. I mean his house in the village, not the watch repair shop. The past few years they've been going to Shouyi's house, since his wife (Cheng Xiu) became the new director, and their house is bigger, with such a big courtyard. Look how small my house is, as soon as they show up there's not even room to sit down. My mother became a Christian early on, and so did (Feng Lan), so sometimes they come here. When they do, they're here for half the day, and I have to take care of the grandchildren while also helping to entertain the guests, so none of the housework can be done. It's not that I don't support them, though. People only come to your house if they respect you.

Despite such complaints, Shoukuan was always enthusiastic about hosting Feng Lan's friends from church, and in everyday life, Feng Lan respected Shoukuan's authority. In this respect, male chauvinism (*dananzizhuyi*) was particularly pronounced in their household. On many occasions, while Shoukuan was chatting with me or someone else and Feng Lan would come and ask him about something, or remind him of something that he needed to do, he would reply impatiently, "Why can't you do it yourself?" or "Can't you see I'm talking to guests?" or "Why are you always gabbing?" When that happened, Feng Lan would usually just turn away silently and go do something else.

Similarly, I asked several of the Christian women, "Who should be in charge of the household?" Almost all of them said the husband should be in charge. Only a few women said, "Either (husband or wife) could be in charge, depending on which one is more reasonable or capable." In reality, however, things were not as they said. During villager team discussions of public affairs such as the installation of tap water or township requisitioning of village land, I noticed that every household representative in attendance was a man, without exception. Even decisions pertaining to production, such as what kind of crops to grow, when to plant them, and what brand of seed, fertilizer, or pesticide to buy, were all made by the men of these Christian households, including Shoukuan and Feng Lan's. When it came to the production process itself, however, most of the farmland in Cheng Village was used for growing vegetables, and most of the actual work was done by women.

In Shoukuan's household, sexism was also evident in their interactions with relatives. Although when Feng Lan wanted to express disagreement with Shoukuan over some matter, she would say that both God and Chairman Mao called for gender equality, when it came to major events such weddings, like other villagers, she unconditionally participated in all events involving

Shoukuan's relatives within five generations, also maintaining cordial relationships with those affinal kin in normal times (giving gifts and granting favors), outside of those events. Toward her own consanguineal kin, however, she only maintained relations within three generations. As for funerals, she attended the ceremonies for everyone in Shoukuan's clan branch, but toward her natal family, she only attended funerals of relatives within five generations. When it came to everyday mutual aid, such as helping out with the construction of houses, the couple said they had to help Shoukuan's relatives within the "five degrees," but only Feng Lan's consanguineal relatives within three generations. And when the clan genealogies were updated, Feng Lan and their daughters-in-law and granddaughter were only included in the records of Shoukuan's clan branch (and not in those of her father's).

Like Ms. Mai and other Christians in the village, Feng Lan preferred boys to girls, believing it was worth violating Family Planning policies in order to give birth to a boy if necessary. She and Shoukuan estimated that one-third of the families in Cheng Village and Duqiao Residential Committee had had over-quota births in order to parent a boy. Feng Lan even said candidly, "Only boys count toward carrying on the family line." For that reason, she fully supported Shoukuan organizing expensive firework ceremonies for each of their grandsons, despite the family's poverty at the time. Some of the other Christian women reservedly expressed contradictory sentiments, such as Ms. Zhang, who said "As long as they're born, both boys and girls are good… but boys are still a little different."

Feng Lan also told me that, with a very small number of exceptions, other Christians in Cheng Village still placed great value on the ancestors. The difference from ordinary villagers was that the Christians did not burn incense, spirit money, or other "articles for use in the afterlife" (*mingyongpin*) such as paper clothes or houses. They did, however, "honor" (*jisi*) the ancestors with prayer and "offerings" (*jipin*) of food, alcohol (or non-alcoholic beverages), and fruit before dinner at the beginning and end of the lunisolar year. Feng Lan explained:

> Of course Christians respect the "great-grandparents," it's just that in the West they use flowers whereas our ancestors are more accustomed to alcohol and fruit, but it's the same idea as offering flowers. When we speak of "worshipping" (*bai*) great-grandfathers, it means the same thing as "praying" (*daogao*)[3] for them.

As far as the clergy of Duqiao Church of the Gospel was concerned, what Feng Lan said was clearly wrong. She was aware of their opinion, so she said, "Don't tell the people at the church about this." They were actually not unaware that this was a common phenomenon among rural Christians, but they just said, "There's no way around it, they won't change even if you talk to them about it." In the summer of 2012, one member of the clergy told me that he had criticized Feng Lan for not being pious enough. This was because her house faced a road, and in order to block the road's "negative energy," Shoukuan had followed a geomancer's advice and installed a tile inscribed with the words "Mount Tai Exorcism Tablet (*shigandang*)" on the corner of the wall. The clergy member felt that Feng Lan should have made Shoukuan knock down the tile, but she did not do this.

According to the clergy's standards, most of the Christians in Cheng Village were "impure" in their conduct. During weddings, for example, several young Christians would hold banquets in their clan temples in addition to the wedding ceremony in the church. These banquets involved basically the same rituals as those of other villagers, except for the omission of bowing to red candles and praying to Heaven and Earth. A few Christians even told me that the reason they had embraced the religion was to ask God to change their "bitter fate" (*kuming*). When I visited the village in the fall of 2010, I also noticed that when Christians such as Feng Lan and Cheng Ju discussed a series of abnormal deaths that had occurred in Jiangbei a few years prior, they would use terms like "karmic response" (*bao*), even saying that the concept of karma was consistent with the Bible.

Nature and Fate

Many villagers had good reason to describe Shoukuan as "optimistic" or "having an accepting and positive attitude" (*huoda*). Regarding his family's poverty, he would often say, "In this life, we can't avoid tasting the sour, the sweet, the bitter, and the spicy." Once while chatting with me the summer of 2012, he said sighed:

> We're just travelers passing through this world, with no idea where we came from before birth or where we're going after death, but that time must be much longer than this life. Our different fates in this world are determined by our different essential natures (*benxing*). For example, my nature is to be honest and simple (*laoshi bajiao*). Same with my two younger brothers. I'm not an obsequious bootlicker (*pai mapi*), so I lost out during the collective era. I won't act against my conscience, so I lost out after decollectivization. I knew I would benefit from (licking boots and acting against my conscience), but I couldn't do it. Lack of ability (to be obsequious) is part of it, and (my) essential nature (to be honest and simple) is another part of it... . If you want freedom or fairness, that's also in a person's nature. If your nature is to think (people) shouldn't be free or (treated) fairly, then you won't feel unfree or (treated) unfairly. If your nature is this way, you'll try to do things in this direction, so your fate will develop in this direction. We often say "doomed by fate." This (expression) is both right and wrong. As far as I see it, half of a person's fate is determined by their previous lives, but the other half is determined by their actions in this lifetime. Your nature determines your fate, so if you can grasp hold of your nature, haven't you determined half of your fate?

It was at this point that I finally understood why Shoukuan had often used the term "essential nature" to explain the events that had befallen him and people around him. In his eyes, it was also Feng Lan's nature that explained why she had gone from a believer in the Three Religions and Nine Schools of Thought, like him, to a Christian. He said, for instance:

> It's in her nature to rely on others. Women are all like this: They rely on their husbands, but if their husbands aren't capable, and if the government (*guan laoye*) can't be relied upon either, then they turn to gods (*shenxian laoye*), and if Chinese gods don't work out, they turn to foreign (gods). If they've exhausted other options and there's nothing else they can rely on, then they believe in the latter (i.e. become Christians).

Shoukuan even believed that the deaths of Shoushu and Shouzhong were to some extent caused by their essential natures. He did not seem willing to discuss this in much detail, simply saying, "They were just too honest and simple, unable to be flexible." Shouzhong "didn't know how to look after himself," being unhealthy but never doing anything about it, to the point that up until his death he did not even know what sickness it was that ailed him. Shoushu was "too rigid": When everyone else had abandoned their fields on the other side of the river, he persisted in farming his, plus he failed to pay attention to safety, "like a child who never grew up."

In addition, Shoukuan used this principle of "one's nature determining one's fate" to provide a detailed explanation of two other famous cases in Cheng Village. The first concerned the story of Cheng Chengyou raising his little brother Chengbang, and the latter repaying this kindness by taking care of Chengyou's son Nanshan. This was the same Nanshan who had often met with punishment by "ascending the longan tree" in the 1960s-1970s. In 1983–1984, Chengbang helped Nanshan to build a two-story red-brick house. Since Nanshan was already past the ideal age for seeking a marriage partner, his progress in "forming a household" did not proceed smoothly, and his parents and friends thought he might remain single for the rest of his life. In early 1987, at the age of 37, he married a 31-year-old woman from the same hamlet, Nantang. (Some villagers said it was for health reasons that she too had passed the ideal age for seeking a partner.) By the end of that year, she had given birth to a son. (Two years later she also mothered a daughter.) Due to her advanced age, Chengbang again provided funding so she could go to the Wu County People's Hospital and give birth there. (At the time, it was still unusual in Cheng Village for women to give birth in hospitals, considering the expenses involved.)

In 2002, Chengbang retired from his post in the Guangdong Provincial Government, and shortly thereafter his wife did the same. Of their four children, two were working in the United States, one in Hong Kong, and the other in Guangzhou. Chengbang continued paying the tuition for both of Nanshan's children to attend school, from primary all the way up through

An Ordinary Peasant 187

college. In 2008, Nanshan's son graduated from a certain railway vocational college, and Chengbang used his connections to help him obtain a job at a certain rapid transit company. In 2010, Nanshan's daughter graduated from vocational secondary school, and Chengbang again used his connections to help her obtain a clerical position at a certain foreign-invested enterprise in Dongguan. Over the past few years, Chengbang and his wife have been living between the United States and Hong Kong, having Nanshan and his wife take care of their home in Guangzhou. They even pay them a basic living stipend, so when Nanshan and his wife return to Cheng Village, they treat it as a vacation.

Many villagers regard the life experiences of Chengyou and his son Nanshan as a typical example of "karmic rewards for good deeds." But why did they perform good deeds in the first place? Shoukuan believes this can only be explained by their essential natures, with good natures giving rise to good fates.

The other case Shoukuan used to explain this theory was related to his nephew Cheng Jingjun. Jingjun joined the army in 1977 and served in the Sino-Vietnamese War of 1979, where he received a medal for meritorious service. After being discharged and returning to Cheng Village, Jingjun won the approval of other villagers through his diligence, ability to endure hardship, and flexibility of thinking. He was also generous and eager to help other villagers. On occasion he even dared to stand up and speak on behalf of peasants who had been treated unjustly by the township or village cadres. The cadres, for their part, were willing to treat him with respect since they felt he had seen the world and received military honors. In Cheng Village, therefore, especially Jiangbei, Jingjun enjoyed a great deal of popularity and some degree of prestige. His wife was also rather kind, and villagers considered her a "good person."

Besides growing rice and vegetables in his fields, Jingjun also contracted the use-rights to a plot of hilly woodland for planting bamboo, and he engaged in the buffalo business, purchasing calves to raise at home until they were old enough to sell. In 2000, he withdrew from these sidelines, rented a piece of uncultivated land, and converted it into a fishpond, also building a small chicken farm nearby. Two years later, he rented another patch of woodland for planting tangerines. In 2007, this orchard produced over 20,000 *jin* of tangerines. Many villagers felt this type of operation would be nearly impossible for two farmers to run on their own. They figured that Jingjun and his wife must truly be hardworking and healthy. As it turned out, however, Jingjun fell ill with severe hepatitis. After this was discovered in 2007, he spent nearly 200,000 yuan on medical fees at a special hepatitis hospital in Guangxi, but he still ended up dying before the end of the year. According to the doctor's analysis, the disease may have been related to Jingjun's working too hard and drinking too much alcohol over the course of many years.

Whenever this topic came up, many villagers would say wistfully that although Jingjun and his widow were good people, their fates were bad—as was the *fengshui* of their home, in all likelihood. Even the widow felt this way, although she also insisted that the doctor's explanation made sense too. Later, when their two daughters left the village to work, Jingjun's widow sold the fishpond and chicken farm, focusing her energy on growing rice and vegetables and managing the orchard in a painstaking effort to make enough money for her son's tuition at a foreign language school in Tongcheng. In 2010, her son graduated and went to work at a foreign-invested enterprise in Dongguan, and the family's situation began to improve. Two years later they demolished their old house and built a three-story red-brick one. At this point, other villagers said, "good people are rewarded, after all."

Shoukuan also believed in fate and karma, but he felt that fate was not entirely determined by one's previous lives. One day in the summer of 2009, for example, he pointed out that Jingjun's illness was related to his inability to control his essential nature:

> His nature was too forthright (*haoshuang*), so his personality was restless (*zao*). He spoke in a deep and raspy voice, and he did everything like there was no tomorrow (*bu yao ming*), with a belly full of impulsive energy (*manli mengzuo*). Of course this was bad for his health. He also drank like there was no tomorrow, over a *jin* (half a liter) of liquor at a time for three meals a day. How could drinking like that not damage one's liver? His life was partly hooked by King Yan (God of the Underworld) and partly by his own actions. His nature was just too forthright, plus he'd served in the army and fought in a war, so he fancied himself something like a bandit... . His heart was kind, and he was a sincere and loyal person. I figure his descendants will probably reap the rewards (of his kindness).

In the fall of 2011, ran into Jingjun's son and daughter on their way home to Cheng Village, and we talked about preparations for the construction of their new house. Later, I mentioned this to Shoukuan and others, and he commented, "Didn't I say his descendants would reap the rewards?"

Shoukuan was not the only person who believed that one's nature determined one's fate. Many middle-aged and older villagers also felt that this idea was reasonable. Even Shouyi, who normally placed special emphasis on individual abilities and believed that his wealth derived mainly from his "brains," also agreed with Shoukuan on this matter. Shouyi said that the main reason he could enjoy good fortune was that his nature was not bad, and although he made money from others, it wasn't "money earned with a guilty conscience" (*kuixin qian*), and even less was it "money earned with a dark heart" (*heixin qian*). (He seemed to have forgotten that two days earlier in Wucheng he had said that he had a "guilty conscience" about his sexual activities.) He gave the example of a man from Duqiao Residential Committee with experiences similar to his own, including participation in the armed struggles of 1967, where he too played an important role. In a battle with the "rebel faction" of a neighboring county, this man had killed someone who was kneeling on the ground begging for mercy. The case was never investigated. In the 1980s, the murderer became one of the first people in the area to get rich, like Shouyi. In the 1990s, however, his family encountered a series of misfortunes: Shortly after his daughter was married off to distant Henan, she divorced; his elder son became epileptic and disappeared, then his younger son came down with dementia; the man himself died young from cancer. Shoukuan commented:

> This man was truly cruel by nature. The person was already kneeling on the ground, begging for mercy, yet he still didn't give him a break. How hard his heart must have been, how cruel. As a result, his evil deeds led to karmic retribution for everyone in his family. If he hadn't acted so cruelly at the time, things might not have turned out so badly.

While we were discussing what had happened, Shoukuan said that although "one's nature is harder to change than the rivers and mountains," it is not completely impossible to change: As long as a person's heart turns toward the good, the person's nature can also change for the better. Besides, he kept emphasizing, the world is fair, every action has its appropriate effect (karmic reward or retribution), so "When we talk about unfairness, actually in the end there is fairness. In the end everyone dies, the question is how they die." Shouzhi, who was also part of this conversation, agreed with Shoukuan but purposely teased him, "When why hasn't Sanlu received retribution for its powdered milk?" Shoukuan replied in a serious tone:

> There will be justice in the end, for sure. It's just that the time hasn't come yet. The way it is now, you poison me, then I poison you. Don't think only the rich can poison people, earning money with a dark heart, and that no one can turn around and poison *them*. I don't believe the rich all have "exclusively provisioned" (*tegong*) rice, vegetables, oil, water, and even air. Unless they all flee to America right away before they're affected too deeply by the poison, and then never come back, they can't escape it either, right? If your nature is bad and you hurt others, then you also hurt yourself. This is determined by fate, you can't escape it. Even if they flee to American, they can't escape it, it's just a matter of time.

On many occasions, therefore, Shoukuan insisted that his "honest and simple" nature was actually a good thing, even though it also led to his fate of poverty. A few days later, I saw him carrying a shoulder-pole of chopped greens, preparing to dump them out, and I asked why. He explained that he had planned to sell them, but then he found out that the "low toxicity" pesticide he had been using on them was fake. When they were cooked, the color and smell were wrong. He sighed:

> In the past when we said "fake pesticide" we meant that it didn't kill pests. Now "fake pesticide" means that after it kills the pests, the vegetables

can kill people too. The hearts of these people (producers of fake pesticide) are so bad, don't you think? Their natures are even more toxic than this pesticide—they'll die young... . If your pesticide kills people, you too will meet with retribution and die young, for sure. Just consider me unlucky. I'm not going to sell these vegetables, I'll just use them to fertilize the fields. Even if it makes me poorer, I'm not going to compromise my nature. Oh me, I guess this is just my fate.

I noticed, however, that many middle-aged and older villagers, including Shoukuan, would sometimes explain the relationship between "one's nature" and "one's fate" in a different way. Often when I ran into them working in the fields and greeted them by asking, "Still at it?," they would reply to the effect of, "There's no way around it, we peasants were born with the fate of working. We're so used to work that it feels wrong if we don't do it." Many of the people who said this were from relatively well-off families. According to Shoukuan's theory, this seemed to be a case of "fate determining one's nature."

Notes

1 Shoukuan explained that after the implementation of "the three rights and the four fixed (factors of production)," during busy farming seasons, in order to motivate team members to work harder, each team assigned a certain number of work-points to a certain task, which was then contracted to certain team members on a voluntary basis or by drawing lots. Work-points were calculated through democratic evaluation. For example, digging ordinary dry-crop fields was normally paid 10 work-points per half *mu*, but if the soil was particularly hard to dig, they might pay 12 work-points per half *mu*. Since the tasks and work-points were already set, those with better tools could save energy and time.
2 *Translator's note*: Runtu (闰土) was a character in Lu Xun's 1921 short story "My Old Home" (故乡). The Three Religions (or "Teachings") are Confucianism, Buddhism, and Daoism. The Nine Schools of Thought are the most influential nine of the "hundred schools of thought" from the Eastern Zhou period (eighth to third century BCE). Here, however, this phrase denotes the indiscriminate worship of various supernatural entities without any systematic religious belief or practice.
3 *Translator's note*: This word for prayer (祷告) is mainly used by Christians. In other contexts throughout this book, the English word "prayer" is also used to translate non-Christian words such as *bai* 拜, but here *bai* is translated as "worship" in order to highlight the distinction Feng Lan is making between Christian and non-Christian terms.

7 The Younger Generation

Investing

In contrast with the older generations, the life experiences of younger villagers were quite different. Their footprints and horizons extended far beyond the Cheng Village. Most of those I encountered in my research, however, in one sense or another continued down the path forged by their parents and grandparents, so could be considered a "sequel" to the story of their elders.

In this sequel, villagers saw Cheng Fudao as carrying on the "legend" of his father Shouyi in the manner of a celebrity. Although in their eyes, Fudao was a "big boss" (Ct. *dai lou*) with all the money he could want, he often expressed anxiety about his lack of capital. On several occasions he said that by the time he had entered the stone-processing industry in 2000, he was already ten years behind the really big bosses, and so remained stuck at the least profitable segment of the production process.

Historically, Wu County already had a tradition of stone processing. In the 1980s this shifted to more decorative work, but the equipment remained traditional. In the early 1990s, a few township and village enterprises and private bosses that already possessed sufficient capital, began to import processing equipment from abroad, vastly improving productivity. At the same time, as the Pearl River Delta's construction sector developed rapidly alongside the quality of interior finishing, the stone processing industry expanded dramatically. By the late 1990s, those bosses who had been the first to amass large amounts of capital began to import stone materials from abroad, processing them and selling the products to markets all over the world.

When Fudao joined the industry, the biggest ten or so bosses already controlled the most profitable lines. First, Fudao explained, natural stone imported from abroad would be processed into slabs between 8 and 27 square meters each (known in the industry as *huangliao* or "slabs"), which would be used as material for further processing by other enterprises down the line. When this natural stone was cut, sometimes it would be found to contain flaws or even to be useless, so this segment of the production chain was particularly risky. Second, such slabs would also be imported from abroad to Customs, from where they would enter the domestic wholesale market. Periodic fluctuations in the market and various Customs procedures sometimes led to overstock, posing risks to capital turnover. Third, large waterjets were used to cut slabs into semifinished products. Waterjets were expensive.[1] Fourth, some enterprises took leftover stone from these other processes, pulverized it, and pressed it into flagstones. This process required a large investment and sophisticated technology. Fudao admired the profitability of these lines, and these entrepreneurs were often members of the Political Consultative Conference or the People's Congress of Wu County or even Qi Prefecture, so whenever they needed help from the government, things proceeded smoothly. However, insufficiency of funds prevented Fudao from ever hoping to compete in those lines.

In 2000, the craft of cutting stone with smaller waterjets began to be adopted in Wucheng's stone processing sector, but these required more investment and skill than the use of electric saws. Fudao did not even have enough money to use small waterjets for more profitable lines such as carving statues or flooring patterns, as his wife's brother did, so instead he just produced ordinary decorative items such as flagstones and stone strips. He often lamented that his financial situation limited him to watching idly as opportunities brushed shoulders with him. In 2009 he finally invested 2 million yuan on two waterjets, but even then, he could only work on small-scale projects.

From 2000 to 2005, Fudao and his wife's brother would process semifinished stone they bought from big bosses in Wucheng. When it came to selling their products, at the time they had not yet formed their own network, so their business was never very strong.

> There was a little profit, but not much. Each year we would gross less than a million yuan, but after taxes and expenses like buying a house and a car, treating clients to restaurant meals and playing cards with them (deliberately losing as a way to give them kickbacks), hardly anything was left.

In 2006, Fudao and his brother-in-law began to purchase slabs wholesale, directly from the Xiamen stone market. They would then transport the slabs back to Chengjiao Township in Wu County, cut them into flagstones, and sell them as finished products. That same year, the Pearl River Delta's real estate sector began heating up, creating enormous opportunities for Fudao. By that time, Fudao had accumulated experience with everything from enterprise management to securing orders, and his marketing network was beginning to expand. Although he mainly dealt only in ordinary construction materials with lower profit per item than large-scale waterjet carvings, therefore, he managed to earn considerable profit overall, as long as he could maintain a large enough sales volume. Over the following years, his factory finally managed to begin netting over a million yuan each year. At this point in the conversation, Fudao's father Shouyi added:

It was more like 1.2 to 1.5 million yuan, to be precise. We don't normally quote this number to anyone else. We Cantonese try to maintain a low profile when it comes to business. We don't like disclosing it publicly. Only in silence can you make the big bucks. Especially in the presence of an official, we would just say we make five or six hundred thousand. Over that, we'd have to pay more taxes.

Fudao pointed out, however, that sometimes while discussing business with a client, they might do the opposite, since only by exaggerating their assets and profits could they obtain more orders, or better orders. "In short," he said "less out is more in. This is different from what you professors say, that 'one plus one equals two'."

In running the stone materials factory, Fudao continued upholding Shouyi's principle, "Don't mix kinship with business." Fudao adopted a trendy online manner of speaking to explain, "Do things according to the laws of market economy, do things according to the requirements of the laws of capital accumulation." From 2000 to 2013, Fudao never hired anyone from Cheng Village to work for his enterprise, except for one middle-aged woman from Nantang whom he hired as a cook. He said that migrant workers from Hunan, Sichuan, Guizhou and Guangxi were willing to work for lower wages, they were obedient, and, since they were working outside their place of residence, they did not dare to "act up" (*tiaopi*). If he hired local villagers, however, although their relationship would be clear, it would always be hard to avoid the admixture of other elements, so it would be more complicated to deal with them than with strangers. For example, he said:

Here (in my factory) I never make unreasonable demands for overtime or rushing to complete an order in time, and normally the management is meticulous, with clear operating specifications, so we've never had any accidents that caused injuries. But we still need to take precautions just in case. If something like that happened, outsiders (non-locals) would follow the government's procedures, "using public methods for public affairs" (*gong shi gong ban*), so it would be easier to deal with. With local workers it would be more complicated. I have a friend (who owns the factory) across the street (from mine). Two years ago, two workers there sawed their fingers off. In dealing with that, it was clearly more complicated with the local worker than with the outsider. It's not just that (the owner) had to pay higher compensation to (the local worker), (he) also had to buy gifts and (visit the worker and their family) in the hospital and at home, not just once but many times... . (This is true) also when it comes to everyday management. If there's a rush or you're short on labor, locals may deliberately choose that occasion to say they have something to take care of at home and ask for leave. Then you're in trouble no matter if you grant the leave request or deny it. If you deny it, (you'll be seen as) unneighborly and it will hurt your reputation—it won't sound good when people start talking about it. If you agree, then you won't be able to hand over the products according to the terms of contract, so you'll offend the client and have to pay compensation, but that's just your own problem and doesn't affect the worker.

According to Fudao's analysis, the only employee who could be easily substituted at a moment's notice was the cook. If the cook suddenly asked for leave, you could just order food from a restaurant. This was why the cook was the only worker he hired from Cheng Village.

In the factory, Fudao was mainly responsible for going to purchase materials in Xiamen and to deal with clients and obtain orders in the Pearl River Delta, so he was out of town for about half of every year. His wife was mainly responsible for bookkeeping, everyday management of the workers, and dealing with certain clients who came to pick up their orders from the factory. Fudao paid two Hunanese workers the high wage of 8,000 yuan per month to carry out technical operations and equipment management. Ordinary workers responsible for polishing, cleaning, etc., were paid between 2,000 and 4,000 depending on their level of familiarity with the work (or sometimes they were paid at piece-rate). In recent years, there have usually been about ten employees working at the factory.

Fudao's successful investment not only brought him wealth but also changed his life. He said:

> When it comes to dining, for example, I used to never drink alcohol or eat chili peppers, but after over ten years of "experience in battle" (*jiu jin sha chang*), now I can eat your (Hunanese) "steamed fish head with pickled peppers," and Sichuanese "beef boiled with peppers." And now I drink alcohol several times a week, even more on holidays. You know, we ordinary Cantonese people don't normally make a fuss about drinking, never pressuring others to drink, much less playing drinking games. But things are different when it comes to business *yingchou* (socializing for the purpose of developing connections or asking for a favor). If you're treating a (state) official to dinner, then it's even more (intense), with drinking games and imported liquor. You know in Duqiao if we drink at all it's usually just a little rice wine. Now all (we in business circles) drink is cognac. I bet it's fake nine times out of ten.... As for sleep, in the countryside I never went to bed too late, but now I'm in the habit of going to bed at one or two in the morning, and then sleeping until nine or ten. I've completely become a night owl. There's no way around it—this is how *yingchou* works.

When I asked why there was "no way around it," Fudao said the main reason was that the scale of his business was "neither big nor small." This scale of business could resolve problems related to materials, sales orders, labor issues, taxes, land use, and even environmental issues only through extra-institutional, "flexible" means, to some extent or another. If the business were bigger, he could "drink red wine in a refined manner, go to bed early every day, get up early and practice t'ai chi, and have subordinates do everything else." If the business were smaller, on the other hand, it would not require so much *yingchou*.

Fudao also mentioned several unsatisfactory things about his investment in stone processing. First, after 2006, many big bosses in the industry began to invest in real estate, and then quite a few bosses operating at about the same level as Fudao simply withdrew from the industry and put their wealth into real estate as well. When he bought his third residential property in the second half of 2006, the average price of housing in Wucheng was only 1,600 yuan per square meter, but by the next year, it had doubled. By the second half of 2012, it had risen to 6,500. During a conversation that fall, he estimated that the profit rate for real estate investment was at least twice that of ordinary stone processing. He said with a bit of chagrin:

> I've not heard of anyone in this industry (stone processing) whose assets have repeatedly doubled over the past seven years... . I can say without exaggeration that at least half of Wucheng's real estate sector is in the hands of bosses from the stone industry. The big bosses speculate in land, the middle bosses in construction, and the little bosses in housing. At the time I was just too simple and honest, thinking I had only just established a foothold in stone (processing), so I should keep my feet on the ground and continue with that. I had already bought three properties in Wucheng, all duplexes of about 200 square meters. My plan was to live in one and give the others to my sons. That was still the thinking of a peasant smallholder (*xiaonong siwei*): to buy a house and live in it, without thinking of it as an investment or speculation. I was already a little boss, but my thinking wasn't liberated enough to make big investments. All I could do was piddle around and make enough money to afford two meals a day.

Fudao finally consoled himself by saying, "people can make plans, but the results are up to Heaven. You can only have what you're fated to have." When I pointed out that he had already made plenty of money, he laughed, saying, "No one complains that they've got too much money. It's like with opium: The more you make, the more you want. There's no end to it."

Fudao also lamented that as his business grew and his network of connections expanded, he had more friends but those he could really talk to truthfully grew fewer and fewer. He once told a friend:

> We used to say a relationship would become as solid as iron after two men "shouldered rifles together" (originally referring to comrades at arms, but here to paying for sex together), but now, when it comes to matters of competition in business, (forming bonds in this way) doesn't seem to make any difference (they are still just as cut-throat toward one another).

At the same time, he emphasized that on many occasions, it was still necessary to "treat" business contacts (to service from a sex worker) in order to foster trust, even if it was bound to be limited trust. Sometimes this type of *yingchou* took place so frequently that he lost all desire to participate. His wife knew what was going on, to some extent, but she said, "Revolution depends on one's own initiative. Nothing will ever be accomplished just by trying to control others." At the same time, she said that even if she could not control Fudao's *yingchou*, if he went so far as to get a mistress (*ernai*), she would divorce him and take their sons with her, along with half his property. What both husband and wife cared about but had no time to control was the two sons' education, with which they had no choice but to ask the grandparents on both sides of the family to take turns helping out. Fudao said, "Children these days are hard to handle... . I'm really a little bit afraid of the saying that 'a family's wealth can't survive beyond three generations'."

Shouyi's first and second daughters each opened a garment factory in Tongcheng, the first with a total asset value over 20 million yuan, the second about 2 million. The third daughter worked in her eldest sister's factor as a manager, relying on the salary to support her family. On multiple occasions, Shouyi pointed out that only his third daughter had graduated from high school, while his other three children had only graduated from middle school, explaining to me, "This proves that school is important, but too much school is no good. That's how we Cantonese people are: We don't care about formalities, only what's practical. People with too much schooling have to come work for us... ."

Working

For most young people in Cheng Village nowadays, the only option is to *dagong*: to leave home and look for a job on the labor market.[2] Shoude's second son Jingdao, his daughter Jingsi, her husband Chen Sheng, Shoukuan's eldest son Jingzu, and Shouzhi's son Jingshan and his son-in-law Li Sheng all belonged to this enormous group of villagers.

Jingdao was born in 1968. After graduating from high school at Duqiao Secondary, he "played" at home for over two years, then in 1990 went out to work. His first stop was Xiaolan Township in Zhongshan, where he worked at factories in the footwear, garment, and hardware industries, saving up a little money in the first few years. According to his recollection, his pay at the athletic footwear factory was 800 yuan for each of the first three months, a probationary period after which it rose to 1,000 yuan per month. (At the time, Jingdao's high school teachers in Duqiao made only between 500 and 600 yuan a month.) Lodging was included but workers paid between 7 and 8 yuan per day to eat in the factory's cafeteria. Since they often had to work overtime, Jingdao rarely had occasion to spend money, at most going out once a week to watch a movie at one of the small VHS cinemas (*luxiangting*) popular at the time, for 3 to 5 yuan. In this way, he could save up 600 or 700 yuan each month. After a year and a half, he left the shoe factory to run a sewing machine at a garment plant. Looking back at that time, he said:

> I switched jobs at the time for two main reasons. One was that overtime was too intense at the shoe factory. Usually, we had to work every night but Sundays, and other than that, we were working all the time that we weren't eating or sleeping, fourteen hours a day or even more. Overtime pay was calculated at a piece rate, so the more you worked the more you earned, but normally this came out to only 2.5 or 3 yuan per hour. The second reason was that while working (at the shoe factory) I had to stand all the time, and after a while I felt I just couldn't handle it. I only managed as long as I did because of my youth—no way I could do that today. You Northerners (Ct. *loujai, loumui*) are tough, but it's hard for us Cantonese people (Ct. *lougwong*). My co-workers from Hunan, Sichuan, Guizhou, and Jiangxi could get by sleeping only three or four hours a night during rush orders, but I just couldn't keep doing that. Nowadays this kind of (factory) is called a "sweatshop," but already at that time I felt that the job was not fit for humans. Although the wages were pretty good, that kind of job was just not for me.

Jingdao's wages at the garment plant were about the same as at the shoe factory. Before long, he began feeling extreme discomfort from sitting in one place about fourteen hours every day. Before the year was out, therefore, he switched to the hardware factory, where wages were lower, but he was somewhat freer to move around at work.

When he returned to Cheng Village for Tomb-Sweeping Day in 2011 and was recounting his experiences working in the early 1990s, Jingdao said:

> It was really just too hard at that time, I can't find the words to express it. People were numb, as if they were made of wood, not thinking about anything but work. Even when we ate we couldn't tell you what it tasted like. Privately everyone would curse, saying, "These bosses make so much money with dark hearts, their family lines should be cut off (*duan zi jue sun*)." I get scared when I think about it, even now. I really don't know how I managed to get through it. Sometimes I see people online saying how great Xiaolan (Township) is, and it pisses me off. Damn, how could it have become so great if they hadn't squeezed so much blood and sweat out of my body? Why are they so damn cocky (Ct. *diu*)? I'm not kidding, there was really blood and sweat involved. Sweat requires no explanation, but also many of my co-workers got injured on the job, their hands cut or crushed in machines—how much blood was that? To say nothing of the youth taken from those girls in the prime of their lives. (The factories) made clear that they only recruited (workers) between the ages of eighteen and twenty-five.

Although it was hard, at least Jingdao managed to save up some money from this work in the early 1990s. He used these savings to renovate the house in Jiangbei and the watch repair shop in Duqiao, installing tile floors, leather sofas, audio cassette tape recorders, and color TVs that attracted a great deal of admiration from other villagers. Shoude and his wife were overjoyed, often using Jingdao's example to criticize their elder son Jingxiu. At the same time, they helped Jingdao search for someone to marry, although he personally was not interested. He said there were plenty of girls "out there" (in Zhongshan where he was working) who wanted to date him. His parents felt, however, that the "northern girls" (Ct. *loumui*) out there would not be reliable, and it would be inconvenient to visit relatives so far from home.

In 1994, Jingdao finally caved in to his parents' nagging and got engaged when he returned home at the end of the year, getting married shortly after the Chinese New Year. The bride was from another village in Duqiao and had been in the same grade with Jingdao during middle school, just happening to meet him again while working in Xiaolan, Zhongshan. The wedding burned through the remainder of his savings.

Over the following few years, it grew more and more difficult for Jingdao to make ends meet. First, the couple had a daughter and a son in 1996 and 1998, so household expenses suddenly rose. Second, from 1996 to 2000, the wife stayed at home to nurse and take care of the children, so she had no income. Third, Shoude and his wife shared a hearth with Jingdao, but their farming and watch repair shop did not generate enough income to cover much of the household's expenses. Finally, and more importantly, Jingdao's wages never rose as he had hoped. Throughout the second half of the 1990s, he tried several jobs in Changping, Huangjiang, and other parts of Dongguan, but never saw a significant increase in pay. In 2000, he switched to another shoe factory working about eleven hours a day (the longest he could handle, he said) for 1,800 to 2,000 yuan a month. Once adjusted for inflation, however, this was even lower than he had made in 1990, while at the same time, the prices of most goods had doubled. He said that this period in the late 1990s was the hardest in his life.

In 2001, Jingdao and his wife went out to work together, leaving their two children with Shoude and his wife. Their wages finally rose in 2005–2006, amounting to a gross income of 7,000 yuan a month between the two of them. Jingdao felt that even adjusting for inflation, this was a little higher than what they had made in the early 1990s. Meanwhile, however, their household expenses continued to increase. The two children's pre-school cost over 1,000 yuan per month, as did living expenses. Once they began primary school, although there was no tuition, they still had to spend over 100 yuan per month on snacks. Jingdao commented:

> Nowadays it seems like you have to spend a lot of money every time you turn around and you've never got enough. Thank goodness my dad

fathered us in a good location, near the street (i.e., the market town). Otherwise, in our township there are some villages far from the street, so when kids go to pre-school or primary school, the old people have to rent a place nearby to accompany them. They can't take care of the farming, and they have to buy rice and vegetables in town. All these expenses add up.

In recent years, Jingdao and his wife have continued working in Dongguan, Zhuhai, and other cities, but their life has not improved substantially. He has considered demolishing Shoude's old shop in Duqiao and building a three-story structure, renting out the first floor, and living on the second and third floors. This would cost about 250,000 yuan, however, and he has never managed to come up with enough money to carry out this plan.

Jingzu's experiences have been quite similar to Jingdao's. In the early 1990s, he used the money he had gradually saved up from working to add a second floor to the one-story red-brick house his father Shoukuan had already built. After that, however, Jingzu and his wife became constantly weighed down by their three children's medical expenses and tuition. By 2013, Jingzu's red-brick house had still not been completely finished: The walls had not been painted and the floors had not been tiled, in keeping with the fashion of the times.

When analyzing the reasons that his income from working had been lower than expected, however, Jingzu was more inclined to blame the limitations of his own capability. While chatting in the fall of 2008, he commented:

> It's hard to say. It's always hard for society to be fair. But for capable people, the more unfair society is, the more money they can earn. It's only we simple and honest people who think society should be more fair. (If we) depend on our fathers, then our fathers aren't as (capable) as other people's fathers. (If we) depend on relatives, then our relatives aren't as (capable) as other people's relatives. (If we) depend on education, then we're not as good at school as other people. (If we) depend on cheating, stealing, or other dishonest methods, then we're not as good at those as other people. You can get rich in those ways, but you've got to have enough capability and guts. If you're neither as capable nor as brave as others, then how could anything change? Just gradually live out your days, it doesn't matter.

Compared with Jingzu and Jingdao, Jingshan's experiences of working seem to have been a little more positive. He said that those other two men were "simple and honest," and that was good, but beyond a certain point these qualities make one inflexible (*daiban*). He also felt that Jingdao and Jingzu should have accumulated skills and experience within a single industry and then tried to become department supervisors, or at least skilled workers making prototypes of the company's products. In that case, their work would have become easier, and their wages would have risen significantly. At the same time, however, Jingshan said:

> Of course, it really is hard when you're first starting out. You have to be able to endure more suffering than other (workers), and your mind has to be more flexible. With so many (workers), who doesn't want to work less hard for more money?

Jingshan believed that his own experiences followed a different path. From 1994 to 1996, right after completing middle school he got a job at a garment factory in Guangzhou. He purposely switched from post to post at the factory until he had learned all the skills involved in production. He also often learned from the master craftsmen (*shifu*) who made prototypes. Several of these craftsmen consciously avoided revealing their own skills, so instead Jingshan learned other knowledge from them besides tailoring skills, such as the characteristics of different types of cloth, information about prices, etc. Starting in 1997, Jingshan got a job at another garment factory where he was responsible for helping the department manager purchase cloth and solicit wholesalers. Since he continued working there for more than ten years, winning the respect of the boss, his pay always stayed around twice that of ordinary workers. In 1998, he married a woman from Eastern Guangdong he had met at the factory. The next year they had a son, and in 2006 they had a second son, in violation of Family Planning policies, so they were fined 20,000 yuan. If they took both their children to attend school in Guangzhou, he said, it would have been too expensive (even if they managed to obtain Guangzhou *hukou*), whereas they could afford it with plenty to spare if they left them in Cheng Village for Shouzhi and his wife to take care of them, as they do now. He only had to work for seven or eight years, he figured, to save up enough money to build a house in the village, but he did not want to demolish the old house and build a new one. One day in December 2012, when we met up in Guangzhou, Jingshan said:

> At this point I'm suspended in mid-air (*bu shang bu xia*). I don't want to return to the countryside, but I can't settle down in the city.... Maybe when I get old and I have no choice but to return, it will just happen naturally.

Li Sheng was Jingshan's brother-in-law (his little sister's husband), and they had attended middle school together. From 1994 to 2000, Li had worked at a seafood market in Guangzhou, making 1,500 to 1,800 yuan per month. In 2001, he returned home and got a job at a stone-processing plant in Duqiao. Although his pay never rose much above 2,500 yuan a month until 2012, he was content because the job was close to home, and he could ride a motorcycle to work every day.

Shoude's daughter Jingsi and her husband Chen Sheng opened a small restaurant along the national highway running through Duqiao in 1996, but this investment failed. Again and again, Jingsi went to the police station to ask the officers to pay the 40,000 yuan they owed for meals they had eaten on credit at the restaurant, but to no avail. During one of these visits, in the Fifth Month of the traditional calendar in 1998, the police chief said they still didn't have the money, but he had just installed an air conditioner in the office, so they no longer needed their electric fans. She could have them if she wanted. Jingsi berated the chief and took the fans, giving one to Shoude. Shortly thereafter, as mentioned above, the Chengjiao Township Family Planning officials came and detained Shoude, pressuring the family to pay 50,000 yuan in fines for Jingsi's over-quota births. After that, not only did Jingsi and Chen Sheng fail to obtain the money that the police owed them, but they also had to go out and work to pay off the fines. One day in the summer of 2009, when I just happened to ask Shoude about the fan on the floor of his watch repair shop, he replied resentfully, "This fan has a complicated history. It's worth over 20,000 yuan." From 2000 until the past few years, Jingsi and Chen Sheng have been working at a stone-processing plant in Duqiao, each doing some relatively light work there for about 1,500 yuan a month. After all, Jingsi said, their children are already grown, so that salary is enough to get by. She did not want to think much beyond that, instead just looking forward to having grandchildren.

Hanging Out

Shoude often said that his eldest son Jingxiu was "both good and bad." I asked other villagers, "What does Jingxiu do, after all?" They said, "He's a person who just hangs out (*huangyou*, literally "wobbles"), wandering from place to place." Sometimes, when I ran into Jingxiu and asked, "What are you busy with now?" he would say, "Nothing, just hanging out."

What did they mean by "hanging out"? Villagers told me that, normally, if a person "doesn't keep their nose to the grindstone," instead just "fishing for two days and then drying the net for three," idling about when they are not working, that was called "hanging out." A more serious form of hanging out was "failing to occupy oneself with proper work," which could even involve illegal activities.

As the villagers saw it, Jingxiu belonged to the less serious version of "hanging out." After getting married in 1986 and fathering a son the next year, he rarely engaged in farmwork and instead always looked for some easier way to make money. Every time he tried to do business, however, he failed. Not only did Shoude scold him about this many times, even Shouyi clearly advised him that if he wanted to do business, he had to be willing to endure some hard work at first. Shouzhi also offered, of his own initiative, to teach him how to raise squab pigeons, but Jingxiu felt that the pigeon trade was not profitable enough, that he could not get rich that way, so was unwilling to learn. Instead, he preferred to spend his time playing cards with other young people in the village or the town. Shouzhi criticized him, "I can see you've got the fate of a poor-and-lower-middle peasant, yet you act like you're the son of a high-ranking official." Jingxiu turned a deaf ear to these exhortations, leaving the farmwork and childcare to his wife, and sometimes asking Shoude to pay for their children's tuition. For the first few years, his wife complained about this, but eventually she just gave up.

According to Jingxiu's own words, he had worked from 1994 to 1998 in Zhuhai, Shenzhen, and other cities. (Other villagers could not recall whether he had actually left the village to work.) Unfortunately, he was not someone who could endure hardship, so never saved up any money. As he put it, construction work expended too much physical energy, plus the southern sun was too hot, so he could not handle it. Although jobs in garment and shoe factories shielded him from the sun, his personality could not endure sitting in one place without moving for more than ten hours a day. Jobs running errands required communication skills, which he also lacked. He often switched jobs, therefore, rarely staying at any one for more than half a year. Among these, many of them followed the convention of withholding the first month's wages until the first year had been completed, so if you quit before that time, those wages would be docked. Jingxiu said he was an accepting person, so often he preferred to accept such losses rather than putting up with abusive bosses for any longer. For the last few years of that period, he just performed "odd jobs," never working on the assembly line and only taking temporary jobs that lasted a month or two, or even day labor. In contrast with his younger brother Jingdao, who only returned to the village for Spring Festival, every year Jingxiu would quit a job in the middle of the year and return to the village for a couple weeks at a time.

In 2003, Jingxiu's son Yuanwen graduated from middle school and left home to work. Jingxiu announced that he already had a "successor to relieve him" of work, so he would never again have to endure the hardships and frustrations of working for someone else. Over the past ten-plus years, he has been living in Shoude's blue-brick house in Jiangbei, but most of the farmwork is still done by his wife. Occasionally, he works at a stone-processing plant in Duqiao, performing work normally done by women, such as polishing and cleaning. He rarely keeps even this kind of easy job for very long, and many bosses call him to help out only when there's a rush order. He does not smoke or drink, but he spends most of what little money he does make on mahjong and cards, and he never buys gambling chips. He believes that buying chips is a stupid way of giving money to others, since everyone's luck evens out over time, although with a little skill one can make a little money. On many occasions he argued that his hanging out was reasonable, for example in the summer of 2011, when he said:

> There's nothing wrong with hanging out. It's not like I do anything too bad, I just like to gamble a little. High-stakes gambling is no good, if you lose you might destroy your whole family, only big bosses can afford that. With low-stakes gambling, everyone knows each other, we just win and lose small sums depending on luck and skill, conceding defeat when we

lose.... You can't get rich working for a wage, I could see that much after my first day out there. At the time I kept saying, "It would be easier to get rich playing the lottery than working." You see all those people tiring themselves out with work, and all they have to show for it is an extra house. Why not just live in my dad's blue-brick house? When he passes away, it will be mine, and the shop (in Duqiao) will be my little brother's. These blue-brick houses with reinforced concrete floors will probably last one or two hundred years. If my kid is capable in the future, he can build his own house, but if not, he can just continue living here. What's the point of working myself to death just to build a new one? We only live once, just as grass only lives for a year. It isn't easy, the important thing is to live in a way that's relaxed, that's free and comfortable (*zizai*). If I were really capable of succeeding at some trade, it would actually be worth tiring myself out over it, but you can't get rich from farming or working for a wage, so what's the point of shouldering a millennium of worries when you can't even live for a century? People laugh at me for being lackadaisical, but I laugh at them for failing to see the truth.

It was said that Jingye was another young villager who liked to hang out but did not do anything too bad. I never met Jingye, but I heard many stories about his "hanging out" experiences from his father Shoukuan and his brothers Jingzu and Jingzong. Prior to gambling away his father's money that had been meant for buying chickens and feed, Jingye often went out to work. In the fall of 2008, when Jingzong came home for National Day, he told me about his brother:

He can't handle hard work. As they say nowadays, he's a typical "moonlighter" (*yueguangzu*, workers who live from paycheck to paycheck). He's already spent all his money before receiving the next month's wages. He's well practiced at pool and computer games, and he only smokes quality cigarettes, eats quality food, and drinks quality beer, not settling for the cheap stuff. For the first few years (he was out working), when he ran out of money he would *kuo* (transliteration of "call" popular among migrant workers of that generation) me to bum a little cash. It's not like I was making a lot of money, and after I got married, I started ignoring him. He's the sort of person who would come often, not to visit our parents, but just to take a break, since he could live and eat here for free. After a while he would get bored and leave again.

Jingzu mentioned, however, that after he had gambled away their father's money, he did not come home for a long time, but he was just hanging out in Dongguan, unwilling to work in any given factory for very long. He said:

Every year I would see this prodigal son in Dongguan on several occasions. He often hopped from job to job, quitting a place as soon as anything bothered him about it. For all this, I never saw him find a very good job. When it came to enjoyment, though, he only wanted the best. White dress shirts, formal trousers, black leather shoes, carefully styled hair, he looked like the senior assistant to a big boss—very handsome. Whenever we were together, people always thought he was my nephew. But his pockets never had more than a few bucks in them.

What especially disappointed his parents was not only this, but that he never got married, up until the present. Every time Jingye came up in conversation, Feng Lan would sigh, "Nothing good has ever come to people who only know how to hang out all the time." Shoukuan would then console her, saying:

> As long as he doesn't break the law, let him hang out. At least we already have grandchildren. It's his own business if he doesn't get married. What can we do with a wastrel (*langzi*) like that? When we get old and our feet are facing the sky, we won't have anything to worry about. Let him do as he pleases.

When young villagers hang out, however, it is not always the case that they stop short of breaking the law. Sometimes, if one is not careful, somebody ends up "hanging out too far" (*huangyou chuge*). For instance, according to the limited data collected from the people I talked to, between 2007 and 2013, at least seventeen young villagers were conned into joining pyramid schemes in Nanning, Liuzhou, Dongguan, and other cities. What enticed them into joining was a simple promise: Invest a few tens of thousands of yuan, find other people to invest, and before long they would achieve their dreams of fabulous wealth. After being "brainwashed," they would begin constantly trying to convince their friends and relatives to join, even after people had pointed out that this was a pyramid scheme, remaining transfixed until they had completely used up all their hard-earned cash and that of their loved ones, and then finally discovered that it was all an illusion.

Chengren's grandson Jinghua went so far as to "hang" his way into prison. After graduating from middle school in 2001, he was always hanging out in Duqiao's market town, where his favorite thing to do besides gaming in internet cafes was to play cards. His brother's life as a migrant worker held no interest for him. His father Shouwang said:

> He got some money from home (asking his parents for money) and bought a motorcycle. As soon as the sun set, he would go out biking with his disreputable friends (*hupeng gouyou*). They would mess around all night, not coming home until sunrise. I told him this would come to a bad end, sooner or later, but he wouldn't listen.

One day in 2005, several migrant workers from out of town, who worked at a stone plant, were eating and gambling at a restaurant along the highway, when a dispute broke out with the owner. This restaurant belonged to the "turf" looked after by the owner's son and his "brothers"—including Jinghua. The quarrel turned into a fight, and one of the workers suffered a severe injury, leading to the arrest and conviction of the owner's son and Jinghua. The owner spent a large sum of money hiring a lawyer, who reduced the son's charge to "accomplice" with a sentence of only one year in prison followed by one year on probation. Jinghua, however, was charged as the main assailant and sentenced to eight years in prison.

When some young villagers who hung out in town got together with those from other villages, they became known as "gangsters" or "hoodlums" (Ct. *laanjai*). When I first arrived in Cheng Village and stayed at the "brigade headquarters," there was an old building next door that used to be the Duqiao Township Health Center, but now all the doors and windows were missing. At first, I assumed that when the center had moved to its new location, the old doors and windows had been installed on the new building. Much later I heard villagers say that this "masterpiece" was the work of gangsters who hung out in town. A few nights after the center had moved in 2006, several "druggies" removed all the doors and windows and sold them at the scrapyard. For each item they could receive 50–60 yuan, enough to buy two doses of drugs.

On the second day of Month Two of the traditional calendar in 2008, Shouzhi's family conducted a firework ceremony for their new grandson. At the ceremony, one of Shouzhi's nephews, a drug user from Jiangbei, partook of the alcohol there and ended up passing out in a corner of the temple. With great embarrassment, he said to Shouzhi, "I'm so sorry, Uncle! I took too much rat poison (i.e., heroin) and made you lose face in front of all these relatives." The following year, Shouzhi and I ran into this man at the entrance to the Jiangbei temple. By that time, he was all skin and bones, with glassy eyes. Shouzhi urged him to get clean, but the man just said, "It's too late, it's already impossible for me to quit. I'll probably die soon anyway." Then his words became kind-hearted:

> I really regret not working when I still had a chance. If I had just done my job in a factory, I wouldn't have spent my time out there hanging out, then I wouldn't have started using this damn thing. This life is already over. In my next life I won't dare to touch it even if I'm beaten to death.

In April of 2010, he actually did die, Shouzhi told me, after hanging out for many years.

With the exception of dramatic incidents like this one, ordinary villagers' normal reaction to drug-related "hanging out" is fear. Out of concern for retribution, they are afraid to publicly acknowledge the existence of drug users. In

2007, a middle-aged resident of Jiangbei accused a "druggie" from elsewhere of coming to Cheng Village to steal things. (Later this accusation led to the man's arrest.) When the man heard about the accusation, he went and stood in the shadows of the trees at the entrance to the village, and then assaulted the villager on his way back from town, taking a keychain and looping it around his penis. The villager went to the Tong Prefecture People's Hospital and spent several hundred yuan on surgery to have the keychain removed. In addition, since "young people who hung out" were likely to cause trouble, Duqiao Secondary School worried that it would be unsafe for students to walk home at night, so they discontinued evening study hall for day students from Cheng Village, Xujiao Village, and Duqiao Residential Committee.

A small number of young people who hung out also enticed certain "honest and simple people" to take risks in the hope of getting rich. One resident of Jiangbei named Cheng Qiufu was considered an honest and simple person by his neighbors. His family was poor, so they hired an underground matchmaker to find him a bride from Vietnam. At first, Qiufu was afraid she would run away, so he kept a close eye on everything of value in the house and asked his neighbors to help keep track of her activities. After living together for four years, the couple had two children. Since they could not obtain a marriage certificate, the children had no household registration (*hukou*), which caused a lot of problems in their lives. Nevertheless, Qiufu felt content, since at least he had a complete family. One day after they had been married about four and a half years, however, when Qiufu was out working in the fields, the woman took all the cash and valuables in the house and disappeared without a trace. Two years later, as the family remained mired in poverty, Qiufu turned his eyes toward the "young people who hung out," trying to solve his economic problems once and for all by selling heroin. In 2004, on his third trip transporting heroin from Guangzhou to Duqiao, he was arrested at the bus station, and to this day he is still in prison. His two children and their elderly grandfather continue to be destitute.

Stewardship of the Land

In recent years, basically the only people who still farm in Cheng Village are over the age of fifty. Among younger people, there are only a small number of women who continue to look after their homes and tend the fields. One of these women is Cheng Jingxian, Shouzhi's daughter.

According to her household registration, after Jingxian got married she became a resident of Xujiao Village, but she spends most of her time during the day at her parents' house in Cheng Village. Villagers often joke that "she commutes to work at her parents' house every day." She declines to comment on these remarks, just explaining that she's in charge of farming her parents-in-law's land in Xujiao while they take care of cooking and other housework. In recent years, it has actually become quite common for women in the area to continue living with their parents after they marry into another village.

I interviewed several such women in Cheng Village, who said they met their husbands while out working, and their in-laws live in a village they have only visited a few times. Either they continue working in the city, or they chose to stay in Cheng Village, since that way they do not have to adjust their patterns of everyday life, plus they can minimize the chances of coming into conflict with their in-laws. This explains the surprising discovery that many children, growing up in the homes of their maternal grandparents, say that they have never seen their paternal grandparents or other relatives, or that they had only seen them a handful of times. Locals feel that, like young men who go out to work, women such as Jingxian who marry into other villages still belong to Cheng Village—that they "never truly left."

Jingxian was born in 1979, graduating from middle school in 1995 and then going to work at a shoe factory in Dongguan. Before long, she realized that she simply could not handle such a heavy workload. Looking back, she said:

> I had never done such hard work in my life. When I was in school, the most I did was to help my parents with some light farmwork, but they did the rest. My brother also helped out, so I didn't have to do anything too hard. So when I went out to work (at the factory), I couldn't get used to it. The work itself wasn't that heavy, physically, but the problem was that we had to make the same motions over and over for more than ten hours without stopping, either sitting or standing continuously—we couldn't even switch positions. There was always someone watching, and you had to ask permission if you needed to use the toilet. The work drove me to tears many times. I just wanted to go home as early as possible. But then I was afraid people would laugh and gossip about me, saying "you just went and hung out for a while and then came back?" So I just gritted my teeth and held out for a year, and after that I just stayed in the village. I bought some gifts for my parents and spent the rest of my wages on clothes, shoes, bracelets, necklaces. I didn't save up any money.

From 1996 to 1998, Jingxian helped her mother Li Jing farm vegetables and tend their tangerine orchard, planted on a little over two *mu*. At the end of 1997, when Jingshan came home for Spring Festival, his middle school classmate Li Sheng came over to visit, and then he met Jingxian. Li Jing was impressed by Li Sheng, so she urged Jingxian to marry him, which she did at the end of 1998. After that, Li Sheng went back to work in Guangzhou, and Jingxian continued living and eating with her parents most of the time. Shortly thereafter, Li Jing told her daughter she did not need to help out so much with the vegetables, reminding her that she needed to go help her in-laws in Xujiao with their own farmwork. At that point Jingxian began taking charge of the main manual labor involved in planting and harvesting her in-laws' vegetable fields. They were overjoyed, saying they could manage the everyday upkeep of the fields while she helped her parents.

In 2000, Jingxian went to work together with Li Sheng at a seafood market in Guangzhou. This time, she said, the goal of going out to work was to live together with her husband and conceive a child. They had been married for two years and still not conceived, so people in Xujiao were beginning to gossip, conjecturing that there was something wrong with her body or their relationship. A few months later, she became pregnant and went back to Cheng Village to prepare for the birth, her parents-in-law often coming to visit. In early 2001, she gave birth to a son, and Li Sheng moved back to Duqiao, where he got a job at a stone plant. In the summer of 2008, Jingxian got pregnant again. One evening when Li Sheng came to pick her up in Cheng Village, I asked whether they were still subject to reproduction quotas. Li Sheng replied:

> Of course we are. Now the township government doesn't care about enforcing Family Planning, they just want to collect fees (for over-quota births). After the baby is born you just pay the fine and that's it. We already set the money aside long ago: 30,000 yuan. Even if you don't have the money it doesn't matter—nowadays the less money people have, the more babies they have, since the government can't do anything about it. It can't demolish their houses or detain them (anymore). If it fines them, they don't have any money to pay. The government can't do anything about it. They have land to farm, so they won't go hungry. As for whether the children can attend school and move up in the world, (the parents) can't do much for them... . Isn't that why we live in this world—to have children and grandchildren as descendants? 30,000 yuan is a small price to pay. It's not like in the past when people were searching for food in the mud. With income from work in the city, 30,000 isn't a small amount, but it's not so much we can't afford it. She (Jingxian) can only produce enough from farming for us to survive. Of course this is important too. If we had to buy all our rice and vegetables, my paltry wages might not be enough for us to afford over-quota births.

Jingxian gave birth to her second son in early 2009. Her parents-in-law were overjoyed, she said, telling her, "From now on you're only responsible for overseeing the overall direction of farming. We'll do all the specific work... . You should focus on raising the two kids and educating them." They hoped that their grandchildren would become people with accomplishments rather than merely tending the fields at home.

Jingxian believed that tending the fields at home was part of the cooperation between husband and wife. As she saw it, if the income from wage labor was relatively high, it would of course be better if both husband and wife could work together in the city and bring their children with them to raise there. If the income was insufficient for raising children in the city, then only the husband or the wife should work in the city, not both of them. Otherwise, the children would become "left-behind" (*liushou ertong*), and the old people at home were completely incapable of providing adequate education for the children. In situations like the one with her and Li Sheng, therefore, only if the man went to work in a factory and the woman tended the fields at home could they both earn money and be able to take care of the family at the same time, especially the children. As she explained one summer day in 2009:

> For a family to do well, the children must be near (at least one of the parents). If the wages are too low, then it would be better for the woman to stay at home and do a little farming, or even do nothing at all, as long as she can take care of the children. Nowadays very few young people farm at home, everyone goes out to work, or they're just hanging out. This is wrong. Never mind the rest, it's bad for the children. It's usually the woman who stays at home, and if she's industrious, then she can do something else while she's raising the children. If not, then childcare is enough. Like in our case, with both parents at home, the children don't dare to act up, and if they do anything bad, at least there's a standard they don't stray too far from (*you ge pu*). They're afraid of their dad. Those children without a dad at home, and especially those with neither parent at home, at a very young age they've already started gaming, playing cards, smoking, cavalierly grabbing a handful of cash from the house and going to buy junk food every day—the old people can't do anything about it. There's no way around it: If you don't work, you won't have any money, but if you do work, there's no one to raise the children, and if they go bad, then you've worked in vain. So I have no choice but to tend the fields at home. We can't make any money from farming, I'm just trying to keep the fields from growing over, and we can eat our own rice, vegetables, and fruit—safer than what you buy at the market. But all this depends on my husband working.

I once asked Jingxian why she did not rent a little land from other villagers and use machinery to farm it. She said there were two main reasons. One was that one woman could not farm a large amount of land on her own. The other was that many villagers were afraid that in the future it would be too much trouble to get their land back, and its economic value was low, so they would rather leave it fallow than rent it out. She could rent fields from relatives, but those were few and scattered throughout the village, so she could not use them for concentrated cultivation.

During the Spring Festival of 2010, Jingxian proposed a plan for raising pigs where she would use the old pig pen that Shouzhi had abandoned years ago, along with pens she would borrow from two neighbors in return for cartons of cigarettes. Jingshan, who had returned home for the holiday, disagreed with this plan. He said that Jingxian would need their parents help, but they were already tired enough from helping her take care of their grandchildren. If she really wanted to raise pigs, therefore, she should do it in Xujiao. Jingxian responded that she understood she had married into another village, but she was not trying to lay claim to her birth family's land. Besides, their father's health was poor, and although Jingshan and his wife and paid for his medical expenses, they never had time to look after him at home, so she was the one who was always taking care of this. After they had quarreled for a while, Jingshan's wife urged him to step back from too much involvement in household affairs, considering he did not have time to farm. She told him not to try to control everything like a traditional male chauvinist. Shouzhi and Li Jing also spoke up on Jingxian's behalf, saying that Jingshan's wife also worked in Guangzhou, and there was too much for the two of them to do at home by themselves, so Jingxian helped them by visiting Cheng Village every day. If she raised pigs in Xujiao, she would not have as much time to come visit.

And so, Jingxian began raising two sows and six pork pigs. It was unavoidable that this would cause at least a little inconvenience for her parents. In the mornings, Jingxian had to deal with the children's breakfast in Xujiao and usually could not ride the motorcycle over to Cheng Village until after ten o'clock, so it was usually Shouzhi who fed the pigs. At noon, Jingxian would cook lunch for her parents, in the afternoon she fed the pigs their second meal, then in the evening she would take the children back to Xujiao. If it got too late, Li Sheng would pick them up in Cheng Village after he got off from work. In her spare time, Jingxian would help her parents in their vegetable garden, or, while watching television, help her mother make little bamboo steamers used for food delivery.[3] As for the fields in Xujiao, as her parents-in-law said, she was only responsible for "the overall direction," such as planting, harvesting, and other heavy manual labor, with everyday upkeep taken care of by her in-laws.

In 2010, Jingxian earned 4,000 yuan from raising pigs, of which she gave 1,000 to her parents "as a token of respect" (*xiaojing*). Shouzhi and his wife used this money to buy each of their four grandchildren a set of clothes for 100 yuan per set. In 2011, the price of pork fell and Jingxian lost 2,000 yuan. The next year she made 3,000 yuan. She explained that she had never expected to make much money from this, but just wanted to contribute to the household budget in some way besides tending the fields. Li Sheng's work was still the main source of income.

Although Jingxian persisted in tending the fields at home in the countryside, she also felt it was bad to be too "country" (*tu*—literally "soil"). One afternoon in 2011, Shouzhi was supervising his grandchildren as they did their summer break homework, and Jingxian was making steamers with her mother as they watched television. A series from Hong Kong was playing, in which the female lead said, "Even if it doesn't have *candles* it's still *sweet*." Jingxian said it sounded like the character used a couple English words in the Cantonese sentence—what did they mean? I translated the two words, and then she sighed, saying she was so "country" that she could not even understand Cantonese TV. She worried she would eventually be "culled" (*taotai*) by society. I joked that the problem was just that "they're not speaking human language," but Jingxian responded seriously:

> I feel so country messing around in the mud every day. Never mind Hong Kong, I'm much more country even than people who go out to work. When they come back from the city, they know this, they know that, but I don't know any of it. Which brand of purses people are using, which brand of dresses people are wearing, their shoes and make-up are some international brand or other, even if they're fake. At home tending the fields, (my life) revolves around the hearth and the children. When I go out, my purse is a plastic bag, my clothes and shoes have no brand name, and I rarely even use make-up. After a few years of this won't I be so country that I'll just be covered in dirt? I'll get older faster than them too… . The good thing is that we have a TV and plenty of time to watch it. They don't have time to watch TV when they're out working. Otherwise we'd be even more country. At least we can keep up with the times, more or less: If you can't eat pork, at least you can see pigs running down the road. When it comes to Korean shows, I can guarantee I've seen more than them, at least that's one fashion where I'm ahead of them. Otherwise, I'd truly be as country as can be. My mom likes to watch dramas about the Qing court (*qinggongxi*), but I don't like them—too country. All the men care about is taking the imperial exams and being emperors, and all the women care about is helping their husbands and educating their sons, depending on their husbands for everything.

Schooling

In the cycle of life experiences, after attending middle school or high school, most young people in Cheng Village join the workforce. Many older villagers hope, however, that their offspring will improve their lives by doing well in school. When I was researching the "ancient village," several villagers kept emphasizing that crumbling remains of a building at the center of the settlement used to be a school (*shuyuan*), showing how important education was to their ancestors. During the collective era, Cheng Village finally got its own primary school, and Duqiao opened a middle school, later adding a high school. Other than joining the army, education was basically the only way people could leave the village, and even the army required at least a middle school diploma. From the early 1980s to the mid-1990s, although a minority of villagers managed to get rich with only a middle school or even primary school education, people still felt that the main way for their offspring to improve their lives was through more advanced schooling.

An important shift occurred in the mid-1990s. Qianjin's son Yuanfang, Shoukuan's third son Jingye, Jingxiu's son Yuanwen, Jingdao's son Zhiyuan, and Fudao's son Siyuan have all been trying to catch up with this shift.

Jingye was one year older than Yuanfang, but due to poverty he took a year off from primary school, so he entered middle school at Duqiao Secondary the same year as Yuanfang, 1994. According to the elderly teacher Mr. Liang, who still worked there, due to fiscal changes in 1994, rural secondary school teachers such as those in Duqiao could no longer receive their salaries on time, with a series of new state directives announcing a rise in salary that never happened. Meanwhile, the middle and primary school teachers in Wucheng and Chengjiao had no problems receiving their salaries. Rural teachers therefore did all they could to transfer to urban schools, leading to a glut of teachers in those schools and a shortage in rural schools. Duqiao Secondary School had no choice but to recruit a large batch of new teachers, a portion of whom were teachers pinched from secondary schools in Hunan, Jiangxi, Guangxi, and Guizhou, and another portion of whom were local high school graduates. In addition, Mr. Liang said, other than a minority of teachers who continued teaching diligently for reasons of conscience, many of the others began to slack off in their work. Occasionally some of them would apply for leave to "jump into the sea (of business)" (*xiahai*), while others were only on temporary employment contracts in the first place, and some of these would suddenly leave in the middle of the semester to go work in the Pearl River Delta. This situation did not begin to improve until 2001.

Yuanfang said, even as a student at the time, he could tell that the teachers' ability was limited. For three semesters at Duqiao Secondary School, for example, his English courses were taught by a substitute teacher. He and classmates such as Jingye discovered that the teacher could not even speak English, so he just had the students listen to recordings and recite the textbook, and he could never explain the grammar clearly. When they practiced after class, the teacher was often unable to provide any assistance. In the standardized examinations at the time, Chinese language, mathematics, and English were considered the most important courses. In addition, Yuanfang said, the general academic ethos (*xiaofeng, xuefeng*) of Duqiao Secondary was subpar. Discipline was lax, and many male students often smoked behind the school buildings or in the woods, even skipping class to play computer games in town. Bigger and stronger students would bully the others, extorting their pocket money to buy snacks or cigarettes without anyone putting a stop to it.

During the winter break after the third semester of middle school, Yuanfang told his parents that either he should transfer to another school or simply drop out and go out to work, like some of his classmates. His father Qianjin, serving as a village cadre at the time, sought out a township cadre and arranged for Yuanfang to be transferred to a private school for the children of migrant workers in Wucheng (where there was tough competition for enrollment), with a tuition of 1,500 yuan per semester (approximately double that of public secondary schools), plus 300 yuan for the dormitory, not including other living expenses. In 1997, Yuanfang tested into a vocational secondary school in Guangzhou. Qianjin felt that it was ultimately worth it to send his son to attend middle school in Wucheng at the time. Especially in contrast with Jingye's "hanging out" everywhere, Qianjin sighed, at least Yuanfang was able to climb up a step and improve his life a little compared with the previous generation. Shoukuan agreed with this statement, to some degree, sometimes saying that the reason Jingye preferred to hang out was related to the bad habits he learned in secondary school.

Yuanwen attended middle school at Duqiao Secondary a few years later, from 2000 to 2003. By that time, he said, the teachers' ability was not too bad, most of them being young graduates of proper educational colleges or vocational secondary schools. From the perspective of villagers concerned with matriculation rates, however, they did not see any substantial improvement. On Grave-Sweeping Day in 2013, I ran into Yuanwen in Cheng Village, and he recounted:

> I don't know why, but in any case the teaching results were poor, with very few students making high scores (on national standardized examinations). Families with even a little bit of money spent it on sending their kids to school in Wucheng. Only the poorest students went to school here (in Duqiao). It's true, as people say now, my classmates consisted almost entirely of "losers" (*diaosi*)[4]—it was basically a concentration camp for losers... . Maybe it was related to the students' foundations in primary school: Now in the city students start learning English and computers in their first years at school. When we were in primary school, all we did every day was play in the mud, catching frogs and dragonflies, so when we got to middle school, English, biology, physics, chemistry, what have you, they were all completely new to us, so it was hard to keep up. The academic ethos was bad too, and there was nothing the teachers could do about it. Teachers would take those students with slightly better scores, those with a little hope of matriculating, and move them to the front of the class. Those in the back would just play computer games, Rubik's cubes, some would even play cards. When things got out of hand, the teacher would say, "Those of you who aren't studying need to keep it down. If you don't want to learn, at least don't cause problems for the other students." Otherwise they just left them alone. If they skipped class, the teachers didn't even try to look for them, so they didn't have to deal with them. They didn't dare—if the students got angry, they would hit the teachers, and the police couldn't do anything about it. It's true, students would hit teachers. Really the students were hurting themselves, you can't blame the teachers.

Among classmates, although Yuanwen's marks were better than average, when it came time for the high school entrance exam, he did not even come close to the score necessary for matriculation, so had no choice but to take the only other "highway to success": leaving home to work in the city. Yuanwen said that of his sixty middle school classmates, only fifteen continued their schooling, with three going on to secondary vocational school, ten to regular senior high school (*gaozhong*) at Duqiao Secondary (five of whom later went to technical colleges), and two to regular senior high school in Wucheng (of whom one later went to a second-tier university and one into a third-tier college). During the Spring Festival of 2013, Yuanwen and some of his middle school classmates organized a ten-year graduation reunion in Duqiao. Other than a few classmates for whom no information was available, everyone compiled the information about most of their classmates' current situation and discovered that almost all of them were still "losers." Yuanwen said, on the one hand, everybody was overwhelmed at the reunion, some of them had already gotten married and had children, others were "drifting" (*piaozhe*) in the Pearl River Delta, still others were hanging out in other cities, lamenting that they had been so care-free (*xiaosa*) back when they were in school that now they could no longer afford to take it easy. On the other hand, everyone agreed that even if they had studied more diligently, their fate might have been about the same, so they should just accept it. They played mahjong all night and then went their separate ways.

I once discussed the example of Yuanwen with the teacher Mr. Liang, and he said that in the 1980s quite a few students at Duqiao Secondary tested into four-year college programs (*benkesheng*), but now even Wucheng's private school for migrant children had a higher matriculation rate. He explained:

> The reasons for this are complex. As a teacher, I feel that first I have to acknowledge a certain degree of responsibility. The teachers here, including myself, have limited abilities (*shuiping*). But as far as that goes, our abilities were even lower in the 1980s, but then it wasn't like it is now, so the key is that we didn't try hard enough in our teaching.
>
> Overall, however, this is related to government policies. Now they're doing all they can to build schools in the city. The government's money is all being poured into "key secondary schools," the better the school the more money it can get. Naturally that means that rural schools can only get worse and worse. But urban schools are always limited, aren't they? If rural children try to go, it's really hard to obtain a spot, and the only other option is to spend money on an elite (private) school. What can be done? I'm also confused by real estate ads that say things like "student spot property" (i.e., if you buy that property you can obtain a spot at a public school as a resident of the school district), but the prices are super high. I don't understand why the government doesn't make the quality of schools a little more equal so ordinary people can send their kids to decent schools. Shouldn't it allow everyone to attend school at a low cost rather than a high cost? Why is it the reverse of that?
>
> Another factor is that rural parents don't place very high a value on education. Nowadays, education really is a competition on the basis of capital (*pin ziben*). For urbanites, tuition itself is just "a single hair from nine oxen" (a drop in the bucket) —most of their investment on

education goes to hiring all kinds of tutors, paying for all kinds of after-school courses, and buying all kinds of top-end supplementary resources. Many rural parents can't afford those things, and some of those who can afford them still aren't willing to make that kind of investment. Some parents think it's enough just to get a little education, to learn to read, write, and say a few sentences in Mandarin so they can communicate with people outside (the village). Some even think they can get rich without education.

Mr. Liang felt especially pained about Duqiao Secondary's low matriculation rate, which has never risen substantially since it fell in the mid-1990s. In recent years, according to official figures, thirty to forty high school students have tested into "universities" (*daxue*) each year, but according to Mr. Liang, all of these schools have actually been technical or vocational colleges rather than universities. Although there should be more to education than merely preparing students to test into post-secondary schools, he said, students who do not matriculate are less likely to find "a way out."

In addition, Mr. Liang mentioned, many students have reported to him that the knowledge and skills they learn at many technical colleges are not useful. After they graduate, there is little difference from simply going straight out to work after high school, plus their parents have to pay 30,000 to 40,000 yuan in tuition. As a teacher, he supports vocational education, but he feels it is unfair and a waste of potential human resources to limit rural children to that path. (He repeatedly emphasized that many rural children are quite smart.) I told him about a three-year survey of general education classes for every major at Sun Yat-sen University, which found that only 30 percent of students came from the countryside, and only 15 percent had lived in the countryside for at least fifteen years.[5] Mr. Liang was not surprised by these findings at all. As far as he knew, there were students from Duqiao Secondary who went to Sun Yat-sen every year in the 1980s, but not a single one in the past twenty years, and very few even among those who attended high school in Wucheng after completing middle school at Duqiao. Among all the rural secondary schools throughout Wu County, Duqiao was above average, which is why it retained its high school. Mr. Liang reckoned that "if you want to go to Sun Yat-sen from Wu County, basically the only way is to attend middle school in Wucheng." He added wistfully that under current conditions, where vocational education was not able to provide practical skills, it has even become hard to say whether going to school is still a useful way for young people in the township to improve their lives—unless they manage to attend secondary or even primary school in the county seat.

Shoude, who had accompanied me in this interview, said the situation the teacher had described basically matched his own understanding, although he wondered whether Mr. Liang's specific choice of words might have been a bit extreme due to his concern for rural education. I later asked Shouyi, and he also agreed that the teacher's analysis was correct, citing an example: In

2005, he proposed sending his six-year-old grandson Siyuan to attend Cheng Village Primary School, but his son Fudao and his wife vehemently disagreed. They could not obtain a seat at a public school in Wucheng, and they worried the boy would not be safe at a private school for migrant children, so instead they sent him to a "closed management" (*fengbishi guanli*) elite school. The total tuition from primary to graduation from middle school amounted to 300,000 yuan (including room and board on weekdays during each semester), with additional charges for themed activities each semester (such as field trips in the spring and autumn, outings to Guangzhou, etc.). In 2010, Fudao also sent his second son (born over-quota in 2004) to the same school. Fudao said his goal in doing this was not for his sons to "read too many books" (obtain an advanced education), since they would probably not need to rely on education to improve their lives and fates in the future. Instead, he just hoped that his children could grow up in a good environment and at least avoid the acquisition of bad habits. In the end, Shouyi conceded that Fudao's choice was the right one, and he was glad that his grandsons could speak English, play piano, and paint.

In contrast with Siyuan, Jingdao's son Zhiyuan said that they "belonged to two completely different worlds." He was raised by his grandparents Shoude and Cheng Ju, attending primary school in Cheng Village and secondary school in Duqiao. Most villagers educated their children in basically the same way as Zhiyuan rather than that of Siyuan.

Life and Pulse

No matter how difficult life may be for the young people of Cheng Village, the material conditions of life are much better than they were for their parents and grandparents. When middle-aged and older villagers discuss the younger generation, they often say, "they've never tasted bitterness" (endured hardship), taking every occasion to "appreciate today's sweetness while recalling yesterday's bitterness," describing how hard it was back then, when sometimes they did not even have enough food to eat. Shouzhi does this as well, but Jingxian has her own take on her father's "grumbling." Of course, what old people say is true, she said, and it makes a certain degree of sense, but they cannot grasp that now young people have their own headaches to worry about. People change as the times change, and people at every age in every era have different problems.

What are young people's headaches. When I raised that question, Jingxian gave several different responses in different settings. Most of them could be summed up as "not having enough money," "powerlessness," "boredom," and "always feeling that something is missing." Upon further inquiry, she provided concrete explanations of the latter two responses.

"Boredom" or "meaninglessness" (*meijin*) did not mean unwillingness to work. Especially under conditions where she still had to raise her children, there was no doubt that she and Li Sheng had to muster their resources and come up with all kinds of ways to get work done. She often felt, however, that this kind of life was meaningless: No matter how hard they worked, it seemed hard to imagine how their lives could be improved substantially. Jingxian even said that the only future she could imagine in a few decades was the same as her mother's, raising her grandchildren, her entire life revolving around pots and pans every day:

> It feels like I can't accomplish anything in this life other than mothering two sons and raising them up. It's just a repetition of the previous generation's life, and that of my grandparents, just circling around this world and then going back (through death). What's the point (*shenme jin*)? If I were like those rich people, or like you academics or people with careers, at least I could say I accomplished something, there would be some point (to my life). With people like us, our lives are really just aimed at having food to eat and clothes to wear. Sometimes when I think about it, it's truly depressing.

Li Sheng, who was also present, criticized Jingxian:

> You're being a bit negative. Isn't that what life is about for everyone? Isn't that true for the rich as well? Can they bring (their wealth) with them into the grave? "You can't take it with you in life or in death" (as the saying goes).

Jingxian defended her position:

> We can't take it with us in death, but why can't we have it in life? Take Fudao's son, for example: He was already rich when he was born, so in the future he doesn't need to worry about making money, he can just live off the interest (from loans). Isn't this "taking it with you in life"?

Li Sheng responded that, no matter whether one's life is meaningful, parents do all they can for their children. Jingxian said, "Of course they do, but that's a separate issue. Doing all you can is one thing, boredom and the sense of meaninglessness is another."

As for the statement that "it always feels as if something is missing," one summer day in 2012, Jingxian explained that this refers not to concrete things like money, but to the sense of enjoying interesting experiences in life and opportunities to see the world outside the village. In her opinion, going out to work did not count, since it was only an effort to seek out subsistence. I asked, "You mean traveling?" She said:

> Maybe. Yes, traveling is basically what I mean, but then again it isn't. If you travel to this city and that is just to work, then it doesn't count. You only go there to get food to eat and clothes to wear. How could you be

in the mood to go around and appreciate the scenery, to experience life? For example, if you were a construction worker on the Canton Tower, of course you could see the Pearl River, but this feels completely different than if you go up (in the tower) to drink tea and watch the river. What's lacking isn't the scenery, but the feeling.

There's a TV series called *The Passionate Years*. Nowadays our living conditions are fine, but there's no passion (*jiqing*). To put it more seriously, we're like the zombies in (the computer game and TV series) *Plants vs. Zombies*: We can move, but we don't have life. All we think about every day is how to make money, coming up with all kinds of ways to improve our food, clothes, and lodging. To put it more lightly, it's like our saying from rural superstition, "you've lost your soul (*hun*)." Everything is fine in terms of food, sleep, and money, but we're missing a soul.

After further discussion, Jingxian concluded that a good life would include both "life" and "soul." Life was like a person's body, while soul was like a person's pulse. If a person's body could move without a pulse, then they were a "zombie." In describing young people's feelings about life, she said:

There's an expression about the "life-pulse" (*mingmai*): If you have life then you have a pulse, and you only have life if you have a pulse. Sometimes I think our lives are much better than those our parents experienced back then, but sometimes I feel that now we have life without a pulse.

In contrast with what Jingxian imagined, however, rich young villagers like Fudao did not always feel that life was meaningful. On the contrary, he often complained that life was "meaningless"—at least as often as people like Jingxian and Li Sheng did.

Since Fudao was usually busy with all kinds of things related to his business, and often out of town, I had few opportunities for formal, quiet interviews with him. We mostly met at his stone-processing plant or in a restaurant. On several occasions while we were talking over a meal, Fudao would be interrupted repeatedly by phone calls, regarding either the coordination of work at the plant or something his business partners wanted to discuss. After hanging up the phone, he would often say, "I can't even eat a meal in peace," adding that every day was like this, that such a life was not meant for humans and truly meaningless. This did not mean that he would not answer the next phone call, or that he would not come up with every reason he could to increase his bargaining power, quibbling over every detail with his partners in an effort to maximize his interests. Often in the middle of a meal, he would go so far as to tell me, "Sorry, I need to make a phone call, I'm afraid I'll forget later on," and then call someone and talk on the phone about business for as long as twenty minutes.

On the evening of the twenty-fourth day of Month Twelve on the traditional calendar, I was preparing to eat dinner at the home of Shouzhi, where

I was staying. Fudao came to the village and invited me to go eat at his father Shouyi's house instead, since it was rare that he "had a chance to come eat at home." At the dinner table, he said:

> Tonight, I finally don't have to drink imported liquor. I know you Northerners like to drink *baijiu* (Chinese liquor), and actually I do too, I hate imported liquor, but normally I have no choice but to drink it for business socializing (*yingchou*). If I'm not socializing, I either eat in the factory or at a restaurant, so busy I only have enough time for fast food. It's a rare pleasure to enjoy a meal with a glass of *baijiu* in peace… . Drinking a little and chatting like this can relax and purify the mind. Don't think about the fact that I make more money than you, in my heart I truly admire you academics, you don't have to worry so much. Sometimes I think, if it weren't to make more money for my children, I really wouldn't want to live this kind of life anymore, overwhelmed with stress all day long, either calculating how to make money off of someone else, or calculating how to keep them from making too much money off of me. It's meaningless and tiring. My body is tired, and my mind even more so. It's true I've made some money, but other than that, it feels like my life is empty… . In the future you should just come and tell me about the Buddhist scriptures.

Before dinner was finished, Fudao answered another phone call about "meeting up with a few friends for *xiaoye* (a late-night snack, often involving alcohol)." At first, he told them he had already started drinking so could not drive, plus he was accompanying a friend at home, but the others just told him to bring me along, and they would send a car to pick him up in the village. After hanging up, he said, "Eating *xiaoye* with this gang of ruffians (Ct. *seuijai*), I'm afraid I'll have to down at least one bottle of imported liquor. Just as we were getting into a nice conversation, it's been ruined again. So pointless." Half an hour later, however, he cheerfully left the village with his friends.

Unmarried villagers younger than Jingxian and Fudao seemed to be much less concerned with such problems. During a visit to Cheng Village on Grave-Sweeping Day 2013, I ran into Yuanwen and asked if, when meeting up with middle school classmates, they discussed such topics. He said that those who had already married had some sense of responsibility, but other than money, all they complained about were some trivialities. People like himself who had not married were frustrated mainly about not earning enough money, and there was nothing else they could complain about around people in their age group. He said:

> For unmarried people, if one person has enough food to eat then the whole household can eat their fill, and family affairs are handled by the parents. What's the point of taking things so seriously? Why not seize the opportunity to have fun? When we get married, we won't be so free.

For teenagers like Yuanwen's cousin Zhiyuan, they did not even have a clear idea about this topic yet. They were influenced, however, by young adults like Yuanwen. One day in August 2013, I ran into Zhiyuan, who was about to begin his third year of middle school, and asked about his plans in life. He figured that he had no hope to continue in school, considering his marks, so he planned to go out to work after completing middle school,[6] saying, "This is the fate of us young people from the countryside, what other kinds of plans could we have? Except not to be born here again in the next lifetime."

While we were talking, Zhiyuan was also reading a story on his knockoff phone. I asked whether he was reading a novel by Jin Yong (Louis Cha), but his response was rather sophisticated: "Jin Yong? No. His crappy stuff is too realistic, not imaginative enough, just like a history textbook. I prefer time-travel novels about officialdom (*chuanyue guanchang xiaoshuo*), they're super imaginative."

Zhiyuan said that basically all of his classmates liked reading time-travel stories of one kind or another, with many girls reading romantic fiction, while the boys preferred martial fantasy (*wuxia*), science fiction, or officialdom literature. During his first year of middle school, Zhiyuan read science fiction about time-travel to the future (rather than time-travel to the past). During his second year, after Yuanwen introduced him to time-travel literature about officialdom, Zhiyuan came to regard his classmates' taste for romantic fiction, martial fantasy, and science fiction as a sign of their immaturity—only time-travel officialdom literature was compelling. He told me about several novels that Yuanwen had introduced him to, saying they were popular among the people he went out to work with in the city, including titles like: *Lust and Caution of the Officials' Way*, *Power and Seduction in the Officials' Way*, *Ambitious Heroes of the Officials' Way*, and *Reborn into a Distinguished and Decadent Career*.[7] Each numbered over a million words and was downloaded from the internet up to several million times. Zhiyuan said that he understood clearly that these stories were fantasy through and through, and yet he often imagined himself traveling through time while reading them.

Zhiyuan often recommended novels he liked to his classmates. As a result, eight or nine girls and more than ten boys in his class had come to like this genre. He explained:

> At first, I expected the girls would say these novels were too sexist, that they wouldn't like them. It never occurred to me that they would like them too. Later I learned that they felt, if the male protagonists truly loved all the female protagonists, if they were sincere, plus if they had more money than they could spend and enjoyed limitless wealth and power, then why was it necessary for them to get married? Modern society doesn't need to be so feudal and conservative—as long as the love is genuine, the formalities aren't important. If other people want to gossip about it, let them.

The Younger Generation 221

Prior to this, I had read *Lust and Caution of the Officials' Way* and recommended it to Fudao, but he said that after reading less than 10 percent of the book he lost all interest, that it was "nothing but the idle dreams of losers (*diaosi*)."

Later, I skimmed some of the other novels mentioned by Zhiyuan, and their plots were similar to that of *Lust and Caution of the Officials' Way*, with the following synopsis:

> The male protagonist is born into a certain family, which disowns him because he rebels and refuses to pursue a career as an official. He dies, but at the moment of death he enters a time portal and is transported back to the 1980s or early 1990s, where he decides to try a different way of life as a rural cadre. Since he knows how society will change in the future, he is always able to make more effective decisions than his competitors in officialdom, so he is quickly promoted again and again. His abilities at work are outstanding, he can manage interpersonal relations with ease, he values the interests of the masses, he has a sense of justice, he has sworn brothers, and throughout his career he helps the area under his jurisdiction to prosper and to be restored from chaos to social order.
>
> He is an ideal man, better at fighting than the special forces, a sophisticated connoisseur of poetry, music, and art, speaks fluent English, and knows world history like the back of his hand. He is also highly enlightened in Buddhism and Daoism, putting to shame monks who have been meditating and studying for decades. He has countless lovers, all as beautiful as goddesses, some of them forced by poverty into prostitution or becoming someone's mistress, others being the daughters of important officials, or very super rich families, or the campus queen of some university, or someone else's wife or mother. He possesses extraordinary sexual prowess, often making love four or five times a day for two to three hours at a time. (The frequent sex scenes are suggestive rather than explicit.[8]) Out of pure love, these lovers are willing to do anything for him, but without ever harboring expectations or pressuring him into marriage. He supports them in business as they grow extravagantly rich or become important officials and world-class artists.
>
> In the end, he becomes the life-pulse of the family that had disowned him, which finally comes to accept, value, and rely on him. His travel back through time was determined by fate, or it was the result of some entity outside the world that changed his fate.

Notes

1 A waterjet cutter is a high-tech tool that uses pressurized water to cut stones. Its advantages include the ability to cut stone into any shape at one time, plus it does not generate heat or dust, so it is safer, more flexible, more efficient, and less harmful to the environment than an electric saw.

2 *Translator's note*: In the 1980s–1990s, term *dagong* (打工) was adopted from Cantonese in contrast with Mandarin terms for working such as *gongzuo* (工作, a more general term for work), *shangban* (上班, to work in an office for a salary), or *ganhuo* (干活, to work manually, usually farming one's own land rather than working for a wage or salary). Originally this term was adopted to describe the precarious status of rural residents who went to look for blue- or pink-collar jobs in the emerging private sector, with the expectation that they would eventually return to farming their own land in the countryside. They were not considered "workers" (*gongren* 工人), since that term was limited to permanent blue-collar employees of state-owned enterprises, who were usually registered as urban residents and assigned their jobs by the state. These "new workers" from the countryside were therefore described colloquially as *dagongzhe*—"people who work," but in the sense of competing for jobs on the labor market. Officially they were called *nongmingong* (农民工), literally "peasant-worker" but normally translated as "migrant worker." By the 2010s, when the labor market had become universal and differences between sectors less clearly defined, the term *dagong* had come to be used for most types of wage labor, including state-sector, white-collar, and agricultural jobs. In this book, however, *dagong* refers to the earlier sense of rural residents competing on the labor market for temporary blue- or pink-collar jobs at private enterprises. When it is necessary to be clear, I use the Chinese romanization *dagong*, but otherwise I translate it as "to work" or "wage labor.".

3 These were a kind of bamboo products designed to be used as steamers for breakfast foods. In 2007, the price of each steamer was 0.3 yuan. By 2013 it had already risen to 0.8. Normally, they could make 15 to 20 steamers per day.

4 *Diaosi* (屌丝, literally "penis hair") was a sarcastic expression used online to describe people who were poor, ugly, short, or stupid.

5 The scope implied by this survey consisted of students who had completed their mandatory education at rural schools (beginning primary school at age six or seven and graduating from middle school at age fifteen or sixteen). From this we can deduce that about 15 percent of the students attended middle or even primary school in urban areas, although their household registration remained rural.

6 In July of 2014, as I was writing this chapter as a visiting scholar in London, Jingxian told me via QQ that her nephew Zhiyuan had already gone to work in Zhuhai.

7 *Translator's note*: The Chinese titles are: *Guandao zhi sejie* (官道之色戒), *Guandao zhi quanse liaoren* (官道之权色撩人), *Guandao zhi xiaoxiong* (官道之枭雄), and *Chongsheng zhi fengliu shitu* (重生之风流仕途).

8 Zhiyuan likened them to "softcore pornography" as opposed to "hardcore." When this second-year middle school student raised such topics, not only did he seem well versed, he discussed them without a hint of embarrassment.

Part II
Reflections

8 The Paradox of Transition

Smallholders

Since the nineteenth century, the fate of Chinese smallholding peasants (*xiaonong*) in the turn toward modernity has attracted a great deal of attention. Chen Hansheng (1984: 16–18) argued that the basic reason smallholders had fallen behind was the serious inequality between landlords and peasants (*nongmin*) with regard to land ownership. The potential solution was peasant revolution. Liang Shuming (2006a: 348) and James Yen (1989: 172–173), however, argued that the basic reason was actually peasants' "ignorance," so they called for peasant education, especially vocational training. Fei Xiaotong (1999a: 189, 201) argued that the outflow from the countryside of factors of production, especially financial resources, had trapped peasants in what Tawney (2014: 83) had called the "predicament" of agricultural development, so Fei advocated rural industrialization. Peasants "suffering from land hunger" were "shackled to the land" (Fei Xiaotong 1999a: 439 and 476; 1999b: 133), so they preferred "the economy of killing time" (*xiaoqian jingji*). In the 1980s, Fei Xiaotong's (1999c: 218, 372; 1999d: 87) discussions of "leaving the soil without leaving the countryside" deepened his thinking about rural industrialization. However, China's export-oriented economy and urban development gave rise to migrant peasant-workers (*nongmingong*) who "left both the soil and the countryside" (Huang 1997: 3), becoming an important factor in "China's transformation" (Murphy 2009). Throughout rural China, it became common for women and the elderly to do the farming. Philip Huang (2007: 476; 2010: 127, 103) called this "the institutionalization of semi-industrial, semi-agricultural (*bangong bangeng*)" households, but it achieved a "hidden revolution" in the agrarian economy's transition from labor-intensive to capital-intensive production, causing an "historical watershed" in China's development. The smallholding economy's transition brought an immense change in the economic beliefs of individual peasants, a change often criticized as a descent into materialism (Yan 2014).

Rural politics have also undergone several major changes. In the early modern period (1840–1949), China's state bureaucracy began attempting to reach down to the countryside, but rural communities actually remained the

DOI: 10.4324/9781003353072-10

political stage of local gentry and lineage elders (Fei Xiaotong 1999f: 340–343; Huang 2003; Duara 1996: 13; Shue 1988: 106–107). Top-down state power and bottom-up lineage and gentry powers together formed a "dual-track politics" (Fei Xiaotong 1999f: 340–343). At the level of village politics, this was expressed as "lineage politics" and "rule by lineage elders" (1999g: 344, 368). This analysis has been supported by the work of Francis Hsu (2001), Lin Yaohua (1989), and Martin Yang (2001) on kinship ethics and "the pattern of father-son identification." On this, Liang Shuming (2006b:85–86) believed that the crux of Chinese culture was its foundation on ethics, so "all politics was ethics." The 1980s saw the initial establishment of grassroots (i.e., township-level) political power in the countryside and villager self-government (Zhang 1992: 473–480; Xu 1997: 22–25). Villager self-government, in particular, was even considered to be the starting point for China's bottom-up democratic constitutional government (Xu 2003). Cultural resources such as social memory and symbolism began to play a role in the transformation of rural politics (Jing 2013: 160–170). According to Liu Xin, the failure of political education movements led to a sort of "immoral politics" (2000: 157). The establishment of state power came to include "sending law down to the countryside" (Su 2000: 40–43), molding "citizens" and changing communities' public authorities (Feuchtwang 1997). Like the "confusion of tongues" described by Clifford Geertz (1999: 12; 2000: 243), confusion among overlapping sets of rules caused problems for governance. Within a system of "pressure politics" (Rong et al. 1998: 27), peasant petitioning of higher authorities (Ying 2001; Zhao 2006) and "rightful resistance" (O'Brien and Li 2004) became attention-grabbing phenomena. Interpersonal networks of reciprocity (*renqing*) continued to influence grassroots politics (Liu 2008; Tan 2016a), with some observers calling them "the lineage politics of a new era" (Feng 2010).

On the social level, early modern rural China was characterized by "the differential mode of association" (*chaxu geju*): "Like the ripples that form when a stone is thrown into the water, each person is the center of the circles that his social influence pushes outwards" (Fei Xiaotong 1999d: 334). Daniel Kulp (2006: 121) and Maurice Freedman (2000: 2) therefore emphasized that the key to understanding Chinese society is familism and clans. Rubie Watson (2008: 230–241), however, discovered that clans "united by trials and tribulation" were also divided by class. In the family, the power of the father and the husband plays the dominant role (Fei Xiaotong 1999a: 26–29; 1999f: 72–74). The principles for managing interpersonal relations within a family emphasize the centrality of filial piety, self-restraint, diligence, and sexual restrictions (Pan 1993: 129–232; Liang 2006b:67–122; Fei Xiaotong 1999g: 316–381; Hsu 2001: 205–221; Hsu 1990: 66–71). These structural analyses were supported by the fieldwork of Gallin (1966), Potter (1970), Pasternak (1972), Baker (1979), Hsieh (1985), and Chuang (1981), among others. Within the context of the modern market economy, the importance of property increased for individuals within families (Gallin1966:143–144; Cohen 1976). Under the influence of urbanization, Han Chinese villages comprised a dispersed modality of the family (Chuang 1972 and 1981). Among the younger generations of villagers, there was a clear increase in their sense of self-determination, as discovered in the research of Diamond (1975), Croll (1981: 185), Wolf (1985), Davis and Harrell (1993), and Yan (2006: 72, 153). According to Stafford (2000:122–126), women played an important role in maintaining the networks of reciprocity involved in care and communication. Feminist scholars such as Gates (1989), Judd (1989), Bossen (1999), and Evans (2008) demonstrated that women's true liberation remained an unfinished task. According to Wu Fei (2009: 117, 32–38), however, hierarchy and the relative strictness or relaxation of relations between genders and generations within the family could not be understand purely in terms of power, since they were also closely intertwined with people's conceptions of ethics, justice, fate, reason (*qingli*), propriety (*liyi*), and survival (*guo rizi*). Outside the family, Yan Yunxiang (2006: 207–208, 243) argued, under the "cold logic of the market," villagers had already become "individuals without public morality." According to Liu Xin (2000; 2005: 144–145), villagers already lived under the shadow of the self, their personalities unstable and in flux. By contrast, Ellen Oxfeld (2013) contended that peasants still "remembered the source of the water they drank," following traditional Confucian values. As for the role of money in interpersonal relations, Mayfair Yang (2009: 135–141) noticed a shift in the nature of gifts from "use-value" to "exchange-value," while Yan Yunxiang (2000: 64) used the term "instrumental gifts" to describe gifts whose exchange involved self-interest. Victor Nee (1985: 171–178), Xiang Biao (2000: 448–450), Zhang Li (2014: 59–61), Wu Chongqing (2014: 141–155), and I (Tan 2016b) all observed another situation where villagers relied on traditional social networks to withstand the market risks posed by the principles of monetary exchange. Hans Steinmüller (2013: 174) also discovered that, due to the divergence between official pronouncements and local practice, activities considered by the formal bureaucracy as "feudal" or corrupt could also be understood as traditional etiquette or obligatory reciprocity when it came to local knowledge. In addition, some researchers observed that the stratification of rural society marked by money gave rise to social attitudes of "depression" (*yumen*) or "hatred of the rich" (Xue 2009), where those who suddenly became rich could not avoid feelings of anxiety (Osburg 2013).

With regard to beliefs, overall, Chinese peasants' traditional concern for ancestors surpassed that of religion. Fei Xiaotong (1999g: 333) argued that in early modern Western societies people came together through an "organizational mode of association" (*tuanti geju*), like straws forming a bundle and bundles forming a haystack. That sort of society required a God to command independent individuals, one that "treats everyone with justice, impartiality, and love" (341). In rural China's differential mode of association, by contrast, society was:

> composed of webs woven out of countless personal relationships. To each knot in these webs is attached a specific ethical principle. For this reason,

the traditional moral system was incapable of producing a comprehensive moral concept. Therefore, all the standards of value in this system were incapable of transcending the differential personal relationships of the Chinese social structure (344).[1]

Liang Shuming (2006b:88–89) believed that morality replaced religion in rural China, since a society "based on ethics" enabled people to achieve meaning and contentment in their lives through secular "human relationships" (*renlun*, relationships defined by Confucian principles). Francis Hsu (2001: 205) also emphasized that peasant worship of ancestors strengthened the social structure based on "the pattern of father-son identification," and vice versa: "Setting out from the whole organized through kinship, the pattern of father-son identification is merely a bond required within a large family, on the one hand connecting to a multitude of ancestors, and on the other to countless descendants." "The family is part of familial religion, and familial religion is part of the family" (210). Research by Lin Yaohua (2000: 189) and Freedman (2000: 58) on familial institutions and lineages showed that ancestor worship's notion of "incense fires" (*xianghuo*) was most important for peasants. Aside from ancestor worship, C.K. Yang (2007: 225, 260, 270–274) was one of the earlier scholars to conduct systematic research on religion in Chinese society, discovering that, like ancestor worship, religion in Chinese society was closely related to Confucianism and the moral order of "human relationships"—so it was a "diffused religion." Shortly thereafter, Arthur Wolf (2014: 160, 169) argued on the basis of fieldwork in rural Taiwan that, although ancestor worship was no doubt important, when descendants neglected offerings or failed to continue the family line appropriately, the ancestors would punish them, so it was not without utilitarian elements. Emily Ahern (1973:154, 200) went so far as to argue that the central logic of ancestor worship among Han Chinese peasants was utilitarian, and if there was no property to pass down, then it was not necessary for descendants to make offerings. Li Yih-yuan (2002: 154–155; 2006) pointed out that ancestor worship in Han culture included three types of relationships: parental (*qinzi*), genealogical (*shixi*), and power-based—with the parental relationship as the norm. According to Li Yih-yuan (2002: 154–155, 2006), Wolf's evidence was based on migrant society in Taiwan, so the element of parental relationships was weak, and Ahern's evidence was based on extreme cases where abnormal kin relations predominated, so the ancestor worship she studied was mainly characterized by power relations.[2] Looking at studies by Gallin (1966: 142–145), Pasternak (1972: 65–69), and Chuang (1981), it is clear that Li's analysis possesses strong and comprehensive explanatory power. Other scholars (Sangren 1987; Dean 1993, 1998, 2003; Feuchtwang 2008; Faure 2009) examined the relationship between state and society, discovering many shadows of the state in folk beliefs. James Watson (2006: 57) called this "standardization of the gods," while David Faure and Liu Zhiwei (2013) pointed out that, in the context of Chinese history and culture, a more accurate term would be "legitimization of the gods." Chau (2006: 214) and Notar (2006: 136) emphasized, however, that when the state permeated rural folk beliefs, it created a power structure in tension with rural society. Liu Xin (2005: 144–145, 146–152) attempted to demonstrate that peasants only cared about "the today-ness of today" rather than considering the past or the future, completely falling into "nothingness." Yan Yunxiang argued that the world of peasant beliefs had already been shattered by the market economy (2006: 205–206). Tan Chee-Beng (2012), Julie Chu (2010: 165–217), and Zheng Zhenman and Zheng Li (2012) discovered, however, that folk beliefs remained the foundation for maintaining networks of relationships among both overseas Chinese communities and among peasants in southeastern China. In addition, the spread of Christianity in rural China began attracting attention again. Some researchers expressed concerns that the religion was again becoming an "instrument" of Western invasion of Chinese society (Chen 2012), since historically when Christianity entered rural China, conflicts with lineages never ceased (Zhang Xianqing 2009: 80–83). According to Lu Yunfeng (2010), Li Huawei (2012), and Hu Weiqing (2013), peasant conversion to Christianity was related to the experience of hardships. Considering, however, that the state was where peasants had conventionally placed their hopes of overcoming hardships (Guo and Sun 2003), there should be other reasons worth investigating behind the recent turn to Christianity.

In sum, relative to the traditional "economy of killing time" that was "shackled to the land," its "dual-track politics," its social structure based on the "differential mode of association," and its belief system centered on ancestor worship, after undergoing the twin influences of revolution and the market, contemporary rural China clearly underwent a great transformation. Is it truly the case, however, that the continual intensification of modern factors led to revolutionary changes in the smallholder economy such that contemporary peasant life has become limited to rampant materialism, political conservatism, egocentrism, the collapse of beliefs, and a concern only for the present moment—as many researchers have argued? The history and present reality of Cheng Village and Duqiao Township cast doubt on such assessments.

Agriculture and Industry

This book does not aim to examine whether the agricultural economic institutions established by Land Reform had a sufficient basis in class differentiation. The support among residents of Cheng Village for the 1950–1951 "redistribution of the fruits of labor," however, and the Peasant Association head Chen Xin's decision to kill himself after being accused of seeking personal advantage from that campaign, both demonstrate a high degree of identification with the ideals of Land Reform among ordinary peasants. Although the later formation of agricultural cooperatives and then the commune system overcame the natural and market risks that individual households faced in agricultural production, it did not fundamentally prevent the outflow of economic resources from the countryside. On the contrary, agricultural surplus was extracted in even larger measure than before. The residents of Cheng Village never again saw an "economy of killing time." The "exaggeration wind" and Cheng Chengren's strict implementation of policies were both extreme footnotes to this shift in economic logic. The end of hunger among peasants after the mid-1970s could be a testament to agricultural growth, but in Cheng Shoukuan's memory of that thirst for "freedom," it is not hard to detect peasants' ardent desire for an economic form with the household as its unit of production.

In the mid-1990s, agriculture began to recede from importance as a source of income for most families in Cheng Village. Yet most residents still have not dared to completely give up their land. When it comes to the transfer of land-use rights, especially irreversible transfers, the villagers are still inclined toward caution as if protecting their lives. There have been a few struggles between the township government and the villagers over the confiscation of land. Basically, these have been less about land rights and more about the value of land-based agriculture as a "lifeline" for the security of peasant families. Since peasants divide their land into one type for "survival" and another for "making money," the villagers are not so tenacious about the transfer of use rights for hilly woodland. In a moderately developed area like that of Cheng Village, therefore, there has emerged a paradox in the mobility of economic factors. On the one hand, agriculture is already incapable of absorbing the countryside's main workforce and providing a dignified life, so many peasants have left the villages to work. On the other hand, in pursuit of financial speculation, many bosses have occupied scarce resources in the countryside, such as farmland and high-quality water, in the name of building factories and developing large-scale agriculture (often actually leaving the occupied land unused in the end). Compared with the historical experience of the unidirectional outflow of production factors from the early modern countryside, the economic situation seems more complicated in moderately developed parts of contemporary rural China. As industrial and commercial capital tries to invest in rural land, there is not much resistance regarding woodland, but when it comes to the "red line" of cultivated land, a contradiction emerges between efficiency and the protection of life. As far as capital is concerned, efficiency is the root of life. For peasants who still cannot completely cast off farmland for their survival, however, who persist in being "semi-agricultural" (*bannong*), they maintain an escape route for the preservation of life. Although the "millennial woes" of Cheng Village's ordinary peasants—whose "lives never last a century"—have not yet been resolved, as far as their semi-agricultural aspect is concerned, capital-intensive efficient agriculture may end up taking those lives.

On the level of micro-production, however, ordinary village families in a semi-agricultural condition paradoxically make all kinds of careful calculations to maximize efficiency whenever possible. Chengren, for example, began in the 1980s to use synthetic fertilizer not only in his rice farming but also in his vegetable cultivation. After fertilizer and pesticide became more affordable in the mid-1990s, it became even more common for everyone to apply those inputs to their crops in larger quantities than necessary. When it came to planting trees on their hilly woodland, if they could afford it they would choose to plant tangerine trees, which had a higher economic value and also required large amounts of fertilizer and pesticide, or even eucalyptus trees—known as "water-sucking pumps." The decision to plant these crops, which Cheng Shoukuan complained would "squeeze every nutrient and every drop of water from the soil," became the most vivid portrait of an agriculture oriented toward short-term micro-efficiency. Still more ironically, after most village households had decreased the pressure of population on the land through semi-agricultural arrangements, farmers "could not even earn ten cents" per *jin* of vegetables, whereas the rural vendors, transporters, wholesalers, and urban retailers all "took a yuan here and a yuan there." Young people who knew something about modern animal husbandry, such as Cheng Jingxian, sometimes earned a little money and sometimes lost money, at most daring only to treat pig farming as a way to supplement the family's income, relying on the husband's wages from working in the city as the backbone of the household economy. In such a semi-agricultural condition, although these smallholders in a moderately developed region had achieved a "hidden revolution" in the intensification of capital involved in agriculture, they remained far from any "historical turning point."

If we use the term "industrial" (*gong*) in a broad sense to encompass all non-agricultural economic activities, then the peasants of this moderately developed region began pursuing "semi-industrial" (*bangong*) livelihoods as soon as decollectivization was completed in the early 1980s. Cheng Shouyi and Cheng Shoukuan became carpenters, Cheng Shoude opened a watch repair shop, Cheng Chengxin occasionally undertook infrastructure construction work, and even Cheng Chengren, always regarded as "rigid" and "inflexible," began to run a stall selling tobacco in Duqiao and neighboring market towns. It was not easy, however, for people in Cheng Village to cast off the shackles of the land, transitioning from agriculture to other activities. Shouyi belonged to a small minority of villagers who managed to escape poverty and become rich through industry, and the secret to his success lay not in industry itself but in his social networks. The wisdom of experience had taught him early on that "connections" possessed the potential for conversion into capital.[3] As a victor, however, Shouyi sometimes forgot that connections often depended on specific conditions besides the individual ability to "operate" them, so not everyone could have such good connections.

Aside from individual households going into industry, commune and brigade enterprises had originally provided another path for peasants to cast off the shackles of the land. After they began in the late 1970s, in fact, Cheng Village's collective enterprises all developed quite well. However, these enterprises could not become as successful as the township and village enterprises (TVEs) in southern Jiangsu, Wenzhou, or the Pearl River Delta, beginning to decline in the early 1990s before collapsing in the mid-1990s—just as slogans about TVEs were at their peak. The reasons for their failure in this moderately developed region seem to include both objective and subjective ones. Externally, from the late 1970s through the 1980s, Cheng Village's collective enterprises faced only a basically local market, but these conditions changed drastically in the mid-1990s. More importantly, in the late 1990s, the grassroots government vigorously promoted TVEs throughout the region as a solution to fiscal shortfalls. The little vitality Cheng Village's enterprises had possessed ended up consuming itself by "killing the chicken to get the eggs." Internally, in the 1970s–1980s, an important premise for the existence of collective enterprises was the frugality and honesty of brigade (and later village) cadres. In the mid-1990s, the cadres' corruption and lack of transparency ended up crushing the enterprises.

Without opportunities to participate in industry by "leaving the soil without leaving the village," the only path left for most peasants was to leave home and look for work. Throughout waves upon waves of labor migration over the course of twenty-plus years, however, very few managed to convert completely from agriculture to industry. Among the households of migrants such as Cheng Jingshan, Cheng Jingdao, and Cheng Jingzu, none of them completely abandoned agriculture. There were also many young people such as Cheng Jingye and Cheng Jingxiu who divided their time between working and "goofing off"—because they were either "lackadaisical" or "did not take anything too seriously." This was not unrelated to their subjective values, but it was also intertwined with their particularly low wages: Since they could see no long-term prospects in their jobs, industry became less valued in their lives.

For the grassroots government, "economic development" was the most important slogan. Needless to say, "economy" should be "developed" for people: Development should be the means, with people as the end. What was surprising, however, was that in Duqiao's mixed economy of agriculture and industry, in the pursuit of efficiency, it often became unclear whether development was a means or an end—and sometimes the two became obviously reversed. In the push to develop Cheng Village's "ancient" settlement, the focus was not the protection of traditional architecture or culture but the fraudulent scheming of Duqiao's leaders. My purpose here is not to morally criticize grassroots cadres for their motives. Although ordinary villagers were concerned with different goals than those of the cadres, their affirmation of "development" itself was very much along the same lines. At root, if "antiquity" could not be converted into money, then the actual age of the village was irrelevant. Cadres such as Cheng Chengxin could see clearly the profound contradictions within this situation, so he bluntly interpreted "development" as "digging up the land." This quickly became the township government's "golden opportunity." All of this involved "playing edge-ball," however, as they side-stepped the formal institutions of tax collection and land-use restrictions in order to sacrifice basic farmland. It was a sort of "partial efficiency" (Zhang Yonghong 2009).

In blindly promoting township enterprises to achieve development, moreover, Duqiao's government quickly ransacked the countryside including Cheng Village, while also putting itself deeply in debt. Failing at industry and wrecking the existing "semi-agricultural" economy, these measures further led to a situation where "bosses were bigger than Heaven," so the grassroots government had to "wholeheartedly serve the bosses." In the face of fiscal shortfalls, the government went all out to promote ceramics production, poisoning the air. For the peasants, who "went to any lengths in pursuit of development for the good of their descendants," what could be more sadly ironic than such pollution "cutting off the family line" in this way? Under the ruling logic of efficiency, however, it was not only grassroots government but also ordinary peasants who never attempted to break free from this paradox. For example, many villagers sold vegetables saturated with toxic agrochemicals. As farmers, villagers knew that the earth could not be "squeezed" to death in this way, just as women should not be fed too many chemical supplements in order to squeeze more babies out of them. After abandoning "the economy of killing time," most families adopted farming methods that "walked the road" of development "into the darkness"—as Cheng Shoukuan put it.

Both grassroots cadres and ordinary peasants often "bit the hand that fed them," criticizing the development that had improved their lives in some ways for causing new problems. Their response was not, however, a return to asceticism (Wang 2009: 43), but instead an embrace of the consumerism that had begun to spread from the cities to rural areas. Since the semi-agricultural, semi-industrial mixed economy was still relatively under-developed, the tension between desires and consumption capacity created yet another paradox. Even after Cheng Shouyi became rich, he always felt he was not making enough money. Although he opposed people "flaunting" their wealth, it was only during the moment of spending money that he truly felt wealthy. He believed that prostitution and overindulgence hurt the body, but he twisted Confucius' words ("desire for food and sex belongs to human nature") and the School of Principle's teachings ("maintain the Heavenly principles and extinguish the human desires") to absolve himself. Although Cheng Shoude was open-minded and easy-going, he was not unaffected by the pressure of being judged according to how much he consumed materialistically. In the processing of agricultural products such as Sanlu powdered milk, far more profitable than growing vegetables, the producers unscrupulously "poisoned" their customers in pursuit of profit. Ironically, Cheng Shoukuan rejoiced that his family was so poor that his grandson could not afford to drink milk, saving them from the danger. Cheng Shouzhi's desires for consumption could not be satisfied by his low income from a mix of agricultural and industry, so he became obsessed with playing the underground lottery. Although Cheng Fudao had already become a millionaire, he sometimes grew weary of a life that revolved around trying to make money every day, yet this could not change his thinking about consumption. As for sexual consumption, he loved to talk about it, but he lamented that it could not solve the problem of trust among business associates,[4] and that it had exhausted his sexual desire. Shouyi's Hunanese mistress said that when she was being consumed as a commodity, she became another person, so her self was no longer her true self.

Rule

In Cheng Village, when local power transferred from the hands of the clan elite to those of the cadres who "redistributed the fruits of labor," at least on the level of political discourse, "the people's self-rule" (*renmin dangjia zuozhu*) replaced "rule for the people" (*wei min zuo zhu*) by gentry and clan elders. In terms of orientation, "self-rule" flowed precisely toward the centralization of power. This paradox derives from the fact that after state power descended down into rural society, the first thing it had to do was to wrest power from the hands of the gentry and clan elite. Otherwise, the state would not have had any power to share democratically. One of the "tracks" within "dual-track politics" was dismantled, and the state's political ideology was no longer Confucian, but peasants still imagined rural politics according to the "dual-track" way of thinking, even believing that "the people's self-rule" followed the same logic as "the state's rule for the people."

The rural political practice of centralism ultimately clarified to the peasants that there was a difference between the needs of the state and their own. The "exaggeration wind" and grain extraction in the midst of starvation made this as clear as day. The residents of Cheng Village, however, did not attempt to change rural politics according to ideas of "democracy," instead maintaining that grassroots cadres were not "ruling for the people." This left a space of traditional "feudal thinking" in rural politics, and a key question became how to restrain and monitor the centralist cadres. Cheng Chengren punished Cheng Chengliu as a "bad element" even though ordinary peasants did not approve. The exaggeration wind's impact on the village was also inseparable from grassroots cadres. Cheng Chenggong detained people right and left, making them "ascend the longan tree," and during Family Planning he threatened people to the point that they committed suicide. For this the villagers called him a "thug." Needless to say, during a time of extreme starvation, not only did cadres such as Chen Lin "eat and take more than their share," they even chose to burn the ration tickets they had embezzled rather than sharing them with ordinary villagers. Cheng Shouyi resisted Chengren's cavalier use of the label "bad elements" as a weapon against Cheng Shoukuan, even leading the Red Flag faction in armed struggle against the East Wind in response to such injustices, but when he achieved a management position in the reservoir construction project, he used it to embezzle large sums of public funds. All this shows that the practices of grassroots power truly did display a touch of "patriarchal socialism" in "ruling for the people" (Stacey 1983: 15; Walder 1996: 251). Worth noting, however, is that rural political centralism's impact on relationships among ordinary peasants was not as profound as has been suggested by the discourse of class (Siu 1989: 170; Madsen 1984; Chan, Madsen, and Unger 1984). Chengren continued to value "loyalty among sworn brothers," Shouyi used his relationships with friends in the Four Cleanups work team to obtain a cadre position, and Shoude relied on his relationship with a classmate to flee political turmoil, and to obtain food and money when his family was in need. Not only were these relationships not completely destroyed, in part they even permeated the political practices of centralism.

After Cheng Village implemented the institutions of villager self-government (such as village committee elections), in the eyes of both village cadres and ordinary villagers, there was no doubt that Chengxin became the most "successful" cadre. His most important capital for conducting village politics, however, all derived from the former system of communes and brigades. For one thing, his reputation as "a man of his word" was related to his many years of service as a brigade cadre. For another, his main "political accomplishment" was running the village enterprises, which had been set up on the basis of the earlier brigade enterprises. After the various "democracies" of villager self-government were implemented, however, things did not become any easier than before. Although ordinary villagers felt that he was not a "good person," he still managed to occupy the center of power under the new conditions of periodic elections. This may have been because the villagers' "democratic consciousness" was not yet fully developed, as people often say (He and Lang 2002: 5). The paradox remains, however, that on the basis of villagers still lacking such consciousness, the top-down power apparatus and the discourse of intellectual circles both hope that grassroots cadres' "rule for the people" will push forward democracy, thereby enabling the majority of ordinary villagers to achieve "self-rule."

It is one thing to ask whether villagers are content, but another to ask whether they would be willing to stand up and effectively exercise the power of democratic oversight. Almost everyone in Cheng Village believed that cadres such as Chengxin had been corrupt in running the village enterprises, and in private they often talked about the cadres' prolific spending on food and drink in the market downtown, travels, and purchase of social insurance, and even their sale of collective assets at discounted rates. However, not a single villager ever stood up publicly, said what they knew and demanded an explanation, even if a perfunctory one, from the cadres. Instead, everyone chose to stay quiet on formal occasions. When Shouzhi led people to oppose the seizure of land for "Brigade Street," because of this he lost the opportunity to run as a candidate in the village committee election and was even accused of "sabotaging" the election. On another occasion he had attempted to petition higher authorities for an explanation about the non-payment of grain subsidies to several hamlets after the Wutong River diversion project, but in the face of the community of interests composed of the grassroots government and village cadres, no explanation came.

In Cheng Village's self-government, therefore, against cadres who do not "rule for the people," ordinary villagers do not have so many colorful "arts of resistance" (Scott 2007: 3). Their most common response to various grievances about cadres in self-government affairs is not resistance but silent "endurance." They hope that "good people" will serve as cadres or control public media, "ruling for the people." Of course there is no lack of "good people" in the countryside, but as soon as the majority of ordinary villagers pin their political hopes on such people, they have already become more distant from the center stage of villager self-government. To some degree, the practice of villager self-government is still stuck within the paradox between "the people's self-rule" and cadres' "rule for the people."

If this is what village politics looks like, then what of grassroots government? In Duqiao, as described above, after the 1980s and especially in the 1990s, the central work of grassroots officials consisted of three main types of activities: developing the local economy, collecting taxes and fees, and implementing the Family Planning Policy.

As it became more and more difficult to collect taxes and fees, the township government found it harder and harder to govern. In order to complete its tax-collection responsibilities, the logic of Family Planning work quietly underwent an inversion. Originally the collection of fines for over-quota births had been a means to the end of limiting the number of births, but when those fines became one of the life-rafts helping township governments to complete their tax-collection responsibilities, they gradually became the main goal of Family Planning work in practice.[5] According to formal regulations, Family Planning was one of the key policies for which no wiggle room was allowed. These conditions of governance, formed with the aim of generating revenue for the township government, were not suitable for explicit presentation to higher-level offices of the state. On the contrary, since they concerned the funding for the activities of so many township cadres, even if higher-level personnel got wind of the actual situation through back channels, they could not bring it up lightly and address it explicitly but could only feign ignorance. Whenever higher-level offices organized inspection tours, therefore, the interaction between higher and lower levels of government became a mere ritual of grassroots governance.

Many township officials felt they were "cast into an arena where they had no choice but to fight," so they "had no choice" but to act in this way. Objectively speaking, under such a "pressure system," "there were a thousand threads above and one needle below": Township officials had heavy responsibilities coupled with very little room to maneuver, so there truly were ways in which they had no choice. At the same time, however, this also involved the township bureaucratic system, along with the interests of individual officials. When Duqiao's officials requisitions the peasants' land at low prices, the Bureau of Land Management tolerated their shady behavior in "playing edge-ball." If the higher-level offices had not feigned ignorance, not only would the township have lost the room for development through the "informal economy" related to land requisitions, even the local governance centered on such development would have been impossible. Matters became still more awkward in certain phases of the process. In their rush to complete the tax and fee quotas most heavily weighted by higher levels in the evaluation of political accomplishments, township officials "had no choice" but to resort to "pulling taxes," "buying taxes," and even hiring "gangsters"—who were supposed to be a target of repression in rural governance—as "tax assistance personnel."

Considering that paradoxes constantly emerge within the administration of grassroots government, officials must become adept at mitigating contradictions, incorporating into their governance behaviors that contain multiple layers of paradox, while also preventing such paradoxes from being made public. Otherwise, at minimum this would lead to embarrassment, and at worst this would lead to a failure of governance, not only preventing the officials from accumulating political capital in the form of "achievements," but possibly even foreclosing their careers. The Duqiao Township leaders' proposal to develop the "ancient" settlement of Cheng Village as a tourist site, for example, contained multiple layers of consideration: If it succeeded that would be good, but even if it did not, it could solve the problem of requisitioning the village land in the old riverbed, "combining the false with the true" and generating political capital in any case. As an "insider," Wen Zhibin must have understood such duplicitous planning, otherwise he would have been expelled from the political arena. This "winning hand" could not be revealed, so he had a "love-hate relationship" with journalists. Somewhat ironically, under these conditions, no matter how adept at governance the political elite were, the ability to create and maintain good "achievements" and convert them into political capital also depended to some extent on "officials' luck."

In practice, then, rural politics was not as black and white as Confucian ethics, which clearly distinguished between "good" and "evil": Political differences, the pursuit of self-interest, factions formed on the basis of kinship networks, exclusion of outsiders and solidarity with insiders—all of these were public and out in the open. The process of modern state power "reaching into the countryside" was clearly a process of breaking this sort of political modality. A case in point was Chengren's rise to the status of local political elite on the basis of class rather than of morality. This was even clearer in political disputes and struggles between factions, as in the Cultural Revolution, which all revolved around differences in "revolutionary" status rather than differences based on kinship. However, networks of private relationships clearly played a role in politics as well—even in as extreme a situation as armed struggle, where clan membership and relationships among classmates were still valued. The implementation of villager self-government gave the people of Cheng Village a new opportunity to defend their interests through kinship networks again, and to express them politically. The debates among villagers generated by the village committee elections, the tourism development plan, and the requisition of land for the ceramics factory, and the competition these elicited among cadres, and between cadres and "the masses," clearly demonstrated that factions formed on the basis of kinship networks not only existed within villager self-government, but they were in fact quite important. Although these factions were based on kinship networks, however, many practical considerations of interests were also mixed in. The relationship between village cadres and ordinary villagers was not equal, giving factions a three-dimensional structure. Within factions a sort of "patron-client relation" emerged (Walder 1996: 12). It is worth noting, however, that in rural politics, patron-client relations did not exist in a pure form, instead often involving reciprocity, or at least being packaged as relations of reciprocity. Chengxin took care of ordinary villagers, through various acts of "helping out," so they had to "help him out" by planting tangerines for him.

In the sphere of grassroots officialdom, which was more bureaucratic than villager self-government, the more rationalized institutions of administration did not lead to the disappearance of factions. The main reason factions emerged there was the severe imbalance in the "supply and demand" relation between opportunities and the political capital of "achievements": "Joining a faction" or "entering a circle" could create more opportunities to obtain a promotion, rather than evincing any inherent "evil" of grassroots officials in a moral sense. Those who were "bookish," incapable, or insufficiently "observant," such as Li Zhewen, who was seen as "aloof" and ignorant about joining factions, ended up "specializing" in writing up paperwork for many years with a status no better than a contract worker in a printing office. To a certain extent, factions composed of personal networks, dominated the political fates and lives of township officials. Political relationships that were so important and structurally existent were not, however, acknowledged in formal settings, since at root the "private" was seen as being illegally embedded in the "public." This was a paradox. A deeper paradox lay in the fact that the reason for this embedment was to take care of "public" matters, to some extent. Against the background of a transitional era, a great deal of grassroots work only came into being due to lack of resources. When investment could not be attracted, there was "no choice" but to force through "development" at the expense of the land and the environment. There were not enough tax sources, yet they "had no choice" but to complete high tax-collection quotas. In the face of these responsibilities that could be completed only through "playing edge-ball," "being flexible," or even resorting to illegal methods, superiors could not rely on formal institutions and orders, but instead needed "private" relationships to make sure their subordinates would do whatever was necessary to get the work done. In order to reciprocate, when their subordinates needed support, of course the superiors would help them out.

Without a doubt, the most common and "natural" private relationships were based on kinship. In Duqiao, we observed the intersection of fraternal relations between Chengheng, Chengxin, and the brother of the head of the Water Conservancy Station. Such relationships were limited in number, however. In a grassroots bureaucracy such as Duqiao Township, it was more common to see relationships based on fictive kinship. Other important mechanisms for maintaining factions were the communities of interest formed around classmates or "comrades-in-arms" (people who had served in the army together) with a foundation of trust, or even around certain big bosses. After Chen Jinhua's schoolmate became the mayor of Duqiao, the two men "naturally" joined the same faction. He Ping took care of Li Zhewen for a similar reason. Fang Lizheng and He Ping could be considered as belonging to the same "faction" since both were the close friends of several stone-processing plant bosses in Wucheng, although they belonged to different "circles" in other respects. It is not unreasonable, therefore, to describe county-level politics (including grassroots officialdom) as the current era's "lineage politics," but perhaps its more fundamental characteristic is "limited factional politics."

The Self

After 1949, the stories about the close relationship between the brothers Chengyou and Chengbang clearly demonstrated familial traits such as filial piety, self-restraint, diligence and thrift, and respect for "human relationships." As rural society changed rapidly in the 1950s–1970s, however, political power replaced wealth and all other standards, beginning to influence social stratification and bring many familial changes. This could be observed in the families of Shoude and his brothers. Shoude persisted in the traditional familial principles of "human relationships," whereas Shouli was eager to escape from such responsibilities, even while using the right granted by those principles to criticize relationships within the extended family. In contrast with Shoude's family, concerning relationships within the household, Chengren's family could be considered to have thoroughly carried out "revolutionary" principles. In the 1970s, he made full use of his power as a father to influence his children's marriages. Shoukuan, whose family was similarly poor, took a different approach. He was an open-minded person, sticking together with his brothers Shoushu and Shouzhong through thick and thin. Chenggong, on the other hand, provided a counterexample, not only neglecting the uncle-nephew relationship with Nanshan, but also often looking down on his brothers.

In relationships outside of the family, if Shoude had been a little more concerned about his own practical interests, there is no doubt that he should have cozied up to Chengren, who possessed "revolutionary" power. Instead, however, he chose to maintain friendly relations with people such as Shoukuan. In his interactions with Shouyi, Shoude was clearly influenced by "revolutionary" ideas, actively supporting the Red Flag faction, but he never expressed an impulse to benefit personally, instead merely serving as a "dark counselor." In comparison, when it came to benefitting personally, Shouyi's choice was obviously more effective. Needless to say, after Chengxin had no choice but to quit his job and return to Cheng Village, for his own good he began to express boundless "loyalty" to the very Chengren he had so despised in his heart.

After the Reform and Opening, especially starting in the mid-1990s, at the same time that villagers such as Shouyi were beginning to get rich, his ego rapidly became inflated to the point that it became a threat to his own family. Of course Shouyi had his own unique theory of "the self." The Hunanese woman who had served as his mistress told him that, during sexual intercourse with a client, she became another person rather than her true self. Shouyi not only believed this statement, but even believed that in his exchanges of money for sex, what he purchased was neither a physical body nor a subject with a brain, but an abstract "service." Paradoxically, however, Shouyi too would sometimes say wistfully that he did not know which was the "real self." Shouyi's family was well-off economically, for which many villagers admired him, even while muttering disapproval about his familial relations. His wife Cheng Xiu would throw a fit every few days, but she tried to do all she could to maintain the household, where power was extremely unequal. While she prevented the family from collapsing, her mental state was highly imbalanced, so she turned to religion. Ironically but understandably, Cheng Fudao's wife classified his extra-marital relations into two types: those involved in "business socializing (*yingchou*)" necessary for the accumulation of capital, and those that might pose a threat to the family. The former could be treated as if they did not exist, but the latter could not be tolerated. In the households of ordinary young villagers such as Cheng Jingxiu, Cheng Jingdao, Cheng Jingshan, and Cheng Jingxian, in comparison with those of their parents and grandparents, relations between husband and wife were much more equal, but relations between generations were inclined toward the younger ones. In contrast with the situation hidden under the power of kinship and only exercising "power behind the scenes" (Li 2010: 234), affinal relations were tending to become part of the family's explicit power at center stage.

Cheng Village's young people expressed their concepts of self more directly and prominently. Whether it was those who went out to work "simply and honestly"—such as Cheng Jingzu, Cheng Jingzong, Cheng Jingshan, or Cheng Jingdao—or those who chose instead to "hang out"—such as Cheng Jingxiu or Cheng Jingye—all of them placed a higher value on their relationships with friends and classmates, assigning them positions closer to the self than kin. With regard to immediate and extended families, young villagers' attitudes toward the family were much more apathetic than those of their parents and grandparents. Among members of rich families, like Fudao and his three sisters, other than symbolic gifts, there was no circulation of capital for business to make up for any given member's shortfalls. The same was true for middle-income families, like those of Shoude and Shouzhi. There was a clear separation between the household budgets of the brothers Jingxiu and Jingdao. And this was even truer for poor families like those of Shoukuan, where the three brothers Jingzu, Jingzong, and Jingye drew explicit lines between the affairs of each household. Among siblings in the younger generations, then, the self had distinct boundaries with the nuclear family as its unit—a characteristic I have called "nuclear-family-centered" (Tan 2010: 448–449).

In spheres colored more deeply by self-interest, such as grassroots officialdom, the phenomena of egocentricity and utilitarianism appear to have been even more pronounced. Although Chengxin said that the small size of Duqiao's township government limited the opportunities for repeatedly switching factions according to self-interest, it was obvious that the creation and maintenance of factions were inseparable from officials' utilitarian calculations centered on the self. Overall, in the structure of concentric circles centered on the self, the principals for deciding which people to place in closer positions were primarily instrumentalist ones—a phenomenon I have called "the multilayered instrumental mode of association" (Tan 2010: 440).

As for the structure of social strata, prior to 1949, Cheng Village had been sharply divided into rich and poor families. This much can be observed in the stories about the parents of Shoukuan, Shoude, and Nanshan. However, these same stories also demonstrate that clan organizations functioned, however weakly, as networks of social protection against such inequality. After 1949, the egalitarianism implied by the discourse of "class" suppressed the division between rich and poor. At that time, stratification became expressed through political status and power rather than through wealth. Overall, rural society entered an era of basic economic equality. After decollectivization in the 1980s, political *status* ceased to be a standard for social stratification, but political *power* remained important, with village cadres enjoying a high status in the rural social structure. For ordinary peasants, of course, wealth became a more important standard. Those well-off economically, such as Shouyi, became "ten-thousand-yuan households" admired by their neighbors. Middling families, such as Shoude, who depended on farming and running the watch repair shop, still managed to build new houses although money was tight. Chengren too managed to buy modern appliances, such as a television, on the basis of farming and small-scale business. Poor families, such as those of Shoukuan, Shoushu, and Shouzhong, clearly improved their living conditions through farming and occasional wage-labor to supplement the household income. Almost everyone believed that their economic situations would improve, but they were unprepared mentally for the more dramatic inequality that was to come.

In the 1990s, especially starting halfway through the decade, Cheng Village's social structure changed rapidly. The village cadres enjoyed advantages not only as measured by their power, but also as measured by their wealth. What bothered ordinary villagers the most was that this wealth did not derive from hard work or business acumen. At almost the same time, the village's collective enterprises all failed and closed down, and certain departments of the township government directly seized peasants' income from business. For example, Cheng Jingsi and Chen Sheng saw their restaurant driven out of business by the police repeatedly eating there without paying, for which the couple had no recourse, and then had to face an enormous fine for over-quota births. (In terms of procedural justice, of course, it is hard to identify any direct connection between these two incidents, as if there were a conspiracy. What matters in investigating social attitudes, however, is the belief by the people involved that the fine was a way the township officials had sought to exact revenge upon the couple.) In addition, many grassroots officials used direct or indirect means to obtain at low rent villagers' individual or collective woodland, fishponds, duck farms, etc., and thereby to reap high profits, or abused their power to monopolize business in spheres such as farm supply, construction materials, restaurants, private education, etc.

Ordinary villagers' attitudes also changed rapidly with regard to the stratification of wealth that was *not* related to power. No one denied that Shouyi was talented when it came to business. When other villagers such as Chengren still lacked the understanding or ability to obtain important resources such as loans by giving gifts, Shouyi was already well versed in using money to make connections and open up channels. In his antique business, the secret to success was "the double scam." Other villagers expressed mild disapproval about this, saying that Shouyi "ate both black and white," with some degree of unfairness in how he made his money. In terms of attitudes, this shows that people belonging to lower social strata harbored strong suspicions about the means whereby members of higher strata obtained their wealth, and about their wealth's legitimacy. What bothered ordinary villagers even more about those who "got rich first" such as Shouyi was the way they spent their money. Not only did he often go to the city to hire sex workers, date a married woman for over a decade, and support a mistress for several years, but he also arrogantly tried to use all kinds of grand "theories" in order to justify this behavior.

However, no matter whether it was those such as Shoude who emphasized relaxation, or those such as Shoukuan who were often ill-tempered and occasionally complained about unfairness, or those such as Shouzhi or Yang Xianzong who were easily excited—none of them would break out of their everyday life and go petition higher authorities about corrupt cadres or try to exact revenge upon the rich. Shoude advocated "doing more and worrying less," relaxing the mind and nurturing the body, "living out one's days." Shoukuan also emphasized that if one just managed to get by, "the well water would not impinge upon the river" (one would not interfere with the affairs of others). As for Xianzong and Shouzhi, although they got worked up about the injustices they saw around them, ultimately, they felt it was more important to take care of their own health and enjoy good food during holidays than to complain. Of course these responses were not without a certain cynical attitude about "setting aside things of no personal concern," but the key point seemed to be "endurance." When it became hard to catch up with those who had "gotten rich first" through conventional methods, there was no lack of people who began to adopt risky measures in pursuit of sudden wealth. This imbalanced attitude was exemplified by the popularity of the underground lottery and pyramid schemes, as well as by Cheng Qiufu, who stepped onto the path of selling drugs after being tricked out of his wealth by the Vietnamese bride.

Beliefs

In the oral histories of Cheng Village, people's descriptions of their past beliefs and those of their ancestors were not very detailed. The large and small temples and other old buildings left behind in the village functioned mainly, to varying degrees, as public spaces for clan groups, but symbolically they were expressions of ancestor worship. Many objects were partially destroyed during the Cultural Revolution, but quite a few peasants quietly dismantled some of the artifacts and kept them hidden, so today one can observe "ancient" objects that have been restored throughout the village. "Son-Adding Day" (*tiandingjie*) on the second day of Month Two of the traditional calendar is both a celebration of male offspring and a way of worshipping the ancestors. After the discourse of class entered the village, kinship networks and ancestor worship were negated in principle. Although the forms of worship changed, however, their core did not disappear. In order to pray for a son, Shoukuan followed others' advice and secretly made offerings to the ancestors. This story illustrates that his family was not the only one that still believed in the connection between ancestor worship and the continuation of "the incense fires"[6] during that era.

After the discourse of class receded, villagers quickly revived the use of household altars. This process occurred so fast and universally that it would be hard to imagine it as the rebirth of a tradition that had been completely cut off (Siu 2003). Instead, this was the "resuscitation" of "dormant" practices of ancestor worship (Tan 2010: 376). The activities for updating the genealogical records organized by Shoude and others proceeded so smoothly that even township cadres admired their ability to mobilize people, but the real reason for their success was that the vast majority of villagers harbored a profound concern for worshipping the ancestors. Of course, the persistence of this concern did not mean that ideas about ancestor worship had not changed over time. Contemporary villagers' beliefs about the practice are much weaker than those of their grandparents.

Aside from the ancestors, many middle-aged and older villagers said, "there are deities everywhere you look," meaning that all kinds of natural entities were worthy of veneration. In this respect, when it came to everyday concerns about livelihood, no stories were closer to their hearts than those about *fengshui*. If you look at the "ancient village," its overall layout shows that the ancestors placed great value on the concepts of geomancy. Even when the discourse of class inundated Cheng Village, beliefs about *fengshui* were never completely discarded, instead being discussed only quietly in private. Starting in the 1990s, peasant households' concern for their individual houses' *fengshui* not only (ironically) destroyed that of the village as a whole, but ultimately that of their own houses. In addition, bodhisattvas, Daoist gods, spirit mediums, and even ordinary passersby could all be considered "deities" or "spirits" with whom villagers might communicate, depending on the circumstances. Even in grassroots officialdom, which in principle permitted only materialist doctrine, it became common for cadres to beseech deities for "officials' luck."

In addition to *fengshui* and deities, villagers believed that "karmic response" was a mysterious mechanism that permeated natural space and time. There were many types of karma, or relations of cause and effect, but the basic understanding concerned whether one's "mind" was "upright." In the sphere of kinship networks, such relations were rather concrete, as in "repaying kindness" or "avenging a grievance." Outside of kinship, however, this also involved more mystical "karmic rewards and retribution." Of course, villagers both believed in karma to a certain degree, and yet did not completely believe in it. At the same time, in social relationships dominated by money and power, they could not hope for karma to change very much in order to make society more fairer. As Shoude said of Chengren, however, it was unfortunate that the latter never believed in karma, since such a belief would have provided his mind with a sense of balance.

Some of the other villagers, especially middle-aged and older women, chose organized religions such as Christianity. In their words and self-understanding, these villagers all believed they were truly Christians rather than merely pretending to adopt that identity. From the perspective of their specific religious behavior after conversion, however, many other elements were combined in their practices. The number of peasants who practiced Christianity had already been small in early modern Cheng Village, and the number became even smaller during the era when the discourses of class and materialism became widespread. After those discourses receded, Ms. Mai became an active proponent of the religion, but few villagers accepted her gospel. In the 1990s, especially starting halfway through the decade, only a few middle-aged and older women converted. Looking at their conversion processes, every one of them was related to major setbacks or changes in life, and to experiences of "magical efficacy" (*lingyan*) when there was nowhere else to turn in a time of crisis. It could be said that "hardship" was one of the social foundations of their turn toward religion, but it was not the hardship itself that directly pushed them in that direction. It was only when they were forced to face hardship as isolated households, or even as individuals, that the distance from religion truly diminished (with Christianity as merely one of the religions they could have chosen). Furthermore, in rural areas where male chauvinism (*nanquanzhuyi*) was particularly prevalent, women—especially middle-aged and older women—were situated in a disadvantaged position in the household, becoming the group most sensitive to hardship.[7] This characteristic created the impression that they were "disingenuous" in all of their religious activities, to the point that the clergy at the Duqiao Church of the Gospel believed that the ideas and behavior of Cheng Village's Christians were "really too non-standard," mixed with all kinds of "impurities." Since this sort of behavior was so universal, however, the clergy had no choice but to tolerate these impurities in a bid to spread the gospel.[8] The emergence of this religious "market," as Stark and Finke (2004: 44–45) have emphasized, when operated well with the "suppliers," attracted more potential "customers"— related to the believers, but at the same time it cannot be ignored that the role of demand may have been more fundamental. Moreover, in peasants' religious practice, sometimes objective social tensions and subjective dilemmas lead to new embarrassments. As with "the Three Religions," it seems impossible for Christianity to easily get rid of the paradoxes for peasants on a fundamental level.

By contrast, peasants seemed more willing to believe in the idea of "fate" or "destiny" (*ming*). As they saw it, fate formed a subjective arrangement with a mysterious "Heaven." People could not change fate but could only change their "luck" (*yun*) in minor ways. Even the latter were limited, since luck was still fundamentally controlled by fate. At the same time, they did not believe that different fates would result in the same outcomes in life. On the contrary, the impermanent affairs of the external world would only lead to greater differences between the life outcomes of those with different fates. Under conditions determined by fate, however, people still had to exert all their energy to give themselves limited lives, and this was what gave meaning to life. This sort of paradox could be partially observed in the lives of villagers of different types. Many villagers believed that Shouyi's wealth was determined by fate. He had started out the same as Chengren, focused on rural politics, when one disturbance about embezzlement followed by Chengren's attack turned his disaster into good fortune. In comparison with Shouyi, Chengren did not lack for ability, but when the social context changed so dramatically, all of his efforts ended up leaving him unhappy in his last years. Chengxin lacked merit but had good fortune, and the only "reasonable" explanation that ordinary villagers could accept was that his fate was good. Chengxin did not believe in fate, but he believed in luck to the point that after "eating state grain" (obtaining a position on the state payroll), he grew enthusiastic about taking care of the incense fire halls, worshipping the ancestors and bodhisattvas, and paying attention to *fengshui*. The space between fate and luck was full of paradoxes, but when ordinary villagers whose lives were going smoothly tried to reconcile the tensions between phenomena of fate in life, such as good fortune without merit, bad fortune despite merit, good fortune with merit, or bad fortune without merit, they consciously or unconsciously ignored these paradoxes.

As for the meaning of life, there was clearly a huge gap between the views of the younger villagers and those of their parents and grandparents. Long ago, they had already stopped defining the meaningful life as one where people had enough food to eat, instead setting their expectations much higher. What was surprising, however, was that many young people's lives were repeating the stories of their parents and grandparents, in some sense. In the eyes of ordinary people, Boss Fudao was said to have plenty of money and yet understood clearly that money could not bring sufficient meaning for his life, so he felt "empty" and became interested in Buddhism. Although he lamented that "such a life is meaningless," he expressed no intention of changing his way of life. Ordinary young people were more inclined to believe that a life "without enough money to spend" or "without power" lacked meaning, that it was "boring" or "seemed to be lacking something," and that contemporary peasants had "life" (*ming*) without a "pulse" (*mai*). Still younger villagers who had just graduated from secondary school were even less willing to talk about the long-term future, feeling that the topic of life's meaning was too "heavy" for them, while only the alternative lives created in time-travel officialdom novels were meaningful. Of course, other villagers such as Jingxiu saw through the "empty parlor tricks" of life's meaning, adopting a cynical attitude of not caring and spending their lives "hanging out." It was not easy to keep oneself above everything, however, and Jingxiu still had many fierce criticisms of social injustice. Holding that life's meaning was "empty" and yet criticizing so fiercely—was this not also another paradox?

People's Lives

From the perspective of life histories or biographies, all of these smallholding peasants were deeply embedded within structural factors such as economy, politics, society and beliefs. These factors themselves were not static, moreover, being instead the results of historical accumulation.

Economically, Chinese smallholders seemed to exhaust their agricultural surplus while supplementing industry during the collective era, but before they had a chance to be repaid (*fanbu*) by the industry they had nurtured, they rapidly entered a market system where agriculture and industry were unequal. In the face of nature and the market, the agricultural risks to individual households increased sharply, and many smallholders became "fated" to lives without vitality. A situation where "if you didn't farm, someone else would farm" made competition even more chaotic. Although a "hidden revolution" of capital intensification took place, it remained far from constituting a true "historical turning point." In oscillating between "semi-agricultural" and "semi-industrial," the role of "semi-industry" consisted mainly of raising income levels, while that of "semi-agriculture" was to lower the risks to survival and protect the bottom line of life. Smallholders went from being "shackled to the land" to being "semi-agricultural, semi-industrial," and the "economy of killing time" gave way to a consumerist economy, satisfying the demand of constantly expanding desires. They "risked their lives" squeezing resources from the soil, but the paradox was that the actual result of continuous increases in productivity was to "hurt each other though born of the same root."[9] Even if smallholders managed to seize the few opportunities that existed to achieve capital accumulation, they abandoned agriculture and converted completely to industry, yet they still did not manage to resolve the economic paradoxes centered on consumption any better than before. When capital accumulation reached the point that every day revolved around making money at the expense of others or preventing them from making money at one's own expense, feelings of emptiness ensued. Moreover, this emptiness could not stop the desire to consume, instead only accelerating its expansion, giving rise to an attitude that only cared about the experiential moment of consumption and could not tell which "self" was the true one.[10] This sort of desire also permeated deeply into the behavioral logic of grassroots government, where "development" went from being a means to being a goal, giving rise to the paradox of using means that "cut off family lines" to achieve the goal of "promoting development for the residents' children and grandchildren."

On the political level, the main historical tendency of village governance has been to part with "dual-track politics" and "clan elders," and to pursue modern "democracy." Within the framework of "the people's self-rule," however, ordinary peasants used their imagination of fictive kinship and ethical politics to see "parental officials" as the expression of "rule for the people." The more recent forms of "villager self-government" drew closer to procedural democracy in the modern sense. In moderately developed areas based on the "semi-agricultural, semi-industrial" mixed economy, however, the focus of attention for ordinary peasants was not on the governance of village affairs, and they still hoped that political elites would "rule for the people." Similarly, township governance heavily relied on "digging up the land." "Seeking out an explanation" (*tao shuofa*) from higher and higher levels of the bureaucracy, including through petitions, became a more important option for ordinary peasants, but most of them lacked proficiency in "the arts of resistance," so they often failed. On the other hand, life was not easy for grassroots officials themselves: If they could not compete successfully within the arena of officialdom, they would turn to relatives and especially classmates, "comrades-at-arms," *laoxiang* (people from the same native place), fictive kin, or networks of interest mediated by capital, forming factions based on reciprocity, in order to satisfy the need for mutual trust and "tacit understanding" (*moqi*). Not only was this at odds with the spirit of modern democracy, but it was also limited in its application. "Officials' luck" remained a curse from which they could not escape.

On the social level, divisions into rich and poor did exist among members of the same clan in early modern Cheng Village, but wealth was not the only standard for social stratification. Within households, the power of fathers and husbands was paramount, emphasizing filial piety, self-restraint, diligence and thrift, etc.—basically consistent with the analysis of earlier scholars. After the discourse of class entered rural society, the importance of political status and power in social stratification were raised to unprecedented heights, but the "cellularization" (*xibaohua*) of rural society remained far from complete. After rural reforms such as decollectivization, wealth became valued by people as a marker of the structure of social stratification. After the 1990s, wealth became the only standard for social stratification, and an important change occurred in the methods whereby privileged groups obtained wealth. In terms of attitudes, people occupying disadvantaged positions within the social hierarchy gradually adopted a "zero-sum game" view that "we lose whatever the rich gain." Nuclear families were still characterized internally by "tenderness" (*wenqing momo*), so it is hard to generalize about peasants' personalities using terms like "individualism" or "the shadow of the self." In a cold way, money quickly permeated social relations outside of the family, but peasants still consciously or unconsciously tried to intermix oppositional pairs such as "cold and warm," "expressive and instrumental," "use-value and exchange-value," or "calculation of interests and loyalty to sworn brothers." Of course, the paradox lay in the fact that it was not easy to smoothly combine all these elements that completely contradicted one another. Paradoxical tensions therefore emerged in the form of irony, embarrassment, cynicism, or direct conflict.

With regard to beliefs, among the transformations in the various beliefs of the peasants of Cheng Village, ancestor worship had changed the least. Folk beliefs such as *fengshui* and karma were still often used by villagers to explain or arrange their living spaces and lives. In the processes whereby folk beliefs combined with local society, however, the state was always present, rather than a "civil society" excluding the state. Looked at from another direction, the state's influence on folk beliefs was limited in that it could not truly replace ancestor worship with materialism, nor could it convince peasants as a whole to abandon folk beliefs. Instead, Christianity, as an organized religion, spread rapidly throughout rural society. Under the mechanisms of rural social bonds centered on the nuclear family, when peasant households encountered unfavorable situations in life that could not be resolved through appeals to the state, the clan, or even the immediate family, middle-aged and older women turned to Christianity based on the logic of "living out one's days." In addition, some peasants truly believed that the meaning of life was to enjoy material possessions and seize the day, or they felt that life was pointless or depressing and that it lacked a "pulse," or they became long-term cynics. This type of attitude even pervaded grassroots officialdom.

It would clearly be too arbitrary and one-sided, however, to hastily conclude from this that contemporary rural beliefs have already "collapsed" completely, or that they have universally descended into "nihilism." The completely opposed faces of nihilism and transcendence coexist in the attitudes of contemporary peasants, forming layer upon layer of paradoxes in their lives. However, paradoxes also provide basic reasons for people to live out their everyday lives in cynical or tolerant ways.

In a word, paradoxes have structurally emerged in the economy, politics, society, and beliefs in which contemporary Chinese peasants are situated. However, peasants are absolutely not passive structural entities. On the contrary, they have an entire set of explanations and attitudes, full of subjective agency, about the economic, political, social, and cosmological structures around them, and about their own lives.

Here subjectivity and agency refer not to the abstract sense in which humans are contrasted with animals or other objects, from a philosophical perspective. Nor does it refer to the relative sense in which all Chinese people are contrasted with foreigners from a psychological perspective. In fieldwork on rural society, when we investigate and interpret peasants' lives, desires, and social attitudes, although no one's life experiences are isolated but emerge instead from social interaction, they will always be rather specific and contextual. And if we use life histories to narrate the political, economic, and sociocultural conditions of the age in which they are situated, the origins for this method may be traced back to the historiography that the Grand Historian Sima Qian used in writing the "Basic Annals," the "Hereditary Houses," and the "Ranked Biographies" (Sima 2013). As a text, the *Records of the Grand Historian* is a history comprised of biographies. What it ultimately presents is obviously not just the life stories of many individuals, but an organic whole. That history uses biographies as a point of entry with the goals of "understanding the relationships between Heaven and people, and the changes from the past to the present" (Sima 2014)—seeking out "orthopraxy" (*zhengtong*), i.e., the secret of political legitimacy, in order to achieve good fortune for the lives of "the common people" (*cangsheng*).

During the early modern era, Chen Yinke tried to build a bridge between modern conceptions of biography and Sima Qian's concern for orthopraxy in the study of life histories. In his *Alternative Biography of Liu Rushi*, the main narrative thread is the life story of the courtesan Liu Rushi in the late Ming and early Qing (Chen 2009a). Pan Guangdan (1994: 327), who advocated "humanistic historiography," combined the methods of social structure and sexual psychology to investigate the brief life of the Late Ming woman Feng Xiaoqing (1993: 1–66). His student Fei Xiaotong (1999g: 387) carried on his method of combining social structure with culture to analyze life aspirations, arguing that traditional Chinese peasants within the "economy of killing time" held an attitude of "unconditional contentment" toward their lives. Here "contentment" did not meant that all of their desires were fulfilled, but only that a portion of their limited desires were fulfilled on the basis of training in a culture of diligence and thrift (Liang 2006b: 177). In their lives, people valued "directing force inward," emphasizing reflection, self-blame, self-restraint, yielding to others, learning to lose, diligence and thrift, industry and frugality, self-motivation and enterprising spirit (Liang 2006b: 177–181). Ma Guoqing (1999: 219; 2009: 73) specifically looked at how after Confucian culture had transformed lineage-based society, there was "analogous reasoning within the analogies" (*lei zhong you tui*) that comprised social relations, and that "the Confucian rites lay within this analogous reasoning" (*tui zhong you li*)—a structure of attitudes where "the analogies were oriented toward groups" (*lei yi qun wei ben*) and "analogous reasoning was based on the family" (*tui yi jia wei zhou*). When Wang Mingming (2010: 7) researched life histories, he advocated placing emphasis on grasping the meaning of life, with "life" understood as both individual and social, or worldly, rather than in the sense of an individual opposed to society.[11] Wu Fei (2009: 117), on the other hand, investigated the meaning of "living out one's days" in biographies from the perspective of death (suicide).

When we focus on life histories and their meaning, it is not hard to discover that from the perspective of cultural "ideal types," the highest ideal that Confucianism set up for traditional Chinese lives was the "sage" (*shengren*). The life philosophy of the sage was not only to "live with integrity" (*chengyi*) and "rectify the mind" (*zhengxin*), but was also closely connected to "governing the country" and "pacifying the world" (*ping tianxia*)—looking upwards—and to "cultivating oneself" and "managing the family"—looking downwards (Zhu 2011a: 5). From the pre-Qin feudal (*fengjian*) era until the mid-Tang dynasty, peasants were largely dependent upon aristocrats and remnants of the earlier *menfa* "eminent families" (Chen 2009b: 260; Yang 2011: 1–58; Tian 2012: 315–320). Beginning in the Song dynasty, rural grassroots communities entered a phase of "commonerization" (*pingminhua*), the commodity economy became more and more developed, and land annexation grew widespread (Xu 2006: 175–176; Liang 2006: 176–190). Facing a social reality where people's material desires were quickly expanding, the Neo-Confucian School of Principle proposed restricting "human desires" and manifesting "the Heavenly Principle" (Zhu 2011b: 79). The Song, Ming, and Qing establishment of "community compacts" (*xiangyue*), clans etc., institutionalized this restriction and put it into practice (Lü 1993: 188–191; Wang 2011: 132). Up until Liang Shuming's early modern Rural Reconstruction Movement, the sagely spirit of community compacts continued to be highly valued.[12]

It was also during this era that a major debate broke out in Chinese intellectual circles regarding science and "perspectives on life" (*rensheng guan*). Those who advocated "advanced" Western culture argued that correct perspectives on life could be derived from scientific cognition, and that only when individual democracy and freedom were achieved could life become good (Ding 1997: 44). Tracing this back to its source, such perspectives on life that championed the individual in Europe and the Americas were related to Christianity. In Christian culture, it was believed that everyone was guilty of "original sin," and the process of gaining meaning lay foremost in seeking out salvation from Christ and obtaining a final judgment on the Day of Reckoning (Augustine 2009: 169–171). Of course, only a small minority of Chinese peasants were Christians, and the more direct way that Western culture influenced their lives was through secularized mass culture. In terms of intellectual sources, the subjective person that mass culture propagated was the "secular person" (*suren*) no longer plagued by guilt. The most extreme and representative reflection of this subjectivity was the famous phrase "God is dead" (Nietzsche 1989: 1).

In secularized philosophy, whether it is Marx's (2000: 62) radical philosophy of political struggle, Durkheim's (2001: 9–12) "professional ethics" where each person followed one's "calling" (division of labor), Weber's (2004: 272) individual "ethics of responsibility," or Simmel's (1991: 44) somewhat tragic individual "ethics of life"—all of these have enjoyed a definite market in China since the early modern era. In addition, looking at those theories that criticized the "maladies" of contemporary society, it is not hard to discover that the "sick people" they illuminated have also existed in contemporary rural China. For example, Herbert Marcuse (2006: 55, 234), one of the representative figures of the Frankfurt School, commented that contemporary people "no longer imagine another way of life but rather imagine freaks or types of the same life,"[13] so the hope of saving these "one-dimensional men" lay in marginalized groups such as vagabonds, outsiders, and the unemployed: people of "the Great Refusal." In conclusion, he quoted the famous words of Walter Benjamin, "Only for the sake of the hopeless ones have we been given hope" (Marcuse 2006: 234). Later, Foucault (1999: 219–255) argued more radically that under the discipline of all-penetrating power, "man" possessing subjectivity had also "died" (2010a: 26; 2010b: 97). Baudrillard (2006: 45, 103) argued, however, that after capital had satisfied people's basic desires, it would create new desires on a larger scale, directing consumption into a state of "simulation" without subjectivity. According to Derrida (2001: 246, 236), in "logocentrism," the more you did the more wrong you were (*zuodeduo, cuodeduo*), and only when labor "ended" could meaningful life begin. According to Lacan and Žižek, on the other hand, all of this was in vain: In the "fantasy" created by capital (Žižek 2014: 144), "the ego" was just "the psychotic subject" (Lacan 1988: 66), and if the "pathology" were not eradicated, the meaning of one's life would just be empty talk.

The lives of contemporary Chinese peasants are clearly "secular, common, or this-worldly" (*su*) in comparison with those of the sages. If you ask them to identify as "sinners," that would not be easy, but the term "secular people" would be more acceptable. If you emphasize the "private" desires of secular people, however, letting those desires expand without limit, they easily become "sick people." In a secular world, the questions of how to pacify the mind, how to establish meaning in one's life, or how to obtain the good life—all of these remain open-ended.

Looking at the empirical material in the "Text" portion of this book, almost every peasant's biography is full of changes, some of them even quite dramatic. When it comes to making choices in life, many of the peasants have wavering, contradictory, or paradoxical attitudes. Through the tinted lenses of this chapter's theories about economic, political, social, and cosmological dimensions, it is not hard to see that these attitudes are not simply habits of individual psychology, but have deeply embedded economic, political, social, and cosmological roots. When reflecting on peasants' biographies, then, with a foothold in the philosophies of everyday life that they value, examining these paradoxes from perspectives such as the relationships between people and things, people and people, people and the mind, people and the state, people and history, and people and life, both of the opposing dimensions that exist at the same time in these pairs must be taken into account equally.

Notes

1 *Translator's note:* English translation from pages 73 and 78 of Fei 1992.
2 Yü Kuang-hong (1986) directly criticized Ahern (1973: 154, 140, 141) for deliberately distorting the facts in order to make a far-fetched argument: limiting the norms for inheritance to wet-rice fields, and failing to acknowledge that dry-crop land, factories, and brick kilns could also be inherited; using data from only four lineages in the village, excluding material about the Li-surnamed lineage (mentioned elsewhere in the book), which contradicted her conclusions; and emphasizing the Shandong proverb "without property, there are no ancestors," mentioned by Johnston (1910: 285), even though the latter had clearly indicated that this proverb was only used when a lineage was faced with extinction.
3 This is similar to what scholars often call "social capital" (Lin 2005: 18).
4 Liu Xin's (2005: 49) study of the relationship between officials, sex workers, and bosses in a certain city in southern China, Guo Yukuan's (2012: 250) study of business socializing (*yingchou*) in Wenzhou, and Osburg's (2013: 176) study of the business activities of the new rich in Chengdu all demonstrate that such phenomena are not isolated cases. Similar to the mechanisms of "communities of complicity" (Steinmüller 2013: 227), these are mainly oriented toward the establishment of close relationships in order to promote cooperation in business. Fudao's point here, however, was that his efforts to build relationships through the shared consumption of sex had been limited in their effectiveness.
5 Now that China has shifted to a three-child policy, it should be pointed out that this book's attention is focused on the practical logic of policy implementation rather than questions of whether such policies have been appropriate from a demographic perspective.
6 *Translator's note*: Here and throughout the book, "incense fires" (*xianghuo*) has the extended meaning of continuing the family line (since only descendants can keep the fires burning), so the connection implied here is that if a family worships their ancestors, the latter will repay them by granting the birth of sons, who can continue the family line and keep the incense fires burning.
7 Similarly, modern feminism has raised sharp criticisms of the scant attention to women in the traditional anthropology of religion (Bowie 2004: 109).
8 This is not unique to Duqiao, with other studies showing that it is often normal for the motivations behind religious belief to be mixed and complex (O'Dea 1970: 243; Johnstone 2012: 87).
9 *Translator's footnote*: The quotation (同根相煎) is derived from the "Quatrain of Seven Steps" (七步诗) from the *Romance of the Three Kingdoms*, where the author's persecution by his brother is likened to beans being cooked over the fire of beanstalks, "born of the same root." Here the phrase refers to the paradox of agrochemical inputs eventually hurting both soil and farmer.
10 This kind of desire created through contrast is essentially "mimetic desire" (Girard 2006: 17), or a "simulation" systematically imposed upon people (Baudrillard 2006: 115), rather than a real need of everyday social life.

11 Wang Mingming (2010: 5, 236–339) advises choosing an informant who is important but not someone whom everyone regards as an "abnormal person," research their entire life, and then write an analytical demonstration of their life history in the manner of Sima Qian. This doubtless has its advantages, but in this book, I have not completely followed this sort of advice for the following three reasons: First, with research on the life histories of people who are still alive, it is hard to identify an end-point. Second, social structure, culture, and attitudes are all processes that continue from the dead to the living, so it seems unnecessary to insist upon delimiting the end of one person's life. Third, people's lives and the social structure, culture, and attitudes they involve are all the products of interaction among many people, so simultaneously investigating the life histories of multiple people who have interacted with one another might create more of a sense of social depth.
12 Liang Shuming thus became known as "the last Confucian" (Alitto 1996).
13 *Translator's note*: I modified the original English version of this sentence (changing "images of" to "imagine") to match the syntax of the Chinese translation quoted here. The original English and its context are: "The vamp, the national hero, the beatnik, the neurotic housewife, the gangster, the star, the charismatic tycoon perform a function very different from and even contrary to that of their cultural predecessors. They are no longer images of another way of life but rather freaks or types of the same life, serving as an affirmation rather than negation of the established order" (Marcuse 1991: 59).

9 From the Past to the Present

The Two Dimensions

Based on empirical narratives in the first seven chapters of this book, we combined methods of empirical and theoretical analysis in Chapter Eight, analyzing the contradictory, paradoxical, and dilemmatic situations that peasants in a changing countryside encountered in the spheres of economy, politics, social relations, and beliefs. We also analyzed the contradictory attitudes that emerged in relationships between people and external objects, other people, their own minds or inner worlds, the state, history, and *ming* (life, fate, or destiny). In this final chapter, we can now approach the two-dimensionality of peasants in a changing countryside, attempting to draw some conclusions about their lives, desires, and social attitudes.

From the perspective of everyday life, the relationship between peasants and external objects entered a dynamic process during the ongoing era of transition.[1] Economically, the countryside began to change from being self-sufficient to being part of a larger macroeconomic cycle, and peasants were no longer tethered to the land, and rural households became "semi-agricultural, semi-industrial." This "dual" mode of existence decreased peasants' reliance on their village communities, but except for a tiny minority, most still depended on the land for survive to one degree or another. As they moved between the two modes of existence, and even if they did not leave their hometown to work in the city, peasants were already bombarded with media messages celebrating consumerism. The "economy of idleness" once associated with smallholding peasants gradually disappeared thanks to the combination of the mixed economy of agriculture and industry "education" by the modern media, and this disappearance in turn drove peasants to reconfigure their lives around the consumer economy. In contrast with the self-sufficient smallholder economy, the mixed economy of agriculture and industry brought peasants rapid increases in their material wealth. Due to the transition from the "economy of idleness" to the consumer economy, however, the acceleration of peasants' desire for material wealth outstripped the rate at which their incomes were rising. The tension between material desires and income was expressed on the social level as the standards for defining social stratification became more

DOI: 10.4324/9781003353072-11

homogenous, with wealth becoming the main one. For most peasant families, however, very few could completely free themselves from the land and agriculture. Regardless of their subjective attitudes, therefore, the basic situation that the vast majority of peasants had no choice but to face objectively was: First, material wealth had become an important standard for judging whether one's life was a success or a failure; and second, income increased much more slowly than desires.

In this context, the principles whereby peasants interacted with objects displayed a trajectory of sharp change. It became a universal, unconscious decision to "risk one's life" squeezing all one could squeeze out of the soil, which had previously been regarded as "the root of life." Contrary to intentions, however, since agriculture itself had been relegated to the position of a weak sector in the modern economy's division of labor, when individual farming households tried to exploit nature by "draining the pond to catch the fish," although gross output increased, this did not directly translate into an increase of economic income. The bigger contradiction, moreover, lay in the difficulty of sustaining development. At the same time, grassroots governments were also influenced by this situation. As the major promoters of local economies under market conditions, the desires of grassroots governments expanded rapidly in the same way. Whether it was pressuring the people to try to get rich or becoming involved in informal or even illegal economic activities, all were the outcome of grassroots officials' efforts to fulfill those desires. Since the material foundation of moderately developed regions was limited to the mixed economy of agriculture and industry, aside from land, natural resources, and environmental capacity, they enjoyed few advantages for particularly rapid economic development. As a result, adopting the attitude that "human desire is a Heavenly Principle," it has become common for grassroots governments to use "flexibility," "skirting the rules," and even illegal methods to bypass laws, regulations, and policies concerning the protection of land and environment in order to push forward development. As for ordinary peasants who have not benefited from this type of development, and who have on the contrary been hurt rather badly by it, this is a paradox of using means that "cut off the family line" to seek out the ends of "doing anything to achieve development for future generations." The basis of this paradox is the mechanism of combining government and business.

The process of transition in rural grassroots politics has basically followed the trend of turning from "dual-track politics" and "the rule of elders" to modern democratic governance. This process has been tortuous, however. When state power went down to the countryside, it aimed to promote "the people's self-rule," but it also had to take the power previously enjoyed by lineage elders and concentrate it in the hands of the state. Ordinary peasants tended to understand this change according to the logic of new state cadres "ruling for the people" out of the goodness of their hearts. After "collectivism" limited freedoms and villagers longed for a return to household production, village-level governance adopted the form of villager self-government.

The top-down system of rural governance did not truly change, however, and most of the responsibilities ultimately rested on the shoulders of grassroots officials. In order to meet administrative goals and develop the local economy, grassroots officials had no choice but to rely on village cadres. It was also hard to achieve these dual goals through conventional techniques of governance. Many irregular means, including "digging up the land," were therefore adopted, inevitably leading to contradictions between cadres and "the masses." The "two levels of rural organizations" (i.e., township and village) also had room to pursue their own interests. Grassroots officials' universal practice of "doing business on the side" and the frequency of outright corruption both led to discontentment among the peasants. Yet peasants did not participate in many active democratic actions, since there were few situations where their "arts of resistance" could be effective. Although there was no lack of overlap between the state's promotion of "the people's self-rule" and peasants' desire for the state to "rule for the people," there were still many gaps between them.

Of course, the moral goodness or badness of grassroots officials was not the crux of all the problems of rural governance. The "pressure system" was also a "curse" for them. In the face of scarce political resources, competition among grassroots officials expended a lot of energy as well. Even more so, under circumstances where they lacked the resources for rapid economic development, when grassroots officials pushed the economy to make repeated "great leaps forward" through "flexibility," "skirting the rules," and even methods that directly violated formal institutions, they still had to face a few risks and uncertainties. In the arena of grassroots officialdom, it was "natural" for rural governance and political competition to emerge on the basis of relationships with kin, classmates, "comrades-at-arms," fictive kin, and even networks of interest mediated by capital. Such factional politics clearly ran contrary to democracy. At the same time, in practice, when it came to reducing the risks of governance for individual officials and strengthening their ability to compete politically, this space was also limited, in fact. Therefore, they often still had to pin their hopes to "officials' luck."

The mixed economy of agriculture and industry, and grassroots politics, where moral goodness and badness were intertangled, together became important driving forces for the transition of rural society, while also limiting that transition to some extent. From the vertical perspective of social bonds (*jiehe*), there were two main factors that made peasants' attitudes imbalanced: First, the disparity between rural social strata was too big. Second, the acquisition of privileged group status within the rural social hierarchy involved an admixture of unjust factors. Turning it around, the disparity between rural social strata was even used to prove that the "honesty and simplicity" previously valued by ordinary peasants was now an expression of "uselessness" or "inability to be flexible." When values such as "integrity" and "uprightness" not only were no longer encouraged by the rural social structure, but even became objects of critical reflection, ridicule and contempt, in terms of attitudes, it became hard for relations between people and things to avoid upsetting balances such as "the unity of Heaven (or Nature) and people" or "unconditional contentment." Besides pushing peasants to squeeze as much as they could out of the natural world and compelling grassroots officials to take development to the extreme, the changing relationship between people and things also transformed the logic of interaction between people, to some extent.

When peasants placed a higher value on material interests, and when they obtained a better position in the rural social hierarchy with material wealth as its main marker, rational calculation blended into the relationship between self and other. Outside of the family, especially the nuclear family, whether people were close in terms of Confucian "human relationships" (*renlun*) or purely "outsiders," everyone who fit this principle of rational calculation often became the object of active efforts to maintain close interaction, but this was not true the other way around. Villagers who could follow or come close to following this principle, were not only regarded as "observant" or adept at "being flexible"—objectively they were indeed more capable of benefiting in social competition. By contrast, those villagers who could not completely follow this principle were regarded as insufficiently "observant," ignorant of how to "be flexible," or too "bookish." Accordingly, in social competition they really did not perform as well as they hoped to. However, it was not easy to truly follow this principle. Under this principle, most villagers ultimately could not satisfy their material desires through the efforts of their nuclear families. For those who had not yet completely left behind the village, therefore, maintaining basic interactions grounded in reciprocity was still a basic necessary of everyday life. Within the nuclear family, moreover, and between the elder generation and their direct descendants, duties based on the "human relationships" were still clearly observable. Even for those villagers whose material desires and wealth were growing rapidly, although they often treated others in a purely instrumental fashion (for example, treating sex workers as objects for the fulfillment of carnal desires), they also occasionally reflected on what their "true selves" might be.

After focusing on the fluctuation and struggle between "human relationships" and instrumentalized ones for a long period of time, peasant attitudes fell into a paradox of self-reflection, to some extent. On the one hand, the will of "secular people," depending on external forces to achieve upward mobility, came to regard "the rites of the sages" (*shengren zhi li*) such as self-restraint, self-encouragement (*zimian*), and critical reflection as markers of the backward ignorance of how to "be flexible." On the other, they also felt that the tender "human relationships" were close and natural, and they were even inclined to search for their "true self" and to carry out everyday life without calculation. Those who had already achieved rapid wealth still felt physically and mentally exhausted in everyday life, so the meaning of life needed to be redefined outside of material things. Ordinary peasants—under conditions considered insufficient compared with those above, but well-off compared with those below—felt that it was necessary to find meaning within everyday life, even if it was just self-consolation. Between continuing "in the shadow of the ancestors" and leaning toward material pleasures in the present, although there was conflict between these two inclinations, peasants were still trying to attend to both at the same time, rather than completely focusing on the latter. It would be hard to say, then, that peasants' everyday life had already become completely subservient to material desires, looking only toward themselves in the present, rather than concerning themselves with others.

In everyday life, of course, it was truly difficult to use an attitude of forbearance and concern for one's descendants to overcome the attitudes of depression, anger, and even resentments between rural social strata. Nor was it an easy thing in interpersonal relations outside the family to strike a balance between oppositional orientations such as "expressive and instrumental," "use-value and exchange-value," or friendship and the calculation of interests. Other than the satisfaction of material desires in the present, then, there truly was uncertainty about what kinds of things could be transcendent in one's life. According to the "rites of the sages," what transcended one's life was to serve as a good intermediary between the ancestors and one's descendants, expressed as male-centered ancestor worship with regard to beliefs, and expressed as the lineage or clan with regard to the grassroots community of everyday life. Due to the weak economic foundation and the strengthening of identification with the nuclear family, the lineage community has not yet revived its previous degree of importance at present, but ancestor worship has continued, especially with regard to the clear expression of ideas about "incense fires." This might be understood as a "little tradition" leaving its imprint in the countryside after "the rites of the sages" had disappeared from the "great tradition." Folk beliefs held by villagers, however, did not exhibit a sense of locality in the manner of "civil society," however, but were premised on the presence of the state.

When "human relationships" coexisted with instrumental ones in everyday life, rather than the former guiding the dynamic processes of social bonds, religion became one of peasants' "life-rafts" when attitudes in life lost their balance—even including belief systems (such as "cults") with strong corporatism and major doctrinal differences from formal religions. In comparison with the universal popularity of "the Three Religions," the rapid spread of Christianity was particularly striking. Looking at the beliefs and practices of rural Christians, they were actually still situated between God and the ancestors, and there still seemed to be many social and cultural difficulties with truly transforming peasants into "sinners" on the level of attitudes. The key could be the relationship between the "impure" concept of "the ancestors" and the philosophy of everyday life. Transcending one's life by relying on the concept of "sinners" alone could not fundamentally solve the problem of life's meaning for peasants. Although all kinds of religion and folk beliefs had found a certain market in the contemporary countryside, peasants were still confused about the point of transcending the carnal pleasures of the present. In attitudes about life's meaning, this condition was often expressed as "boredom," "meaninglessness," or even "life without a pulse." Pointing out the blind spots of peasants' everyday beliefs, then, and the cynicism and, to some degree, nihilism of their focus on material pleasures in the present does provide insights. It is worth noting, however, that peasants' everyday life also included another aspect that emphasized "human relationships" within the family, intergenerational transmission, and transcendence of one's individual life. This point should not be overlooked.

Based on this two-dimensionality regarding economy, politics, social relations, and beliefs, peasants' attitudes toward the relationship between people and history was also two-dimensional. Peasants' historical sensibility had previously focused on the alternation among different "ways of the world" (*shidao*) each "giving order to chaos" (*zhi luan*) in their own way, with the "evolutionary theory" of state power attempting to change this situation, but with limited effects. Later, the "materialization" of the rural social structure, and the rise of instrumentalism in the logic of interpersonal affairs, ultimately focused peasants' sense of history on attention to the present way of the world, to the point of "biting the hand that fed them." Peasants hoped that the way of the world would become more fair or just, but also that it would become more free, with contradictions often emerging between these two ideals. While criticizing their powerlessness, some young villagers turned toward cynicism or fantasies about traveling through history to reorient the way of the world.

In the tension between the broad trends of "the ways of the world" and the paths of individual people's lives, the principles whereby fate or destiny was believed to take shape were also directly related to peasants' desires and social attitudes. On this point, the influence on peasants of "the rites of the sages" lay in the importance they placed on people's lives in this world. In the "little tradition," however, peasants still needed to ground their fates in sources preceding this life, and to establish the direction of their fates after the end of this life, in order to maintain a balanced attitude in the face of paradoxes such as "merit without good fortune" or "good fortune without merit" in their lives. Although "advanced" ideas about materialism entered the countryside, the concept of fate never truly disappeared from peasants' everyday lives. What truly began to negate the cycles of fate before, after, and during people's lives was actually that peasants, under conditions of "freedom," were steered toward searching for the basis of their fates in this life through the disparities between rural social strata that kept expanding every day. The problem, however, was that people's lives in this world were replete with paradoxes. Peasants' explanations of how their fates took shape thus vacillated between previous lives and this one. Accordingly, peasants demonstrated both a reflective dimension that asked, "Is anyone born an aristocrat?" (*ning you zhong hu*, i.e., hierarchy is unnatural and can be changed), alongside a fatalistic or cynical dimension.

In sum, taking "the sages" as models for emulating in one's life was previously an important point of reference for peasants with some degree of "countryfied, utilitarian and secular" (*tuqi, suqi*), but this was not always true in everyday life and has become especially difficult in the present era of transition. The idea of secular people born into this world as "sinners," understood as an "advanced" model for a modern person's life, has been making inroads into the everyday life of Chinese peasants. In this, there has been no lack of a social basis for "pathological" factors in the countryside. The rites of the sages that valued "human relationships" previously had a complete logic for the interaction between people and things, other people, their own minds, the state, history, and fate. Now, however, one new logic after another has been trying to demonstrate that these relationships should be different. When the "principles" (*li*) change, so too should the "rites" (*li*) change. Contemporary peasants' life philosophy, however, has not completely changed into an "other," with their lives being reduced to a single dimension that is pathological, empty or nihilistic, or a simulation. On the contrary, peasants are two-dimensional with regard to economy, politics, social bonds, beliefs, and their approaches to history and fate. In their efforts to live their everyday lives, these two dimensions, with tensions and sometimes even contradictions between them, coexist within the same people's lives, where they are used to regulate desires and social attitudes. This is what is meant by "two-dimensional man."[2]

The Sagely and the Secular

From an ideal perspective, "two-dimensional man" is the product of the transition from a society centered on the sages to one centered on secular people. In this transitional society, reflections on individual people's lives, and on their desires and attitudes, have two types of typical orientations. One is complete criticism from some sort of moral high ground. The other is complete affirmation based on absolute pluralism and liberalism, saying "anything goes." The formation and characteristics of two-dimensional people show clearly that such reflections must be investigated dialectically.

Accommodation to the needs of natural cycles through self-restraint, or more precisely the restraining of one's desires, is no doubt beneficial for the sustainable use of things. To some extent, however, this is also what caused the "high-level equilibrium trap" in China's traditional rural development (Elvin 1973: 298–299). Peasants' cycles of life were not unrelated to this. On the one hand, peasants emphasized compliance with the inherent nature of things, along with self-exertion and diligence, meticulously cultivating the soil, and maximizing output under the premise of sustainable use, with the space for increasing the marginal returns of labor ultimately approaching zero. On the other hand, peasants' emphasis on frugality, their equal division of wealth among all sons, and their "economy of idleness" led to a constant expansion of population, to the point that diligence and thriftiness could no longer ensure their survival from day to day. Between generations, moreover, it became common to see dramatic differentiation into rich and poor among descendants of the same ancestors. From the perspective of governance, the excessive costs of the bureaucratic system, with its detailed division of labor, were bound to overwhelm rural society. Under conditions where agriculture dominated the rural economy, then, what China practiced was "minimalist governance" (Huang 2007: 414). On the basis of kinship networks complemented by locality-based ones, peasants achieved grassroots self-government by consulting "the rites of the sages" upheld by the state's "great tradition" while relying on "little traditions."

Ultimately this arrangement of rural society was broken when state power went down to the countryside. Of course, this process did not proceed entirely smoothly. At first, state power did not bring new governance resources from the top down, nor could it effectively organize rural society by providing more resources from the bottom up. Later, this process lacked a sufficiently relaxed environment in China. After the new world system formed, traditional states had no choice but to become swept up in the process of competition within the framework of modern sovereignty. State transition (from empire to independent nation-state) urgently needed governmental power to be extended to the countryside in order to consolidate resources from broader areas, to push forward modernization, and thereby to strengthen sovereignty. When the state finally achieved this, then the rapidly concentrated allocation of resources and the promotion of rural economic development were not only necessary for peasants to survive but were also a strategic necessity for state transition. The facts demonstrate that under conditions without sufficient new technologies for utilizing land, the organization of rural society into units (*danweihua*) was the secret recipe for the construction of water conservancy infrastructure, the expansion of land area under cultivation, and the elevation of agricultural output. At first, the reason peasants were willing to participate in this process was the combination of utilitarian factors, such as the acquisition of land, and ideological motivation, such as the hope of achieving "self-rule." However, when the state took away the agricultural surplus after output increased, and especially when "centralism" made peasants unfree, contradictions finally emerged between everyday life and the "great tradition's" discourse of "class." These contradictions found concentrated expression in the figure of the grassroots cadre who could not "serve the people," which became the concrete object of peasants' critical reflection on centralism. In addition, the "human relationships" that survived in peasants' "little traditions" also played a definite role in resistance to the discursive practices of "class." These relationships not only practically restricted and questioned that discourse's efforts to make rural society one-dimensional, but they also became the attitudinal foundation for the discourse's later disappearance from rural society.

The partial affirmation of peasants' private, material desires was certainly a sort of progress. Of course, against the background of the state's transitional strategy, the accumulation of heavy industry had already been basically completed by that time, and the state's reliance on agricultural surplus had begun to decline. However, peasants mainly viewed these changes from the perspective of everyday life. The affirmation of private, material desires that had been repressed and the safeguarding of basic survival seemed clearly to be in accordance with the "Heavenly Principles." Moreover, since a vast industrial sphere had emerged outside of agriculture, it finally became possible to move toward a mixed economy of agriculture and industry. This meant that it was finally possible for peasants to jump out of the "developmental trap" caused by the newly increased population "eating away" the fruits of rural economic growth. All of this was clearly not something that could be accomplished by restricting the ego's desires and conforming to nature. Later, when "semi-industry, semi-agriculture" had already become the economic base for rural households, peasants began to partially abandon the land in order to improve their everyday life, satisfy their material desires, and achieve their ideal lives. In this, there was an active dimension to peasant attitudes. Considering that peasants had come to rely on more than the land and the village community, they no longer cherished the land as much as their ancestors had done, and to some degree it may have been inevitable that the village moral system would also lose its power over individualized peasant households.

Furthermore, ordinary peasants' attitudes were rather imbalanced toward the drastic increase in immediate material desires. Relative to privileged groups within the rural social hierarchy, their desires were still limited, so there was good reason for such an imbalance to exist. In contrast with those who had become obsessed with carnal pleasures, ordinary peasants objectively had little choice but to retain the attitude of "unconditional contentment." In contrast with those who had acquired material wealth by sidestepping "integrity," "uprightness," and the legal system (including grassroots officials who acted as "governmental businesspeople"), how could ordinary peasants not be "simple and honest," or "ignorant of how to be flexible"? In light of these comparisons, there was clearly a deep-seated basis in reality for peasants to have imbalanced attitudes and consider their lives to be far from ideal, rather than merely being a result of the sudden expansion of material desires to the point that people became "as discontent as a snake trying to swallow an elephant." From this perspective, regarding the difficulty of fulfilling desires, governmental corruption, the snobbishness of the privileged, lack of meaning in people's lives, unfairness or injustice, the fickleness of fate, etc., most peasants' discontentment or cynicism also involved a touch of critical reflection upon society's transition. Although these reflections were not necessarily systematic, rational, or even appropriate, if we were just to criticize them, that too would be biased.

Of course, to affirm the liberation of peasants' desires from self-restraint, and to note their historical rationality, is not the same thing as approving of "unbridled desires" (*wuyu hengliu*). To say that stepping out of self-restraint is reasonable is not to say that it is reasonable to make demands on "the other" (whether those be people or external objects) by any means whatsoever. In other words, under conditions where it is hard to become a "sage" or a "sinner," it is reasonable to be a "secular person," but this absolutely does not mean that one should be secular to the point of becoming a "sick person."

In this sense, however, there are truly cases where contemporary peasants have gone too far. The universal growth of material wealth has not directly led peasants to simply believe subjectively that their lives have become more ideal, that their desires have been fulfilled in everyday life, or that their attitudes have become free from worry. On the contrary, since the speed and scope at which material desires have increased has far outstripped people's positions in the social hierarchy, not only has a bigger gap emerged between the desires of ordinary peasants and their actual conditions, but the privileged groups in rural society have also become even more discontent with what their lives have given them. Mental instability has further aggravated doubts about the meaning of life in the present world. Although the bonds between ancestors and their descendants still provide a certain peace of mind, that is not enough. There is a social basis for the Three Religions, for Christianity, for cynicism, and for "de-historicized sensibility" (in the form of literature on time travel). None of these, however, can fundamentally dispel peasants' anxiety about material wealth and the uncertainties of their lives. From this angle, two-dimensional people truly do have a pathological aspect.

The pathological aspect of two-dimensional people has been formed through the process of social transition, or at least we can say that it was not formed overnight. In fact, when the discourse of class went down to the countryside, it was fundamentally different from peasants' philosophy of everyday life, and there were some conflicts between the two. The lives that the discourse of class tried to construct were in some ways similar to those advocated by the sages, as, for example, in the negation of private, material desires. In this respect, the former went even further than the rites of the sages. The ideal of being "revolutionary to the depths of one's soul" was harder and more thorough than calling for integrity and uprightness in everyday life. Of course, all of this has its specific historical causes that cannot be addressed in detail here. In the process of practice, however, it created two consequences for peasants. One was that because it negated "private desires" too stridently, it departed from the warmth of familial relationships in peasants' everyday lives. This meant that even when peasants were willing to accept the discourse of class on an intellectual level, it became hard for them to carry it out in practice. Even the most "revolutionary" cadres still depended upon "private" relationships (involving desire) and nurtured them. Another consequence was that when peasants' everyday lives fell into difficulties because of "revolutionary ideals," and especially when grassroots cadres—as representatives of class discourse—were ultimately shown to have not only failed to uproot their private desires, but even to have been motivated by such desires more than ordinary peasants, the discourse was negated. As a result, one large-scale, intense political movement after another could not get rid of peasants' private, material desires, and instead they partially destroyed the basis for the rites of the sages that had previously existed in everyday life.

The use of money to measure all value and serve as a bridge for social exchange further eroded this basis on a deeper level. It is worth noting, however, that money could not carry out this function of its own accord. The precondition for this potential function to be activated was again the transition of the state and society. The state's tentacles at the rural basic level, i.e., grassroots officials, became "governmental businesspeople" in practice, rather than having the peasants rule themselves as called for in ideology, or "ruling for the people" as expected according to the rites of the sages. The rural social structure maintained a dynamic link with those officials, and the importance of the ends of getting rich overshadowed the means for achieving that. When the gap between rural social strata kept growing, a huge pressure formed in the attitudes of not only ordinary peasants but also privileged groups. That acquisition of material wealth became the marker for measuring the success of a person's life, rather than the degree to which the means for acquiring wealth conformed to morality or the law. In a chain reaction with this mechanism, the principle of utility permeated the logic of peasants' everyday life and personal interactions to a greater extent. Under this precondition, it became more common for their relationships with the state, history, and fate to become more confused and chaotic on the level of attitudes, to the point of pathology.

In sum, if we examine rural people's lives, desires, and social attitudes dialectically from a perspective of society's "great transformation," it is not hard to discover that we must pay attention to both dimensions that exist symbiotically within "two-dimensional man" while in opposition to one another at the same time, rather than just focusing on one dimension or the other. Contemporary academics have been inclined to use one-dimensional discourses to analyze peasants' desires and social attitudes, in ways that may be worth supplementation or critical reflection. If we expand our field of vision to encompass longer stretches of history, we can see that "unbridled desire" is not a unique concern of contemporary intellectuals about contemporary rural society. Prior to transformation according to the standards of secular people, rural society had already undergone many changes, among which those in the Song dynasty were particularly striking. One important goal of the reforms proposed by Song Confucians was, under conditions of "unbridled desire," to "rearrange" (*andun*) peasants' everyday lives such that their minds could be stabilized and rectified. Since the situation of "unbridled desire" was a product of rural social change, in order to impose appropriate limits (rather than trying to get rid of private, material desires), solutions should be sought through critical reflection on social change. Since unreasonable factors in grassroots governance and the rural social structure have played an important role in the excessive growth of peasants' desires and the instability of their social attitudes, then using these as a point of entry for rebuilding rural governance and communities of everyday life seems to be a way for the problem to be partially solved by its own source. If instead we merely criticize or approve of it wholesale, that would not only be insufficiently dialectical, but would also be hard to make pertinent. At root, from the perspective of peasants' everyday life philosophy, if we affirm secular people's normal private, material desires while also appropriately restraining them according to the rites of the sages (in terms of ideal types, this could be called "treating the secular as sagely"), this may not be too lofty for ordinary people to understand or put into practice, while also preventing excessive this-worldliness (*su*) from falling into pathology.

Trapped

Although the process of rural social transition leading to the emergence of two-dimensional people has fluctuated over time, the pursuit of modernity has been a constant. Even when the discourse of class negated peasants' private, material desires, that too was a sort of modern idea. It did not ask peasants to practice self-restraint according to "the rites of the sages," but to control desire for the modern state and for the contribution of surplus products of their labor. Two-dimensional people have therefore also been rooted in modernity at the same time. The reason that modernity could ultimately become a diffuse pressure on peasants' lives, desires, and social attitudes is precisely its dependence not on class discourse or simple, direct, "centralist" controls over the body and mind, but on widening the disparities between rural social strata through granting peasants "freedom," which gives abstract, quasi-magical powers to the objective implement that symbolized this disparity—i.e., money. Monetary mechanisms not only dominate the economic sphere of everyday life, but at the same time they also forcefully permeate every other sphere, whether explicitly or implicitly. In other words, of course modern monetary mechanisms do not constitute a perpetual motion machine that can maintain its operation of its own accord. Their mechanism of propulsion lies in the state's use of rural governance to transform both grassroots politics and society in the state's own process of transition. Money has used its unique, indiscriminate mediating mechanism toward other values to dominate the "life-pulse" of grassroots cadres, and at the same time to assess and rank every ordinary peasant.

Of course, no matter whether we are describing grassroots cadres or ordinary peasants, it would be hard to call either of them passive recipients or objects of transformation by modernity. In the face of monetary mechanisms of mediation, the more capable the rural political elite are, the more adept they are at "being flexible" or "skirting the rules" to achieve the goals of "digging up land" and obtaining the magic wand of money. In everyday rural life, the more "observant" or "aware of how to be flexible" peasants are, the more skillful they are at using the cold mechanisms of monetary mediation to suppress the "tenderness" of "human relationships" in order to achieve the goal of getting rich quick. Subjectively, of course, neither cadres nor ordinary peasants are necessarily willing to completely prostrate themselves in the face of money. In reality, cadres try to serve the people and promote development for the coming generations. It is just that, in moderately developed regions, this space is often limited. In their logic of personal interaction, cadres do not completely ignore the "tenderness" of "human relationships." In the face of limited political resources and the risks of "being flexible," "skirting the rules," and "digging up land," the cold principle of utility unintentionally spreads throughout the process of forming and maintaining factions. As for ordinary peasants, they clearly attempt to combine cold money with warm relations of reciprocity. To some degree, however, the need to accumulate money compels them to consciously assess and construct all kinds of social networks in order to obtain useful resources from them.

"It is easier to summon a god than it is to make him leave," as the saying goes. As soon as the dominant status of money is established, it becomes inevitable that its oppressive aspect will emerge. Relative to money's dominance and instrumentality, the question of whether one depends on labor, or whether one's labor is equivalent to the money received, has already become unimportant, with the acquisition of money itself becoming the only logic that counts. In the everyday life of rural society, however, the space for directly relying on labor to satisfy ever-expanding monetized desires is often limited. This makes people, including both privileged groups and ordinary peasants, universally complain of feeling exhausted, and attitudes of disappointment, depression, and emptiness are already widespread. This sort of attitudinal predicament that privileged groups face, besides creating pressure for their own egos, also creates pressure that directly targets ordinary peasants. It has become a goal to be pursued by the latter, even something that proves whether a person has face and whether their life has meaning.

As a mechanism for organizing the economy and its social hierarchy, under these conditions, monetary mediation has gradually begun to clamp down upon everyday life, forming one set of interlocking traps after another, all replete with two-dimensionality. In these traps, the desire for money among cadres and peasants has become stimulated to an unprecedented extent, but opportunities to satisfy these desires cannot not increase at the same rate. As a result, almost every individual and stratum has become trapped. As with traps that become tighter the more you try to escape, however, the efforts of individual peasants and each stratum to quickly escape from the trap, through labor or other methods, actually aggravate the degree to which they are trapped. On the level of social attitudes, then, this could be called a "trapped society."[3]

The "trapped society" is both a practical result of the everyday life of two-dimensional people and also, of course, is closely related to the dimension of valuing immediate material desires that has emerged with the rise of modernity. This has been precisely the focal point of all kinds of critical narratives about "one-dimensional man" and one-dimensional modernity. Actually, however, the concept and phenomenon of "two-dimensional man" has significance for critical reflection upon such narratives.

In rural everyday life, although two-dimensional people do manifest alienation, rationalization, objectification, or even pathologization, they also possess a dimension that struggles to uphold a "true self" or "essence." Even if they become obsessed with carnal desires, they also carry out this kind of critical reflection to some extent or another. Social networks based on kinship, locality, or reciprocity, albeit instrumental, play a big role in the process of the rise of monetary mechanisms of mediation. At the same time, they also provide an everyday-life safety valve or shock absorber for the "losers" in lives mediated by monetary mechanisms. In the arena of rural governance, although rational bureaucracy has been on the rise, traditional forms of authority involving patriarchy and charisma not only continue to exist, but they can even be combined with grassroots officialdom in order to conduct the responsibilities of governance. Those tenets of interpersonal relations and other beliefs that are deeply embedded in the hearts of villagers (although replete with contradictions) provide expansive and deep soil for religious, quasi-religious, and patriarchal modes of control. The tension between "the people's rule" and "rule for the people" shows that the rise of modernity has led to the possibility that the arena of governance can become closed off, on the one hand, but at the same time can also generate the democratic participatory force that opens the door of governance, on the other. This is a two-way process.

Classic social theorists and more recent critical theorists developed profound critiques of the secular or "sick" people created by the rise of modernity. There is no doubt that these made sense when it came to reflecting on grand concepts such as freedom, democracy, equality, or justice, and on the hypocrisy of treating such concepts as sacred tenets. In the everyday practice of two-dimensional people, however, another type of discourse emerges every day in "countryfied" forms, such as ironic jokes and rhymes, bantering doggerel, and sarcastic metaphors. As two-dimensional people see it, the more closed-off a formalized discourse is, the more explicitly or implicitly popular the critical, reflexive discourse related to it will be. This logic echoes the saying, "Wherever there is oppression, there is resistance." Modernity leads secular people to become homogeneous "sick people," but these can only give rise to two-dimensional people, since they cannot avoid encountering the resistance of the "true self" or "essence" that comes from within everyday life.

Although classic social theorists provided insights on the question of how to overcome problems of modernity, they left behind a series of questions about how modernity is related to the practices of everyday life, which are worth exploring further. On the basis of modern everyday life, the path of class struggle and political liberation targeting "alienation" (Marx 2000: 59) has left behind the practical predicament of how to normalize institutions of mobilization and struggle. Now that modern factors have accumulated to the point that there is a surplus beyond basic subsistence, two-dimensional people have often been inclined to reflect upon the overcoming of modern society and its superior alternatives, under the precondition that the order of everyday life remains relatively stable. Similarly, the use of professional and moral education to address social anomie in the rise of modernity (Durkheim 2000: 313, 113) has also left behind the question of how morality could become an organic component of ordinary people's everyday life, including under conditions of insufficient "organic solidarity" in heterogeneous societies. Moreover, there are still unresolved questions regarding how education in professional ethics might escape from the vicious circle of class reproduction, where "sons get the same jobs as their fathers," and thereby enable ordinary people to accomplish their life goals and sort out their social attitudes in everyday life. As for using the method of individual performance based on an "ethics of responsibility" to break free from the "iron cage" of rationality (Weber 2007: 188), that seems closer to a sort of moral admonition, with weak and dissipated power for critical reflection. Similarly, Simmel's (1991: 44) formula for an individual "ethics of life" encourages people to find meaning that transcends immediate material desires by feeling the value of life, but within the tranquility of everyday life, it remains unclear how people can find the motivation to actively reflect on its value.

Of course, no matter how they put it, when classic social theorists reflected on modernity's tendency toward unidimensionalization, they emphasized the vast majority of ordinary people. By contrast, when many critical theorists reflected on the "unbridled desires" and repression of human nature that modernity had brought with it, although there were big differences among their approaches, all pinned their hopes on marginalized groups outside of mainstream society, and on those groups' ideas.

Regarding the problem of modern rationality's control over and transformation of secular people into "sick people," the alternatives posed by these theorists did not look to ordinary people in everyday life or their ideas about self-salvation. On the contrary, reflections on "one-dimensional man" argued that only vagabonds and outsiders, the exploited and persecuted people of different races and skin colors, the unemployed and the unemployable possessed the hope of curing the malady of one-dimensional modernity through "the Great Refusal" (Marcuse 2006: 234). Although their reflections were profound and powerful on the level of criticism, on the constructive level they not only overlooked the critical abilities of ordinary people, but they also ignored socially marginalized groups' abilities and practical avenues for enduring the weight of modernity's "salvation." In societies where modernity was on the rise, the degree to which people depended upon specific other people fell significantly, while the degree to which people depended upon society rose drastically. (Peasants' turn from agriculture to the mixed economy of agriculture and industry was just one aspect of this change.) This meant that connections dependent upon private individuals weakened, while interaction dependent upon the public became more important. The orientation of the "Great Refusal" clearly ran in the opposite direction.

As for calls to deconstruct centralizing, totalizing grand narratives, these have also been quite profound for revealing the living people that have been disciplined by dispersed, modern mechanisms of objective power (Foucault 1999: 353). Deconstruction itself, however, is not equivalent to salvation.

On the contrary, after all relevant value systems have been deconstructed, ordinary people's lives lose their coordinates for orientation. Although it is easy for purely individualized, fragmented subjectivity to achieve "orgasmic" experiences (Foucault 2002: 591), how to incorporate it back into a sustainable everyday life often becomes a major problem. In the same way, although pointing out the death of both God and Man-as-subject is meaningful for reflecting upon modernity's illusory aspects, relying merely on appeals to abandon greed and face the absence of the self's subjectivity (Baudrillard 2006: 166) cannot function more effectively than moral appeals. Calls to emphasize attention to "difference" and "différance" in order to help people search for "traces" of meaning (Derrida 2001: 112) unintentionally negates the value of labor in people's lives. From the perspective of everyday life, its paradox lies in the fact that without labor, people's lives are divorced from everyday life, to say nothing of meaning. Further, treating modernity's social maladies with psychoanalytic methods (Lacan 2006: 80–81) poses the question of who is treating whose illness. Moreover, when "pathology" derives from the modernity of the system, how could there not be tension with individualized treatment?

The knowledge that modern people are two-dimensional allows us, first of all, to negate the following type of statement: that "two-dimensional man" is a temporary feature of transitional societies, and that after modernity develops for a longer period of time, he will ultimately become one-dimensional man. Further, regarding modernity's inclination toward unidimensionalization and the repression of people's subjectivity, the lesson of "two-dimensional man" is that ordinary people in everyday life can and, by rights, should themselves become the protagonists of critical reflection. Just as in the "great transformation," after society is squeezed by the market, it will rise up of its own accord and protect itself (Polanyi 1957: 130), the prescription for overcoming the maladies of modernity lies mainly not in other places, but in modern everyday life itself. In this process, since the state possesses subjectivity that transcends society, it is more appropriate for shouldering the responsibility of serving as a vanguard for reflecting upon and optimizing formulas for modernity. As noted above, only state governance can rectify the minds of the people. Rectification of the mind (*zheng xin*) can then manage the family (*qi jia*) and establish destiny (*li ming*). Once the mind is rectified, the family is managed, and destiny is established, the hope emerges for the "trapped society" to become untrapped. Here it is worth pointing out that since those connected to the modernity within everyday life are two-dimensional people, reflection too lies not in a "Great Refusal" but in a "Great Dialogue." First, through dialogue, social discourse becomes pluralistic, and seeking common ground while preserving differences breaks out of ideological autarky. Second, through dialogue, social structure becomes flexible and fluid, breaking the rigidity of social strata. Third, through dialogue, life values become diverse, breaking the grip of monetary mediation mechanisms on human dignity.

Governing the Country

In modern society, there is no doubt that the state is the most important platform for different groups and strata to carry out public dialogue, communication, and consultation. At the same time, it is also the seat of public power that transcends any single individual or stratum. Especially when it comes to ordinary peasants, the state is the precondition for their lives and for their everyday life. For reflection upon state governance, the significance of "two-dimensional man" within the changing countryside is that it demonstrates the tension between both extreme directions (the promotion of either extreme altruism or extreme egocentricity), on the one hand, and peasants' lives and everyday life, on the other.

In grassroots rural governance, if the state unilaterally negates the immediate material desires in peasants' everyday life, the practical results often turn out the opposite of what was intended. Since peasants have no way to "get rid of private desires" (*qu si*) to a corresponding degree, it is hard for them to achieve transcendence over the self and its desires in their lives. Not only will they be unable to achieve "loftiness of character" (*chonggao*) in the way state governance wishes, but they might even question or ridicule loftiness, pursuing more urgently the private, material desires that have been excessively repressed. Under these conditions, although the state can provide peasants' everyday lives with a certain degree of equality, since peasants' private, material desires have become the target of state governance, what the state provides can only be the equal repression of desires. Of course, it is not as if peasants cannot repress desires in everyday life for the state's grander, longer-term goals. However, the vast majority of ordinary peasants are not ascetic monks, after all. Therefore, two premises are necessary: first, that everyday life based on the family can function normally; and second, that the private, material desires of privileged groups in the rural social hierarchy be repressed consistently. If ordinary peasants have not even solved basic problems of subsistence, that runs counter to the former. In this way, rural social attitudes will inevitably become unbalanced. Peasant consciousness in pursuing the fulfillment of basic desires in everyday life will naturally evolve into critical reflection targeting grassroots governance, and with attitudes yearning for the state to "rule for the people," they will look forward to a transition of state governance. In peasants' philosophy of everyday life, this could be called the propensity of the way of the world, which may be followed but not opposed. With regard to the state, the propensity of the way of the world that peasants recognize is "the will of people" (*renxin*). The human-mindedness of the way of the world is concerned with the legitimacy of the state, and more directly with the reasonableness and effectiveness of governance. Therefore, the question of whether this Great Dialogue between ordinary peasants, rural privileged groups, and the state can take place smoothly, and whether communication and consultation based on this dialogue can occur, concerns the question of whether ordinary peasants can live well and achieve their ideal lives, as well as the question of whether the state can achieve human-minded "governance of the world."

In rural grassroots governance, however, if the state were to unilaterally affirm the immediate material pleasures in peasants' everyday lives, the practical outcome would also be contrary to intentions. Especially in moderately developed regions that lack the objective conditions for rapid development in the first place, if grassroots cadres were to unilaterally emphasize the logic of satisfying immediate material desires in local development, although it might bring the rapid growth of material wealth, it could only "dig up the land" by "flexibly" sidestepping or directly violating broader policies and the legal system. As a result, the faster this sort of growth is, and the more grassroots officials' private, material desires are satisfied, the more the law is undermined. In order to obtain more political capital and opportunities for promotion in the bureaucracy on the basis of manipulating this sort of "flexibility" and violation of the law, the phenomenon of grassroots factional politics becomes all the more rampant. In practice, since the public rights of grassroots government can be flexible and violate the law for the public goal of local development, local officials significantly expand the scope for the private use of public rights. As soon as state governance becomes distorted in grassroots officialdom, no matter whether peasants call on officials to serve the people through "(the people) ruling themselves," or pin their hopes on officials showing mercy by "ruling for the people," either way, things become extremely difficult. Ultimately, the more grassroots governance departs from the public goals of state governance, the harder it becomes for peasants to live well and achieve ideal lives, and the more imbalanced rural social attitudes become.

A similarly important problem lies in the state's unbalanced emphasis on immediate material desires in rural grassroots governance, objectively leading to rapid expansion of disparities between strata in rural society. Moreover, among the privileged groups in the rural social hierarchy, their means of getting rich also include "being flexible" and violating the law. Their intentions in getting rich are not necessarily sincere, their minds not necessarily upright, and if the state cannot restrain or punish them in time, not only will this form a living, bitter irony for peasant lives that are sincere and upright, though situated at the bottom of rural society, but it will also stimulate the further expansion of more intense desires among ordinary peasants. Resources and opportunities in rural society are limited, however, especially in moderately developed regions. At a time when the standards for rural social strata are becoming increasingly limited to the "single-plank bridge" of material wealth, it is inevitable that only a small minority of peasants will be able to cross this bridge over to the upper strata, while most ordinary peasants can only yearn for money and sigh. Therefore, now that the state is emphasizing "giving priority to efficiency with due concern for fairness" in its push for social transition, it is necessary to have specific mechanisms to ensure that "due concern" is implemented in peasants' everyday lives. Otherwise, it would be easy for grassroots governance to abbreviate the policy so that only the first half is implemented without the second half. As soon as efficiency surpasses fairness, the political-economic proposition of "whose efficiency" emerges. In the rural social hierarchy, if efficiency belongs only to a small, privileged minority, there can be no doubt that the higher the efficiency, the more frustrated ordinary peasants will feel in their everyday lives, and the more imbalanced rural social attitudes will become. Not only will ordinary peasants bite the hand that feeds them, but even privileged groups will also become smug about their advantages. Since their efficiency came too easily and unjustly, the privileged not only demonstrate contempt for the law, their conflicts with everyday life also become bigger, their minds less stable, their families less peaceful, and their lives harder to find transcendence, since their desires expand more easily.

Using everyday life as a benchmark, then, it would be inadvisable for the state either to simply negate peasants' private, material desires in rural grassroots governance, on the one hand, or to simply affirm them, on the other. Taken to the extreme in either direction, peasants' everyday lives would sink into dire straits, and it would become even harder to achieve the ideal life, making the state's governance in the countryside contradict peasants' sense that the present era is an historical golden age. In other words, a reasonable frame of reference for the state to implement rural grassroots governance would be peasants' everyday lives and normal desires in life, rather than either "the rites of the sages" or the desires of secular people.

If we further analyze state governance, it is not hard to discover that the concept and phenomenon of "two-dimensional man in a transitional countryside" also bears significance for reference in reflecting upon the rule of law and democracy—the pillars of modern state governance.

The transition from the "rule of rites, ideals, or customs" (*li zhi*) to the "rule of law" has always been considered an important standard for modern state governance. The presupposition about people's lives that underpins this idea is the transition from "sages" to "secular people." If we presuppose that people are sagely, education (*jiaohua*) should be emphasized, and society should be governed by rites. If we presuppose that people are inherently secular, institutions (*guifan*) should be emphasized, and society should be governed by law. In the process of the rise of modernity, the idea of sageliness came to be considered "backward," or at most something limited to the sphere of morality, and the secular people born from the status of "sinners" came to be considered "advanced" markers of self-determination. Without a doubt, the laws and institutions defined by the state as "advanced" and based on the desires of secular people appeared extremely important for replacing the "backward" rites expressing the "human relationships" of the sages. In rural society, itself a classic symbol of "backwardness," the tension between these two has been even more pronounced. Setting aside the social costs necessary to support this transition, the weakness of peasants' awareness of the law has been a real problem necessary to address first. In reality, peasants are not, in their everyday lives, opposed to all laws. Even under conditions where the state's laws contradict many principles of everyday life, peasants sometimes change in ways that actively draw themselves closer to the laws. With regard to the principle of gender equality, for example, many changes of perspective have already taken place. In some situations, peasants have even taken the initiative to bring the legal system down to the countryside in order to protect their own rights.

The real problem, then, lies in those laws that are divorced from everyday life and therefore hard to implement, at least temporarily. In those cases, it must be considered that a reasonable distance be maintained from peasants' everyday lives. Peasant can move toward the rule of law only when the law can be implemented without major changes to everyday life. If the law requires them to completely change their lives, or if even such changes are not sufficient to meet the letter of the law, in practice peasants will either treat it as "wind brushing past the ears," a mere formality, or they will consider it "tyranny" (*kufa*) that completely ignores reality, neither befitting human nature (something not abstract but rooted in concrete sociocultural conditions), nor capable of supporting an ideal life. Even when it comes to those laws that have recognized that the rites of the sages are still meaningful for modern society, and which have attempted to establish some kind of continuity with their historical legacy, if their distance from everyday life is too great, they might be reduced to moral symbolism providing spiritual comfort for the modern rule of law. For example, when "semi-industrial" young peasants cannot afford to look after the elderly due to the constraints of income, holiday schedules, and transportation, how could the law make their family life become more orderly? The rule of rites is therefore not purely opposed to the rule of law, nor does the former naturally precede the latter in an evolutionary relationship of substitution. On the contrary, there are many areas of overlap between the two. Even some of their content that does not overlap is not necessarily opposed but is instead mutually supporting. As for the content that modernity must replace, it is destined to be a gradual process of establishing the rule of law, since the transition of peasants' everyday life is always gradual.

More importantly, in everyday life, ordinary peasants are not truly ignorant of the law. Even if their legal knowledge is inferior, their respect and veneration of the law is much stronger than those of privileged groups in the rural social hierarchy. Grassroots officials "dig up the land" in violation of the law and default on loans, enterprises pollute the environment and violate migrant workers legal rights, individual bosses sell fake and low-quality farm supplies and toxic foods, "observant" peasants run underground lotteries when they can or sell toxic agricultural products when they cannot. Not only is such behavior often allowed to take place unchecked and unpunished by the state, but it also even brings people enormous material wealth in a short period of time. Further, those who get rich in this way not only scoff at the law as being a mere formality, but they also even ridicule people who obey the law for being "ignorant of how to be flexible," saying their thinking is insufficiently "liberated." The principle of "liberating thought" was originally a state mechanism for optimizing governance in the transition to the rule of law, but here it has come to mean "anything goes." When ordinary peasants try to quote the law regarding land in order to prevent privileged groups from "digging it up" and to protect their own rights, upholding their right to villager self-government, the response they get from grassroots officials is "don't be so pedantic," "you need to give us a little face," and so on. In a word, as soon as the law lacks specific measures for just implementation, it may become subject to "selective implementation"—as well as selective "blindness." Needless to say, the problems brought in this way not only damage the prestige of the law in places where "Heaven is high and the emperor is far away," they also cause grassroots officialdom to lose its "human-mindedness," to some extent. As far as ordinary peasants are concerned, although the state's law is good, only "other people" are able to make effective use of the law at the basic level. In this type of attitude, does it not better suit the philosophy of everyday life for peasants to lack awareness of the law, instead pinning their hopes on the state "ruling for the people"?

With modern formulas as a reference, however, peasants' hope that kindhearted people will rule for the people is considered an extremely backward idea that needs to be transformed. This puts peasants in an awkward position. If modern formulas can be achieved only with great costs of time, energy, and even personal safety, peasants' everyday lives cannot catch up. Very few peasants are able to cast aside everyday life, or are willing to pay these kinds of costs to deal with privileged groups in the rural social hierarchy. For the everyday lives of ordinary peasants, less troublesome methods are to be cynical, to endure, to criticize after dinner, and then to expect the government to rule for the people. In this way, it is clearly hard to have a firm social foundation for bottom-up supervision of the power of village cadres and grassroots officials, no matter whether it is to be exercised through villager self-government or through grassroots official governance. Of course, peasants are not eager to give up their rights to democratic elections, decision-making, management, or supervision—if they were, then they would not be so imbalanced in their attitudes. It is hard, however, for peasants' everyday lives to bear democratic rights with high costs, unless there are greater benefits that could be useful for everyday life. In the arena of grassroots officialdom, on the other hand, the phenomenon of "two-dimensional man" is expressed in the form of factional politics. This makes it hard not only for ordinary peasants in everyday life to exercise their rights to democratic elections, decision-making, management, and supervision, but also for them to directly access opportunities for the state to rule for the people. This is because peasants can escape the confines of factionalism and find "parental officials" who can uphold "the way of justice," untouched by grassroots government's factional interests, only by skipping over the township, county, or even higher levels of officialdom. Petitioning higher-level officials is hard, and many peasants ultimately give up after petitioning in vain.

Although the idea of pinning their hopes on kind-hearted officials ruling for the people does not attach importance to democratic elections, it would be hard to say there is no substantial overlap with democratic decision-making, management, or supervision. Although this idea does not meet secular people's formal standards of democratic state governance, it clearly has another logic for democracy. In the philosophy of peasants' everyday lives, the state ruling for the people and ensuring that peasants can live well is precisely the most important expression of "the people ruling themselves." If the state cannot ensure that peasants can live well, then it is not doing a good job of ruling for the people. As soon as this is the case, any amount of formal democracy is considered nothing but a mere formality with respect to everyday life. In the philosophy of secular people, one might not be able to speak of substance without form. For the philosophy of peasants' everyday life, however, form exists only to serve substance; substance is more important than form, and even the most flawless form cannot replace substance. Of course, there are differences between the two: "Self-rule" depends more on the "principle or rationality" (*li*) of the rule of law, while "ruling for the people" places more value on the manifestation of the "rites or customs" (*li*) of "human relationships" in the practice of the state's law. There is considerable overlap, however, between the principle of the law and the rites of the people. If the principle of the law lacks content involving the rites of the people, then it is tyranny or an inhuman institution of management. If the rites of the people cannot merge with the principle of the law, then it is merely moral exhortation that cannot easily be put into practice in everyday life. In any case, it is worth critically reflecting on the division of these two into purely distinct opposites, and on the assertion that the transition from "rule for the people" to "self-rule" is a unidirectional necessity of history.

Managing the Household

The household is the platform upon which people depend in order to carry out their everyday lives, playing a decisive role in determining whether they can achieve the ideal life. A new household is a union of two people, often produced through the original motivations of affection (*qinggan*) and satisfying sexual desire. This is most often a union between a man and a woman. In order for a household to be a unit of everyday life, it must have a certain material foundation. No matter whether it is rich or poor, therefore, relationships within the household always involve property relations. Property relations include rights and duties, the two being interdependent. Under normal conditions, a union between a man and a woman means reproduction. No matter the form of society, then, substantial marital arrangements are necessary to ensure that care for the next generations proceeds smoothly. It follows that, in everyday life, relationships between generations and among kin within the same lineage or through marriage overlap with property relations, to some extent or another.

Both the strengths and weaknesses of everyday life lie in the everydayness of such life. Everyday life provides expectations of relative stability for both of the partners who established the household, but it easily leads to the gradual disappearance of the original motivations for the household's establishment. The passion of sexual desire is not, therefore, a stable force that can maintain a household over a long period of time, so the motivation of affection seems more important. The rites of the sages promoted all kinds of rules about "righteousness, propriety, or loyalty" (*yi*) between husband and wife, their crux being to temper the uncertainty of individual affection. In highly immobile societies where people depended mainly on agriculture for survival, when it came to clearly ordering household relationships, making them more stable doubtless played an important role. Accordingly, no matter whether it was relationships between husband and wife or between generations, or between kin within a wider range, property relations between them were always understood as Confucian "human relationships," rather than merely material ones. Further, all kinds of broader familial relationships formed fictively on the basis of kinship, such as lineage or clan relationships, were endowed with the duties and rights of providing material relief to those undergoing hardships, resolving conflicts, and maintaining order. Turning it around, these extended families were both insurance for managing the household, and folk resources for maintaining social order within a given locality.

In the process of the rise of modernity, secular people have advocated individual equality, including between husband and wife. Rural Chinese society, forced to try to catch up with "the advanced," has also been swept up into this process. At every level of definition, from the household to the clan, the family has been replaced by rural grassroots agents of the state, and equality between men and women has been pulled into mainstream social discourse. For the everyday life of peasant households, which have been extremely dependent upon agriculture and whose populations have been highly immobile, these two basic characteristics still have not changed. Even when women's rights have increased, therefore, they have not formed a relationship of mutual restriction of men's rights. Households have not depended upon contractual cooperation formed by individual rights, but on the maintenance of affection in "human relationships," still the precondition not only for household stability, but also for the maintenance of rural social order. Mainstream social discourse's emphasis on *zuofeng* (behavioral norms)[4] and village public authorities' mediation of household disputes have played a similar role in managing households as lineages and clans had previously done according to the rites of the sages, to some extent.

As peasants have moved toward the mixed economy of agriculture and industry, population mobility has accelerated rapidly. This has marked a major change for basic conditions of the household's everyday life. At the same time, with the "decollectivization and opening" (*qudanweihua*) of villages, the motivation and ability of village public authorities to mediate household disputes has declined. In addition, the life outlook of secular people or even "sick people," as an "advanced" mainstream social discourse, has spread rapidly into the countryside through modern media and the "education" of peasants who have gone to work in cities. The question of how to stabilize and sustain affection and "human relationships" in peasant marriages also has begun to face challenges in everyday life.

In this respect, the privileged groups in the rural social hierarchy have been the most affected. On the one hand, through the process of wealth accumulation, women have lost most or all of the resources they had previously controlled for maintaining marriages. On the other hand, men have obtained sufficient material resources for extramarital sexual relationships while losing almost all the extrafamilial restrictions to which they had previously been subject. Modernity has granted women the concept of equal rights in marriage, but the logic of power and everyday domestic life has moved in exactly the opposite direction. Women actively and formally call for rights, but only to annul marital relationships, and this means the end of everyday domestic life. As soon as this happens, relationships between people are no longer important, leaving behind only material relationships involving the division of property and the allocation of responsibilities for childcare. Otherwise, women can rely only on the affection from the start of the marriage, which has already diminished significantly, to maintain everyday domestic life in a cynical way. There can be no doubt that this sort of relationship is abnormal, with attitudes hard to balance and a life full of regrets. Even if women seek help from "fate" or religion, in order to obtain some degree of psychological consolation, these cannot solve the real problems of managing the household, nor can they achieve the ideal life.

Since ordinary villagers do not have many material possessions, material relations in such marriages are simpler. This does not mean they are easy to deal with, however. In the logic of rights, relationships of responsibility should be clear. In peasants' everyday domestic lives, however, responsibilities are all elastic and ambiguous, whether they be responsibilities for childcare, production, or dealing with kin. Under conditions of material scarcity, questions of who should be responsible for which tasks often become the main source of problems in marriages. These problems are hard to resolve using the logic of confrontation between equal rights. On the contrary, those households with a clearer division of labor, which do not necessarily advocate full equality of rights, often proceed more smoothly in everyday life, with more balanced attitudes and more positive self-evaluations of their members' lives.

In addition to marital relations, intergenerational relations also play a major role in determining whether everyday domestic life proceeds smoothly.

In intergenerational relations, the challenges brought by the phenomenon of "two-dimensional man" are manifested foremost in the nuclear family. The younger generation's private, material desires, which keep expanding every day, drive them to ask their parents to give them more. Overall, this sort of potential contradiction achieves its greatest resolution, within limits, by the older generation's attitude of valuing the continuation of the family line as a transcendence of their individual lives. In everyday domestic life, however, such contradictions do not simply disappear for this reason. Although the older generation is willing to accept this familial situation intellectually and emotionally, at the same time they cannot avoid a certain imbalance in their attitudes, and they complain. When the situation grows serious, family affairs often become complicated. In more extreme cases, young people become unwilling to fulfill their responsibility of paying monetary support to their parents, leading to intense intergenerational conflicts. This could be called the weakening of the sagely virtues before the secular relationships of rights and duties have become established, causing the older generation to fall between the cracks of the transitional "gutter of desire" (*yuhe*) of the younger generation's "pathological" self-interest.

Another challenge that two-dimensionality has brought to intergenerational relations within everyday life in the rural household is the issue of children's education. In ordinary peasant households, since the household economy has already become "semi-agricultural, semi-industrial," the current norm is for the able-bodied workforce to spend most of the year outside the village. "Semi-industrial," however, is not sufficient to enable households to raise children in the city. It has therefore become a universal phenomenon to partially or wholly rely upon the elderly members of the household to raise their grandchildren in the countryside. The elderly are adept at providing for children's basic survival, but it is harder for them to take care of their health and safety, to say nothing of education. In the modern transitional process of education and knowledge systems, it is hard for the elderly to truly play the role of household educators. This has led to serious problems in the education and psychology of children. For ordinary peasants, considering the dual nature of their household economies as "semi-agricultural, semi-industrial," there is little they can do about this problem. By contrast, for those households that already occupy positions of absolute privilege in the rural social hierarchy, but which still rely heavily on elderly family members to raise and educate their grandchildren, this is clearly caused by their excessive desire for immediate material gratification. More ironically, the more a household is like this, the more its members worry that the children will develop problems leading to the family's "wealth disappearing after three generations."

Under conditions where the rise of modernity has caused familial relations to change rapidly, the presumptions of contemporary external institutions have been inclined toward dealing with the "pathological" phenomena that emerged in this process directly according to secular people's standards of modern relations of rights and duties. This involves turning over family affairs to the formal legal system as much as possible, including monetary support and even actual care for the elderly, childcare, and the annulment of marriages. In the process of social transition, however, the accelerated provision of legal resources according to the rule of law requires a process, after all. Under conditions where such resources are insufficient, the practice of the rule of law has no choice but to give up the public duty to supervise and promote harmony in family affairs. Under the logic of pursuing efficiency, the use of formal law to rectify familial relations tends toward treating relations between people as relations between things. In this way, regarding the annulment of a marriage, the practice of the rule of law is inclined toward making the concerned parties divide up their property and draw up a clear, one-off balance sheet of their rights and duties, as if they were material things, as quickly and smoothly as possible. Intergenerational relations are also dealt with in this manner. The law now stipulates that all adults must visit their elderly parents at least once every three months, but this law neglects the complexities of everyday life. Questions such as *how* to look after the elderly, with what attitude, and how to deal with intergenerational relations after the young are forced to visit the elderly—even if details were specified, how could the law truly ensure affection in "human relationships"?

Under conditions where formal rule of law is insufficient, of course the logic of efficiency has its own difficulties in practice. Moreover, it also plays an irreplaceable role as a bottom line, ensuring justice within the household. However, although household "human relationships" are often closely related to material relations, they cannot be managed entirely according to that logic, after all. On this point, two-dimensionality actually demonstrates another aspect of the matter. Although the rise of private, material desires has often led to "pathological" features among peasants, at the same time, the sagely rites have continued to exist, at least to a certain extent. Therefore, the approach of "treating the malady" need not and cannot be limited to further clarifying the rights and duties of secular people, and to using state force to ensure their implementation in everyday life. The state's distance from peasants' everyday life is too great, so if it were to promptly help them sort out household relationships on a daily basis, the costs would be unimaginably high. The original meaning of "the rule of law" itself, moreover, absolutely does not mean that all of everyday life must be governed through formal laws. By contrast, other people in peasant households' kinship and place-based networks are close to their everyday domestic life. On the basis of formal law establishing a bottom line for household justice, the resources of kindship and place-based networks should and are completely capable of being revitalized to help peasant households sort out domestic relationships in everyday life. As noted above, in contemporary rural society, there are still many enthusiastic people willing to participate in kin affairs and village public affairs. As long as there is no contradiction with the law, these sorts of villagers are completely capable of doing large amounts of everyday work to this end with the help of kinship and place-based networks, within the scope of thirty to fifty households—as in a hamlet or a villager team. In fact, this set of mechanisms is already operating, to some extent, but due to the lack of the necessary legal formalities, it is not considered fully legitimate, so its potential has yet to be fully realized.

Judging by the preceding analysis of moralized politics, there are three main reasons that it is hard for the contemporary system of villager self-government to play the aforementioned roles. First, there are not enough cadres for the large scale of the administrative village, with too much distance from the intimate networks of villagers' everyday life—the hamlets or villager teams. Second, it is hard for ordinary villagers to supervise village cadres, whom they do not fully trust (whereas prestige is the precondition for those who participate in sorting out other households' relationships). Third, most of the village cadres' energy has been focused on helping with the duties of grassroots officialdom. Therefore, two ideas are worth exploring. One would be to extend the system of villager self-government downward to become established at the hamlet or villager-team level of thirty to fifty households (with the grassroots administrative tasks currently performed by village cadres then deputized to special personnel). Second would be, on this scale, under the guiding spirit of the rule of law and in a form such as "village affairs directorate," to revitalize and foster the resources of kinship and place-based networks and their ability to help peasants sort out domestic relationships in everyday life. At the same time, these resources could also strengthen and make use of these units' currently scant collective property. As for whether this would give rise to corruption in the same way as villager self-government, there are three points worth elucidating. First, within the scope of thirty to fifty households, in popular organizations based on kinship and place, the members would have a strong sense of belonging. Second, the feasibility of members supervising power would be stronger than in the current system of villager self-government. Third, to fundamentally forbid the existence of public property out of fear of corruption would be a negative way of thinking. (According to this line of reasoning, should the county-level budget be abolished just because there is a risk of corruption among county officials?) The positive approach would be institutional supervision of public power.

In sum, it may be a dead end to purely emphasize relying on individuals within households alone to sort out domestic relationships in everyday life, according to the rights and duties defined by formal law, on the basis of the assumptions of secular people. This is because at most these can only ensure a bottom line of justice within the household. When there is no choice but to implement the law, everyday domestic life and the affections of "human relationships" might end at any time.[5] On the basis of the rule of law ensuring a bottom line, starting with everyday life, dynamically maintaining reasonable desires of household members not only concerns whether domestic relationships are stable, but also whether ideal individual lives can be achieved, and whether rural social attitudes can be balanced. In this respect, the sagely rites and related networks based on kinship and place are still useful.

Establishing One's Destiny

The mind is the ultimate spiritual home in one's life. The spirit finds its sustenance in establishing one's destiny (*li ming*). In this sense, "the mind" (*xin*) refers not to individual psychology, but to the social attitudes of everyday life composed of complex social relationships. People cannot establish meaning in their lives and spiritual sustenance through individual psychology alone, but only within complex social relationships.

In peasants' everyday lives, of course, there are many people who partly turn their spiritual sustenance, i.e., their minds, over to religion or folk beliefs. As noted above, however, religion and folk beliefs also consist of ideas about establishing one's destiny and sorting out one's attitudes. In reality, therefore, practicing religion or folk beliefs is also a path to establishing one's destiny. According to this reasoning, one's destiny is already determined outside of this life by Christ, deities, Nature, or karma from a previous life. In this life, people just need to carry out their everyday lives in accordance with such predestined factors for the mind to be serene of its own accord, and for the spirit to find sustenance. If peasants cannot achieve this state in everyday life, it is believed to be caused by insufficiency of sincerity in their minds. From this perspective, to establish one's destiny through religion or folk beliefs is a shortcut, at least on the surface: All one needs is sincerity for the problem of establishing one's destiny to be solved.

Unfortunately, the actual situation is far from that simple. In peasants' everyday life, it is easy for the practice of religion or folk beliefs to encounter problems precisely on this point of "sincerity." This is because of the contradiction inherent within peasant beliefs. This contradiction is even more pronounced with regard to two-dimensional people in the process of the rise of modernity. On the one hand, in this world, peasant beliefs have a certain ultimate value and adhere to mysterious forces with which people's minds can commune in this life. On the other hand, the vast majority of peasants also believe, to some degree, that this world does *not* contain mysterious ultimate values for which it would be worth sacrificing everyday life for one's entire lifespan. For the absolute majority of peasants, therefore, belief in religion or folk beliefs is not only consistent with everyday life in this world, but it is also even fundamentally aimed at improving everyday life, rather than at becoming an ascetic monk or nun divorced from everyday life. Under conditions where the private, material desires of everyday life are rapidly expanding, the initial motivations for practicing religion or folk beliefs even involve a utilitarian coloring that is particularly pronounced. Following the principles of pragmatism, moreover, it is also common for peasants to practice mutually contradictory or even conflicting religions or folk beliefs. To put it bluntly, two-dimensionality demonstrates that "insufficient sincerity of the mind" is still a common problem that peasants face when establishing their destiny through belief in religion or folk beliefs. For the vast majority of contemporary peasants, then, it would be extremely difficult to achieve the goal of establishing one's destiny by relying on walking only this path.

Of course, with respect to peasants' establishment of their destinies within everyday life, religious approaches are still useful and not entirely meaningless, so grassroots government should adopt a tolerant attitude toward them. Under conditions where peasants' everyday life has all that it needs, religious impulses should not be "blocked" (*du*), but instead the path should be "cleared" (*shu*) for peasants to practice religion and folk beliefs in public. Only by "clearing" can the many "spirits" rise to the surface so they can be put on the right track, legally punishing cults and other underground phenomena disguised as religions. They are like two faces attached to the same body. However, if peasants' main hope of establishing their destinies is attached exclusively to this path, or if it is used to numb their critical spirit in everyday life, then it is also a dubious shortcut in the search for meaning. The struggling aspect of two-dimensional people in this world has already let out an agitated, ponderous cry. For the vast majority of peasants, the basis of their destinies must be established in the everyday life of this world, rather than anywhere else.

In the relationships of this world's everyday life, factors related to social attitudes are mainly concentrated in the three spheres of economy, politics, and social bonds.

In the economy of peasants' everyday life, the problem of establishing one's destiny is first and foremost related to "settling down in a home" (*anshen*). Settling down means that one's material life can achieve the minimum standard that contemporary social life can accept. Besides the bottom lines of food, warmth, and shelter, content such as basic healthcare and education are also important. In the "semi-industrial, semi-agricultural" mixed economy, the bottom line is located in the right to benefit sustainably from land tied to the "semi-agricultural" component. In the present and for a long period of historical time in the future, no matter whether peasants are obtaining income from "semi-industrial" work or from the state, or from the two of them combined, none of these arrangements seem capable of ensuring that several hundred million peasants can safely rely on social welfare to live good everyday lives. This means that as soon as the economy faces significant instability, the bottom line for peasant survival will still be to obtain sustainable, even if extremely low, income based on the land through farming or other methods. Of course, peasants can enter the cities or small towns, but if we survey the situation from a long-term perspective, rather than from a short-term one, their household economies still have a "semi-industrial, semi-agricultural" character, so for peasants, sustainable income based on the land still essentially signifies a bottom line for settling down and establishing their destinies. No matter whether peasants are passive or active, if they enter cities or towns but cannot satisfy the basic material desires of their lives as a whole (including the reproduction of labor-power), and if the cost they have to pay for this is the loss of sustainable income from land, then the basis for settling down and establishing their destinies will be destroyed. If that is the case, their lives can only be concerned with the present, their social attitudes will lapse into feelings of transience, and the bottom lines of rural social order will inevitably become seriously threatened.

On the basis of settling down, peasants clearly have higher expectations about living good everyday lives. Beyond the bottom line of survival, however, "higher" refers not to a certain level of income in an abstract sense, but to *social* comparison, or vertical social bonds (*jiehe*). Peasants' economic concepts and attitudes toward the rural social hierarchy described above demonstrate that they are not at all intolerant of inequality between rich and poor, as if they were absolute egalitarianists or populists crazy about "(everyone eating out of) one big pot." Ascribing these characteristics to peasants, if there is no other intention, at least reflects misunderstanding or bias. In reality, peasants' desire for freedom outweighs that for equality. Not only can they calmly accept a considerable degree of inequality, under conditions where the gap between rich and poor is enormous and privileged groups even generate inequality through means contrary to the "Heavenly Principles," but peasants also criticize them on the one hand, while on the other seeking out methods to balance their attitudes, such as "endurance," "accepting fate," and cynicism. How can one use labels like "absolute egalitarianism" or "populism" to cover up or brush aside such facts? From this perspective, then, with regard to peasants settling down and establishing their destinies in contemporary everyday life, the economic significance of two-dimensionality lays in its demonstration of the urgent need to mitigate the gap between rich and poor, and to strictly control illegal, unjust means for the acquisition of wealth. Otherwise, if "good fortune without merit" were to become the rural economy's new normal, it would become even harder for peasants to balance their attitudes in everyday life, to say nothing of establishing their destinies.

For most contemporary peasants, grassroots politics is still the only sphere of their everyday lives that could be considered as following "the organizational mode of association." This is a public life of existing statutes and later actions according to statutes, different from group life based solely on kinship and place-based relationships. The former consists of public relationships with a morality involving the formal regulations' system of rights and duties, which are equal as long as the members are legal (following the statutes). Although the latter could be considered public, for individual households, the character of their relationships are an extension of private ones, morally distant or close depending on "human relationships," without universal standards. Grassroots politics' transition from lineage-based public life toward one based on the "organizational mode of association" is, without a doubt, an important expression of the rise of modernity. However, since peasants' experience with truly voluntary participation in the differential mode of association is limited, it is still hard for their self-rule based on villager self-government to ensure that the expectation of "good people" as a norm will become stabilized at the center stage of village politics, and that it will not become adulterated over time. When villagers complain that cadres cannot "rule for the people," their confidence to rule themselves also dissolves.

Disappointed expectations of "good people politics" not only inhibits peasants from entrusting themselves to the public life of the organizational mode of association, but also leads to social injustice, stimulating the further expansion of private, material desires and imbalances in rural social attitudes. When peasants thus complain about "the ways of the world," it not only inhibits peasants from establishing their destinies in modern public life, but also weakens the basis for establishing their destinies within their existing sense of history. In the framework of moralized politics, extending villager self-government down to hamlet or villager-team units of thirty to fifty households would make use of the limited but already existing "human relationships," and combine them with the emerging principles of democracy to restrain the political elite's tendency toward "not ruling for the people." For people's lives, this would attempt to combine two-dimensional people's existing dimension of sagely rites with secular political principles, creating a modern "organizational mode" of public life on the foundation of continuing traditional resources. With regard to specific formulas, of course, there are many other models worth exploring. The overall principle could, however, be summarized as: Only when grassroots politics finds ways for both sages and secular people to develop at the same time, rather than one replacing the other, can peasants find a basis for establishing their destinies in public life at the intersection between tradition and modernity.

By contrast, the private social networks based on kinship and place have a more direct relationship with the spiritual sustenance of villagers' lives, without a doubt. When, in everyday life, villagers compare their positions in the rural social hierarchy with those of others, the direct and salient points of reference are those who are relatively close to them in kinship and place-based networks. On the other hand, if they encounter difficulties in everyday life, or even major misfortunes in their lives, those close to them in such networks are also the people to whom peasants will turn for help first. Under the spiritual guidance of the secular rule of law, then, there is profound significance for the spiritual sustenance of villagers' lives to appropriately revitalize and foster kinship and place-based networks of the sagely rites, and to convert them into an everyday quasi-public life with vitality. This is even truer with regard to relationships within the household, since that is the basic unit of villagers' everyday life, playing a special role in spiritual sustenance and the achievement of meaning in their lives. In addition to the secular system of rights and duties clarifying and delimiting the bottom line of household justice, it would be worth exploring methods such as using kinship and place-based networks to semi-directly mediate and sort out disagreements, or using schools and media to foster the spirit of the sagely rites and encourage people to follow them. Here, as with religion and folk beliefs, the keys are sincerity and rectification of the mind. Considering that two-dimensional people still attach their life's meaning to carrying on the ancestors' legacy, plus the national context of the aging population, it seems unnecessary to condemn villagers' notions of continuing the family line.[6] One direction worth considering might be trying to promote the idea that daughters could also be markers of lineage continuation, with equality in the inheritance of property and ritual symbolism, as in adding women's names to the genealogical tables, to tombstones, and to ancestral offerings.

In any case, the characteristics of two-dimensional people show that the vast majority of peasants cannot achieve the establishment of their lives' destinies by relying solely on religion or folk beliefs. They are destined to be able only to "treat the secular as sagely" in everyday life. In this respect, the family has its unique and irreplaceable significance. Society in a transitional countryside is changing drastically, so "settling down" might be accomplished away from home (if people can rely on social welfare) but establishing one's destiny is still something that can be accomplished only at home. Outside the home, one's destiny is incomplete. Further, if the way of the world is hard, or if one's life encounters misfortunes such that it becomes hard to settle down, one's destiny must still be established. Of course, no matter whether one is at home or outside, two-dimensional people have their basis in economy, politics, and social bonds, and their path to settling down and establishing their destinies should be within these relationships, rather than outside of them. In addition, it is not easy to treat the secular as sagely. In one's life there are always ways in which desires conflict with reality, and it is hard to avoid mishaps. These are all uncertainties with regard to settling down and establishing one's destiny, as well as the actual reason for the existence of religion and folk beliefs—including beliefs about destiny or fate. Maybe it is already paradoxical to search for permanence in a world that is always changing. Even so, no matter whether it is the state, the family, or the individual, transcending the present is something that must be done.

At the ultimate level, the worldview, cosmology, and ontology of secular people can surely generate more practical and effective scientific knowledge, but they might damage those social bonds that previously brought individuals together and prevented them from isolation and misery. Contemporary philosophers' critique of "sick people" stems from anxiety regarding the replacement of relationships among people with relationships among things, and the replacement of people with things, to the point that the mind is wandering in the wilderness. In relation to this, the rites of the sages may still have their unique value in overcoming people's difficulties with settling their minds and establishing their destinies, and in overcoming their personality conflicts or even splits—including the split into two dimensions.

In this, "harmonious interdependence among all beings" (*shengsheng hexie*) is a sacred but also a secular condition of "Heaven's (God's) Will" (*tianming*) and people's minds. In relationships among people, this means: If you want to live well, let others live well, otherwise no one can live well. From this perspective, establishing destiny is not a purely individual, private matter, but a major event concerning the relationships between people and external things, other people, their own minds, the state, history, life, and death. No matter whether it is the rational principles of secular people or the customary rites of sages, however, all must face the question of how to implement lofty principles at low cost in the everyday lives of peasants. This may be something that cannot be accomplished purely by relying on the law, on the one hand, or on moral philosophy and education, on the other, but which requires a synthesis of the two, on the basis of a "Great Dialogue," that explores the paths of governing the world and settling the mind, starting with the levels of economy, politics, society, and beliefs in peasants' everyday life. In any case, the ability of the vast majority of peasants to form and satisfy reasonable desires in everyday life, and to arrive at a more serene attitude, is the key to establishing destiny in their lives, and also the key to social peace and state rule.

In closing, let us take Benjamin's aphorism, which Marcuse had applied to one-dimensional man, and adapt it for "two-dimensional man": Only when the vast majority of ordinary people can find hope in everyday life can we finally be given hope!

Notes

1 *Translator's note*: Throughout this book, "transition" (转型) has been left deliberately ambiguous, but its time frame refers to the entire period from the mid-20th century to the present. At times it is associated with Karl Polanyi's concept of "the great transformation" (translated into Chinese with the same term for "transition") from traditional societies (where economic relations were embedded within social ones) to market society (where the market has become disembedded and asserted dominance over social relations). Elsewhere it refers to the long "state transition" from empire to "independent nation-state" (which started earlier, in the Republican era, but continued under the People's Republic). More often it refers to a broader series of changes conventionally associated with the terms "traditional" and "modern," although the author deliberately avoids that use of those labels as oversimplifying, while also avoiding Marxological debates about how to characterize the "collective" era of "planned economy" in relation to the modes of production that preceded and succeeded it.

2 Abner Cohen used this term "two-dimensional man" to analyze how to approach the study of power in complex societies from a symbolic perspective. The two dimensions referred to the need, in research on sociopolitical organization, to attend to both explicit structures and institutions, and to invisible structures and symbols (Cohen 1974: 1–4, 16–17). He also wrote that both Marxist economic analysis and Weberian cultural interpretation were necessary in order to understand power, and that the analysis of lineages in African stateless societies could be applied to research on complex societies (120–126). Cohen's attention to invisible structures, symbols, and cultural interpretation are truly enlightening, but this book has not continued along this trajectory or repeated his approach, instead focusing on the two-dimensionality of economy, politics, society, and beliefs in a rural society's process of transition toward modernity. The difference between our two approaches is clear.

3 Here, "trapped" mainly derives from the "trap" of the vicious circle of competition created by unfair allocation, excessive disparities and pressures between social strata, the low level of resources per capita, and social stagnation (Kuhn 1999: 300).

4 *Translator's note*: Zuofeng 作风 is conventionally translated as "style" in the context of "work style problems" (工作作风问题). During the collective era, cadres' "work style problems" referred to behavior that violated the party's work discipline, such as "bureaucratism," i.e., abusing power or just going through the motions rather

than "serving the people." For ordinary peasants, the term "*zuofeng* problems" often referred to inappropriate sexual relations (extra-marital affairs, promiscuity, etc.). Here, "mainstream discourse's emphasis on *zuofeng*" refers to the continued social enforcement of sexual norms that resemble traditional norms (and enforcement mechanisms) associated with Confucianism.
5 Basically, this is a matter of social attitudes rather than of individual psychology. Therefore, it is not a problem that psychoanalysis can solve, but one that can only call on forces outside the household, with the affection of "human relationships," to help fix the problem.
6 Gender and intergenerational relationships are actually not completely opposed to one another. The promotion of the concept of gender equality does not necessarily require an end to the idea of passing on the family line.

References

Ahern, Emily Martin 1973. *The Cult of the Dead in a Chinese Village*, California: Stanford University Press.

Alitto, Guy 艾恺 1996. *The Last Confucian: Liang Shu-ming and the Chinese Dilemma* 最后的儒家, trans. Wang Zongyu 王宗昱, et al., Nanjing: Jiangsu renmin chubanshe.

Augustine of Hippo 奥古斯丁 2009. *The City of God* 上帝之城, vol. 2, trans. Wu Fei, Shanghai: Shanghai sanlian shudian.

Baker, Hugh 1979. *Chinese Family and Kinship*, London: Macmillan.

Baudrillard, Jean 波德里亚 2006. *Symbolic Exchange and Death* 象征交换与死亡, trans. Che Jinshan 车槿山, Nanjing: Yilin chubanshe.

Bol, Peter K. 2008. *Neo-Confucianism in History*, Cambridge, MA: Harvard University Asia Center.

Bossen, Laurel 1999. "Women in Development," in Robert E. Gamer and Stanley W. Toops, eds. *Understanding Contemporary China*, Boulder: Lynne Rienner Publishers.

Bowie, Fiona 鲍伊 2004. *The Anthropology of Religion: An Introduction* 宗教人类学导论, trans. Jin Ze 金泽, et al., Beijing: Zhongguo renmin daxue chubanshe.

Chan, Anita, Richard Madsen, and Jonathan Unger 1984. *Chen Village: The Recent History of a Peasant Community in Mao's China*, Berkeley: University of California Press.

Chau, Adam Yuet 2006. *Miraculous Response: Doing Popular Religion in Contemporary China*, Stanford: Stanford University Press.

Chen, Baifeng 陈柏峰 2012. "The Spread of Christianity and Becoming Reacquainted with Religion in China" 基督教传播与中国宗教再认识, in Philip C.C. Huang 黄宗智, ed. *Rural China Studies* 中国乡村研究, vol. 9, Fuzhou: Fujian jiaoyu chubanshe.

Chen, Hansheng 陈翰笙 1984. *Landlord and Peasant in China: A Study of the Agrarian Crisis in South China* 解放前的地主与农民, trans. Feng Feng, Beijing: Zhongguo shehui kexue chubanshe.

Chen, Yinke 陈寅恪 2009a. *The Works of Chen Yinke: An Alternative Biography of Liu Rushi* 陈寅恪集·柳如是别传, vols. 1, 2 and 3, Beijing: Sanlian shudian.

Chen, Yinke 陈寅恪 2009b. *The Works of Chen Yinke: Essay Drafts on the Origins of Sui and Tang Institutions, Essay Drafts on Tang Political History* 陈寅恪集·隋唐制度渊源论稿 唐代政治史述论稿, Beijing: Sanlian shudian.

Chu, Julie Y. 2010. *Cosmologies of Credit*, Durham: Duke University Press.

Chuang, Ying-Chang 庄英章 1972. "The Adjustment to Modernization among Rural Families in Taiwan" 台湾农村家族对现代化的适应, *Bulletin of the Institute of Ethnology at Academia Sinica* 中央研究院民族学研究所集刊, no. 34.

Chuang, Ying-Chang 庄英章 1981. "Nan Village Families amid Social Change" 社会变迁中的南村家族, *Bulletin of the Institute of Ethnology at Academia Sinica* 中央研究院民族学研究所集刊, no. 52.

Cohen, Abner 1974. *Two Dimensional Man: An Essay on the Anthropology of Power and Symbolism in Complex Society*, Berkeley: University of California Press.

Cohen, Myron L. 1976. *House United, House Divided*, New York: Columbia University Press.

Croll, Elisabeth 1981. *The Politics of Marriage in Contemporary China*, Cambridge: Cambridge University Press.

Davis, Deborah and Stevan Harrell 1993. *Chinese Families in the Post-Mao Era*, Berkeley: University of California Press.

Dean, Kenneth 1993. *Taoist Ritual and Popular Cults of South-East China*, Princeton: Princeton University Press.

Dean, Kenneth 1998. *Lord of the Three in One: The Spread of a Cult in South-East China*, Princeton: Princeton University Press.

Dean, Kenneth 2003. "Local Communal Religion in Contemporary South-east China," *The China Quarterly*, vol. 174.

Derrida, Jacques 2001. *Writing and Difference*, trans. Alan Bass, London: Routledge.

Diamond, Norma 1975. "Collectivization, Kinship, and the Status of Women in Rural China," in Rayna R. Reiter, ed. *Toward an Anthropology of Women*, New York: Monthly Review Press.

Ding Wenjiang 丁文江 1997. "Daoist Metaphysics (Xuanxue) and Science" 玄学与科学, in Zhang Junmai 张君劢, et al., eds. *Science and Perspectives on Human Life* 科学与人生观, Ji'nan: Shandong renmin chubanshe.

Duara, Prasenjit 杜赞奇 1996. *Culture, Power, and the State* 文化、权力与国家, trans. Wang Fuming 王福明, Nanjing: Jiangsu renmin chubanshe.

Durkheim, Émile 涂尔干 2000. *The Division of Labor in Society* 社会分工论, trans. Qu Dong 渠东, Beijing: Sanlian shudian.

Durkheim, Émile 涂尔干 2001. *Professional Ethics and Civic Morals* 职业伦理与公民道德, trans. Qu Dong 渠东, Shanghai: Shanghai renmin chubanshe.

Elvin, Mark 1973. *The Pattern of the Chinese Past*, Stanford: Stanford University Press.

Evans, Harriet 艾华 2008. *Women and Sexuality in China: Dominant Discourses of Female Sexuality and Gender Since 1949* 中国的女性与性相, trans. Shi Shi 施施, Nanjing: Jiangsu renmin chubanshe.

Faure, David 科大卫 2009. *Emperor and Ancestor* 皇帝和祖宗, trans. Bu Yongjian 卜永坚, Nanjing: Jiangsu renmin chubanshe.

Faure, David 科大卫 and Liu Zhiwei 刘志伟 2013. "Standardization or Legitimization? Perception of the Unity of Chinese Culture from the Standpoint of Popular Beliefs" '标准化'还是'正统化, *Journal of History and Anthropology* 历史人类学学刊, vol. 6, nos. 1 and 2.

Fei Xiaotong 1992. *From the Soil: The Foundations of Chinese Society*, trans. Gary G. Hamilton and Wang Zheng, Berkeley: University of California Press.

Fei Xiaotong 费孝通 1999a. *The Works of Fei Xiaotong* 费孝通文集, vol. 2, Beijing: Qunyan chubanshe.

Fei Xiaotong 费孝通 1999b. *The Works of Fei Xiaotong* 费孝通文集, vol. 11, Beijing: Qunyan chubanshe.

Fei Xiaotong 费孝通 1999c. *The Works of Fei Xiaotong* 费孝通文集, vol. 8, Beijing: Qunyan chubanshe.

Fei Xiaotong 费孝通 1999d. *The Works of Fei Xiaotong* 费孝通文集, vol. 9, Beijing: Qunyan chubanshe.

Fei Xiaotong 费孝通 1999e. *The Works of Fei Xiaotong* 费孝通文集, vol. 12, Beijing: Qunyan chubanshe.

Fei Xiaotong 费孝通 1999f. *The Works of Fei Xiaotong* 费孝通文集, vol. 4, Beijing: Qunyan chubanshe.

Fei Xiaotong 费孝通 1999g. *The Works of Fei Xiaotong* 费孝通文集, vol. 5, Beijing: Qunyan chubanshe.

Feng Junqi 冯军旗 2010. "Zhong County Cadres" 中县干部, Ph.D. dissertation, Department of Sociology at Peking University.

Feuchtwang, Stephen 王斯福 1997. "Peasant or Citizen?" 农民抑或公民?, in Wang Mingming 王铭铭 and Stephen Feuchtwang 王斯福, eds. *Order, Justice, and Authority in Rural Society* 乡土社会的秩序、公正与权威, Beijing: Zhongguo zhengfa daxue chubanshe.

Feuchtwang, Stephen 王斯福 2008. *The Imperial Metaphor: Popular Religion in China* 帝国的隐喻, trans. Zhao Xudong, Nanjing: Jiangsu renmin chubanshe.

Foucault, Michel 福柯 1999. *Discipline and Punish* 规训与惩罚, trans. Liu Beicheng 刘北成 and Yang Yuanying 杨远婴, Beijing: Sanlian shudian.

Foucault, Michel 福柯 2002. *The History of Sexuality, Volume 1: An Introduction* 性经验史, trans. She Biping 佘碧平, Shanghai: Shanghai renmin chubanshe.

Foucault, Michel 福柯 2010a. *Abnormal* 不正常的人, trans. Qian Han 钱翰, Shanghai: Shanghai renmin chubanshe.

Foucault, Michel 福柯 2010b. *Hermeneutics of the Subject* 主体解释学, trans. She Biping 佘碧平, Shanghai: Shanghai renmin chubanshe.

Freedman, Maurice 弗里德曼 2000. *Lineage Organization in Southeastern China* 中国东南的宗族组织, trans. Liu Xiaochun 刘晓春, Shanghai: Shanghai renmin chubanshe.

Gallin, Bernard 1966. *Hsin Hing, Taiwan: A Chinese Village in Change*, Berkeley: University California Press.

Gates, Hill 1989. "The Commoditization of Chinese Women," *Signs*, vol. 14, no. 4.

Geertz, Clifford 格尔茨 1999. *The Interpretation of Cultures* 文化的解释, trans. Han Li 韩莉, Nanjing: Yilin chubanshe.

Geertz, Clifford 吉尔兹 2000. *Local Knowledge: Further Essays in Interpretive Anthropology* 地方性知识, trans. Wang Hailong 王海龙, et al., Beijing: Zhongyang bianyi chubanshe.

Girard, René 基拉尔 2006. *To Double Business Bound: Essays on Literature, Mimesis and Anthropology* 双重束缚, trans. Liu Shu 刘舒, et al., Beijing: Huaxia chubanshe.

Guo Yuhua 郭于华 and Sun Liping 孙立平 2003. "Speaking Bitterness: A Mediating Mechanism for the Peasant Conceptualization of the State" 诉苦：一种农民国家观念形成的中介机制, in Yang Nianqun 杨念群, et al., eds. *New Historical Studies: The Prospects for Multidisciplinary Dialogue* 新史学：多学科对话的图景, Beijing: Zhongguo renmin daxue chubanshe.

Guo Yukuan 郭宇宽 2012. "Conspicuous Consumption and Commercial Cooperation" 奢靡消费与商业合作, in Guo Yuhua 郭于华, ed. *Tsinghua Sociology Review* 清华社会学评论, vol. 5, Beijing: Shehui kexue wenxian chubanshe.

He Baogang 何包钢 and Lang Youxing 郎友兴 2002. *Searching for a Balance between Democracy and Authority* 寻找民主与权威的平衡, Wuhan: Huazhong shifan daxue chubanshe.

Hsieh, Jih-chang C. 谢继昌 1985. "Meal Rotation" 轮伙头制度初探, *Bulletin of the Institute of Ethnology at Academia Sinica* 中央研究院民族学研究所集刊, no. 59.

Hsu, Francis L.K. 许烺光 1990. *Clan, Caste, and Club* 宗族·种姓·俱乐部, trans. Xue Gang 薛刚, Beijing: Huaxia chubanshe.

Hsu, Francis L.K. 许烺光 2001. *Under the Ancestors' Shadow: Kinship, Personality, and Social Mobility in China* 祖荫下, trans. Wang Peng 王芃, et al., Taipei: SMC Publishing.

Hu Weiqing 胡卫清 2013. *Hardship and Beliefs* 苦难与信仰, Beijing: Sanlian shudian.

Huang Ping 黄平 1997. *In Search of Survival* 寻求生存, Kunming: Yunnan renmin chubanshe.

Huang, Philip C.C. 黄宗智 2003. "'Public Sphere'/'Civil Society' in China? The Third Realm between State and Society" 中国的'公共领域'与'市民社会'?, trans. Cheng Nong 程农, et al., in Philip C.C. Huang, ed. *Paradigmatic Issues in Chinese Studies* 中国研究的范式问题讨论, Beijing: Shehui kexue wenxian chubanshe.

Huang, Philip C.C. 黄宗智 2007. *Experience and Theory: Chinese Society, Economy, and Law from the Perspective of Historical Practice* 经验与理论：中国社会、经济与法律的实践历史研究, Beijing: Zhongguo renmin daxue chubanshe.

Huang, Philip C.C. 黄宗智 2010. *China's Hidden Agricultural Revolution* 中国的隐性农业革命, Beijing: Falü chubanshe.

Jing, Jun 景军 2013. *The Temple of Memories: History, Power and Morality in a Chinese Village* 神堂记忆, trans. Wu Fei 吴飞, Fuzhou: Fujian jiaoyu chubanshe.

Johnston, Reginald F. 1910. *Lion and Dragon in Northern China*, New York: Dutton.

Johnstone, Ronald L. 约翰斯通 2012. *Religion in Society* 社会中的宗教, trans. Yuan Yayu 袁亚愚 and Zhong Yuying 钟玉英, Chengdu: Sichuan renmin chubanshe.

Judd, Ellen 1989. "*Niangjia*: Chinese Women and Their Natal Families," *Journal of Asian Studies*, vol. 48, no. 3.

Kuhn, Philip A. 孔飞力 1999. *Soulstealers: The Chinese Sorcery Scare of 1768* 叫魂：1768年中国妖术大恐慌, trans. Chen Jian 陈兼, et al., Shanghai: Shanghai sanlian shudian.

Kulp, Daniel Harrison 葛学溥 2006. *Country Life in South China: The Sociology of Familism* 华南的乡村生活, trans. Zhou Daming, Beijing: Zhishi chanquan chubanshe.

Lacan, Jacques 1988. *The Seminar of Jacques Lacan, Book 1: Freud's Papers on Technique, 1953–1954*, ed. Jacques-Alain Miller, trans. John Forrester, Cambridge: Cambridge University Press.

Lacan, Jacques 2006. *Écrits*, trans. Bruce Fink, New York: W.W. Norton and Company.

Li Huawei 李华伟 2012. "Hardship and Religious Conversion" 苦难与改教, *China Agricultural University Journal (Social Sciences Edition)*, no. 3.

Li Xia 李霞 2010. *Natal Family and Husband's Family* 娘家与婆家, Beijing: Shehui kexue wenxian chubanshe.

Li Yih-yuan 李亦园 2002. *Self-Selected Works of Li Yih-yuan* 李亦园自选集, Shanghai: Shanghai jiaoyu chubanshe.

Li Yih-yuan 李亦园 2006. "Chinese Families and Their Rites: A Study of Several Concepts" 中国家族与其仪式：若干观念的检讨, in Yang Guoshu 杨国枢, ed. *The Psychology of Chinese People* 中国人的心理, Nanjing: Jiangsu jiaoyu chubanshe.

Liang Gengyao 梁庚尧 2006. *Rural Economy in the Southern Song* 南宋的农村经济, Beijing: Xinxing chubanshe.
Liang Shuming 梁漱溟 2006a. *The Complete Works of Liang Shuming* 梁漱溟全集, vol. 2, Ji'nan: Shandong renmin chubanshe.
Liang Shuming 梁漱溟 2006b. *The Complete Works of Liang Shuming* 梁漱溟全集, vol. 3, Ji'nan: Shandong renmin chubanshe.
Lin, Nan 林南 2005. *Social Capital: A Theory of Social Structure and Action* 社会资本, trans. Zhang Lei, Shanghai: Shanghai renmin chubanshe.
Lin, Yaohua 林耀华 1989. *The Golden Wing: A Sociological Study of Chinese Familism* 金翼, trans. Zhuang Kongshao 庄孔韶, et al., Beijing: Sanlian shudian.
Lin, Yaohua 林耀华 2000. *A Study of Lineages in Yixu* 义序的宗族研究, Beijing: Sanlian shudian.
Liu Neng 刘能 2008. *Township Administration from a Perspective of Hierarchy and Social Networks* 等级制和社会网络视野下的乡镇行政, Beijing: Shehui kexue wenxian chubanshe.
Liu, Xin 2000. *In One's Own Shadow*, Berkeley: University of California Press.
Liu, Xin 流心 2005. *The Otherness of Self* 自我的他性, trans. Chang Shu 常姝, Shanghai: Shanghai renmin chubanshe.
Lu Yunfeng 卢云峰 2010. "Hardship and the Growth of Religion" 苦难与宗教增长, *Sociology* 社会, no. 4.
Lü Dajun 吕大钧 1993. "The Community Compact of the Lü Family" 吕氏乡约, in Chen Junmin 陈俊民, ed. *Collated Compilation of the Surviving Writings of the Lü Family of Lantian*, Beijing: Zhonghua shuju.
Ma Guoqing 麻国庆 1999. *The Family and Chinese Social Structure* 家与中国社会结构, Beijing: Wenwu chubanshe.
Ma Guoqing 麻国庆 2009. *Eternal Home* 永远的家, Beijing: Beijing daxue chubanshe.
Ma Wen-yee, ed. 1986. *Snow Glistens on the Great Wall: The Complete Collection of Mao Tse-tung's Poetry*, Santa Barbara, CA: Santa Barbara Press.
Madsen, Richard 1984. *Morality and Power in a Chinese Village*, Berkeley: University of California Press.
Marcuse, Herbert 1991. *One-Dimensional Man: Studies in the Ideology of Advanced Industrial Society*, Boston: Beacon Press.
Marcuse, Herbert 马尔库塞 2006. *One-Dimensional Man* 单向度的人, trans. Liu Ji 刘继, Shanghai: Shanghai yiwen chubanshe.
Marx, Karl 马克思 2000. *Economic and Philosophical Manuscripts of 1844* 1844年经济学哲学手稿, trans. Central Compilation and Translation Bureau, Beijing: Beijing renmin chubanshe.
Murphy, Rachel 墨菲 2009. *How Migrant Labor is Changing Rural China* 农民工改变中国农村, trans. Huang Tao 黄涛, Hangzhou: Zhejiang renmin chubanshe.
Nee, Victor 1985. "Peasant Household Individualism," in William L. Parish, ed. *Chinese Rural Development*, New York: M.E. Sharpe.
Nietzsche, Friedrich W. 尼采 1989. *The Anti-Christ* 上帝死了, trans. Qi Ren 戚仁, Shanghai: Shanghai sanlian shudian.
Notar, E. Beth 2006. *Displacing Desire*, Honolulu: University of Hawaii Press.
O'Brien, Kevin J. and Lianjiang Li 2004. "Suing the Local State: Administrative Litigation in Rural China," in *The China Journal*, vol. 51.
O'Dea, Thomas 1970. *Sociology and the Study of Religion*, New York: Basic Books.

Osburg, John 2013. *Anxious Wealth: Money and Morality among China's New Rich*, Stanford: Stanford University Press.
Oxfeld, Ellen 欧爱玲 2013. *Drink Water, But Remember the Source: Moral Discourse in a Chinese Village* 饮水思源, trans. Zhong Jinlan 钟晋兰, Beijing: Shehui kexue wenxian chubanshe.
Pan Guangdan 潘光旦 1993. *The Works of Pan Guangdan* 潘光旦文集, vol. 1, Beijing: Beijing daxue chubanshe.
Pan Guangdan 潘光旦 1994. *The Works of Pan Guangdan* 潘光旦文集, vol. 2, Beijing: Beijing daxue chubanshe.
Pasternak, Burton 1972. *Kinship and Community in Two Chinese Villages*, Stanford: Stanford University Press.
Polanyi, Karl 1957. *The Great Transformation*, Boston: Beacon Press.
Potter, Jack 1970. "Land and Lineage in Traditional China," in Maurice Freedman, ed. *Family and Kinship in Chinese Society*, Stanford: Stanford University Press.
Rong Jingben 荣敬本, et al. 1998. *From Pressure System to Democratic System of Cooperation* 从压力型体制向民主合作体制的转变, Beijing: Zhongyang bianyi chubanshe.
Sangren, Steven P. 1987. *History and Magical Power in a Chinese Community*, Stanford: Stanford University Press.
Scott, James C. 斯科特 2007. *Weapons of the Weak: Everyday Forms of Peasant Resistance* 弱者的武器, trans. Zheng Guanghuai 郑广怀, et al., Nanjing: Yilin chubanshe.
Shue, Vivienne 1988. *The Reach of the State: Sketches of Chinese Body Politic*, Stanford: Stanford University Press.
Sima Qian 司马迁 2013. *Records of the Grand Historian* 史记, Beijing: Zhonghua shuju.
Sima Qian 司马迁 2014. "Letter to Ren An" 报任安书, Xigutang Guoxue Wang 习古堂国学网, December 30, 2014. www.xigutang.com/guwenguanzhi/6671.html
Simmel, George 齐美尔 1991. *Bridge and Door: Collected Essays of George Simmel* 桥与门：齐美尔随笔集, trans. Ya Hong 涯鸿, et al., Shanghai: Shanghai sanlian shudian.
Siu, Helen F. 1989. *Agents and Victims in South China*, New Haven: Yale University Press.
Siu, Helen F. 萧凤霞 2003. "Recycling Tradition: Culture, History, and Political Economy in the Chrysanthemum Festivals of South China" 传统的循环再生, *Journal of History and Anthropology* 历史人类学学刊, vol. 1, no. 1.
Stacey, Judith 1983. *Patriarchy and Socialist Revolution in China*, Berkeley: University of California Press.
Stafford, Charles 2000. *Separation and Reunion in Modern China*, Cambridge: Cambridge University Press.
Stark, Rodney 斯达克 and Roger Finke 芬克 2004. *Acts of Faith: Explaining the Human Side of Religion* 信仰的法则, trans. Yang Fenggang 杨凤岗, Beijing: Zhongguo renmin daxue chubanshe.
Steinmüller, Hans 2013. *Communities of Complicity: Everyday Ethics in Rural China*, New York: Berghahn.
Su Li 苏力 2000. *Sending Law Down to the Countryside* 送法下乡, Beijing: Zhongguo zhengfa daxue chubanshe.
Tan Chee-Beng 2012. "Shantang: Charitable Temples in China, Singapore, and Malaysia," *Asian Ethnology*, vol. 71, no. 1.

Tan Tongxue 谭同学 2010. *Way of Bridge Village: Morality, Power, and Social Structure in a Changing Countryside* 桥村有道：转型乡村的道德、权力与社会结构, Beijing: Sanlian shudian.

Tan Tongxue 2016a. "The Ironies of 'Political Agriculture': Bureaucratic Rationality and Moral Networks in Rural China," in Hans Steinmüller and Susanne Brandtstädter, eds. *Irony, Cynicism, and the Chinese State*, London: Routledge.

Tan Tongxue 2016b. "Social Ties and the Market: A Study of Digital Printing Industry from an Informal Economy Perspective," in Wu Chongqing ed. *Mapping China: Peasants, Migrant Workers and Informal Labor*, Leiden: Brill.

Tawney, Richard H. 托尼 2014. *Land and Labor in China* 中国的土地和劳动, trans. An Jia 安佳, Beijing: Shangwu yinshuguan.

Tian Yuqing 田余庆 2012. *Aristocratic Politics in the Eastern Jin* 东晋门阀政治, Beijing: Beijing daxue chubanshe.

Walder, Andrew 华尔德 1996. *Communist Neo-traditionalism: Work and Authority in Chinese Industry* 共产党社会的新传统主义, trans. Gong Xiaoxia 龚小夏, Hong Kong: Oxford University Press.

Wang Mingming 王铭铭 2010. *Life Histories and Anthropology* 人生史与人类学, Beijing: Sanlian shudian.

Wang Ning 王宁 2009. *From Ascetic Society to Consumer Society* 从苦行者社会到消费者社会, Beijing: Shehui kexue wenxian chubanshe.

Wang Shouren 王守仁 2011. *The Complete Works of Wang Yangming* 王阳明全集, ed. Wu Guang 吴光, et al., Shanghai: Shanghai guji chubanshe.

Watson, James L. 詹姆斯·沃森 2006. "Standardizing the Gods" 神的标准化, trans. Chen Zhongdan 陈仲丹, in Averill Stephen C. Averill 韦思谛, ed. *Chinese Popular Religion* 中国大众宗教, Nanjing: Jiangsu renmin chubanshe.

Watson, Rubie S. 鲁比·沃森 2008. *Inequality among Brothers: Class and Kinship in South China* 兄弟并不平等, trans. Shi Lina 时丽娜, Shanghai: Shanghai yiwen chubanshe.

Weber, Max 韦伯 2004. *Collected Works of Max Weber, Vol. 1: Academics and Politics* 韦伯作品集I：学术与政治, trans. Qian Yongxiang 钱永祥, et al., Guilin: Guangxi shifan daxue chubanshe.

Weber, Max 韦伯 2007. *Collected Works of Max Weber, Vol. 12: The Protestant Ethic and the Spirit of Capitalism* 韦伯作品集XII：新教伦理与资本主义精神, trans. Kang Le 康乐, et al., Guilin: Guangxi shifan daxue chubanshe.

Wu Chongqing 吴重庆 2011. *Ancient Villages in Southern China: Native Soil and People Stranded on the River of Time* 华南古村落：搁浅于时光长河的乡土与人, Beijing: Beijing daxue chubanshe.

Wu Chongqing 吴重庆 2014. *The Path to Sun Village: Gods, Ghosts, and People in a Post-Revolutionary Society* 孙村的路, Beijing: Falü chubanshe.

Wu Fei 吴飞 2009. *A Fleeting Life in Pursuit of Justic: A Cultural Interpretation of Suicide in a North China County* 浮生取义, Beijing: Zhongguo renmin daxue chubanshe.

Wolf, Arthur P. 武雅士 2014. "Gods, Ghosts, and Ancestors" 神、鬼和祖先, trans. Peng Ze'an 彭泽安, et al., in Arthur P. Wolf, ed. *Religion and Ritual in Chinese Society* 中国社会中的宗教与仪式, Nanjing: Jiangsu renmin chubanshe.

Wolf, Margery 1985. *Revolution Postponed: Women in Contemporary China*, Stanford: Stanford University Press.

Xiang, Biao 项飚 2000. *Transcending Boundaries: Zhejiangcun: The Story of a Migrant Village in Beijing* 跨越边界的社区, Beijing: Sanlian shudian.

Xu Yong 徐勇 1997. *Villager Self-Government in Rural China* 中国农村村民自治, Wuhan: Huazhong shifan daxue chubanshe.

Xu Yong 徐勇 2003. "Villager Self-Government: Innovation in China's Institutions of Constitutional Government" 村民自治：中国宪政制度的创新, *Studies in the History of the Communist Party of China* 中共党史研究, no. 1.

Xu Zhuoyun 许倬云 2006. *Eternal Rivers* 万古江河, Shanghai: Shanghai wenyi chubanshe.

Xue Yong 薛勇 2009. *Hatred of the Rich: Competition between Rich and Poor in Contemporary China* 仇富：当下中国的贫富之争, Nanjing: Jiangsu wenyi chubanshe.

Yan, Yunxiang 阎云翔 2000. *The Flow of Gifts: Reciprocity and Social Networks in a Chinese Village* 礼物的流动, trans. Li Fangchun 李放春, et al., Shanghai: Shanghai renmin chubanshe.

Yan, Yunxiang 阎云翔 2006. *Private Life under Socialism: Love, Intimacy, and Family Change in a Chinese Village, 1949–1999* 私人生活的变革, trans. Gong Xiaoxia 龚小夏, Shanghai: Shanghai shudian chubanshe.

Yan, Yunxiang 2014. "The Moral Implications of Immorality," *Journal of Religious Ethics*, vol. 42, no. 3.

Yang Liansheng 杨联陞 2011. *Elite Families in the Eastern Han* 东汉的豪族, Beijing: Shangwu yinshuguan.

Yang, Martin C. 杨懋春 2001. *A Chinese Village: Taitou, Shantung Province* 一个中国村庄, trans. Zhang Xiong 张雄, et al., Nanjing: Jiangsu renmin chubanshe.

Yang, Mayfair Mei-hui 杨美惠 2009. *Gifts, Favors, and Banquets: The Art of Social Relationships in China* 礼物、关系学与国家, trans. Zhao Xudong 赵旭东, Nanjing: Jiangsu renmin chubanshe.

Yang, C.K. 杨庆堃 2007. *Religion in Chinese Society: A Study of Contemporary Functions of Religion and Some of Their Historical Factors* 中国社会中的宗教, trans. Fan Lizhu 范丽珠, Shanghai: Shanghai renmin chubanshe.

Yen, James Y.C. 晏阳初 1989. *The Complete Works of James Yen* 晏阳初全集, vol. 1, Changsha: Hunan jiaoyu chubanshe.

Ying Xing 应星 2001. *A Story of Migrant Petitioners from the Big River* 大河移民上访的故事, Beijing: Sanlian shudian.

Yü Kuang-hong 余光弘 1986. "No Ancestral Tablets without Ancestral Property?" 没有祖产就没有祖宗牌位?, *Bulletin of the Institute of Ethnology at Academia Sinica* 中央"研究院民族学研究所集刊, no. 62.

Zhang Hou'an 张厚安 1992. *Basic-Level Political Power in Rural China* 中国农村基层政权, Chengdu: Sichuan renmin chubanshe.

Zhang, Hui 2010. "Windfall Wealth and Envy in Three Chinese Mining Villages," Ph.D. dissertation, Department of Anthropology at London School of Economics and Political Science.

Zhang, Li 张鹂 2014. *Strangers in the City: Reconfigurations of Space, Power, and Social Networks Within China's Floating Population* 城市里的陌生人, trans. Yuan Changgeng 袁长庚, Nanjing: Jiangsu renmin chubanshe.

Zhang Xianqing 张先清 2009. *Government, Clans, and Catholicism* 官府、宗族与天主教, Beijing: Zhonghua shuju.

Zhang Yonghong 张永宏 2009. "The Politics of Local Governance" 地方治理的政治, *The Sun Yat-sen University Journal (Social Sciences Edition)*, no. 1.

Zhao Dingxin 赵鼎新 2006. "The Theory of Social and Political Movements" 社会与政治运动理论, *Academia Bimestris* 学海, no. 2.

Zheng Zhenman 郑振满 and Zheng Li 郑莉 2012. "The Transnational Cultural Networks of Qiao Township, Putian" 莆田侨乡的跨国文化网络, *Journal of History and Anthropology* 历史人类学学刊, vol. 10, no. 2.
Zhu Xi 朱熹 2011a. "Commentary on *The Great Learning*" 大学章句, in *Commentaries on the Four Books* 四书章句集注, Beijing: Zhonghua shuju.
Zhu Xi 朱熹 2011b. "Quotation Fifty-Two" 语录五十二则, in Zhang Wenzhi 张文治, ed. *Key Texts of National Studies* 国学治要, vol. 4, Beijing: Zhongguo shudian.
Žižek, Slavoj 齐泽克 2014. *The Sublime Object of Ideology* 意识形态的崇高客体, trans. Ji Guangmao 季广茂, Beijing: Zhongyang bianyi chubanshe.

Index

Note: Figures are indicated by *italics*.

abnormal person 253
agricultural tax 57, 59, 113, 114, 135, 138, 140, 143, 162
alienation 96, 266, 267; worship 28, 90, 98, 158, 177, 178, 181, 184, 190, 228, 229, 243, 245, 248, 252, 258
ancient village 3, 5, 16, 18–23, 25–8, 31, 35–8, 211, 243, 294
anthropology for ordinary people 12
anti-rightist campaign 43
arts of resistance 236, 247, 256

basic desires 251, 270
blowing black the lamp 46
Bianzhi 54, 100
bitter fate 185
book of changes 9
brigade 10, 15, *16*, 25–8, 38–9, 42–55, 61, 63–4, 69–77, 100, 102, 104–6, 109–11, 119, 123–4, 132–4, 136–40, 157, 160, 164–5, 168, 205, 231–2, 235
budget market 173

Cheng brigade 39, 43–51, 53, 55, 70–4, 76–7, 106, 109, 119, 132–3
clan elder 26, 27, 29, 31, 32, 37, 41, 42, 115, 234, 247
collective era 4, 38, 45, 66, 91, 93, 136, 176–7, 185, 211, 246, 286
collectivization 55
commando 70, 72, 97, 163, 177
committee for maintaining order 52
communes 235
commune and brigade enterprises 132, 231
communist party 38, 41, 63, 97, 102, 132, 295

Confucian value 227
construct a new socialist countryside 21, 23

dark counselor 71, 103, 105–7, 239
decollectivization 38–9, 55, 65–6, 75, 77, 95, 119–20, 134, 167, 172, 176, 178, 185, 231
descendant 21–2
the differential mode of association 226, 283
do thought work 140
dual-track politics 226, 229, 247, 255
duan zi jue sun 197
Duqiao commune 45–6, 50, 53, 73–4, 77, 100, 105, 110, 133
Duqiao residential brigade 71–2, 100, 105, 110
Duqiao residential committee 83, 111, 121, 138–40, 165, 184, 188, 206

eaten state grain 100
economy of killing time 225, 229–30, 233, 246, 249
elite school 216
embezzled public fund 95, 167
essential nature 185–6, 188
establishing one's destiny 280–2, 285
ethics of life 251, 268
extended family 178, 239

faction 50, 63, 70–1, 105–6, 151–6, 163–5, 188, 234, 238–9
fake pesticide 189–90
family income 112
family planning policy 53, 107–8, 236

fate 68, 79, 157, 159–61, 177, 185–6, 188–90, 201, 214, 220–1, 225, 227, 245, 254, 259–60, 262, 264, 277, 283, 285
fengshui 7, 12–16, 20, 24, 34, 35, 128, 129, 158, 178, 188, 243, 244, 245, 248
the five degrees 52, 68
folk belief 228–9, 248, 258, 281–2, 284–5
four cleanups campaign 44–6, 49, 103

garment plant 197
gentry power 226
geomancer 12, 178, 185
geomantic knowledge 7
get rid of private desires 270
giving order to chaos 259
governmental businesspeople 146, 262, 264
grave-sweeping day 29, 114–15, 117, *119*, 213
great dialogue 269–70, 286
great leap forward 44, 48, 51
great refusal 251, 268–9
great tradition 258, 261
guanchang jing 16
guanxi 17

harmonious interdependence among all beings 285
Heaven's Destiny 285
household registration 100, 132, 206, 222
household responsibility system 55
human-mindedness 270, 274
human relationships 61, 228, 239, 257–61, 265–6, 272, 275–7, 279–80, 283–4, 287

instrumentalism 259
intergenerational transmission 259

Jianye 147
jiang yiqi 147
jump into the sea (of business) 212

karmic response 185, 244
karmic reward 189
kinship network 261, 237–8, 243–4

land reform 29, 42, 100, 109, 130, 229
lao haoren 156
left-behind 208
life and pulse 216
life history 253

lineage 9, 226, 239, 249, 252, 255, 258, 275–6, 283–4, 290, 293
little tradition 258, 259, 261
loftiness of character 270
loser 213–14, 221, 267

marketing co-op 44, 54, 56, 66, 106, 112, 126, 181
materialist 176, 244
matriculation rate 213–15
meaninglessness 216–17, 259
memorial tablet 4
mianzi 37, 76
middle peasant 48, 70, 103, 202
migrant worker 81, 148, 160, 193, 203–5, 212, 222, 273, 294
ming 3, 9, 20, 28, 98, 115, 184, 188, 218, 245–6, 249–50, 254, 269, 280
minimalist governance 261
minimum social security benefit 61
mount Tai exorcism tablet 185
mu 4, 12–13, 19, 36, 39, 48, 55, 82, 118, 123, 137, 139, 143–8, 167, 170–1, 190, 207

new rural cooperative healthcare 60
nuclear family 241, 248, 257–8, 277

officialdom 16, 126, 159, 220–1, 238–9, 241, 244, 246–8, 256, 267, 271, 274, 280
officials' luck 157–8, 160–1, 237, 244, 247, 256
official-speak 159
old society 4
one-dimensional man 266, 268–9, 286, 292
over-quota births 129, 184, 201, 208, 236, 242
overseas nationals 109, 181

paifang 15
parental officials 247, 274
party committee 16, 21, 23–4, 39, 63, 74, 77, 82–3, 110, 123, 137, 141–2, 147, 149, 150–6, 160, 162
the pattern of father-son identification 226, 228
pindie 174
play edge-ball 139, 157, 232, 237–8
political backer 149
political capital 18–19, 139–40, 151, 158, 237–8, 271

poor-and-lower-middle peasant 202
production team 36, 39, 42, 44–6, 48–9, 53, 55, 66, 74–5, 97, 100–3, 106–8, 111, 119, 121, 124, 130–1, 133–4, 164–6
pull taxes 142, 237
pyramid scheme 204, 243

real estate sector 192, 195
records of the grand historian 11–12, 41, 66, 249, 293
redistributing the fruits of labor 42
relatives within five generations 184
renqing 36, 226
ren zai jianghu, shen bu you ji 17
responsibility field 167
righteousness 65–6, 276
rightist 43–4, 46–8, 52–3, 104–5, 157
rule of rites 272–3

san quan si guding 119
the school of principle 3, 5, 6, 20, 21, 23, 27, 28, 38
secular person 250, 262
selective implementation 274
self-encouragement 257
semi-agricultural 225, 230–1, 233, 246–7, 254, 278, 282
semi-industrial 225, 231, 246–7, 254, 273, 278, 282
shaqi 7
sick people 251, 267–8, 277, 285
smallholder 195, 225, 229, 231, 246, 254
social bond 248, 256, 258, 260, 282–3, 285
social hierarchy 248, 256–7, 262–3, 266, 270–4, 277–8, 283–4
social inequality 174
son-adding 179, 243
spirit 7, 57, 80, 90, 115, 129, 157, 159, 167, 177–8, 180, 184, 244, 247, 249–50, 273, 280–2, 284, 294
stratification 227, 239, 241–2, 247–8
the stone-processing industry 191
student spot property 214
sweatshop 197

taigung 29, 39
taipo 39

task-contracting 166–7
tax and fees reform 59
the three religions and the nine schools of thought 176, 178
the three rural problems 139
three strikes, two build-ups 149
time-travel 220, 246
township official 16, 18–19, 29, 31, 236–8, 242
trapped society 266, 269
true self 93, 234, 240, 257, 266–7
two-dimensional man 260, 264, 266, 269, 272, 274, 277, 286

unbridled desires 262, 268
unit 25, 38–9, 41, 97, 105, 132, 139, 149, 152–3, 230, 241, 261, 275, 280, 284
the unity of Heaven 257
upholding the red flag 93
upscale market 173

vegetable retail stall 172
village committee 3, 6, 10, 21–2, 25, 27, 52, 55, 123, 134–8, 140–1, 143–4, 148, 235, 238
village party branch 10, 13, 25, 118, 135, 148
village politics 42, 226, 235–6, 283
villager self-government 226, 235–8, 247, 255, 274, 279, 280, 283, 284
villager team 38–9, 55, 113, 119, 144–5, 183, 279–80

wastrel 204
ways of the world 126, 259, 284
winds of exaggeration 44
work team 42, 45–6, 48–9, 70, 100, 103–4, 235
worldliness 260, 265
wufu 52, 68

xunfu 9

youth (labor) commandos 70

zhan dui 151
zhang 35
zhimaguan 18

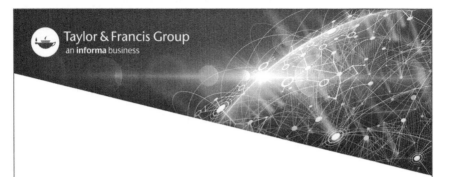